LEGO®
MINIFIGURE
YEAR BY YEAR
A VISUAL HISTORY

Senior Editor Helen Murray
Additional Editors Pamela Afram, Ruth Amos, Jo Casey,
Lindsay Kent, Julia March, Catherine Saunders
Senior Designer Lisa Sodeau
Project Art Editor Owen Bennett
Additional Designers Neha Ahuja, Guy Harvey, Lauren Rosier,
Anamica Roy, Anne Sharples, Rajdeep Singh, Chitrak Srivastava
Senior Slipcase Designer Mark Penfound
Senior DTP Designer Kavita Varma
Producer Louise Daly
Managing Editor Paula Regan
Managing Art Editor Guy Harvey
Creative Manager Sarah Harland
Art Director Lisa Lanzarini
Publisher Julie Ferris
Publishing Director Simon Beecroft

Consultant Giles Kemp
Additional writing Catherine Saunders, Jo Casey, Julia March, and Lindsay Kent
Additional photography Gary Ombler, Thomas Baunsgaard Pedersen, and Tim Trøjborg

This edition published in 2016
First American edition, 2013
Published in the United States by DK Publishing
345 Hudson Street, New York, New York 10014
DK, a Division of Penguin Random House LLC

Slipcase UI: 002-289263-Aug/15

A catalog record for this book is available from the Library of Congress.

ISBN: 978-1-4093-3312-8

Printed in China.

www.LEGO.com
www.dk.com

A WORLD OF IDEAS:
SEE ALL THERE IS TO KNOW

LEGO®

MINIFIGURE

YEAR BY YEAR
A VISUAL HISTORY

Written by
Gregory Farshtey with Daniel Lipkowitz

CONTENTS

1970s

1980s

1990s

2000s

88

2010s

188

BRINGING LEGO® PLAY TO LIFE

IN THE 1960s and early 1970s, the focus in LEGO® building was on constructing models like houses, cars, and trains. But something important was missing: people to live in the houses, drive the cars, and run the trains! If children wanted characters to play in their LEGO creations, they had to make them out of bricks themselves. To address this need for role-play and storytelling, the company first created large, buildable family figures, and later shrunk them down to a size that would fit in better with smaller LEGO models. In1975, a figure was launched with a blank yellow head, a torso with arm-shaped bumps, and a single, solid leg. In 1978, this forerunner to the minifigure was updated with moving arms and legs, hands that could hold accessories, and a face painted with two dots for eyes and a friendly smile. The famous LEGO minifigure was ready to play!

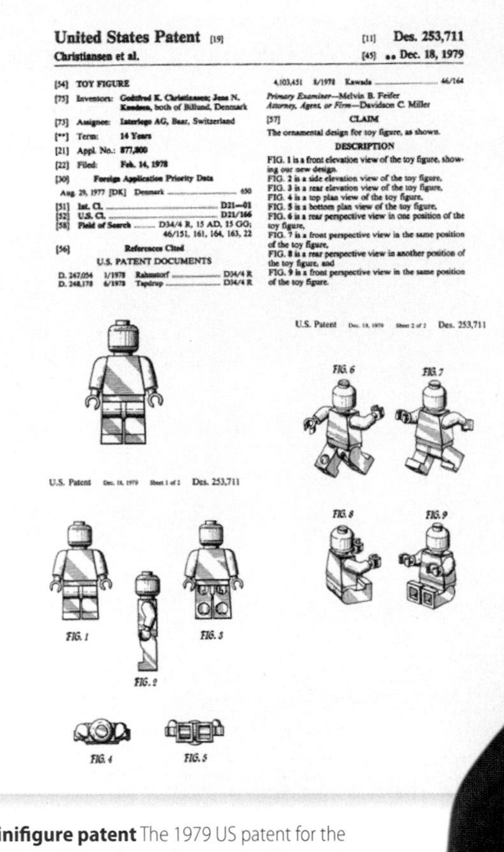

United States Patent [19]
Christiansen et al.

[11] Des. 253,711
[45] ** Dec. 18, 1979

[54] TOY FIGURE
[75] Inventors: Godtfred K. Christiansen; Jens N. Knudsen, both of Billund, Denmark
[73] Assignee: Interlego AG, Baar, Switzerland
[**] Term: 14 Years
[21] Appl. No.: 877,800
[22] Filed: Feb. 14, 1978
[30] Foreign Application Priority Data
Aug. 29, 1977 [DK] Denmark 650
[51] Int. Cl. .... D21—01
[52] U.S. Cl. D21/166
[58] Field of Search .... D34/4 R, 15 AD, 15 GG; 46/151, 161, 164, 163, 22
[56] References Cited
U.S. PATENT DOCUMENTS
D. 247,054 1/1978 Rahmstorf .... D34/4 R
D. 248,178 6/1978 Tapdrup .... D34/4 R
4,103,451 8/1978 Kawada 46/164

Primary Examiner—Melvin B. Feifer
Attorney, Agent, or Firm—Davidson C. Miller

[57] CLAIM

The ornamental design for toy figure, as shown.

DESCRIPTION

FIG. 1 is a front elevation view of the toy figure, showing our new design.
FIG. 2 is a side elevation view of the toy figure,
FIG. 3 is a rear elevation view of the toy figure,
FIG. 4 is a top plan view of the toy figure,
FIG. 5 is a bottom plan view of the toy figure,
FIG. 6 is a rear perspective view in one position of the toy figure,
FIG. 7 is a front perspective view in the same position of the toy figure,
FIG. 8 is a rear perspective view in another position of the toy figure, and
FIG. 9 is a front perspective view in the same position of the toy figure.

U.S. Patent Dec. 18, 1979 Sheet 2 of 2 Des. 253,711

U.S. Patent Dec. 18, 1979 Sheet 1 of 2 Des. 253,711

Minifigure patent The 1979 US patent for the LEGO minifigure design demonstrated its iconic shape, the brick-compatible holes on its feet and legs, and the way its limbs could move.

Girl power The female minifigure went through many concept stages before it was decided that it would share the same standard legs as male minifigures.

BIRTH OF A LEGEND

To create the prototype for the first minifigure, designer Jens Nygård Knudsen and a team of colleagues sawed and filed LEGO bricks into a miniature human form. Three years and 50 additional prototypes carved in plastic and cast in tin later, he produced the updated modern-style minifigure. It debuted in set number 600, featuring a policeman and a buildable brick patrol car.

LEGO Family
A best-selling precursor to the minifigure, the first LEGO Family figures appeared in 1974 in set 200. The set included five family members with posable arms, brick-built bodies, and swappable, reversible hair pieces.

MINI-EVOLUTION

As behind-the-scenes development progressed, the minifigure gained separated legs, multiple moving parts, and a decorated face. Common to all was the stud on top of the head, which allowed a variety of hats and hair elements to be attached, thereby creating different personalities and jobs—and endless imaginative play opportunities for children.

Ring-shaped hands

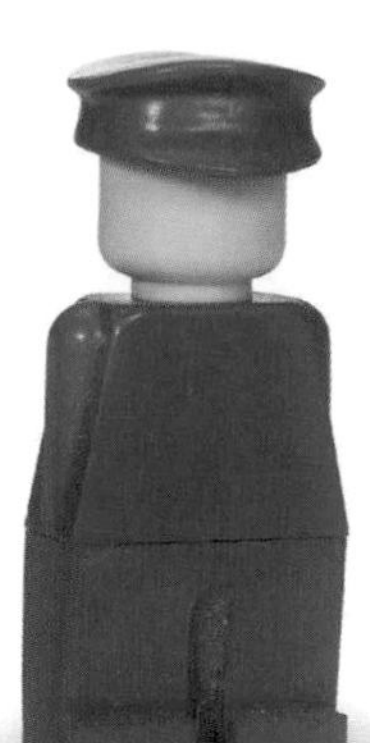

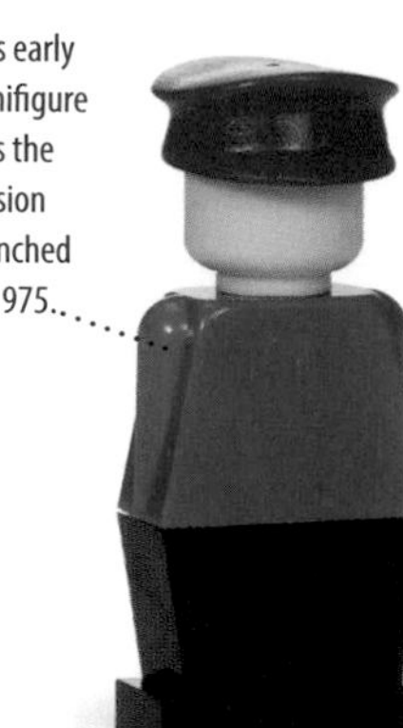
This early minifigure was the version launched in 1975

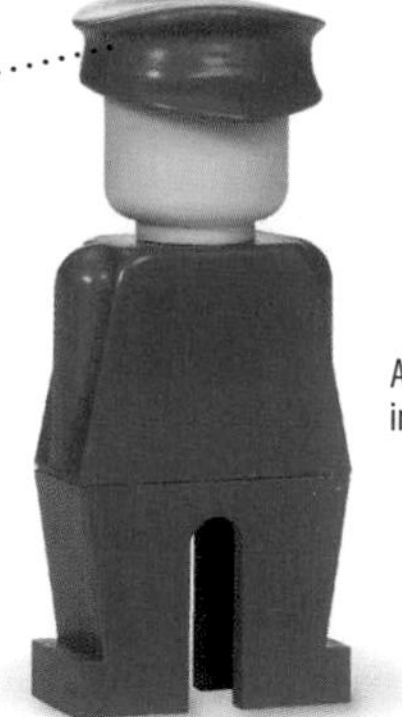
Hat compatible with modern-style minifigures

An experiment in hinged legs

Arms can swing back and forth
Hollow legs and feet fit over LEGO brick studs

Then and now
The 1978 minifigures, seen here, were essentially the same as the ones that can be found in LEGO sets today.

Hand-drawn prototype torso decoration

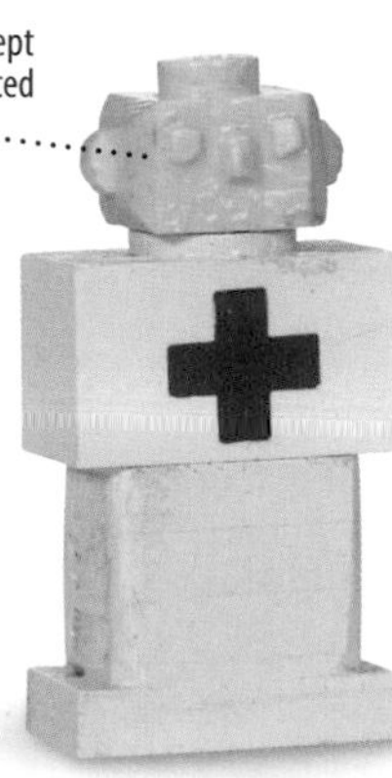
Head concept with sculpted features

WHAT'S A MINIFIGURE?

Size matters Without a hat or hair piece, a minifigure stands exactly four LEGO bricks high. This precise measurement makes it easy to construct LEGO buildings and vehicles that can fit minifigures inside.

A LEGO® MINIFIGURE is a small, posable figure of a person or being. Most minifigures have rotating arms, legs, hands, and heads. They have connectors on their bodies that are compatible with LEGO bricks and other elements. They often represent famous archetypes, such as firefighters, astronauts, and knights. A minifigure can be disassembled and combined with parts from other minifigures to create an entirely new character. The faces of many minifigures carry a friendly smile, but some have other expressions—even multiple ones! Minifigures drive cars, live in castles, fly spaceships, and fill the world of construction with endless possibilities for fun, role play, and imagination.

Stud on top of head can connect to headgear and other LEGO pieces

Build a minifigure
A standard LEGO minifigure comes in three sections when you open a new LEGO set: the head, the torso with arms and hands, and the waist and legs.

Arm rotates 360 degrees at the shoulder
Hand swivels at the wrist

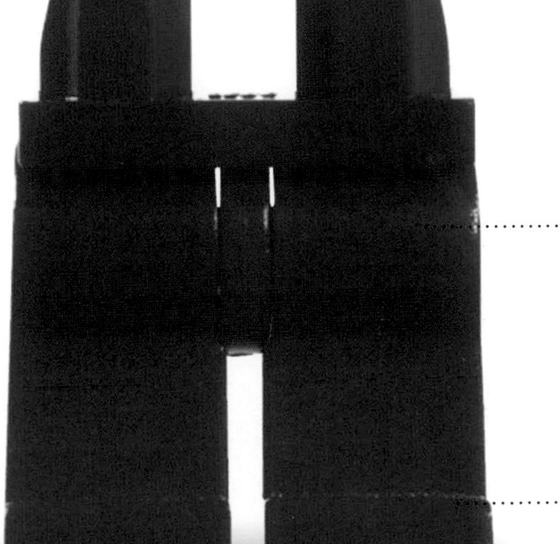
Legs swing back and forth for sitting and walking poses
Holes on backs of legs and bottoms of feet attach to LEGO brick studs

MINIFIGURES AT WORK

LEGO minifigures hail from many different places and times, including the past, present, and future, as well as worlds of fantasy and science fiction. You can tell where a minifigure comes from and what kind of job it has by looking at the details of its printed clothing and its accessories.

A uniform with reflective stripes and a special helmet make it clear that this is a firefighter.

With his coveralls, cap, and shovel, what else could this hard-working fellow be but a farmer?

An ancient gladiator carries a sword and shield, and wears a protective helmet and leather armor.

MEET THE MINIFIGURES...

A minifigure must have a number of essential key minifigure characteristics in order to be considered a true LEGO minifigure. Although all of the characters shown here have different faces, clothes, accessories, and even some body parts, each one is still a minifigure because it is based around the same basic LEGO minifigure design.

The pirate has a hook-hand, a peg-leg, and a printed eyepatch and beard.

This retro robot has a mechanical arm with a claw, a helmet with a visor, and bolts printed on his body and legs.

This mermaid stands on a single-piece fish tail instead of legs.

A queen from LEGO® Castle wears a dress made from a printed sloped piece.

A beastly warrior has an animal head with a reversible minifigure face underneath.

This cheerleader has legs that are printed to look like a skirt and socks.

Some minifigures have short legs to make them appear smaller.

The EXO-FORCE™ heroes are based on the look of Japanese animation.

Minifigures can represent anybody from any country or culture.

Handy A zookeeper holds a banana in one hand and a hungry baby chimpanzee in the other.

MEET THE NON-MINIFIGURES...

Not every LEGO figure is a minifigure! Many other colorful characters inhabit the universe of LEGO building. The LEGO® *Star Wars*® droid and the LEGO® Friends mini-doll are not minifigures because they are not made up of any standard minifigure parts. The skeleton does not have enough standard parts to count as a true minifigure.

LEGO skeleton

LEGO *Star Wars* Battle Droid

LEGO Friends mini-doll

HOW TO USE THIS BOOK

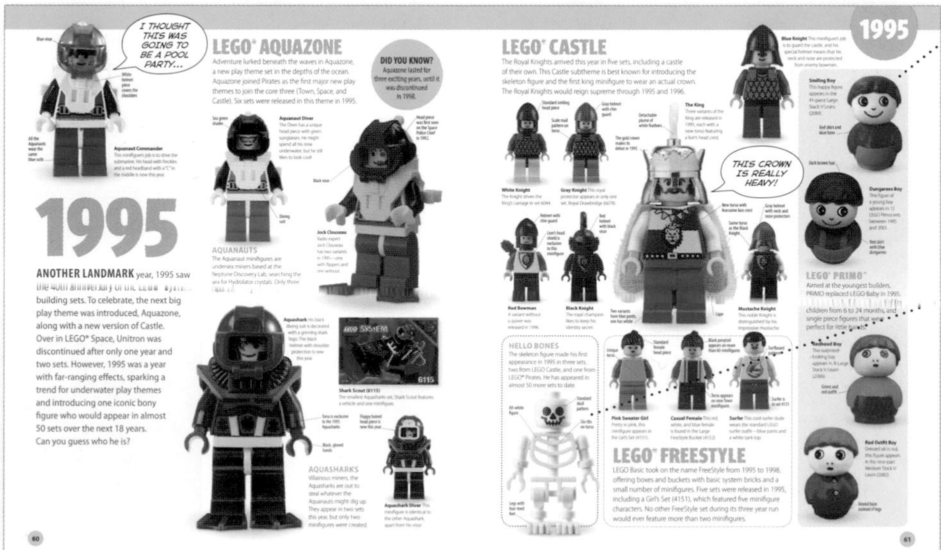
I THOUGHT THIS WAS GOING TO BE A POOL PARTY...
LEGO® AQUAZONE
DID YOU KNOW?
1995
ANOTHER LANDMARK
LEGO® CASTLE
1995
THIS CROWN IS REALLY HEAVY!
LEGO® FREESTYLE

Some themes have a style of figure that is all their own, such as LEGO DUPLO figures and LEGO Friends mini-dolls. These non-minifigure themes appear in gray boxes throughout the book.

Some non-minifigures are designed to fit in and interact with minifigures in their themes, such as LEGO *Star Wars* droids, LEGO Castle skeletons, and LEGO Space aliens. These appear in the book in boxes with a dotted key line.

HAIR, HATS, AND GEAR

The minifigure's head stud lets you attach and swap hundreds of different hair pieces, hats, and helmets. Their hands can hold a wide variety of accessories, and backpacks and armor can be attached to their bodies.

Armor This knight wears a helmet and an armor piece fitted over his torso.

HOW IS A MINIFIGURE MADE?

Many minifigures start out as a rough concept sketch that shows how the character might appear when it's created.

CREATING A NEW MINIFIGURE isn't a quick process. It can take more than a year from the time an idea is first sketched out on paper to the moment a brand-new plastic character is picked off the LEGO® production line to be packed up and shipped to shops all around the world. Many individuals contribute to the creation of a minifigure, from sculptors to graphic artists, as well as the machines that make sure each one is perfectly molded and ready for play. Here's how it's done.

The LEGO Minifigures team hold brainstorming sessions at the LEGO offices in Billund, Denmark.

BRAINSTORMING

When it's time to start work on new sets for a LEGO play theme, the whole design team sits down for a "Design Boost" brainstorming session. They share their ideas to come up with the best concepts for new models and the minifigures that will populate them. If a new set will need one or more new minifigures to be created, then the character design process begins.

DESIGNING

The design team makes sketches and decides what new accessories or body-part elements are needed. For research, they might visit a fire station, or study historical armor at a library. Element designers hand-sculpt organic-looking pieces such as hair at a 3:1 scale out of clay, while more regularly-shaped parts are designed via a computer using a 3D program. Meanwhile, graphic designers create a map of face and body details that will be applied to the minifigure. Minifigures are chosen to be included in a set based on how well they help to tell that set's story. If it is a licensed character from a movie or comic book, then the team collaborates with licensing partners until both are totally satisfied with the design. Finally, a Model Committee checks that everything fits and works properly, and the completed design is approved for production.

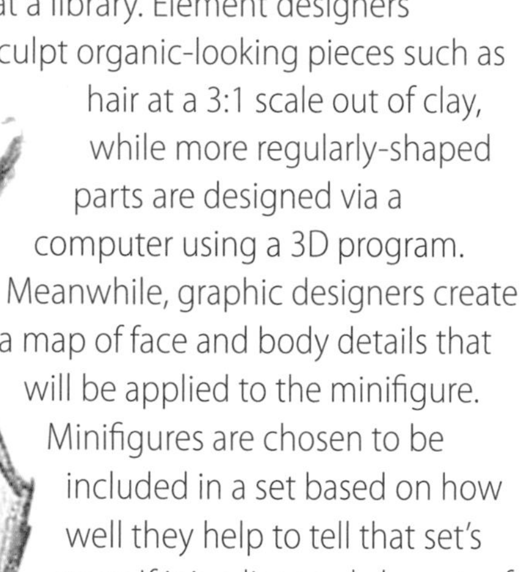

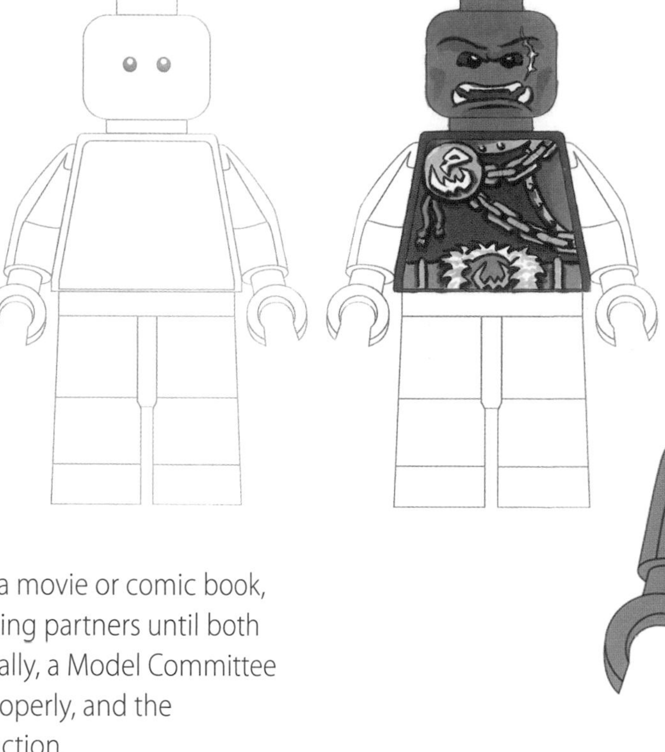

Design work begins on a blank minifigure template, bare of any colors, personality, or details.

A graphic designer comes up with a design for the face and costume of the new minifigure and adds color.

The approved design is refined and finalized on a computer as a 2D version of what the minifigure will look like when it is produced in plastic.

Most minifigures are manufactured at the LEGO Group headquarters in Billund, Denmark. Others come from factories in Hungary, the Czech Republic, China, and Mexico.

MANUFACTURING

Just like LEGO bricks, minifigures start out as piles of tiny, colorful plastic granules, made out of acrylonitrile butadiene styrene (ABS), each one about the size of a grain of rice. These granules are mixed together and heated until they melt and become a plastic goo, which is pressed into shape inside metal molding machines. Automated assembly machines attach legs to waists, hands to arms, and arms to torsos. Decorating machines then use special inks to print faces and clothing decorations directly onto the assembled parts. At last, the new minifigure is complete and ready to be purchased, shipped, and sold.

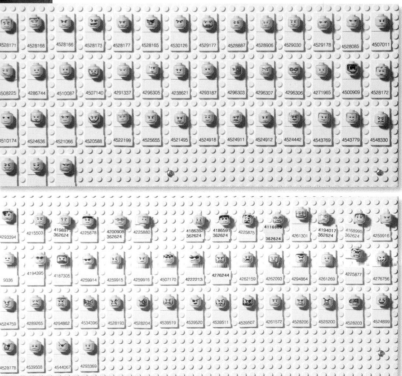

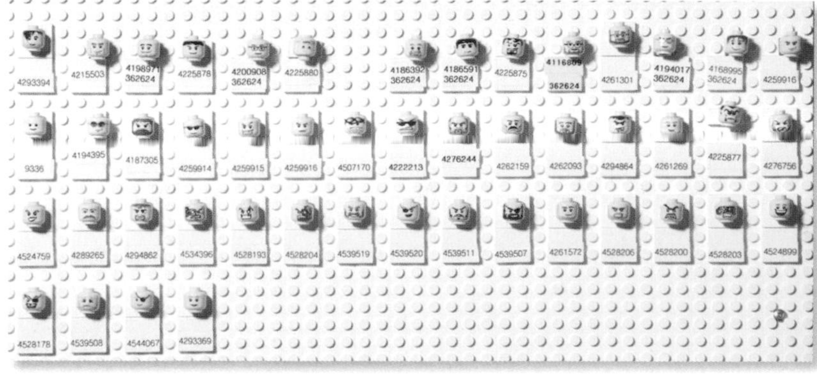

The LEGO employees at the factories use coded display boards to keep track of the many different minifigure faces that are currently in production.

TIMELINE

EVEN THOUGH their fundamental design has remained the same for 35 years (and counting), minifigures have gone through many changes over the decades. This timeline chronicles some of the most important events in minifigure history, including the first new facial expressions and new body parts and the first licensed characters from the big screen, as well as the debuts of classic minifigure elements, accessories, and other LEGO® figures.

LEGO Family figures

1974

- The first LEGO figures—LEGO Family building figures—have round heads with painted expressions, posable arms, and bodies built out of LEGO bricks.

Freddy Fox LEGO FABULAND figure

Handy briefcase to carry everything a minifigure needs

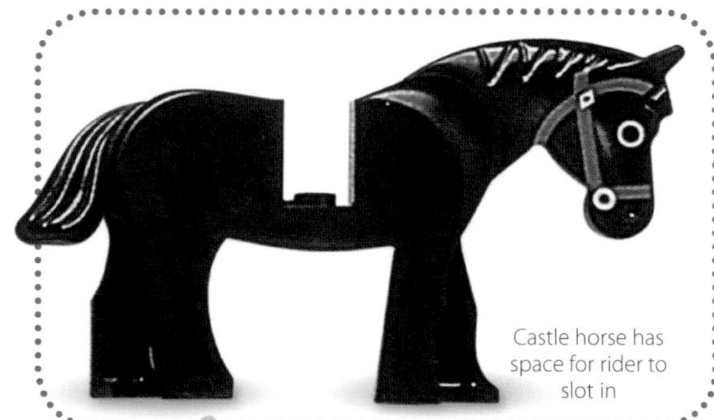
Castle horse has space for rider to slot in

1979

- First yellow Space minifigure.
- First female Castle character.
- First male hair piece.
- First chef's hat.
- Animal-headed LEGO® FABULAND™ figures.

1980

- First top hat.

1983

- First minifigure briefcase.

1984

- New Castle factions and elements are introduced.
- Minifigure-rideable horse.

Monkey figure with curly tail

1989

- LEGO® Pirates introduces the first minifigures with different facial expressions and body parts, such as peg-legs and hook-hands.
- Monkey uses minifigure arms for all four limbs.

1990

- The first LEGO ghost minifigure has a glow-in-the-dark shroud element.
- First time a slope is used instead of legs for a minifigure's dress.

Early three-piece figure with red hat

LEGO DUPLO figures

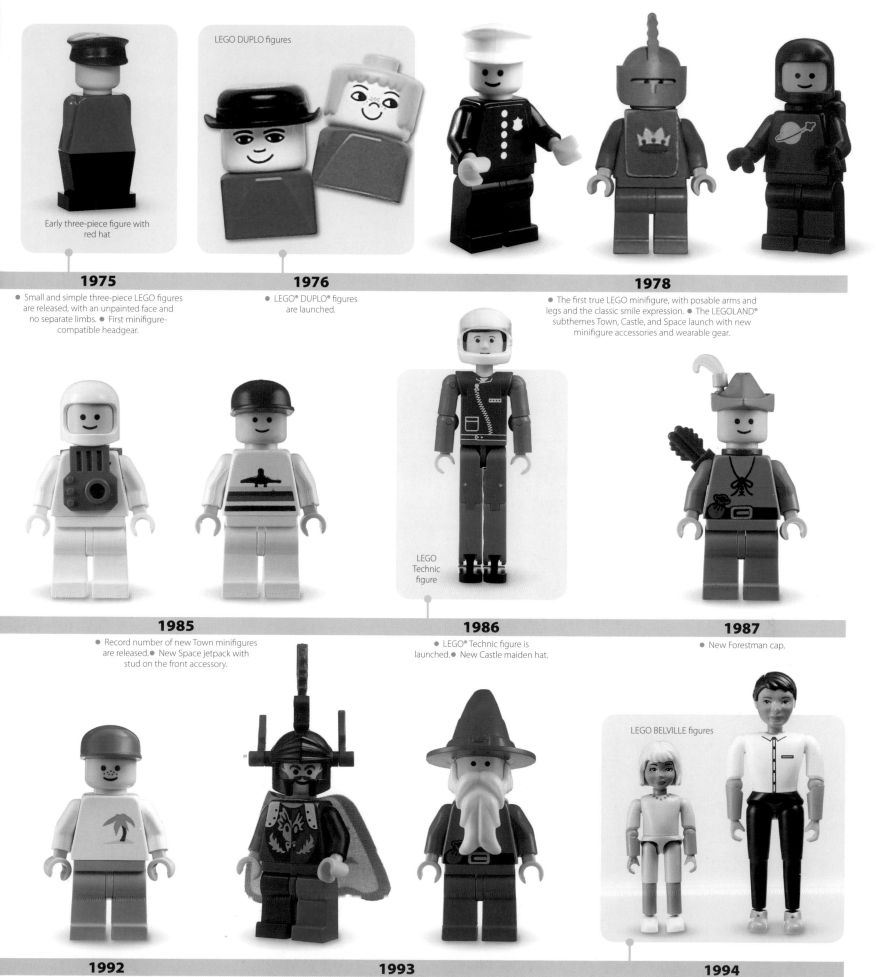

1975

- Small and simple three-piece LEGO figures are released, with an unpainted face and no separate limbs. • First minifigure-compatible headgear.

1976

- LEGO® DUPLO® figures are launched.

1978

- The first true LEGO minifigure, with posable arms and legs and the classic smile expression. • The LEGOLAND® subthemes Town, Castle, and Space launch with new minifigure accessories and wearable gear.

LEGO Technic figure

1985

- Record number of new Town minifigures are released. • New Space jetpack with stud on the front accessory.

1986

- LEGO® Technic figure is launched. • New Castle maiden hat.

1987

- New Forestman cap.

LEGO BELVILLE figures

1992

- First minifigure head with freckles.
- New surfboard accessory.

1993

- First female LEGO Space minifigure. • First separate beard piece. • First minifigure headgear with printing. • First LEGO Town crook. • First fabric minifigure cape.

1994

- First printed minifigure legs.
- First robot minifigure head.
- LEGO® BELVILLE™ figures are launched.

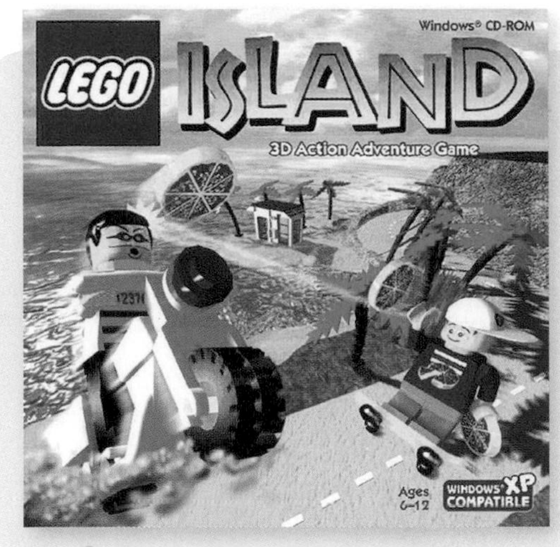
Windows® CD-ROM
LEGO
ISLAND
3D Action Adventure Game
Ages 6–12
WINDOWS XP COMPATIBLE

LEGO® *Island* video game

1995

● First skeleton figure has new body and limb components. ● New diver accessories: helmet, visor, and flippers. ● First minifigure crown.

1996

● First minifigure nose.

1997

● First minifigure with a printed sloped skirt piece. ● LEGO *Island* is the first video game to star (digital) minifigures. ● LEGO® SCALA™ figures are launched.

NBA

2001

● First minifigure with a two-sided face print. ● First glow-in-the-dark minifigure head.

2002

● First minifigures to feature new short LEGO leg piece. ● First super hero minifigure. ● LEGO® Studios werewolf mask transforms an ordinary minifigure into a howling beast. ● Neck bracket element allows objects to be attached to a minifigure's back.

2003

● Minifigures with special arms and spring-loaded legs for holding and throwing basketballs. ● First minifigures based on actual people—with realistic skin tones. ● First minifigure with arm printing. ● The first minifigures on Mars—illustrations of astrobots Biff Starling and Sandy Moondust land on the Red Planet aboard the NASA rovers *Spirit* and *Opportunity*.

2005

● Minifigures with built-in batteries let Jedi lightsabers and police flashlights light up when the heads are pushed down. ● Hand-held magnetic accessory lets Harry Potter™ grab a golden dragon egg. ● First minifigure mermaid tail. ● First viking helmet.

Brightly colored LEGO® Games microfigures

2009

● Tiny microfigures appear in LEGO Games sets. ● LEGO® Space Police features new modified alien heads. ● First hair piece with a hole for accessories.

2010

● LEGO® *Toy Story*™ sets introduce minifigures with extra-long arms and legs. ● A new tentacle-legs element first appears in LEGO® Atlantis. ● Han Solo (from LEGO *Star Wars*) is the first minifigure to be frozen in carbonite. ● The collectible LEGO Minifigures line adds many new body parts and accessories. ● First minifigure legs with side printing. ● *The Adventures of Clutch Powers* is the first feature-length movie starring minifigures.

1998

• LEGO® Adventurers introduces new headgear: wide-brimmed hat, pith helmet, and aviator cap with goggles. • LEGO Castle's Ninja subtheme launches Samurai and ninja gear. • First mummy minifigure.

1999

• LEGO® *Star Wars*® minifigures introduce many new parts and accessories. • First minifigure head to be sculpted into a different (non-standard) shape.

2000

• LEGO® Studios Director minifigure.

Skeleton figure with sword

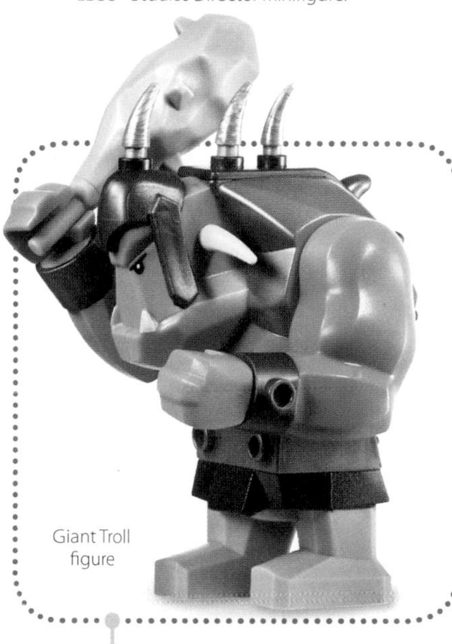

Giant Troll figure

2006

• LEGO® EXO-FORCE™ features minifigures with faces and hair pieces designed after Japanese animation, as well as robot villains with new body, arm, and leg pieces. • First printed hair piece.

2007

• For the 30th anniversary of *Star Wars*, 10,000 gold chrome C-3PO minifigures are randomly packed into LEGO® *Star Wars*® sets, and two 14-carat gold versions are given away. • Skeleton minifigure body is updated so its arms can move. • LEGO® Mars Mission features aliens with transparent glow-in-the-dark bodies. • First minifigures with soft-plastic heads.

2008

• "Go Miniman Go!" event celebrates the 30th anniversary of the LEGO minifigure. • LEGO® Agents introduces a new robotic minifigure arm. • The Castle theme introduces the Giant Troll figure.

Frakjaw and Wyplash from LEGO® Ninjago

Meet mini-doll Nicole from LEGO Friends

2011

• Aluminum minifigures of the Roman gods Jupiter and Juno and the astronomer Galileo are launched aboard the Juno space probe. • A new leg piece gives boots to LEGO Ninjago skeleton figures. • First hair piece with ears.

2012

• LEGO Ninjago introduces snake head and tail pieces, and a torso extender with extra arms. • LEGO® Friends debuts the mini-doll. • LEGO® Monster Fighters features new bat-winged arms and steampunk mechanical leg pieces.

2013

• First minifigure with chicken wings. • New animal minifigure elements in LEGO® Legends of Chima™. • New heads and turtle shells for the LEGO® Teenage Mutant Ninja Turtles™.

1970s

The 1970s were when it all began. First there were big, buildable people with round yellow heads. Then came mini-sized, solid-bodied figures with swappable hats and expressionless faces. Finally, in 1978, the best parts of both were combined to create a smiling little character with movable arms and legs. The LEGO® minifigure was born, and with it came three new lines—Town, Castle, and Space—creating an entire world of constructible buildings, vehicles, and accessories to bring it to life.

Air tank piece attaches with a neck bracket
Black torso with fire uniform sticker was last worn by LEGO firemen in 1981

Fireman Two parts of this minifigure's firefighting equipment—his fire-proof helmet and air tank—are still used by the firefighters of LEGO City today.

1978

THE MODERN MINIFIGURE as we know it was born in 1978, making it one of the biggest years ever for LEGO® building. The new LEGO characters were vastly different from their precursors, released in 1975, which were static, unprinted, and made from bricks. Made up of three separate pieces (a head, torso, and legs), minifigures now had cheery printed faces, and arms and legs that moved to make them posable for play. You might think that that would be enough excitement for one year, but there was more! Three new subthemes were introduced: Town, Castle, and Space—as part of the LEGOLAND® play theme.

TOWN

The first LEGO minifigure ever produced was a police officer minifigure for the LEGOLAND Town subtheme. 1978 would bring much more than law and order, though—fire officers, medics, construction workers, street sweepers, and more would begin populating Town, bringing life to a place that builders would return to again and again.

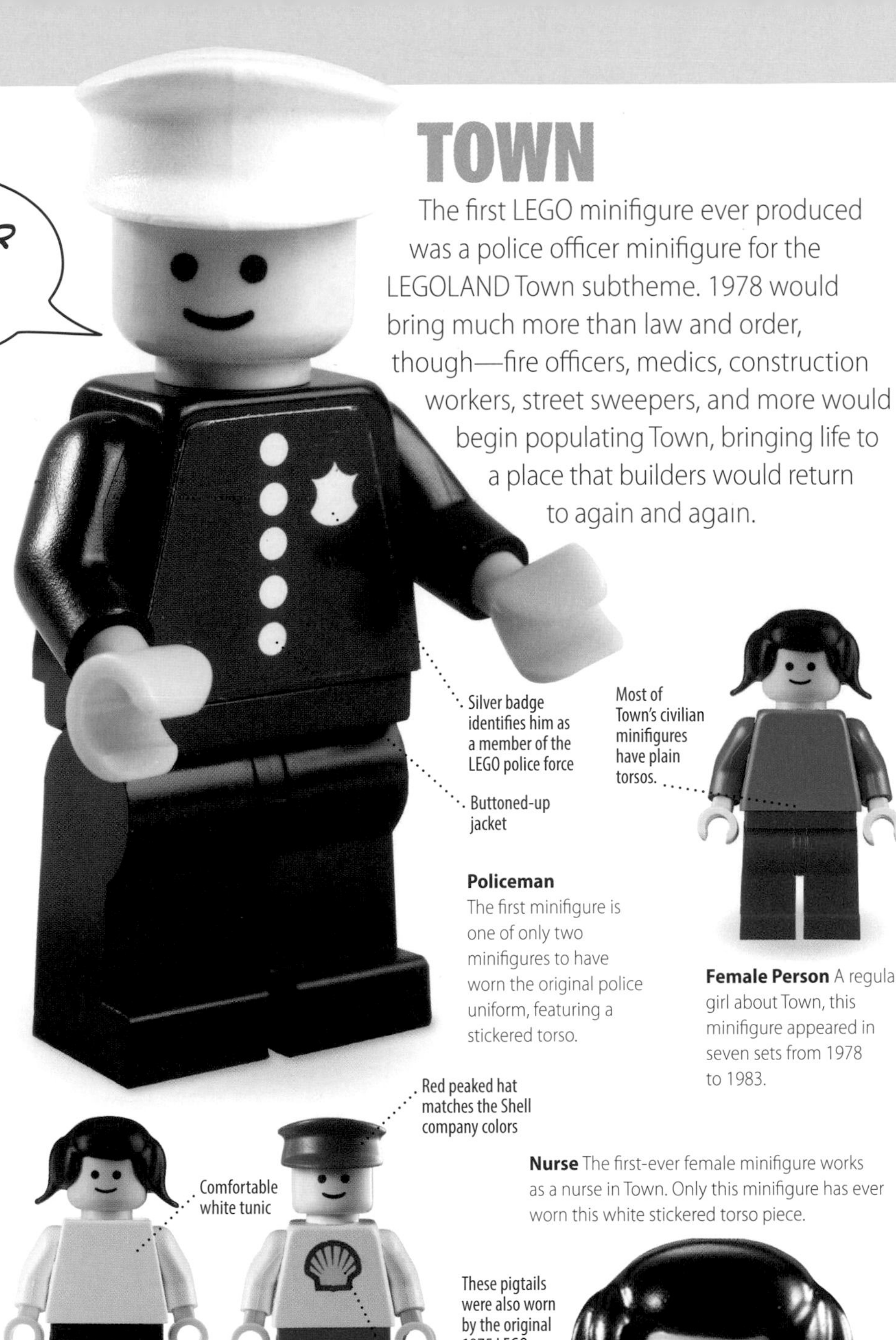

I'M NUMBER 1 AROUND HERE.
Silver badge identifies him as a member of the LEGO police force
Buttoned-up jacket
Most of Town's civilian minifigures have plain torsos.

Policeman The first minifigure is one of only two minifigures to have worn the original police uniform, featuring a stickered torso.

Female Person A regular girl about Town, this minifigure appeared in seven sets from 1978 to 1983.

Comfortable white tunic
Red peaked hat matches the Shell company colors
Company uniform with Shell logo
These pigtails were also worn by the original 1975 LEGO figures.

Nurse The first-ever female minifigure works as a nurse in Town. Only this minifigure has ever worn this white stickered torso piece.

Passenger This female is dressed in plain traveling clothes for her debut on the Passenger Coach (164).

Shell Employee This oil company worker keeps the citizens of Town on the move.

White sailing hat
Star Coast Guard symbol
Medical symbol
Red torso with shirt-pattern sticker is unique to this minifigure.

Coast Guard Captain The head of sea security only appears at the Coast Guard Station (575).

Street Sweeper Town is kept pristine by this busy minifigure in Town Square (1589).

DID YOU KNOW?
All male minifigures wore hats until male hair pieces appeared in 1979.

Workman's cap protects his head
Plain clothes for heavy manual work

Male Person One of the first regular minifigure citizens of Town, this minifigure works at the Cargo Station (165).

Red hat makes him visible on the tracks
Dressed professionally in a jacket over a shirt and tie

Train Conductor This minifigure was the first to feature a torso that was printed instead of stickered.

Town House With Garden (376) Two minifigures live in this delightful house, complete with flowers and sunlounger.

Black cowboy hat matches his sharp suit
Unique stickered torso features a black jacket and red tie.
Red briefcase

Patron This well-dressed man-about-town exclusively appears in the Main Street set (1589). He must have lots of important errands to run!

Helmet with chinstrap

Printed torso features the LEGO Space logo

Protective space suit covers the hands, too

Red Spaceman This trailblazing minifigure was first into LEGO Space and first to wear his helmet, which was in sets until 1988.

Classic, all-white space suit

White Spaceman One of the five original LEGO astronauts, this character appeared in 37 sets from 1978 to 1987.

SPACE

It was time for minifigures to blast off into Space in 1978, when the subtheme's first three sets were launched. The Rocket Launcher (462), Space Cruiser (487), and Space Command Center (493) all featured astronaut minifigures. Each space adventurer wore a full-body spacesuit in a bold color—white, red, yellow, blue, or black—with the classic yellow face peering from the helmet.

LEGO® DUPLO®

The earliest DUPLO figures predate the modern minifigure, having first appeared in 1976. They had a head and a one-piece body, with no arms or legs—a design that would change in the years that followed.

Blue sailor hat identifies him as a seafaring figure

DUPLO Sailor With a wide smile and a freckly face, this happy sailor popped up in five nautical-themed DUPLO sets from 1978 to 1990.

CASTLE

The very first Castle set charged onto the LEGO building scene in 1978. It would go on to become a bestseller for the next six years. Nicknamed the "Yellow Castle," Big Yellow Castle Kingdom (375) featured a working, crank-raised drawbridge and contained 14 knight minifigures (in four different variants) and four brick-built horses, making it great for endless play.

Only this knight has ever worn this visor in light gray.

Defending soldiers wear a purple vest with a crown.

Plume Helmet Knight Part of the blue cavalry that protects the Yellow Castle, only one Knight of this kind appears in the set.

Visor with plume fits over the classic LEGO helmet worn by the astronauts (above)
Shield emblem of the attacking army

Black Cavalry Knight Dressed in black and ready to attack, this Black Cavalry Knight has a foreboding appearance.

I LOVE THE YELLOW CASTLE. THE KNIGHT LIFE IS GREAT!

Helmet with neckguard was first worn by this knight. The piece is still worn by battling minifigures today.

Stickered vest with neck bracket fits over the knight's torso

Blue Cavalry Knight An army of seven of these minifigures defends the Yellow Castle (375) from the invading army.

Helmet for protection against flying arrows
Torso with a royal crest
YOU RANG, SIR?

Knight Modeling a new helmet for the Castle theme, this minifigure appears in Knight's Procession (677).

1979

THE MINIFIGURE CELEBRATED its first birthday in grand style in 1979, with new sets for LEGOLAND® Castle, Space, and Town. In other non-minifigure news: SCALA, a jewelry and accessories line for girls was introduced; LEGO® DUPLO® expanded with two new subthemes, Playhouse and Farm; and LEGO® FABULAND™ was launched, which was seen as a bridge theme for children growing out of LEGO DUPLO. But for many fans, this was the year that showed the minifigure was here to stay.

CASTLE

The second and third Castle sets in history came out in 1979: Knight's Tournament (383) and Knight's Procession (677). They were both released in Europe this year, but would not reach US shelves until 1981. Knights' Tournament came with six minifigures, but no horse figures as we know them today— the horses had to be built using bricks.

Helmet in light gray

Red torso with crest

Procession Knight This Knight has a helmet with neck and nose guards for maximum protection.

CAN YOU ATTACH A HAIRDRYER TO MY THRONE?
Red, short hair piece
Gold necklace
Male hair piece new to this year
Tri-color crest

Princess With her startling red hair, this minifigure is the first female in the Castle theme, paving the way for many more.

Prince This regal Prince sports a new hair piece, which has since become an iconic LEGO element.

DID YOU KNOW?
Most minifigure head pieces have a hole in their stud to prevent choking if swallowed.

SPACE

1979 was a huge year for Space, with a dozen sets released, plus building plates resembling a lunar landscape, and minifigure packs. Unlike later Space subthemes, these sets were free of any kind of conflict or aliens. Astronaut minifigures explored the galaxy with smiles on their faces in spaceships, and are still remembered with fondness by many adult fans.

A yellow helmet matches his head color

Gold space logo

Yellow Spaceman This minifigure is bright yellow—a new color for an astronaut in the Space theme.

454
LEGOLAND
LEGO
Ages 6-12

Landing Plates (454) This set comes with two landing pads, one with a crossroad and one with a T-intersection.

1979

Chef Wearing a new hat, the first chef minifigure is ready to work in Snack-Bar (675), a new set for 1979.

I'M VERY PROUD OF MY NEW HAT!
Iconic chef's hat
Bright red neckerchief
Gray hips and legs
Hard hat for working on-site
Torso with vest print
Peaked cap
Red shirt under blazer

Construction Worker The printed torso on this minifigure is one of many that is new to this year.

DID YOU KNOW? The total number of minifigures produced could fill around 170 standard-sized swimming pools.

Taxi Driver This unusually well-dressed taxi driver comes in one set: Taxi (608).

White crash helmet for when he is riding his motorbike
Black pigtails
Torso with badge and zipper details

Policeman Making his debut this year, this minifigure would be around for nine years.

Baby Part of the short-lived Homemaker theme, this baby has a vest with bib detail.

The same peaked cap as on the taxi driver
Button-up pockets
Same hair piece as the Prince
Blue sweater
Red peaked cap
Sticker with Exxon logo
EXXON

Mechanic This helpful minifigure comes with a wrench in the Auto Service Truck set (646).

Boy This young man is part of a Homemaker set, Family Room (268).

Exxon Worker Sporting a torso with an Exxon sticker, this minifigure is in the Exxon Fuel Pumper set (554).

TOWN

LEGO builders looking to create their own town layout had lots to work with in 1979, with many new sets and updated minifigures. There was a Taxi (608) and a Bus Station (379) so minifigures could get around; a Snack Bar (675) for hungry minifigures; and many more. Only a small number of minifigures were new this year; most were variations on ones released in 1979.

LEGO FABULAND

LEGO FABULAND, with colorful, easy-to-build models and fun animal characters, was introduced to fill the niche between DUPLO and LEGO System models. The popular play theme would last until 1989.

Oversized molded fox head
Red, chunky legs
Bear face with printed snout
Distinctive feline features
Head molded to look wooly
Torso with yellow vest

Freddy Fox Wide-eyed and bushy-tailed, this fox appears in six Fabuland sets including Town Hall (140).

Bernard Bear This friendly bear comes with his own pick-up truck in one set (329).

Charlie Cat This smiling cat works at Fabuland's Doc David's Hospital (34 and 137).

Lucy Lamb This lamb comes with printed eyelashes, indicating she is female.

1980s

The 1980s were a golden age for LEGO® minifigures. Many young builders were discovering them for the first time as the minifigure reached US stores. Although the beloved minifigure's clothes and headgear might be switched around from set to set, the basic style remained the same—until 1989, when the arrival of the swashbuckling new LEGO® Pirates theme changed everything. Suddenly, minifigures could have eye patches, mustaches, stubble, or lipstick, not to mention hook-hands and peg-legs. The possibilities were endless!

HEY, I'VE GOT AN IDEA!
Stripy blue T-shirt

Bill This clever minifigure came with the *LEGOLAND Idea Book*, which followed the adventures of Bill and Mary.

Medical symbol

White Doctor This minifigure likes everything to match—she dyed her hair piece red to go with her cross logo.

Glamorous Lady Wearing a gold necklace that was first seen on a princess in the Castle theme in 1979, this lady appropriately features in Town Square – Castle Scene (1592).

I HOPE IT'S BETTER THAN YOUR LAST ONE!

Glamorous gold necklace

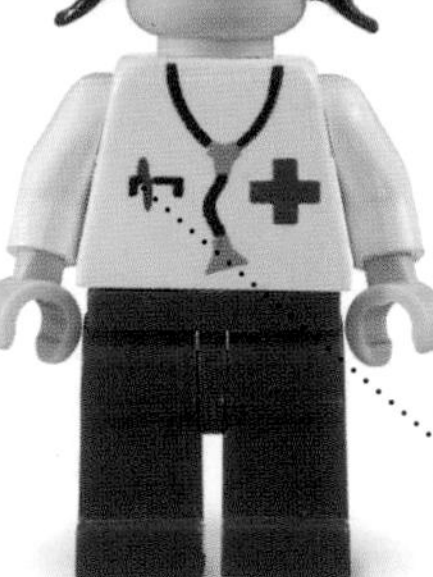
Pen for scribbling medical notes

Red Doctor This doctor is ready for any medical emergency—as long as it can be solved with a stethoscope....

DID YOU KNOW? The pigtails hair piece has appeared in three colors—red, black, and white.

1980

THIS YEAR SAW the LEGO Group continuing to expand, with new factories being built and the brick establishing itself in more and more homes. No new themes were introduced this year, but the LEGOLAND® Town subtheme saw significant expansion. The latest in a line of LEGO Idea Books would also come out, with a story centered on Bill and Mary, the two minifigures packaged with it. But inventive LEGO fans were already coming up with great ideas of their own and experimenting with their new sets and minifigures!

TOWN

The Town subtheme kept growing in 1980, with the addition of a Main Street (6390), an Auto Repair Shop (6363), a Gas Station (6375), and a number of new vehicles cruising the streets. Some minifigures were used in multiple sets or multiple times in the same set, often with only minor variations.

Helmets are vital for high-speed racing
Even the racer has go-faster stripes.

Racing Driver Dressed up in racing gear, this driver has to wait until 1983 to actually race a car in Race Car (6609).

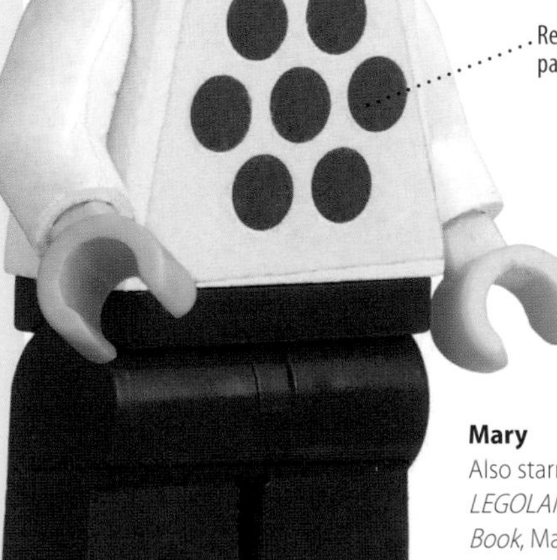
Red pigtails
Red flower pattern

Mary Also starring in *LEGOLAND Idea Book*, Mary is pals with White Doctor and likes to match, too.

Top hat

GOT MY TOP HAT

This black figure represents a statue in the Town Square (1592). Nobody seems to know just who it is supposed to be a statue of, but he had a very nice hat!

Statue This mysterious figure is wearing the top hat accessory for the first time.

Torso with shirt detail

Builder Introduced this year, the Builder minifigure was last seen residing in one of the houses he helped build on Main Street (10041).

EXXON
Exxon logo

Exxon Worker Run out of gas? This helpful lady will be at your service in Exxon Gas Station (6375).

Mærsk Line Worker This minifigure works for container shipping company Mærsk. He appears in the promotional set Mærsk Line Container Truck (1651).

Sky-blue hard hat
I'M SO EXCITED I JUST CAN'T CONTAIN MYSELF.

Black fire helmet

Fire Chief The Fire Chief is the first minifigure to wear the fire uniform. But he isn't the last—it is seen on more than five other minifigures.

Red hard hat
Blue button down shirt

Construction Worker Appearing in more than 20 sets, this minifigure has been catching up on his sleep for the past ten years.

Same shirt as the Builder and Construction Worker

Train Guard This minifigure has guarded trains in more than 12 sets. He ran out of steam in 1985.

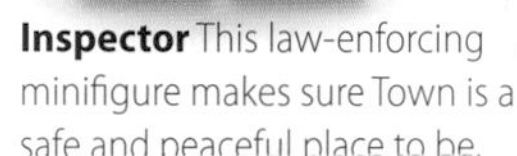
Rare white pigtails piece
Police badge

Inspector This law-enforcing minifigure makes sure Town is a safe and peaceful place to be.

CASTLE GUARD

This guard minifigure does not come from an official Castle set. He was part of two identical sets, both called Town Square, which came out in the Netherlands and United Kingdom only. Although dressed in medieval garb, he is actually wearing a costume and "guarding" a castle in a modern town.

Domed medieval-style helmet
Lion with two hearts sticker

Castle Guard This minifigure has a distinctive design on his torso, perhaps inspired by English King Richard the Lionheart.

1592
LEGO

Town Square – Castle Scene (1592) This set comes with a book shop, castle, and fish-and-chips kiosk, plus 11 minifigures including castle guards and villagers.

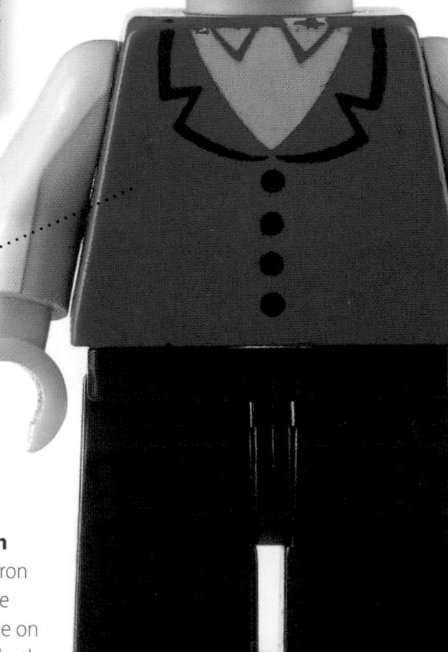
Fancy top hat
Blue vest with shirt underneath

DID YOU KNOW? The LEGO top hat piece has been worn by around 20 minifigures.

Shop Patron The Shop Patron seems to have based his style on the Statue—both wear the same new top hat piece.

ANYONE NEED A HAND?
Plain blue top
Black pants in case of job interviews

Town Guy Unsure of what his job actually is, the Town Guy wears his best hat and pants each day, just in case someone figures it out.

1981

THE MINIFIGURE CROSSED the Atlantic this year, as the three original Castle sets that had taken Europe by storm were released in the United States. The Town and Space LEGOLAND® subthemes continued to expand, bringing with them new and exciting places for LEGO fans to build and play. New police, fire, and medical minifigures joined the ever-growing cast of LEGO characters as Town continued to base imaginative play on real-world places, and the heroes who work in them.

TOWN

You never know what may happen in Town. You could be relaxing in a Summer Cottage (6365), while firefighters race from the Fire Station (6382) to save the day. Got a medical emergency? The LEGO ambulance or the minifigures from the rescue helicopter (6691) may help out. Real life was the key theme this year, and this would continue for years to come.

Policeman's hat
All-weather jacket
Precinct Badge

Police Officer It's quite safe in Town, so the Police Officer spends his time greeting visitors, directing traffic, and eating donuts.

Pigtails are very popular in Town sets
Casual clothing

Red Girl There's plenty to see from her front yard, so the Red Girl spends her time sipping tea and watching her neighbors.

6365
LEGOLAND
LEGO

Summer Cottage (6365) The Red Girl has spent a lot of time perfecting the Summer Cottage's front yard so she can entertain her guests.

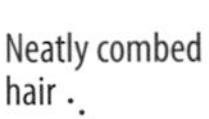
Neatly combed hair
MY FACE HURTS FROM SMILING SO MUCH.

Red Man This minifigure can always be found in some kind of scrape, waiting to be rescued. But he seems quite cheerful about it!

DID YOU KNOW? The rescue helicopter (6691) was the first minifigure-compatible helicopter to be released.

Always smiling

White Top Guy No one knows where this minifigure comes from, or why he's in Town, but he helps out whenever there's trouble.

Neat coveralls

Firewoman Dressed in a basic station uniform, this Firefighter also maintains the fire engines.

Hard hat protects from falling debris
Fireman's uniform
6382
LEGOLAND
LEGO

Fireman This Firefighter's torso printed with gold buttons is featured on nine minifigures.

Fire Station (6382) This station is very busy. There is always something to do, whether it is polishing the engine or manning the radios.

Shell logo
Warm pants for working outdoors

Gas Worker When this minifigure signed up for her job she thought the shell symbol on her uniform meant she'd be working at the beach….

Blue coveralls are perfect for any task

Blue Girl Changing tires or fighting fires, this minifigure lends a hand wherever she is needed.

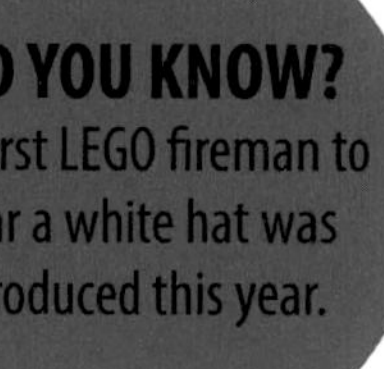

DID YOU KNOW?
The first LEGO fireman to wear a white hat was introduced this year.

Red hat stands out in a crowd
Pocket holds bandages and treats
Symbol indicates he works in the hospital
Standard white medical uniform
I THINK YOUR HEAD NEEDS TO BE REPLACED.

Medic
When there is not an emergency, the Medic drives his ambulance around the town greeting people and offering lifts.

Bright red pants match red emblem on torso

Doctor This torso, with broad collars and a medical symbol, has featured on 12 minifigures.

Even her pigtails are pristine!

Surgeon The Surgeon is always spotless—she hates getting anything on her crisp white uniform.

Pilot's helmet

Helicopter Pilot The Pilot always has his helmet on in case he has to fly at short notice.

Polished tusks
A good listener

Elton Elephant Everyone is friendly in FABULAND, but Elton is also known for his stylish outfits and polite nature. He appears in three sets.

LEGO® FABULAND™

The gentle fun of FABULAND continued this year, with the introduction of cute new characters Elton Elephant, Bonnie Bunny, Boris Bulldog, and Barney Bear, who all showed up to play.

LEGO® BASIC

LEGO Basic introduced figures this year—these colorful finger puppet figures would be a part of LEGO Basic Building sets for decades. These sets were designed to promote creative play and focused solely on building rather than a specific model.

Made from one piece

Female Finger Puppet This figure has appeared in 21 sets. She just loves watching buildings being constructed.

A keen eye for detail

Male Finger Puppet After appearing in 24 sets, this finger puppet is an expert in LEGO architecture.

I LOOK LIKE A DANDY NEXT TO MY BIKER PALS!
Classic helmet in red
Red torso with zipper details

Red Biker This minifigure won't ever get lonely—he featured in Little People & Accessories (1066) with 35 other minifigure friends!

1982

TOWN AND SPACE were the big stories this year. Three new Space sets rocketed into the universe in 1982, bringing with them four astronaut minifigures. Meanwhile, Town fans could explore everywhere from the local post office to the highways and byways of the city. Also released this year was a set featuring an amazing 36 minifigures including a chef, a doctor, a fireman, and a police officer.

Black wrench for breakdown emergencies
White police hat
Black shirt with pockets
Highway logo

Breakdown Repair Man Coming to the rescue of minifigures in broken down cars is this helpful repair man, in Breakdown Assistance (1590).

Highway Patrol Usually seen patrolling the highway in his emergency truck, this minifigure is debuting a new torso with a highway design.

DID YOU KNOW? The first postal worker minifigures were released this year.

Torso also seen on Lord Sam Sinister from the Adventurers theme in 1998.

Driver On his way to the office this minifigure's car breaks down. Luckily, Breakdown Repair Man is on the case in Breakdown Assistance (1590).

TOWN

Town went postal this year! Although there had been other sets in the past with the word "Mail" on a brick, 1982's Mail Truck (6651) and Post Office (6362) models were the first ones to really focus on the mail delivery service. This would later be expanded into the Cargo subtheme.

MINIFIGURES SURE GET LOTS OF FAN MAIL!

Post office logo

Mailman Proudly wearing a new shirt with the post office logo, this minifigure always delivers the mail with a smile.

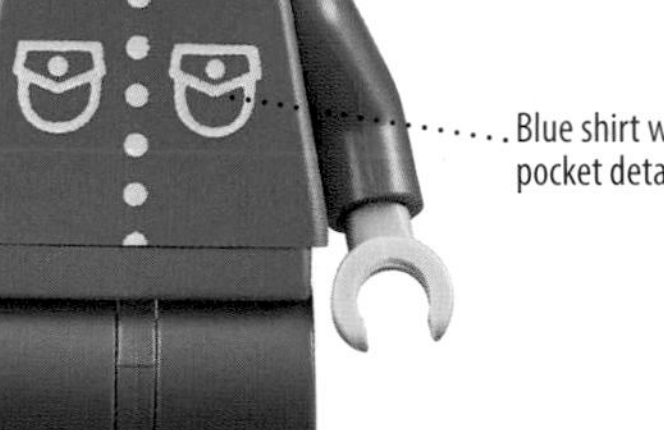
Blue shirt with pocket detail

Postal Worker This mailman looks happy, but really he wishes his shirt had the post office logo on it, too.

6651
LEGOLAND
LEGO

Mail Truck (6651) This set features a truck, a mailbox, and a mail worker minifigure.

Medical red cross logo

Doctor With a stethoscope around her neck and a pen in her top pocket, this doctor is ready to take someone's stats.

I CAN FACE ANY PERIL DRESSED IN MY FANCY UNIFORM.
All-black uniform is set off by gold details and red belt

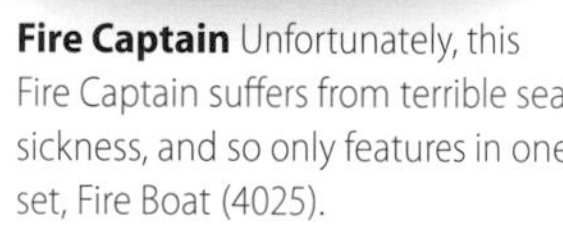

Fire Captain Unfortunately, this Fire Captain suffers from terrible sea sickness, and so only features in one set, Fire Boat (4025).

White pigtails

Red Villager No prizes for guessing what color is this minifigure's favorite! She appears in one set (1066).

White helmet with chin guard

Gold lapel detail on torso

Red belt with gold buckle

Fireman
This fireman gets to the scene of a fire in super-fast time in his helicopter, featured in Fire Patrol Copter (6657).

Utility gray helmet

Monochrome Man
This minifigure likes to blend in, hence his plain black and white outfit.

DID YOU KNOW?
Yellow was chosen for minifigures from the original LEGO color palette as an ethnically-neutral color—to represent all races and ethnicities.

Oversized molded bear head
Big, yellow beak for pecking

Billy Bear
This bear works at the service station in Fabuland, and comes in three sets.

Patrick Parrot
Say cheese! This colorful parrot prefers to be behind the camera in Photographer Patrick Parrot (3782).

LEGO® FABULAND™

FABULAND roared ahead in 1982, releasing 24 figures, more than any other theme. Eleven new sets were added, including a FABULAND House complete with a car.

Stripy Lady This lady is extremely proud of her home—in fact, she loves her Town House (6372) so much she never leaves it.

DON'T I LOOK GREAT IN STRIPES? BE HONEST.

Stripy sweater

Blue jacket with white shirt

Businessman This minifigure thought that his business suit was unique, and was upset to discover that it's been worn by more than ten other minifigures.

White peaked hat

Multi-color Man Hanging out with his minifigure friends makes this guy smile, in Little People with Accessories (1066).

Daredevil Pilot
Complete with aviator-style hat and an impressive mustache, this pilot is ready to take to the skies.

Fearless expression

Firefighter hat

Firefighter These DUPLO figures have much more detailed faces than early minifigures, and include eyebrows, detailed eyes, and a nose.

LEGO® DUPLO®

Little builders got the chance to have some adventure of their own as a fire truck and a plane joined the assortment, complete with Firefighter and Daredevil Pilot figures.

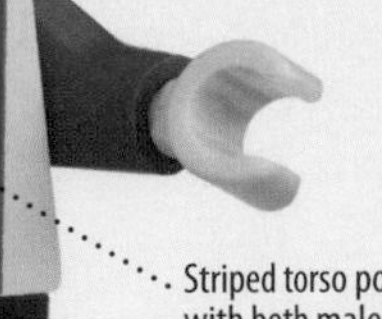
I'M SURE MY RED STRIPE MAKES ME GO FASTER!

Helmet also seen on the Space astronauts from 1978

Striped torso popular with both male and female minifigures

Motorcycle Dude
This minifigure is usually seen with a wrench in his hand—his motorcycle breaks down often.

1983

THIS YEAR, TOWN provided a lot of action and fun with new sets and minifigures, while Space hit the stratosphere with five exciting sets. Castle released only one set, but it was a minifigure collection, so that was definitely worth getting excited about. It all added up to new police, fire, and knight minifigures, plus some new town folk to populate a playscape. Many of these minifigures became highly collectible in later years.

TOWN

Town offered a varied mix of sets this year, including a new Police Station (6384) and Police Car (6623), two construction-themed sets, a Shell Service Station (6371), and a forerunner of the Cargo subtheme, the Delivery Van (6624). Train released a new station, complete with nine new minifigures, and four firemen appeared in a minifigure-only set.

Air tank is full of oxygen

Firefighter
Classic firefighter to the rescue! This torso was first seen in 1980 and it still looks pristine!

Plain white torso has been worn by more than 100 other minifigures

Motorcycle Rider
Uh oh! This guy's motorcycle has broken down. Luckily, he has a trailer to take it to the mechanic, in Motorcycle Transport (6654).

DID YOU KNOW?
The Railway Station (7824) would be the last Railway Station released for eight years.

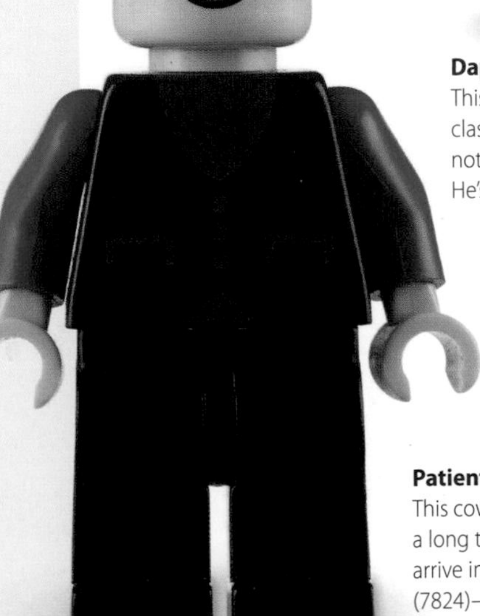

Classic cowboy hat worn by more than 30 other minifigures

Patient Cowboy
This cowboy will be waiting a long time for a train to arrive in Railway Station (7824)—the set doesn't come with a train!

Torso seen on more than 10 other minifigures

Dapper Passenger
This minifigure is wearing a classic policeman's hat. He's not a policeman, however. He's just a train passenger.

Red pigtails are seen on more than 10 other minifigures.

Train Station Worker
The minifigures better have their train tickets at the ready—this worker has a fiery temper.

Gold necklace

Train Passenger
This passenger feels like a princess—her torso was also seen on a Classic Castle Princess in 1979.

7824
LEGO

Railway Station (7824)
Nine minifigures, a ticket booth, and a food stand for hungry commuters are included in this set.

CENTER PARTS LIKE MINE ARE JUST SO HOT RIGHT NOW.

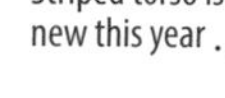

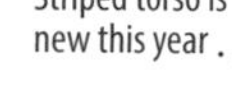

Torso also seen on the Motorcycle Dude

Vacationer This vacationer is staying at her new Holiday Home (6374). She is most excited about her sliding patio roof.

Parted hair piece

Striped torso is new this year

Striped Lady
The first to wear a parted hair piece (a minifigure style that has endured the years), this minifigure is a trendsetter.

DID YOU KNOW?

If all the minifigures ever produced formed their own country, their population would be three times larger than China's.

Service Station Attendant
This helpful attendant is debuting the new style cap, that has since been worn by more than 400 other minifigures.

Company logo

There are no ketchup stains on this chef's whites!

Chef Serving the hungry townspeople hamburgers always puts a smile on this chef's face.

Zippered torso is identical to Service Station Customer and Freight Operator

Hungry Lady This minifigure wants a hamburger and she wants it NOW, in Burger Stand (6683).

Helmet has protected more than 30 other minifigure heads

Service Station Customer
This customer always gets a speedy service at the Service Station (6371).

Visor with grille clips onto helmet

Standard black hair piece

Camera Man This guy used to work at the Hospital (9364) but he was last seen as a camera man in TV Camera Crew (6659).

Red Police hat

Freight Operator A job at the Freight Loading Depot (7838) keeps this minifigure smiling.

Classic Castle shield emblem

Black Knight
This brave Knight's torso was first worn by a knight in 1978, and has only been seen on five other Knight minifigures.

CASTLE

Only one Castle set was released in 1983—Castle Minifigures (6002)—a collection of four Knight minifigures. The two pairs of Knights had different helmets and torso designs, marking them as belonging to different royal factions.

Freight Train Operator
Wearing his blue uniform and yellow cap, this figure keeps all the DUPLO trains running smoothly.

Blue train uniform

LEGO® DUPLO®

This DUPLO figure appeared in two DUPLO Train sets this year, Freight Train (2700) and Passenger Train (2705). He also made an appearance in later years in DUPLO Gas Station (2639) and DUPLO Farm sets.

Classic astronaut helmet • 1978 • Red Spaceman • LEGOLAND Space.

Peaked cap • 1978 • Coast Guard Captain • LEGOLAND Town.

Black fire helmet • 1978 • Fireman • LEGOLAND Town.

Black stetson • 1978 • Patron • LEGOLAND Town.

Norman helmet with neck guard • 1978 • Blue Cavalry Knight • LEGOLAND Castle.

Yellow helmet with blue visor • 1987 • Yellow Futuron • LEGOLAND Space.

Pointed hat with brim and yellow feather • 1987 • Forestman with Pouch • LEGOLAND Castle.

Bicorne with crossbones • 1989 • Captain Redbeard • LEGO Pirates.

Red bandana • 1989 • Blue Pirate • LEGO Pirates.

Tricorne • 1989 • Pirate Blue Shirt • LEGO Pirates.

Horn headdress • 1997 • Medicine Man • LEGO Western.

Helmet with nose guard and bat wings • 1997 • Basil the Bat Lord • LEGO Castle.

Fluorescent bubble helmet • 1998 • Gypsy Moth • LEGO Space.

Nemes headdress • 1998 • Pharaoh Skeleton • LEGO Adventurers.

Pith helmet • 1998 • Baron Von Barron • LEGO Adventurers.

Eagle ceremonial headdress • 1999 • Achu • LEGO Adventurers.

Ninja mask • 2000 • Ninja Princess • LEGO Castle.

White molded helmet and mask • 2001 • Stormtrooper • LEGO *Star Wars*.

Turban • 2001 • Professor Quirrell • LEGO® Harry Potter™.

Full cowl with pointed ears • 2006 • Batman Black Suit • LEGO® Batman™.

Jester's hat • 2008 • Jester • LEGO Castle.

Gold crown tiara • 2009 • Crown Queen • LEGO Castle.

Beret • 2010 • Mime • LEGO Minifigures.

Bearskin • 2011 • Royal Guard • LEGO Minifigures.

Domed sailor's hat • 2011 • Sailor • LEGO Minifigures.

Hard hat • 1979 • Construction Worker • LEGOLAND Town.

Chef's hat • 1979 • Chef • LEGOLAND Town.

Top hat • 1980 • Shop Patron • LEGOLAND Town.

Grille helmet with black plume • 1984 • Blue Knight • LEGOLAND Castle.

Hennin • 1986 • Maiden with Cape • LEGOLAND Castle.

Fusilier hat • 1989 • Imperial Soldier • LEGO Pirates.

Cone-shaped wizard's hat • 1993 • Majisto Wizard • LEGO Castle.

Islander mask and feathered headdress • 1994 • King Kahuka • LEGO Pirates.

Gold crown with white plume • 1995 • The King • LEGO Castle.

Feathered headdress • 1997 • Chief • LEGO Western.

MAD ABOUT HATS!

LEGO® HEADGEAR has been around longer than the modern minifigure. The first prototype LEGO figures, released in 1975, may have had blank faces, but they were also wearing hats! LEGO hats fit on a stud on the top of the standard minifigure head. They are often specially molded pieces, and help to distinguish minifigures from one another by indicating their job or role in the story. LEGO hats and headgear are compatible with nearly all minifigures. There are a few exceptions, primarily licensed characters with specially molded heads, such as Yoda and Plo Koon from LEGO® *Star Wars*®.

Domed molded helmet with neck guard • 1999 • Darth Vader • LEGO *Star Wars*.

Hood • 1999 • Padawan Obi Wan Kenobi • LEGO *Star Wars*.

Half mask with pointed ears • 2006 • Catwoman • LEGO Batman.

Fedora • 2008 • Indiana Jones • LEGO® *Indiana Jones*™.

Asian conical hat • 2011 • Sensei Wu • LEGO Ninjago.

Red crested helmet • 2013 • Roman Commander • LEGO Minifigures.

YAY! SOMEONE TO JOUST AGAINST!
Fixed face grille helmet
Armored breastplate is new this year

Yellow Plume Knight This brave Knight helps to protect the King's castle with his lance and shield in King's Castle (6080).

1984

IN THE EARLY YEARS, LEGO® minifigures rarely ran into conflict or encountered anything that would wipe the big grins off their faces. Space explorers didn't clash with aliens, everything ran smoothly in Town, and the Castle knights only had gentle adventures. However, the peace was disrupted in 1984, as Castle introduced two opposing groups of knights—the Crusaders and the Black Falcons—who could compete in jousts and battle it out with catapults and siege towers.

CASTLE

The Crusaders and the Black Falcons were the first of several groups that would make up the Castle mythos. They arrived with two fortresses, the Knight's Castle (6074) and King's Castle (6080), plus an impressive Siege Tower (6061).

Black plume

Blue Knight The Blue Knight takes his job very seriously, but unfortunately for him, he features in only one set, Knight's Castle (6073).

Plume element introduced this year
Gray grille helmet

Black Knight An accomplished horseman, this Knight shows off his skills in Knight's Challenge (1584).

Red Knight This Knight looks friendly but just try escaping from the Siege Tower (6061) and he quickly turns fierce!

Black Falcon Soldier Proudly wearing the new Falcon crest on his torso, this Soldier is ready to defeat the Knights!

The Black Falcons typically wear black helmets with chinstraps

New cowl element keeps minifigure's head warm
Tie shirt also comes in blue and green

Peasant This Peasant is debuting a new torso with printed pouch and a farmer's cowl.

Brown apron exclusive to this minifigure

Blacksmith Being a Blacksmith is a messy job. Luckily, this minifigure wears an apron to keep his yellow torso clean.

Helmet with neck protector

Black Falcon with Neck Protector This soldier loves a brutal battle—he appears in no less than seven sets.

DID YOU KNOW?
From this year on, Castle factions had unique crests on their armor, shields, and flags.

1984

6030
LEGOLAND
LEGO

Catapult (6030) This set features a catapult with flags and two minifigures to operate it.

Crusader with Quiver This Knight prefers to ride his horse and cart than do battle, in Horse Cart (6022).

Quiver of arrows is a new element this year

Crusader with Neck Protector This Crusader guards the Blacksmith Shop (6040). In 1987, he reappears with a spear in Battering Ram (6062).

WHO'S GONNA ATTACK A BLACKSMITH'S SHOP?

Crusader crest

Helmet with chin guard

Bow and arrow piece is new this year

Lion Crusader This Crusader is debuting the alternative Crusader coat-of-arms—the upright lion.

Ax Crusader If this Crusader knew his archenemies were on the opposite page he wouldn't look so happy!

DID YOU KNOW?
The first minifigure-rideable horses appeared this year, featuring in seven sets.

Fisherman
The last time this figure went to sea, all he caught was a cold. He hopes to be more successful on his next trip.

Life preserver

Diver This deep sea diver is determined not to get stranded at sea, so he is attached to a safety reel.

Diving helmet

LEGO® DUPLO®

LEGO DUPLO sailed the ocean blue this year with sets including Deep Sea Diver (2618) and Sea Explorer (2649). New figures sported diving gear and life vests as they adventured on and beneath the waves.

SPACE

Space returned with eight new sets in 1984, including the Intergalactic Command Base (6971) and the Robot Command Center (6951). Astronaut minifigures appeared in two new colors, as they explored the universe and searched for precious uranium.

Classic Space logo

Black Spaceman
Black is a new color for the Space astronauts this year.

Space suit makes its debut in blue

Blue Spaceman
This astronaut is about to set off on his first mission into space in Space Dart-I (6824).

Cool leather jacket

Helicopter Pilot
This Pilot looks super stylish flying his helicopter in his new leather jacket.

Cap is blue for the first time this year

Coveralls are new this year

Repair Man This handy man can repair anything, from tires and trucks, to trains and tractors.

Red helmet with visor dimples is exclusive to this minifigure

Mailman The Town mail is never delivered late thanks to this mailman.

TOWN

Seventeen new sets hit the shelves in 1984, with the most significant being the first Cargo Center (6391). The subject of mail and package delivery had only been seen once before, in a 1982 Post Office set (6362). This set was followed up with a Delivery Center (6355) in 1985. Cargo later appeared as a subtheme of its own, in 2007.

I'M ALL AQUIVER ABOUT MY QUIVER!
Helmet with chin guard

Crusader Knight with Quiver This minifigure is identical to his Crusader Knight friend, apart from a quiver accessory, which makes him feel special.

1985

THE LEGO® SYSTEM of play with its endless possibilities celebrated its 30th birthday in 1985, with a record number of new minifigures released and the launch of Airport as part of the Town subtheme. Both Town and Space saw strong assortments this year, while Castle took a bit of a back seat before making a comeback in 1986. This year offered further proof that the world of LEGO building and LEGO minifigures would continue to change and grow every year.

CASTLE

This year Castle only released two sets and a minifigure collection. These added to the Black Falcon and Crusader factions, but were smaller models. Prisoner Convoy (6055) featured five horses and four minifigures, and was the only Castle carriage to be drawn by four horses. Black Knight's Treasure (6011) featured only one Black Falcon knight minifigure.

Black Falcon emblem

Black Falcon This knight doesn't feature in any action sets this year, which makes him sad but he doesn't show it.

Crusaders lion emblem

Crusader Knight Not having a quiver accessory is fine by this Knight—he prefers using a spear, anyway.

DID YOU KNOW?
The 1985 Castle sets were released in Europe and other parts of the world, but not the United States.

Jetpack is also seen in gray and black

Solar panel
Lever piece

Blue Droid This Droid accompanies the astronauts on their Solar Power Transporter (6952). Which is good, as he's running out of solar power.

Black Droid This rookie Droid is about to travel into space for the first time, in Space Scooter with Robot (6807).

ROBOTS ROCK

These two robots appeared in Space sets this year. Although neither is officially classed as a minifigure, they represent some of the earlier robots and androids in a LEGO theme.

White Spaceman The Space astronauts breathed a sigh of relief this year—they finally received a jetpack element.

SPACE

Thirteen new Space sets were released in 1985, most of them consisting of a small vehicle with one astronaut minifigure. The larger sets, including the Solar Power Transporter (6952) and FX-Star Patroller (6931), continued the tradition of Space models being modular, with features such as detachable cockpits.

Coveralls with a handy pocket

Coveralls are black for the first time

Caring face
Bright red hair

Forklift Driver This guy hopes to be a car mechanic one day. He's reassured that they have the same taste in clothes.

Car Mechanic This minifigure makes his debut this year. He's handy with a wrench, which is why he works in the Car Repair Shop (1966).

Community Worker Caring for the commuity is this minifigure's specialty, in Community Workers (1063).

DO I GET FREQUENT BUILDER MILES?

Blue helmet also seen on the Classic Spacemen in 1984
Same zipper detail as Helicopter Pilot

Biker This Biker's torso is new this year—it probably won't stay pristine white for long!

Police hat worn by more than 200 minifigures
Horn emblem

Mailman This minifigure's first career choice was a policeman, but he only got as far as buying the hat.

TOWN

Town set a record this year, with an impressive 49 new minifigures released. The big story, however, was the chance to fly the buildable skies of LEGO Air as the first ever Airport set (6392) made its appearance.

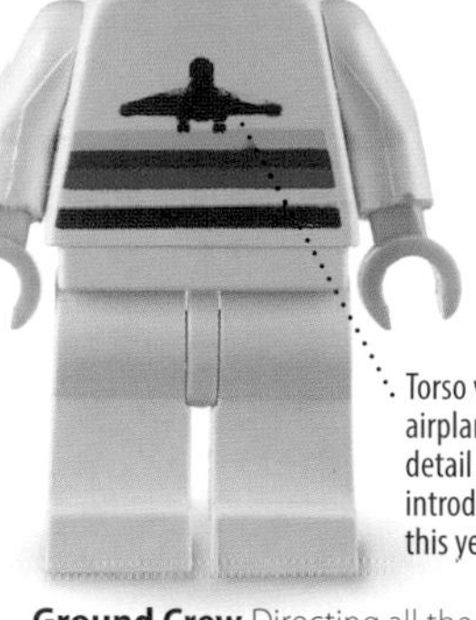
Torso with airplane detail introduced this year

Ground Crew Directing all the minifigure vacationers to the airplanes is a hard job—this guy wishes he was taking off too.

Standard LEGO hair piece

Red helmet is also popular with Classic Space astronauts
Red neckerchief

Gray cowboy hat
Torso only seen on Classic Town minifigures

Cargo Trailer Driver Heavy LEGO luggage is no problem for this minifigure. He just carts it to the airplane in his trailer.

Helicopter Pilot The Pilot takes to the skies, looking stylish in his new zippered torso.

Ice-Cream Server This guy keeps the Town minifigures refreshed with ice cream from his cart.

Container Truck Driver Despite appearances this guy doesn't ride a horse. He actually drives a truck.

Gold buttons
Airplane logo
Pressed black pants

Pilot The frequent flyer is about to take to the skies wearing the Pilot's uniform, introduced this year.

Airport Tower Operator Responsible for directing all the LEGO airplanes, this minifigure is always calm—apart from when she sees another minifigure wearing her hair piece.

Hair piece seen on more than 100 minifigures

6392
LEGOLAND
LEGO

Airport (6392) LEGO building finally took to the skies from this airport, which included eight minifigures, a control tower, an airplane, a helicopter, and even a restaurant for hungry passengers.

THIS CAP GIVES ME HAT HAIR.
Plain white cap
Plain red torso also used on Classic Castle Knights between 1978 and 1981 (underneath their breastplates).

Speedboat Driver Exclusive to set RV with Speedboat (6698), this minifigure can't wait to get out on the water.

I HAVE NO HAIR TO GET HAT HAIR.
Torso used only on Town minifgures
Black helmet with thick chinstrap is new this year.
Hair piece later used in 2001 for Professor Snape from the Harry Potter™ theme
Blue undershirt

Young Man This minifigure is new this year, but is wearing a striped T-shirt, first introduced in 1985.

Motorbike Racer This racer is wearing a new torso this year—maybe the "S" logo stands for speed?

1986

ANOTHER BRILLIANT YEAR for fun and imagination, 1986 saw a wide variety of Town sets, new Crusader and Black Falcon sets in Castle, plus the last classic Space sets. Town and Space also got the first Light and Sound kits, an electronic system that used light and sound bricks powered by a 9V battery box, bringing even more excitement to the LEGO® play experience. Minifigures were joined by new LEGO® Basic, LEGO® DUPLO®, and LEGO® Technic figures as the world of LEGO building continued to expand.

TOWN

Twenty-eight sets appeared in 1986, including the first police station in three years, Police Command Base (6386), a new RV with a Speedboat (6698), and a detailed Riding Stable (6379).

Townsperson She lives in the Town, not Castle, but this minifigure has the same torso as the maiden minifigures from the Castle theme, also first seen in 1986.

Protective hard hat
New torso design this year
White gloved hands

Horseback Rider Giddyup! This horseback rider is well-prepared for a day jumping over brick hurdles wearing his fancy new riding jacket.

Black variant of construction helmet is new this year

Stable Boy Practical blue coveralls are necessary when mucking out stables and cleaning horses all day.

Only two Town minifigures have this torso

Striped Horseback Rider Wearing the same torso as the motorbike racer, but in yellow, this horseback rider isn't as well turned out as the other horseback rider.

6379
LEGOLAND
LEGO

Riding Stable (6379) Two horses have plenty of exercise and a luxurious stable in this set, which also comes with a horseback rider, stable boy, and a hay cart.

1986

CASTLE

Only five Castle sets were released this year, but they included the impressive Black Falcon's Fortress (6074) and the Guarded Inn (6067), which was re-released in 2001 as part of the LEGO Legends series. Two maiden minifigures—with different colored hats—appeared this year, along with new Crusader and Black Falcon soldiers.

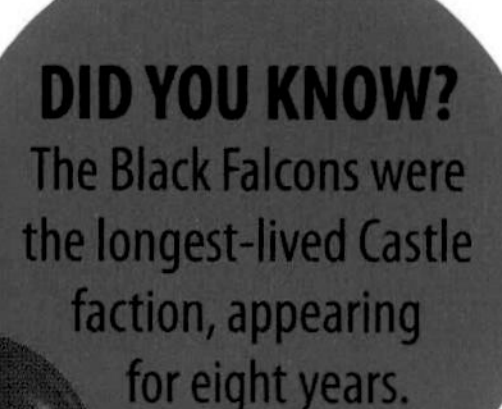

DID YOU KNOW?
The Black Falcons were the longest-lived Castle faction, appearing for eight years.

Hat piece also seen in black on Queen Lenora from the Castle theme in 2000

Maiden This merrry Maiden's cone-shaped hat is new this year.

Helmets are either gray or black

Helmet with neck guard

Showing off his armor wares

Blue plastic cape is attached between neck and torso at the back

Crusader Ax This Crusader has the important job of guarding the Maiden in set 6067.

Crusader Lion The Crusaders' traditional coat-of-arms is an upright lion.

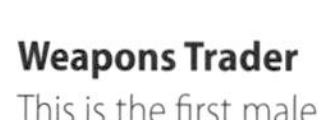

Weapons Trader This is the first male minifigure to wear this hair piece. He doesn't seem to mind, though.

Maiden with Cape This fair Maiden likes to show off her new cone hat to visitors of the Guarded Inn (6067).

DROIDS

These two robots were included in a Space Minifigures set (6702). Droids like these were a popular addition to Space in the 1980s.

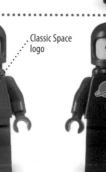

Robot claws

Short Space Droid The short Space Droid may not have a computer on its front, but it does have a flashing red light!

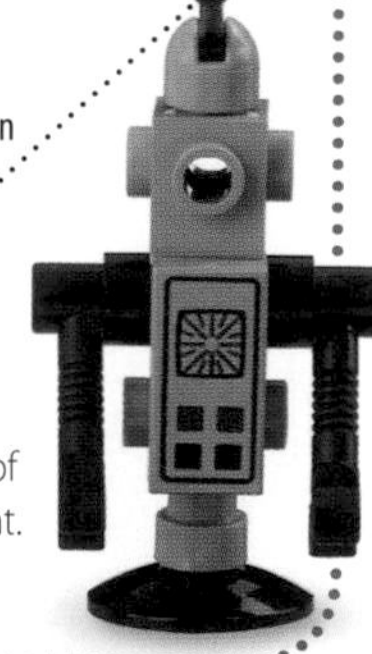

Lever piece commonly used on droids and robots

Tall Space Droid This Space Droid is a bit more technologically advanced than its short friend, with the addition of a computer tile on its front.

SPACE

This would be the last year of Classic Space, before the first factions debuted in 1987 with Futuron. Sixteen sets were released this year, featuring the traditional modular space vehicles and astronauts in primary colors. Major sets this year included Alien Moon Stalker (6940) and Cosmic Fleet Voyager (6985).

Jetpack

Classic Space logo

Bright red spacesuit

Black Spaceman The Spaceman's jetpack was introduced in 1985, but the gray variant is new this year.

Blue Spaceman Wearing a blue space suit, helmet, and air tank, this astronaut isn't feeling blue—he's off to explore space!

Red Spaceman This red Spaceman is the most common Spaceman minifigure, featuring in 46 sets.

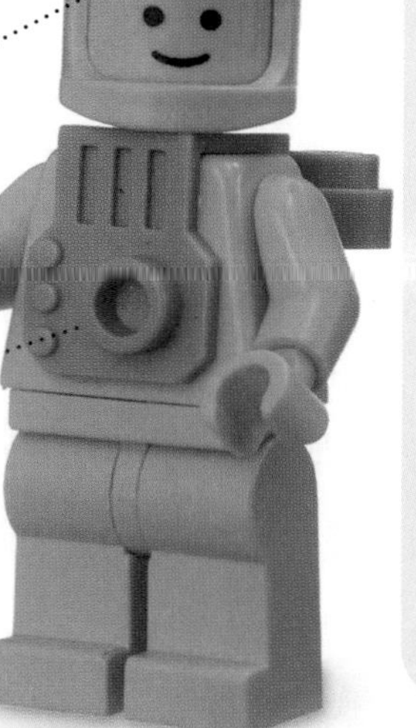

Helmet first released in 1978

Jetpack

Yellow Spaceman This Spaceman's space suit matches his yellow minifigure body perfectly.

Huge smile

Boy This may be the first Basic figure to have legs—but he decides to sit down and fly a Helicopter (390).

LEGO BASIC

This figure was one of the few to appear in LEGO Basic sets, the predecessor to today's Creator line.

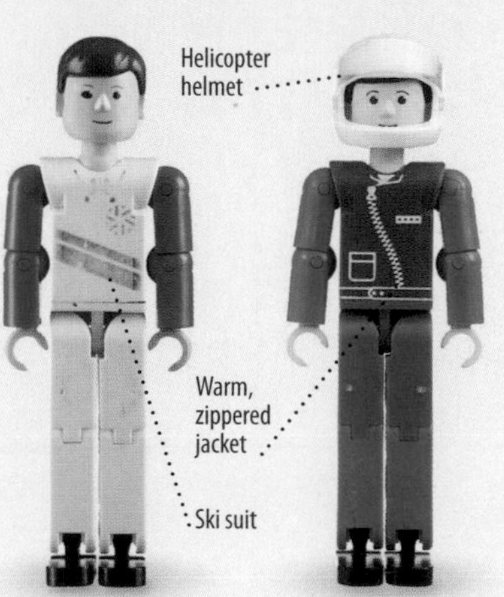

Helicopter helmet

Warm, zippered jacket

Ski suit

Skier One minute this figure is having fun on the slopes on his Snow Scooter (8620), the next he is being rescued by the Air Rescue Unit (8660).

Pilot This figure pilots his Polar Copter (8640) and Prop Plane (8855) making sure the Skier figures stay safe on the slopes.

LEGO TECHNIC

Figures were introduced in 1986 in the new LEGO Technic Arctic Action subtheme, which also featured vehicles and structures designed for an arctic environment. Arctic Action only lasted one year.

Red fire helmet

Firefighter This figure has fought many fires—all with a smile on his face.

LEGO® DUPLO®

This figure first appeared in his fire engine in 1985 in the DUPLO Town set (2611). He continued to help the community in 1986, appearing in Community People (1042) and Community Vehicles (1044).

BOLDLY GOING WHERE NO MINIFIGURE HAS GONE BEFORE!
Helmet with blue visor element is new this year

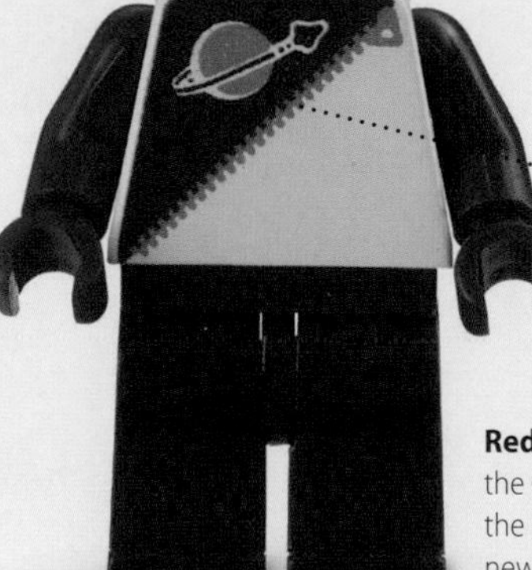
Gold zipper

Red Futuron Moving on from the Classic Spacemen from 1986, the Futuron astronauts have a new, flashy torso design, with gold zippered detail.

1987

NO MATTER WHERE a minifigure went in 1987, he or she was sure to run into adventure. Deep in the woods of Castle, Forestmen minifigures made an appearance for the first time. Beyond the stars, the forces of Futuron and Blacktron were about to have a galaxy-shaking clash. Closer to home, LEGO® Club was founded in this year, and would eventually bring minifigure fun into the homes of millions of LEGO fans. Buckle up your rocket belt and get ready to blast off into 1987!

FUTURON

Premiering with six sets, Futuron centers on peaceful minifigures based on Earth's moon. They have fun exploring the solar system, but constantly have to contend with the wicked Blacktron Astronauts.

Airtank

Yellow Futuron The busiest astronaut out of his space pals, this Futuron has featured in 12 sets. He retired in 1990.

Classic Space logo

Blue Futuron The Futurons all wear the standard helmet worn by more than 300 other minifigures.

DID YOU KNOW? Faces are printed onto LEGO minifigures using a mechanized process called Tampo printing.

6990
LEGOLAND
LEGO

Monorail Transport System (6990) This set features a battery-operated monorail plus five Futuron minifigures.

SPACE

Space introduced its first two competing factions in 1987, the Futuron explorers and the fiendish Blacktron Astronauts. Design of the minifigures, particularly on Blacktron, was a huge advance from Classic Space and helped cement Space as a much-loved LEGO line.

DARK DROID

The Blacktron Astronauts don't carry out all their missions alone—they need the help of this deadly droid figure. The Blacktron Droid was only available in one set, Invader (6894).

Robot arm

Blacktron Droid This Droid is all in black, just like the Blacktron Astronauts, apart from a red translucent piece.

BLACKTRON

The Blacktron Astronauts made their debut in three sets, including their starship, Renegade (6954). These minifigures are in space for profit and aren't going to let the peaceful Futuron explorers get in their way.

Airtank is attached with neck bracket
Torso also seen on the Blacktron Racer minifigure from the 1992 Classic Town theme

Blacktron Astronaut Wearing a new torso with a silver power pack design, the Blacktron Astronaut looks sleek and striking.

Fixed grille helmet
Silver armor

Black Falcon Knight A grilled helmet and armored breastplate should be enough to protect this Knight in battle!

KNIGHT CLASH

The Crusader and Black Falcon minifigures squared off in sets including Battering Ram (1971) this year, with the Crusaders laying siege to Black Falcon strongpoints. The "Black Falcon" name came from one of their sets and was never actually an official name.

Helmet with chin guard
Crusaders gold lion symbol

Crusader This courageous Crusader is on the lookout for Black Falcon knights—their Battering Ram doesn't scare him!

Blue plume

Blue Forestman Wearing his new forestman hat, this skilled archer gets to work, sharpening his arrows.

Green hat matches tunic and pants

Red Forestman This Forestman likes hanging out with his Forestmen friends deep in the woods in set 6066.

FORESTMEN

The Forestmen minifigures made their first appearance in the Camouflaged Outpost set (6066), identifiable by their distinctive hats.

New basket element also seen on the Hunchback from the Studios theme in 2002.

Black Forestman Carrying a heavy basket laden with LEGO bricks on his shoulders is hard work, but this Forestman seems happy enough.

CASTLE

New faces were on the medieval scene in 1987, as the Forestmen minifigures joined the Castle cast. They appeared in only one set this year, but their arrows would continue to fly until 1990. Elsewhere, the Crusaders battled the Black Falcons and would clash with the Forestmen, too, in future sets.

Tie shirt

Forestman with Pouch This Forestman looks after the precious gold pieces they "collect" from the rich in his waist pouch.

Red plume

Brown-hatted Forestman His brown hat distinguishes this Forestman from his Red Forestman friend.

White hat is usually seen on Police minifigures

Double-breasted suit jacket

LOW BRIDGE! EVERYONE TAKE OFF THEIR HEADS!

Boat Admiral As Captain of the Cargo Carrier (4030), this Admiral wears a new suit, with shiny gold buttons and gold anchor logo.

TOWN

Cargo had to be transported, and the Town minifigures were on the job! The Cargo Carrier (4030) appeared this year, complete with a captain and crew. But it wasn't all work in Town—the 4-wheelin' truck tore up the roads, looking for adventure!

Fire helmet
Zippered jacket

Firefighter This minifigure might not look like a classic Firefighter—his zippered torso commonly appears on bike racers—but he's just as brave.

Construction hard hat is white for the first time

Cargo Worker Sporting a new top with anchor logo, this Cargo Worker is ready for his first day hauling cargo at the dock.

Truck Driver This minifigure drives a truck and he's wearing a truck on his tank top—he's probably thinking about trucks, too. He just loves trucks, OK?

Red cap
Truck logo on tank top

Standard black male hair piece
WE ONLY TAKE PLASTIC.
Pocket for essential tools

Mechanic This mechanic's new red coveralls are only seen on Classic Town minifigures, both male and female.

1988

IT WAS ANOTHER exciting year for LEGO® builders. Town was back with the biggest race-themed set produced to date. Castle introduced the brutish Black Knights, and Futuron and Blacktron continued to clash in the far reaches of the Space subtheme. No matter what the situation, though, minifigures were always smiling. The minifigures from the three LEGOLAND® subthemes (Town, Castle, and Space) seemed content to carry on as they were. However, little did they know that this time next year, what it meant to be a minifigure would change forever....

TOWN

It was all about cars and keeping them well-serviced and on the LEGO roads in Town this year. Victory Lap Raceway (6305), with a whopping 13 minifigures, including four racers, mechanics, and spectators, left the starting line, as did the Metro Park and Service Tower (6394).

DID YOU KNOW?
Metro Park & Service Tower (6394) is the first set to feature car wash brushes.

Striped T-shirt

Service Station Worker
Servicing the cars of Town must be a great job—this gas worker can't wipe the smile from her face.

6394
LEGOLAND
LEGO

Metro Park & Service Tower (6394) Keeping all the Town cars running, this set includes a service station, multi-story car park, and six minifigures.

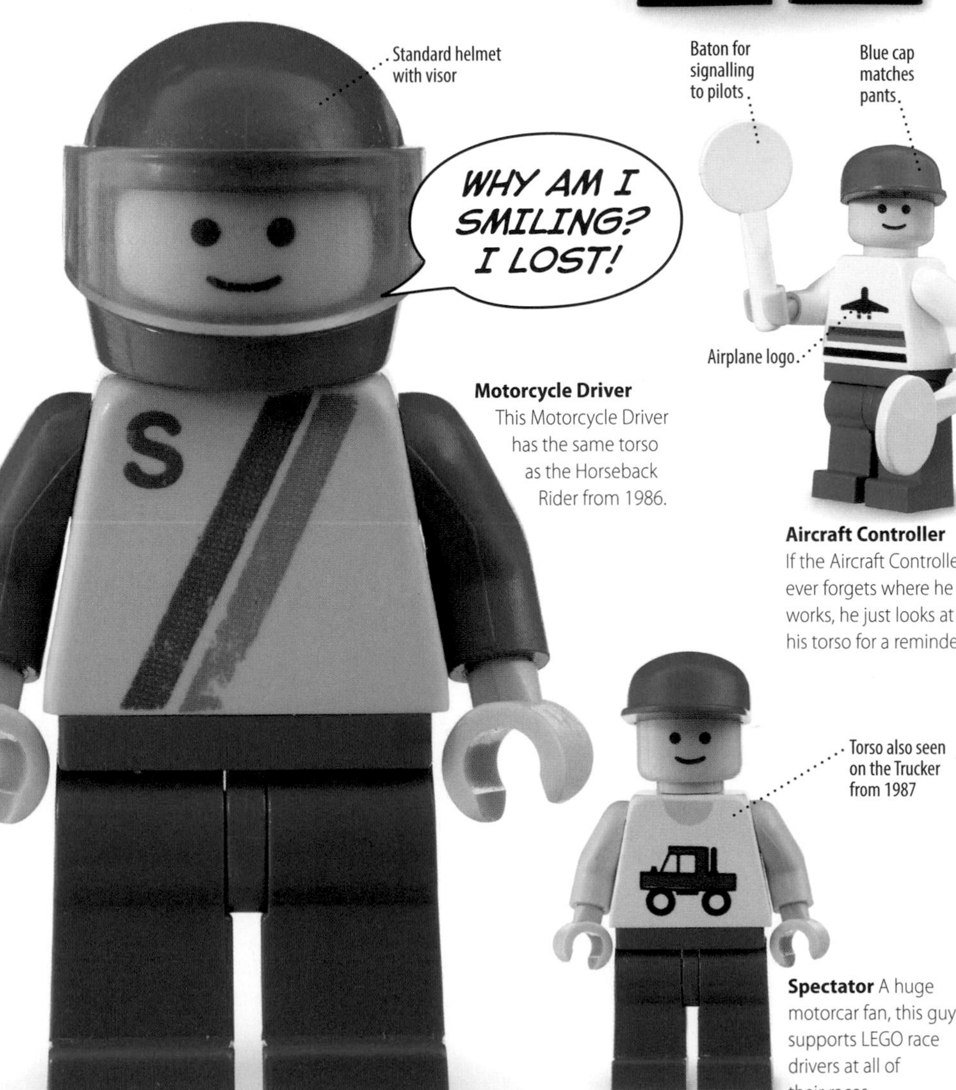
Standard helmet with visor
WHY AM I SMILING? I LOST!
Baton for signalling to pilots
Blue cap matches pants
Airplane logo
Torso also seen on the Trucker from 1987

Motorcycle Driver
This Motorcycle Driver has the same torso as the Horseback Rider from 1986.

Aircraft Controller
If the Aircraft Controller ever forgets where he works, he just looks at his torso for a reminder.

Spectator A huge motorcar fan, this guy supports LEGO race drivers at all of their races.

Red collar

Red Forestman The Forestmen are skilled with a bow and arrow, thanks to hours of target practice in sets like the Forestman's Hideout (6054).

FORESTMEN

Only one set, Forestmen's Hideout (6054), marked the second year of the Forestmen faction. With vines to climb up and targets to shoot at, the Forestmen would be ready to take on any naughty Knights.

Green forestman hat
Pouch is full to bursting
The Forestman's spear always hits its target

Forestman with White Plume This Forestman is a variant of the Forestman with Pouch, seen in 1987, but this minifigure's plume is white instead of yellow.

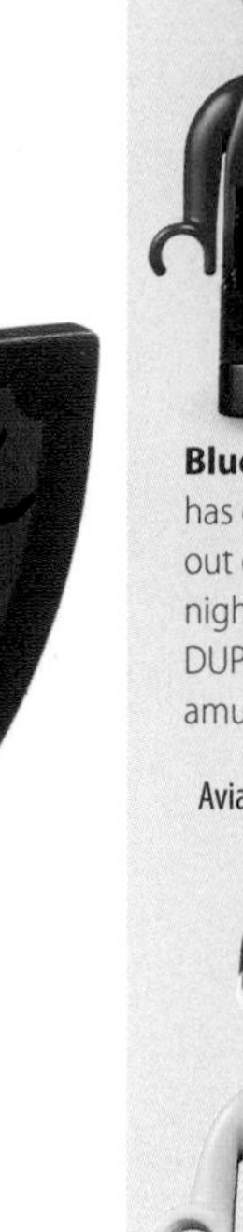

Circus Ringmaster Keeping the Circus Clowns in line as well as making sure his mustache is neatly trimmed is no laughing matter for the Ringmaster.

Bowtie

Blue Clown This Clown has guts—he is blasted out of a cannon every night, much to the DUPLO audiences' amusement.

Aviator helmet
Big bowtie

Red Clown Luckily for this Clown, he just has to ride an elephant while carrying an umbrella, in the DUPLO Town Circus Caravan (2652).

LEGO® DUPLO®

LEGO DUPLO was off to see a show with the Circus Caravan set, one of seven sets released this year. This was the first appearance of the Circus Ringmaster figure.

CASTLE

The Black Knights arrived this year, with their powerful fortress, the Black Monarch's Castle (6085). Guarded by 12 knight minifigures, it was the first of two castles for this popular Castle faction. Beyond the gates, the Black Knights and the Crusaders would oppose each other in the Knight's Challenge joust, before the eyes of two spectator minifigures.

Dark gray helmet with chin guard
Scale mail armor over blue torso
Bow and arrow are perfect for scaring off intruders

Black Knight Guard Wearing his new armor with scale mail, this Knight stands guard outside the Black Monarch's Castle (6085).

Blue torso matches blue pants

Black Knight When they're not clashing with their forest foes, the Knights are busy jousting in sets such as Knight's Challenge (1584).

The Crusaders' crossed halberts emblem

Crusader Ax This Crusader Knight is standing next to his archenemies. Luckily for them, he doesn't realize this.

Long pole with ax attachment
Helmet is seen on many LEGO Knights

Dragon Shield Black Knight The red torso with scale mail pattern that adorns this Knight is new this year.

1584
LEGOLAND
LEGO

Knight's Challenge (1584) Let the games begin! Depicting a jousting tournament, this set includes an audience stand, weapons rack, and a tapped keg, as well as eight minifigures.

Purse pouch

Peasant The humble Peasant is attending a jousting tournament—just as a spectator, however.

Black helmet with neck protector

Black Knight The Black Knight's armor was first seen in 1984, but it still looks just as shiny this year.

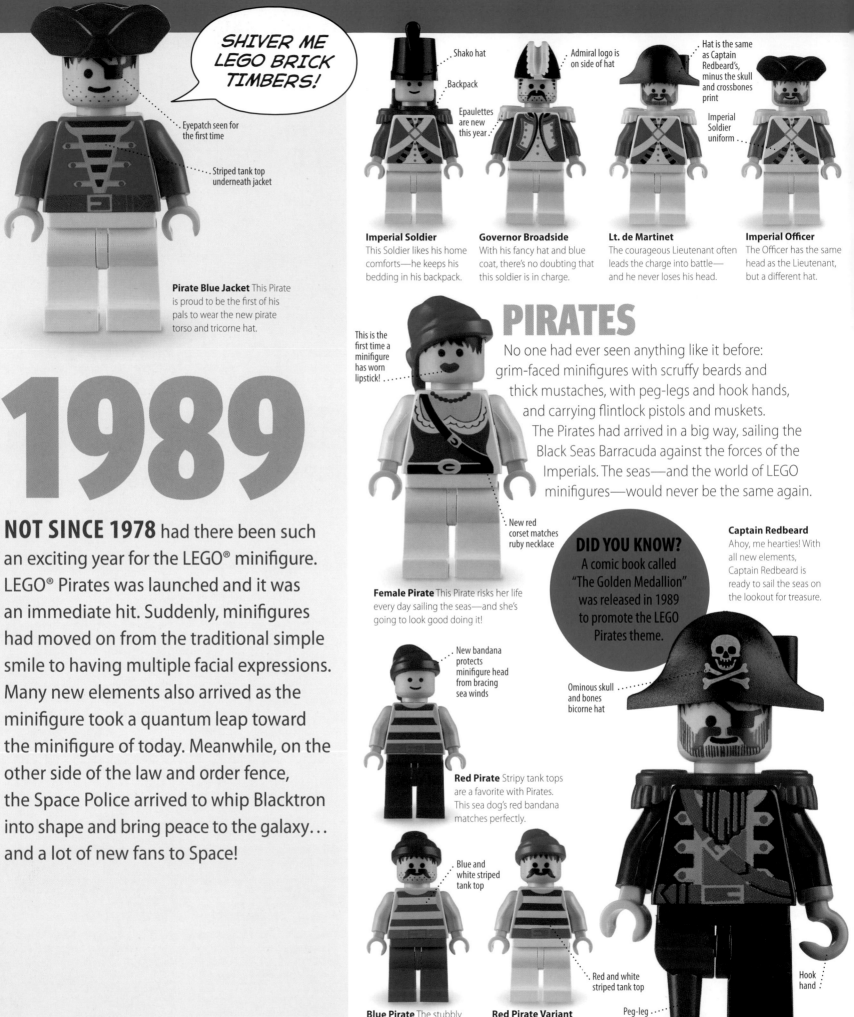

SHIVER ME LEGO BRICK TIMBERS!
Eyepatch seen for the first time
Striped tank top underneath jacket

Pirate Blue Jacket This Pirate is proud to be the first of his pals to wear the new pirate torso and tricorne hat.

1989

NOT SINCE 1978 had there been such an exciting year for the LEGO® minifigure. LEGO® Pirates was launched and it was an immediate hit. Suddenly, minifigures had moved on from the traditional simple smile to having multiple facial expressions. Many new elements also arrived as the minifigure took a quantum leap toward the minifigure of today. Meanwhile, on the other side of the law and order fence, the Space Police arrived to whip Blacktron into shape and bring peace to the galaxy... and a lot of new fans to Space!

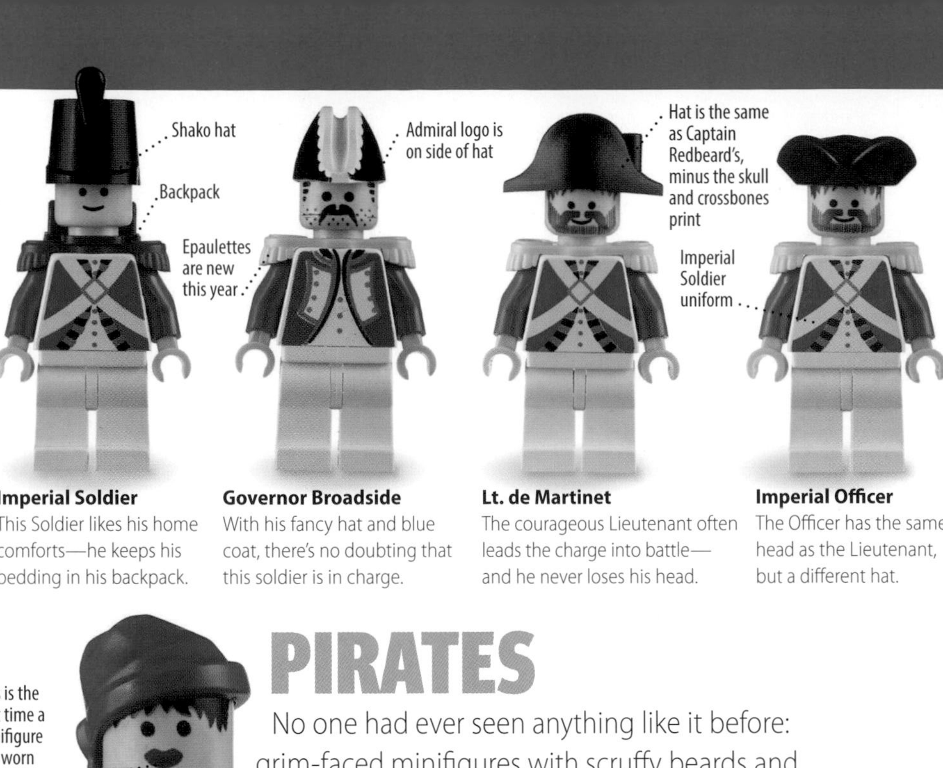
Shako hat
Backpack
Epaulettes are new this year
Admiral logo is on side of hat
Hat is the same as Captain Redbeard's, minus the skull and crossbones print
Imperial Soldier uniform

Imperial Soldier This Soldier likes his home comforts—he keeps his bedding in his backpack.

Governor Broadside With his fancy hat and blue coat, there's no doubting that this soldier is in charge.

Lt. de Martinet The courageous Lieutenant often leads the charge into battle—and he never loses his head.

Imperial Officer The Officer has the same head as the Lieutenant, but a different hat.

PIRATES

No one had ever seen anything like it before: grim-faced minifigures with scruffy beards and thick mustaches, with peg-legs and hook hands, and carrying flintlock pistols and muskets. The Pirates had arrived in a big way, sailing the Black Seas Barracuda against the forces of the Imperials. The seas—and the world of LEGO minifigures—would never be the same again.

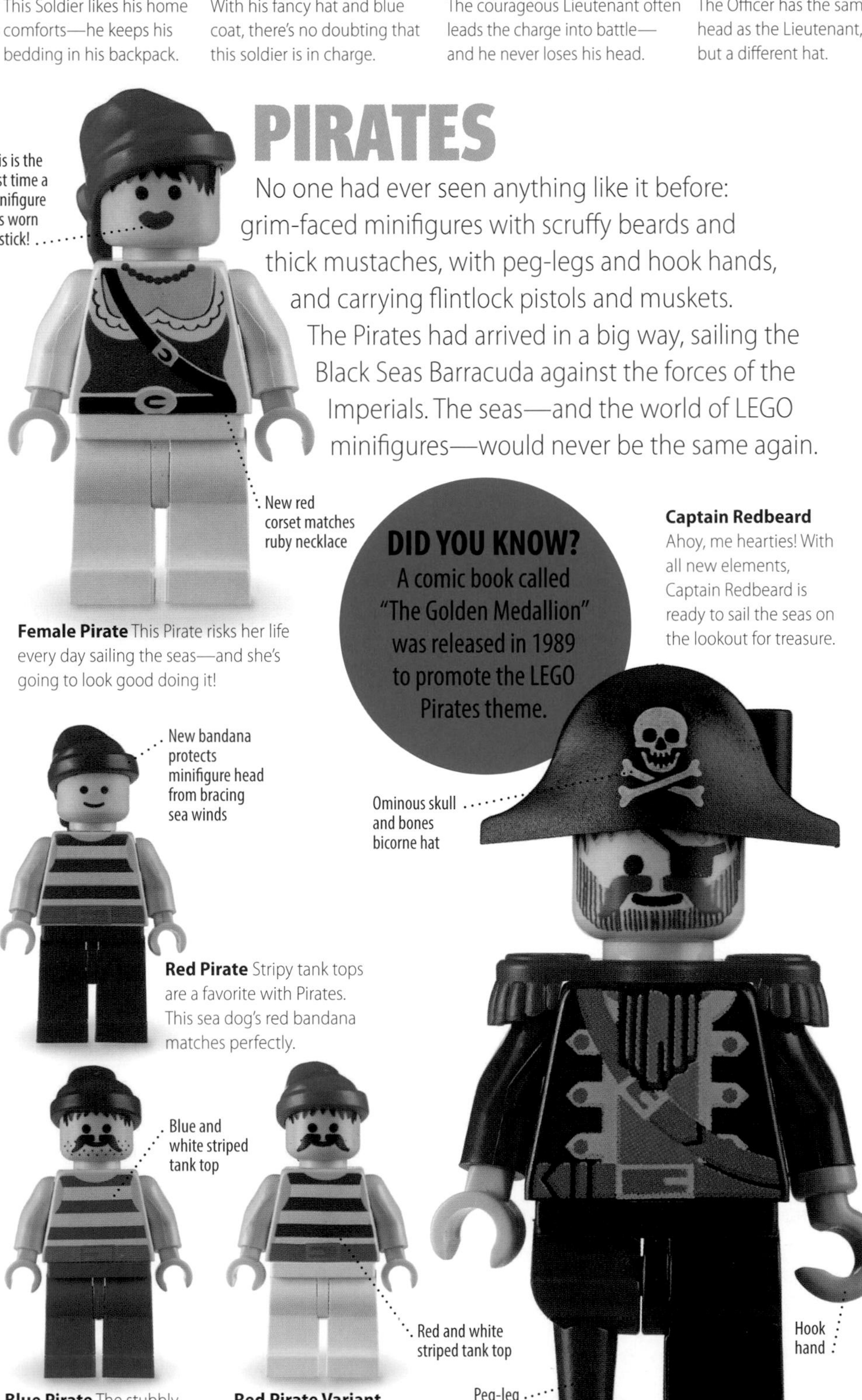
This is the first time a minifigure has worn lipstick!
New red corset matches ruby necklace
New bandana protects minifigure head from bracing sea winds
Blue and white striped tank top
Red and white striped tank top
Ominous skull and bones bicorne hat
Hook hand
Peg-leg

Female Pirate This Pirate risks her life every day sailing the seas—and she's going to look good doing it!

DID YOU KNOW?
A comic book called "The Golden Medallion" was released in 1989 to promote the LEGO Pirates theme.

Captain Redbeard Ahoy, me hearties! With all new elements, Captain Redbeard is ready to sail the seas on the lookout for treasure.

Red Pirate Stripy tank tops are a favorite with Pirates. This sea dog's red bandana matches perfectly.

Blue Pirate The stubbly head with droopy mustache is new this year.

Red Pirate Variant This Pirate is sporting the same tank top as his pal, but he has chosen white pants instead.

Forestman This Forestman has built a fortress with his friends in set 6077 and he's going to do all he can to protect it!

Forestman hat

Yellow plume

Blue collar

Leather belt

Yellow Plume Forestman Making an appearance in just one set, Forestman's River Fortress (6077), doesn't seem to have upset this Forestman.

I'M JUST A SIMPLE HAY HAULER.

Farmer's cowl also seen on the LEGO Castle Wolfpack gang in 1992

Torso is the same as the Forestman, but in gray

Peasant This sneaky smuggler is out to steal what he can—today it's pieces of gold and some hay to bed down on.

CASTLE

The Forestmen were back with their largest set to date, the Forestmen's River Fortress (6077), which they fought hard to protect from the Crusaders. Another set released this year was the Smuggler's Hayride (1974), which featured a peasant smuggler and a wagon with gold bars hidden away. However, the Forestmen subtheme had only one more year to be merry.

LEGO® DUPLO®

These two LEGO DUPLO figures were part of an educational 18-figure set, intended to represent people from all over the globe.

Tie matches pants

Red necklace

Man with Tie This figure makes an appearance in the DUPLO Figures International set (9159) and he's dressed for the occasion!

Woman From the same set as Man with Tie, this figure is dressed more casually, in a yellow top and red pants.

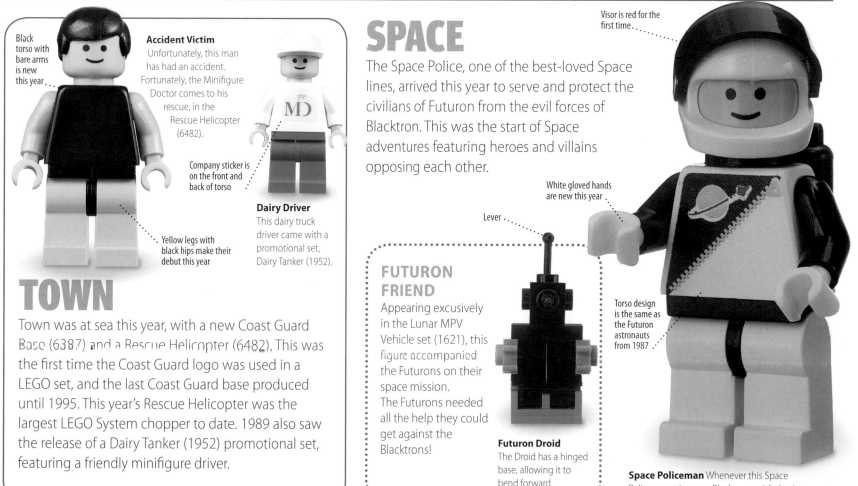

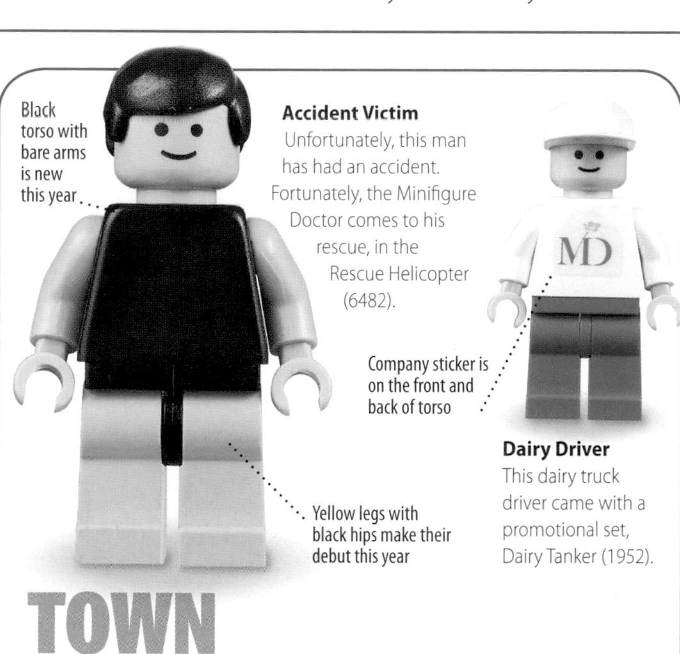

Black torso with bare arms is new this year
Company sticker is on the front and back of torso
Yellow legs with black hips make their debut this year
MD

Accident Victim Unfortunately, this man has had an accident. Fortunately, the Minifigure Doctor comes to his rescue, in the Rescue Helicopter (6482).

Dairy Driver This dairy truck driver came with a promotional set, Dairy Tanker (1952).

TOWN

Town was at sea this year, with a new Coast Guard Base (6387) and a Rescue Helicopter (6482). This was the first time the Coast Guard logo was used in a LEGO set, and the last Coast Guard base produced until 1995. This year's Rescue Helicopter was the largest LEGO System chopper to date. 1989 also saw the release of a Dairy Tanker (1952) promotional set, featuring a friendly minifigure driver.

SPACE

The Space Police, one of the best-loved Space lines, arrived this year to serve and protect the civilians of Futuron from the evil forces of Blacktron. This was the start of Space adventures featuring heroes and villains opposing each other.

Visor is red for the first time

White gloved hands are new this year

Lever

Torso design is the same as the Futuron astronauts from 1987

FUTURON FRIEND

Appearing excusively in the Lunar MPV Vehicle set (1621), this figure accompanied the Futurons on their space mission. The Futurons needed all the help they could get against the Blacktrons!

Futuron Droid The Droid has a hinged base, allowing it to bend forward.

Space Policeman Whenever this Space Policeman witnesses Blacktrons misbehaving, he sees red—literally.

ROBO
ROBO
ROBO
LEGO

1990s

LEGO® mania! The '90s saw an explosion of wild new LEGO play themes, and with them came an even wilder array of new minifigures. Ghosts, cowboys, robots, aliens, witches, and wizards abounded. Minifigures traveled through time, blasted off to futuristic frozen planets, explored ancient pyramids, and went diving to the bottom of the sea. Capping it all off at the decade's end was the biggest news in minifigure history: a famous licensed theme of truly galactic proportions!

TIME TO BLAST OFF INTO THE '90S!
Helmet with visor is vital for space walks
NASA sticker on torso

Shuttle Astronaut This NASA minifigure appears in only one set: Space Launch Shuttle (1682).

1990

AS A NEW DECADE began, LEGO® Town, LEGO® Space, and LEGO® Castle became play themes in their own right, and their minifigures were getting ready for many new adventures. Far up in LEGO Space, M-Tron joined the line up, while the forest-dwelling Forestmen said farewell in LEGO Castle. Over in LEGO Town, everyone was getting ready to travel on a jet plane to visit far-off lands. LEGO® DUPLO® also continued to grow, adding new subthemes this year. With new minifigures in space, on land, and even a new figure haunting a medieval castle, it was a year of action and adventure for builders, young and old.

LEGO TOWN

Builders visiting LEGO Town in 1990 had lots to choose from. They could take off from the airport, visit the Breezeway Café (6376) for lunch, or ride with the police from the Pursuit Squad (6354). LEGO Town continued its tradition of presenting a fun variety of places to play.

Classic female hair piece

Showjumper With a sharp-suited torso and white gloves, this minifigure is competition-ready!

Red neckerchief offsets the chef's whites

Chef This minifigure works at the Breezeway Café (10037) where he serves delicious food to all the minifigure patrons.

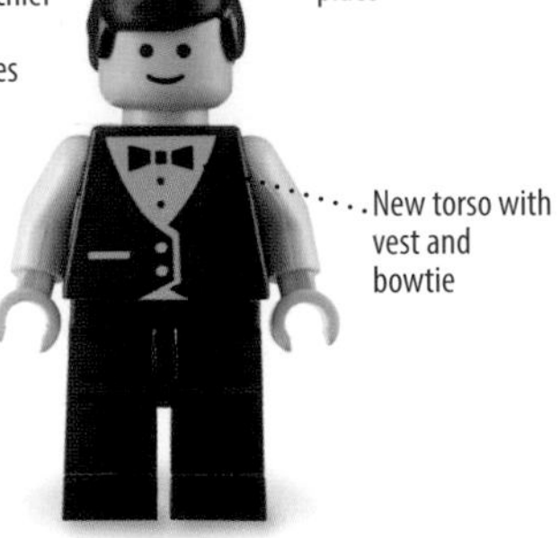
Not a hair out of place
New torso with vest and bowtie

Waiter Sporting formal attire and a slick hairdo, this waiter works in a classy establishment.

Torso with fancy gold trim and buttons

Fire Chief The Fire Chief came to the rescue in only one set, the Fire Control Center (6389).

Helmet protects head in rough seas
Bright yellow life vest makes Coast Guard visible at sea

Coast Guard Wearing a new life preserver accessory, this minifigure is ready for action.

LEGO SPACE

The M-Tron subtheme introduced a new innovation to LEGO building: the use of magnets to hold parts together. It was the first major space theme to feature only vehicles—and not bases—in its seven sets. The Futuron subtheme came to an end this year, after four years in Space.

M-Tron With a new torso and visor color, this minifigure is ready to blast off into space.

Airtanks for a space walk
M-Tron logo

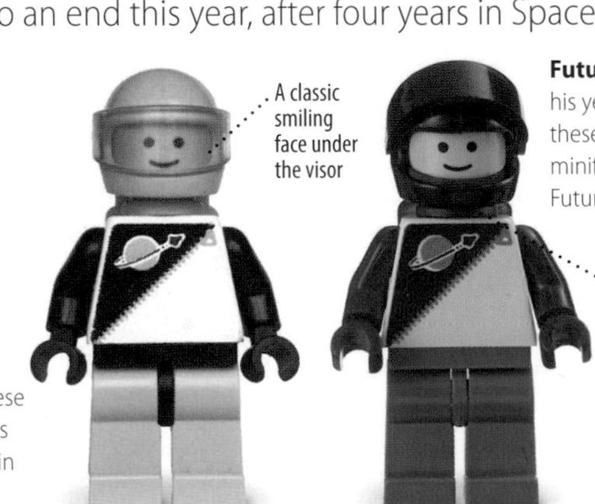
A classic smiling face under the visor
Airtank fixes to back with neck bracket

Yellow Futuron Four of these minifigures appeared in set 9355.

Futuron Alongside his yellow friend, these were the last minifigures for the Futuron subtheme.

BOO!

The first LEGO ghost minifigure mysteriously appeared this year, glowing in the dark in the King's Mountain Fortress (6081). This smiling spirit would be around for the next five years.

Ghoulish face, but still smiling
White minifigure arms

Ghost Underneath the Ghost's new shroud piece is a white torso and a plain black head.

6081
LEGOLAND
LEGO

King's Mountain Fortress (6081) This stone fort comes with eight minifigures including knights, guards, and a princess.

LEGO CASTLE

There was plenty of excitement in the world of LEGO Castle in 1990, with the introduction of the first skirted female minifigure and the finale of the Forestmen subtheme. This year also saw the first castle built on a raised baseplate. It was a merry medieval time for all!

Red Knight The Black Falcons had better watch out—this Knight is armored and ready for battle.

Scale mail torso provides protection

Helmet with covered visor and red plume
Breastplate armor

Blue Knight This minifigure likes his new visor—he is just finding it a bit hard to breathe.

Traditional forestman hat
Quiver full of arrows

Red Forestman This Forestman looks happy—he has smuggled goodies from the Crusaders in Crusader's Cart (1680).

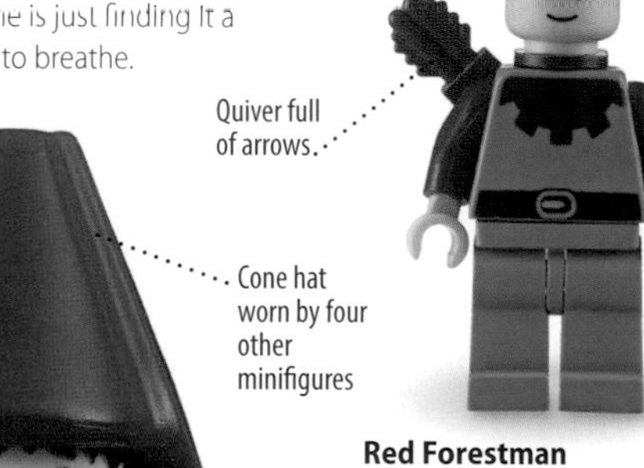
Belt with money pouch

Green Forestman None of the parts are new, but this minifigure features a new combination of pieces.

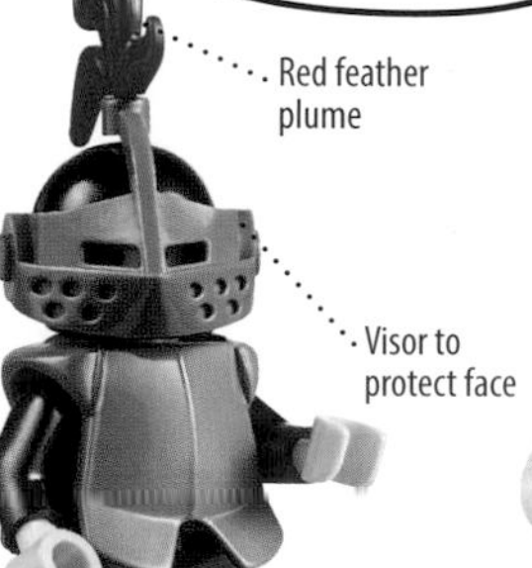
Red feather plume
Visor to protect face

Black Knight Underneath his new breastplate, this minifigure is trembling—he's just seen a spook, in Black Monarch's Ghost (6034).

IS IT A HAT OR A ROCKET NOSE CONE? YOU DECIDE!
Cone hat worn by four other minifigures
New torso with necklace detail

Maiden This fair Maiden has a sloped piece instead of legs—the first time it has been seen.

Hat to keep warm
Corset also comes in red

Forestwoman This Forestwoman minifigure is sporting a new color variation on her torso.

ZOO
Green zookeeper's uniform

Female Zookeeper This figure came in two DUPLO Zoo sets (2669, 2666), and a DUPLO People set (9979).

Yellow hat to keep the elements off
Zoo logo on torso
ZOO

Male Zookeeper This figure is seen in many locations, from safaris to zoo trains—he's a busy guy.

LEGO DUPLO

DUPLO LEGO was made even more fun this year with the introduction of sets based on Zoo and Race. Little builders had plenty to see and do with these new worlds!

2
Number helps identify racer on the course.

Motorcycle Racer This figure appeared in Racer (2609) with a blue DUPLO car.

Red police hat matches tie
TICKETS, PLEASE!
Railway logo

Station Manager
The Station Manager is happy with his new torso—it makes him look and feel important.

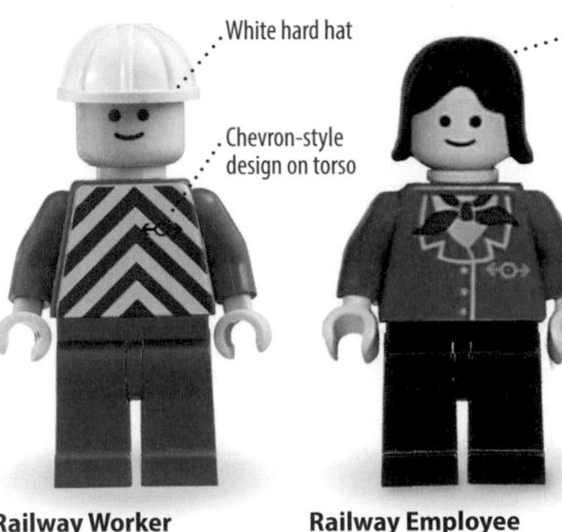

White hard hat
Chevron-style design on torso
Hair piece seen on more than 125 other minifigures

Railway Worker
The Railway Worker is glad he can't see his new torso with chevron design—it makes his minifigure eyes go funny!

Railway Employee
This minifigure is most impressed with the new railway uniform, especially the bright red neckerchief.

Same torso as Railway Worker

Maintenance Man The railway tracks don't repair themselves—this guy does, in Road and Rail Maintenance (4546).

Same red hat as the Station Manager's
Railway logo printed on torso
I NEED A TIMETABLE ACCESSORY!

1991

THE BIGGEST NEWS of 1991 came from the high seas. After the massive success of LEGO® Pirates in 1989, the line had effectively taken a year off in 1990. It came back with the roar of cannon fire this year, and with sets that are still fondly remembered to this day. An old LEGO® Space friend returned, too, as Blacktron was updated and turned into Blacktron II. In LEGO® Town, the Firefighters dispatched a new unit—RSQ911— to save the day.

LEGO® TRAIN

LEGO Train entered a new era in 1991, as 9V train sets took over from 12V and 4.5V. Six new sets appeared this year, including the Metroliner (4558) and the Metro Station (4554), with 19 minifigures between them. These included conductors, railway workers, and passengers. 9V dominated LEGO Train until 2006.

LEGO PIRATES

The second major wave of Pirates sets came out this year, including Rock Island Refuge (6273) and Lagoon Lock-Up (6267). Five sets sailed the Spanish Main, featuring pirate and Imperial Soldier minifigures, and the second female pirate ever released. Hoist the sails!

Red bandana
Belts for tucking in swag

Female Pirate
The only difference between this pirate and the 1989 variant is the bandana color—the other pirate has a blue bandana.

New torso with lime green logo
Jetpack for freestyle flying.

Blacktron II Spaceman This minifigure spaceman thinks the new Blacktron logo is simply out of this world.

M-Tron Spaceman With his new jetpack, this M-Tron minifigure can finally breathe easily in space.

DID YOU KNOW?
So far more than 330 minifigures have worn the standard helmet since its redesign in 1987.

Blacktron II Commander Wearing new bodywear, the jetpack with twin handles, this minifigure is ready for a mission.

Lime green visor to protect his grin

Jetpack with twin handles

Blacktron II logo

LEGO SPACE

Blacktron II rocketed into the stratosphere in 1991, with a dozen sets. This was a remake of the original Blacktron from 1987, and many of the sets were similar to those released previously. The major change was in the look of the minifigures, who all received new uniforms with a black hexagon logo. An M-Tron minifigure was also released—the first minifigure from the M-Tron subtheme to feature a jetpack.

LEGO® DUPLO®

Police became a part of DUPLO Town in 1991, with the release of a new Police Station (2672) and a Police Emergency Unit (2654). New figures included police officers and a prisoner.

2·672
Prisoner number
Silver police badge.

Jailbreak Joe This stubbly-faced figure came in one set: Police Set (2672).

Blue Policeman Part of six sets, this figure was a familiar face on the beat in 1991.

Black cap

Black Policeman If there was a minifigure emergency this guy would be there, in Emergency Unit (2654).

Scale mail decoration on torso

Knight There are no new parts on this minifigure, but it is a new combination of parts.

LEGO® CASTLE

Only one new Castle set was released this year, King's Catapult (1480). Launched as part of the Crusaders subtheme, it featured pieces to build a catapult and one new Crusader soldier minifigure. It was a lonely year for this fellow, but Castle would return in 1992.

LEGO TOWN

RSQ911, part of the Fire subtheme, came out this year, along with some new nautical-themed sets like Cabin Cruiser (4011) and Coastal Cutter (6053). Minifigures learned to love the life preserver, as a total of 10 minifigures wore this accessory in 1991.

Cap to combat glare off water

Boater Part of the Cabin Cruiser set (4011), this minifigure came with a new accessory: a fishing rod.

Yellow life preserver

Policeman The life preserver had only been worn by one minifigure in 1990. The Policeman thinks that safety is always in fashion!

Red helmet with transparent visor
Truck logo

Trucker Just in case he forgets what his vehicle looks like, this minifigure has it printed on his torso.

Classic hair piece

Business suit

Commuter This minifigure came in Metro Station (4554), complete with a new suitcase accessory.

Airplane design on torso

Airport Fireman This is the first fireman to be featured in the Airport subtheme.

Broad-brimmed tricorn hat
ARRRR! NEW LANDS TO PLUNDER!
Frilled shirt

Blue Pirate A new head piece with shaggy hair, a mustache, and beard is exclusive to this rugged minifigure.

1992

THIS YEAR SAW SOME new faces and the return of some old ones. Both LEGO® Space and LEGO® Castle followed the lead of LEGO® Pirates and upgraded their minifigure heads to the more modern look that is visible today. The Space Police subtheme returned (nicknamed Space Police II), while Castle got a brand new bunch of bad guys, and Pirates faced a new military foe. For those minifigures who wanted to get away from it all, the LEGO® Town theme offered up a variety of tropical delights in the subtheme Paradisa.

LEGO PIRATES

The Pirates got a new enemy this year, the Imperial Guard, as nine new sets appeared. The Imperial Guard minifigures were very similar to Imperial Soldiers, featured from 1989 to 1991, with only a change of uniform. They would battle the Pirates for four years before being replaced by the Imperial Armada in 1997.

Brimmed hat keeps rainwater at bay
New torso with striped tank top

Striped Pirate Protocol requires this pirate to maintain a rugged appearance

LEGO SYSTEM
6277

Imperial Trading Post (6277) This is one of the largest Imperial Guard sets. It comes with a merchant ship, rowing boat, and cannons.

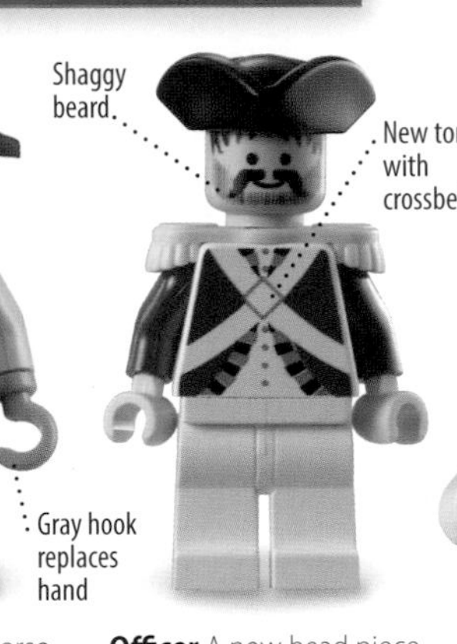

Shaggy beard
New torso with crossbelts
Gray hook replaces hand

Black Pirate A new torso for this minifigure has a black knife tucked into his crossbelt—so the pirate's one hand can be free.

Officer A new head piece with an unkempt hairstyle shows this Imperial Guard focuses on polishing his robes rather than his hair.

Elaborate black bicorn hat
White triple feather plume
Printed sideburns
Ornamental shoulder decorations

Admiral This very important Imperial Guard minifigure has a dashing new head piece and torso.

LEGO SPACE

It was Space Police's turn to get revamped in 1992, with new uniforms and new ships—although no permanent base. Pitted against their enemies Blacktron II, Space Police II would protect civilian space explorers for the next year. The subtheme is remembered by fans for the fact that the ships carried fewer weapons into battle than in earlier space subthemes.

DID YOU KNOW?
Space Police II was the first Space subtheme to replace the classic minifigure head with a more detailed one.

Neck bracket connects air tanks to back

Radio for contacting the base

Space Police Officer This officer proudly bears the Space Police logo on his brand-new torso.

New head piece with printed headset
Formal red epaulet

Space Police Chief This minifigure manages a police station and jail aboard a spaceship.

1992

LEGO CASTLE

LEGO Castle was inspired by Pirates this year, premiering the same kind of printed head pieces as Pirates debuted in 1989. The Wolfpack, robbers and renegades who appeared in two sets in 1992, also featured this year. One Wolfpack minifigure appeared in 1993 before the subtheme came to an end.

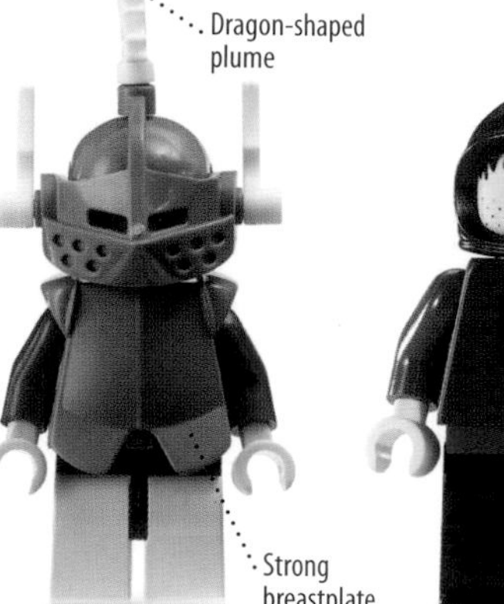
Dragon-shaped plume
Strong breastplate armor

Knight The biggest challenge for this armored minifigure is getting around without making too much noise.

Shaggy appearance
Red belt to hold up pants
A farmer's cowl covers unkempt hair
Wolfpack motif

Brown Bandit The new brown torso worn by this minifigure helps him hide amongst the trees in the forest.

Black Bandit For a fierce bandit, this minifigure has a cheerful expression. This new rugged minifigure was introduced this year.

Reading glasses
Sideswept hairstyle
Sweet frilly shirt

DUPLO Grandma This bespectacled veteran only appears in Grandma's Kitchen (2551).

DUPLO Grandad This figure is featured in two sets: DUPLO Supermarket (9167) and Grandma's Kitchen (2551).

LEGO® DUPLO®

These two figures were cooking up something good in the DUPLO Playhouse Grandma's Kitchen set (2551). Although LEGO DUPLO had no new themes this year, it continued to provide plenty of fun for young builders.

Surfer Girl With a new summery torso, this minifigure heads to the beach in three sets Sand Dollar Café (6411) and Seaside Cabana (6401).

Casual ponytail
Waterproof makeup
Strapless tankini for sunbathing

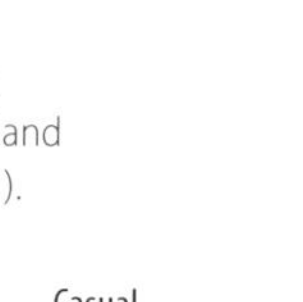
Hard riding hat
Tank top for hot days

Stable Hand This minifigure's head piece and torso were introduced this year.

Octan
Octan gas logo

Octan Worker This is the first new minifigure for the Gas Station subtheme in six years.

Protection against sun's glare

Pool Guy Sleeveless tank top and white pants are perfect attire for a casual sun-lover.

SURFER GIRL NEVER EVER NOTICES ME...

Life preserver
Nautical striped tank top
Black swimming trunks

Speedboat Driver Nothing pleases this minifigure more than feeling the wind in his hair piece as he sails.

Glamorous beach style
Palm Tree motif on new torso

Swimmer This minifigure has a pretty new torso and appears in Poolside Paradise (6416).

Vendor This is the first minifigure to feature freckles. He wears a cap to shield his face from the sun.

LEGO TOWN

Paradisa, a new subtheme of Town, launched with four sets in 1992. Aimed more at young girls, it focused on tropical vacation spots and used plenty of pink bricks. A number of new female minfigures were produced for the line, featuring a new facial design and new hair pieces. The Paradisa subtheme would continue for five years.

New pointed hat piece
Pouch for carrying potions
ADMIT IT, YOU LOVE THE HAT.

Majisto Wizard As the first wizard minifigure, Majisto is as proud of his wizard's hat as he is of his brand-new separate beard piece.

1993

THE STRENGTH OF THE LEGO®

minifigures as a concept rested on the idea that each minifigure could be customized and used in a variety of settings. The ability to add to new and old sets would help to keep long-standing themes looking fresh and current. Both the LEGO® Castle and LEGO® Space themes got new factions and new places to explore this year. From the scorched plains ruled by the Dragon Masters to the frigid wasteland of the Ice Planet, LEGO fans and their minifigures were given plenty of exciting and innovative ways to stir their imagination in 1993.

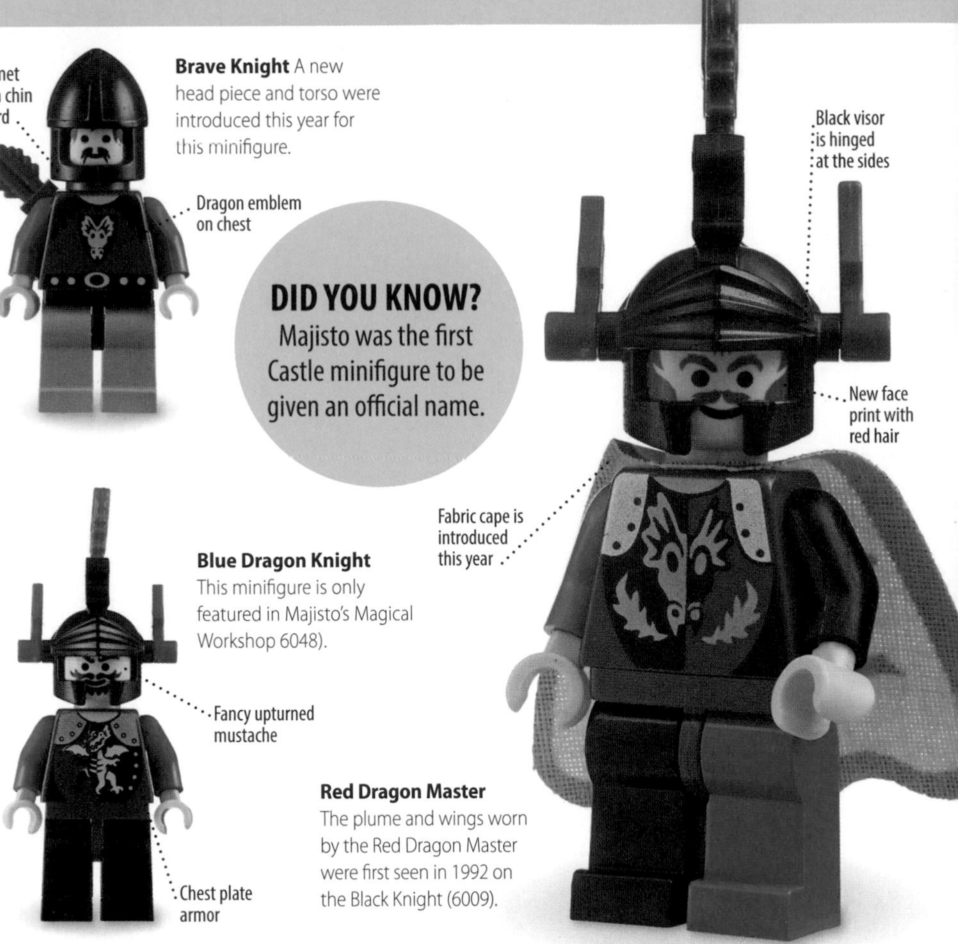
Helmet with chin guard
Dragon emblem on chest
Black visor is hinged at the sides
New face print with red hair
Fabric cape is introduced this year
Fancy upturned mustache
Chest plate armor

Brave Knight A new head piece and torso were introduced this year for this minifigure.

DID YOU KNOW?
Majisto was the first Castle minifigure to be given an official name.

Blue Dragon Knight This minifigure is only featured in Majisto's Magical Workshop 6048).

Red Dragon Master The plume and wings worn by the Red Dragon Master were first seen in 1992 on the Black Knight (6009).

LEGO CASTLE

The beat of huge, leathery wings announced the arrival of Dragon Masters, the newest Castle subtheme. The wizard Majisto sent his dragons into battle in a line that introduced several new minifigures, cloth pieces, and the now famous flame piece to LEGO building. The dragons roared only until 1995.

Dragon-shaped plume

HA! NOW THIS IS WHAT I CALL A HAT!

New shoulder armor printing

Blue Dragon Master Almost identical to the Red Dragon Master, this minifigure also has a red hip piece mismatched with blue and black legs—new for this year.

Fire Breathing Fortress (6082) Featuring six minifigures, this set has a trap door that dumps intruders into a pit.

LEGO SYSTEM
6082

Dragon Master's flag

LEGO® TOWN

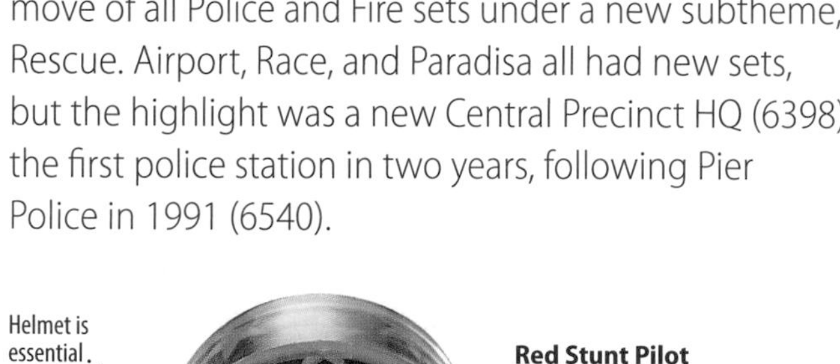

It was a big year for LEGO Town, starting with the move of all Police and Fire sets under a new subtheme, Rescue. Airport, Race, and Paradisa all had new sets, but the highlight was a new Central Precinct HQ (6398), the first police station in two years, following Pier Police in 1991 (6540).

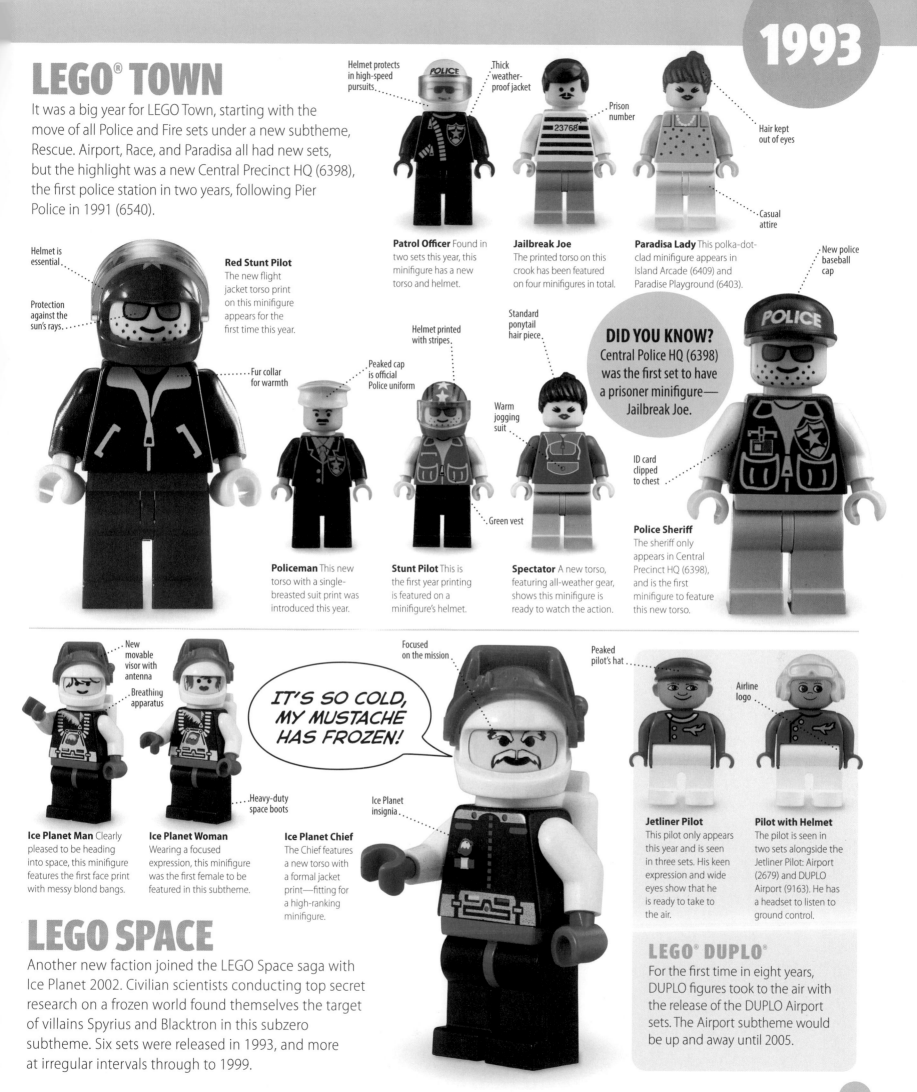

Helmet protects in high-speed pursuits
Thick weather-proof jacket

Patrol Officer Found in two sets this year, this minifigure has a new torso and helmet.

Prison number

Jailbreak Joe The printed torso on this crook has been featured on four minifigures in total.

Hair kept out of eyes
Casual attire

Paradisa Lady This polka-dot-clad minifigure appears in Island Arcade (6409) and Paradise Playground (6403).

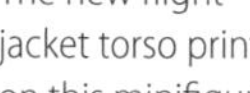

Helmet is essential
Protection against the sun's rays
Fur collar for warmth

Red Stunt Pilot The new flight jacket torso print on this minifigure appears for the first time this year.

Peaked cap is official Police uniform

Policeman This new torso with a single-breasted suit print was introduced this year.

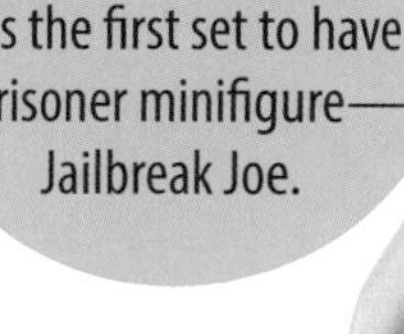

Helmet printed with stripes
Green vest

Stunt Pilot This is the first year printing is featured on a minifigure's helmet.

Standard ponytail hair piece
Warm jogging suit

Spectator A new torso, featuring all-weather gear, shows this minifigure is ready to watch the action.

DID YOU KNOW?
Central Police HQ (6398) was the first set to have a prisoner minifigure—Jailbreak Joe.

New police baseball cap
ID card clipped to chest

Police Sheriff The sheriff only appears in Central Precinct HQ (6398), and is the first minifigure to feature this new torso.

New movable visor with antenna
Breathing apparatus
Heavy-duty space boots

Ice Planet Man Clearly pleased to be heading into space, this minifigure features the first face print with messy blond bangs.

Ice Planet Woman Wearing a focused expression, this minifigure was the first female to be featured in this subtheme.

IT'S SO COLD, MY MUSTACHE HAS FROZEN!

Focused on the mission
Ice Planet insignia

Ice Planet Chief The Chief features a new torso with a formal jacket print—fitting for a high-ranking minifigure.

LEGO SPACE

Another new faction joined the LEGO Space saga with Ice Planet 2002. Civilian scientists conducting top secret research on a frozen world found themselves the target of villains Spyrius and Blacktron in this subzero subtheme. Six sets were released in 1993, and more at irregular intervals through to 1999.

Peaked pilot's hat

Airline logo

Jetliner Pilot This pilot only appears this year and is seen in three sets. His keen expression and wide eyes show that he is ready to take to the air.

Pilot with Helmet The pilot is seen in two sets alongside the Jetliner Pilot: Airport (2679) and DUPLO Airport (9163). He has a headset to listen to ground control.

LEGO® DUPLO®

For the first time in eight years, DUPLO figures took to the air with the release of the DUPLO Airport sets. The Airport subtheme would be up and away until 2005.

1994

THIS YEAR SAW a combination of venturing into new areas and building on what already worked. LEGO® Pirates and LEGO® Space were both back with new subthemes, while LEGO® BELVILLE™, a non-minifigure line aimed primarily at girl builders, started what would become a 15-year run. LEGO® Town was in the air with a new aircraft and stunt chopper, on land with new Fire and Police sets, and at sea with the Coastal Patrol. There were many adventures to be had for LEGO minifigure fans in 1994.

LEGO SPACE

The battle between good and evil raged beyond the stars in 1994, as two new subthemes of LEGO Space were launched. The well-trained Unitron squad found themselves battling the cunning forces of Spyrius. Many LEGO fans still wish more sets had been released for these highly-popular lines.

Head can also be seen in 1996 on a droid in the Time Cruisers theme.

Standard LEGO helmet is totally clear for the first time.

HI, I'M RUSTY... WHAT'S SO FUNNY?

Spyrius Droid
The Spyrius Droid minifigure is all-new, with exclusive torso and legs. This is also the first time a minifigure has printed legs!

Exclusive blue and silver Spyrius printing on helmet

Torso also used on the Spyrius Astronaut

Spyrius Chief
The leader of this year's Space villains has a unique rugged head piece and printed helmet.

Plain red helmet

Spyrius Astronaut
The Astronaut also has a unique head piece featuring a blue headband.

SPYRIUS

On a far-off, desolate planet, a team of spies plot to steal technology from the heroes of Unitron. From their Lunar Launch site, the villains of Spyrius carried out their evil plans in five sets this year.

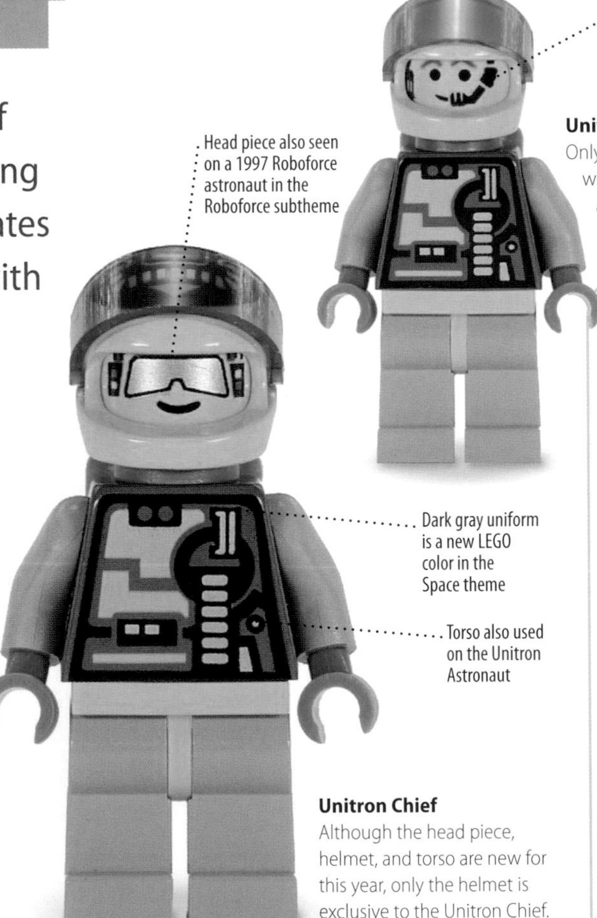

Head piece with headset seen on more than 20 other minifigures
Head piece also seen on a 1997 Roboforce astronaut in the Roboforce subtheme
Dark gray uniform is a new LEGO color in the Space theme
Torso also used on the Unitron Astronaut

Unitron Astronaut
Only two Unitron minifigures were released—the Chief and the Astronaut.

Unitron Chief
Although the head piece, helmet, and torso are new for this year, only the helmet is exclusive to the Unitron Chief.

UNITRON

Unitron took over from Space Police II as the heroes of LEGO Space, but only appeared in two sets in 1994. Their mission was to stop Spyrius from getting their evil minifigure hands on top-secret data.

DID YOU KNOW?
Spyrius was the first LEGO subtheme to feature robot minifigures.

LEGO® TRAIN

The LEGO Train theme had been running since 1965. In 1994, Freight Rail Runner (4564) was the largest of the three sets released that year. The set included three minifigures, a conductor, and two railway workers.

Construction helmet
Torso exclusive to this conductor and the 1991 variant

Conductor
This minifigure is a variant of a 1991 Conductor with black pants.

Construction worker
This minifigure is exclusive to set 4564, but the torso can be see on five others.

LEGO PIRATES

LEGO Pirates returned for its fifth year. This time, the fierce pirate minifigures were journeying to exotic islands and meeting the natives. But were King Kahuka and his tribe friends or enemies? Another exciting Pirates adventure was about to begin.

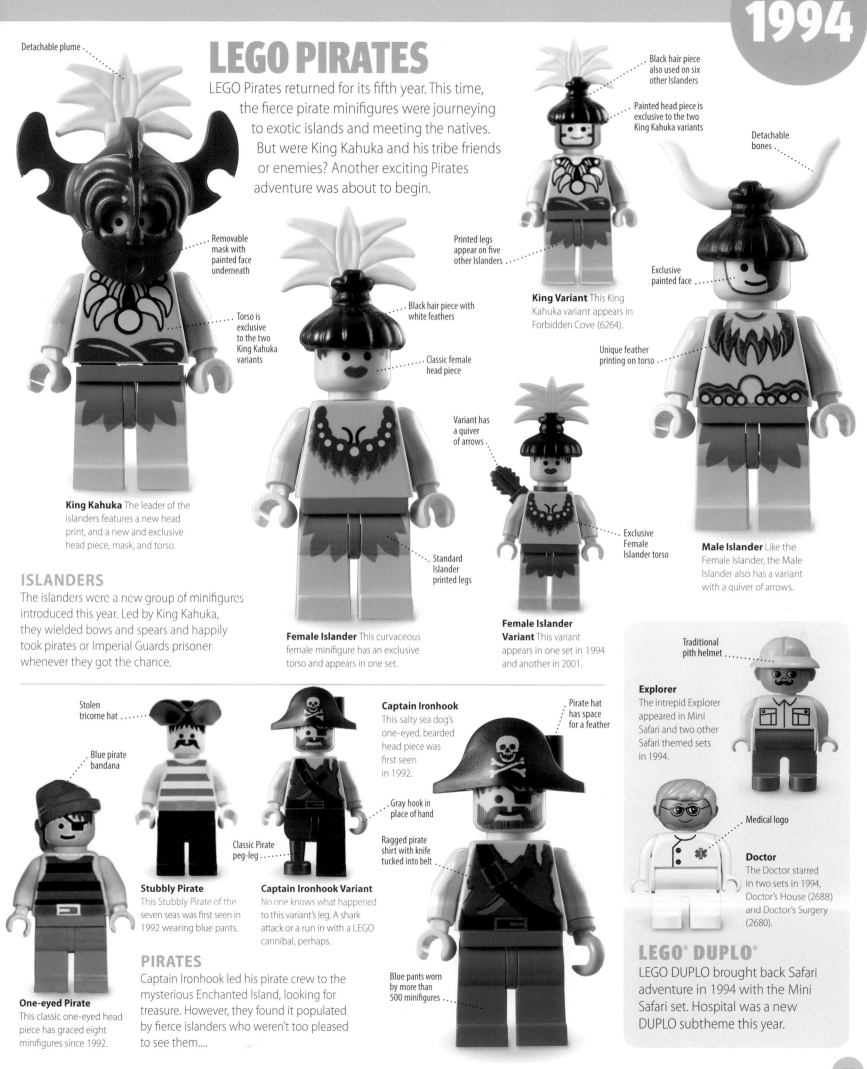

Detachable plume
Removable mask with painted face underneath
Torso is exclusive to the two King Kahuka variants

King Kahuka The leader of the islanders features a new head print, and a new and exclusive head piece, mask, and torso.

Black hair piece also used on six other Islanders
Painted head piece is exclusive to the two King Kahuka variants
Printed legs appear on five other Islanders

King Variant This King Kahuka variant appears in Forbidden Cove (6264).

Detachable bones
Exclusive painted face
Unique feather printing on torso

Male Islander Like the Female Islander, the Male Islander also has a variant with a quiver of arrows.

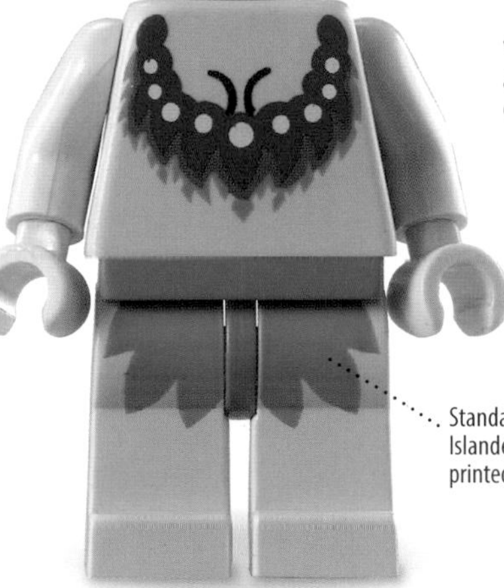
Black hair piece with white feathers
Classic female head piece
Standard Islander printed legs

Female Islander This curvaceous female minifigure has an exclusive torso and appears in one set.

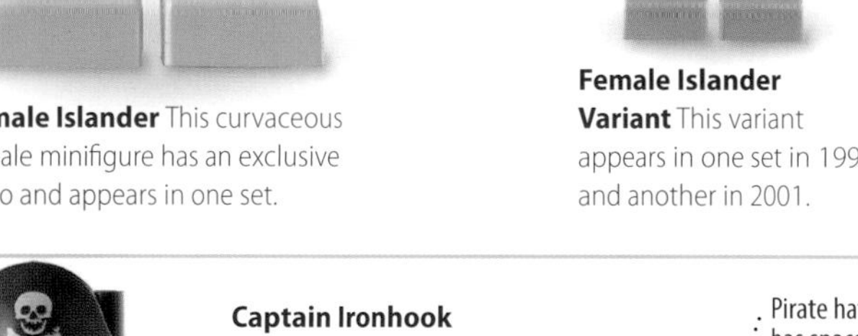
Variant has a quiver of arrows
Exclusive Female Islander torso

Female Islander Variant This variant appears in one set in 1994 and another in 2001.

ISLANDERS

The islanders were a new group of minifigures introduced this year. Led by King Kahuka, they wielded bows and spears and happily took pirates or Imperial Guards prisoner whenever they got the chance.

Blue pirate bandana

One-eyed Pirate This classic one-eyed head piece has graced eight minifigures since 1992.

Stolen tricorne hat
Classic Pirate peg-leg

Stubbly Pirate This Stubbly Pirate of the seven seas was first seen in 1992 wearing blue pants.

Captain Ironhook Variant No one knows what happened to this variant's leg. A shark attack or a run in with a LEGO cannibal, perhaps.

Pirate hat has space for a feather
Gray hook in place of hand
Ragged pirate shirt with knife tucked into belt
Blue pants worn by more than 500 minifigures

Captain Ironhook This salty sea dog's one-eyed, bearded head piece was first seen in 1992.

PIRATES

Captain Ironhook led his pirate crew to the mysterious Enchanted Island, looking for treasure. However, they found it populated by fierce islanders who weren't too pleased to see them....

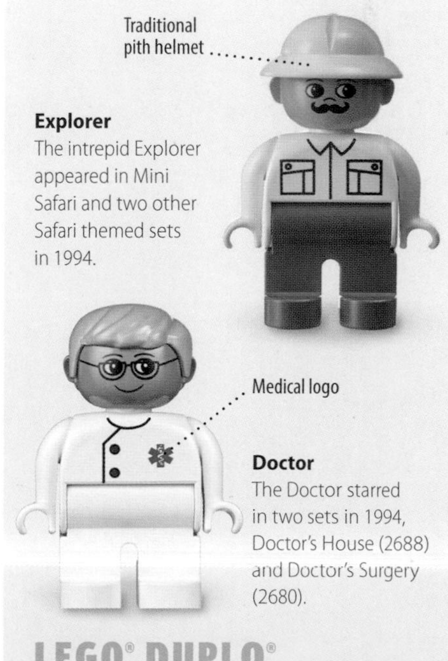
Traditional pith helmet
Medical logo

Explorer The intrepid Explorer appeared in Mini Safari and two other Safari themed sets in 1994.

Doctor The Doctor starred in two sets in 1994, Doctor's House (2688) and Doctor's Surgery (2680).

LEGO® DUPLO®

LEGO DUPLO brought back Safari adventure in 1994 with the Mini Safari set. Hospital was a new DUPLO subtheme this year.

1994

Torso is used on four other Firefighter minifigures

Firefighter The Fire minifigures have a new torso in 1994, featuring a flamingly good new badge.

Adult Male This posable male appeared in Pretty Wishes Playhouse (5890) with an adult female, a girl, and a baby boy.

Young Female Three variants of this figure were released between 1994 and 1996, wearing pink shorts (above), a pink skirt, and a yellow skirt.

LEGO BELVILLE

A combination of traditional LEGO bricks and new pink and purple elements, BELVILLE also featured larger, doll-like figures with more joints for greater posability. Early sets were themed around everyday family life.

Horseback riding jacket

Horseback Rider This lucky figure has a horse to ride and a foal to pet in Prize Pony Stables (5880).

Pretty Wishes Playhouse (5890) This set features four figures, a swimming pool, parrot, and pet dog.

LEGO SYSTEM
Belville
5890

Helmet is exclusive to this minifigure
Gold badges

Fire Chief The Chief stands out from his crew thanks to his new torso with formal collar and matching helmet.

LEGO TOWN

LEGO Town had something for everyone this year: five sets were released in the Rescue subtheme, including Flame Fighters (6571), which featured a fire station, fire truck, and helicopter. Auto fans had three Race sets to build, while those in need of a vacation could take a jet plane from the Century Skyway airport to the idyllic Paradisa.

Standard helmet seen on almost 90 minifgures in a range of colors
OKAY, WHO BURNED THE TOAST?
Torso with tire pressure gauge is new this year
Black gloves

Fire Mechanic This mechanic minifigure appears in two sets in 1994, Flame Fighters and Hook and Ladder (6340)

Unisex shirt torso is new this year

Townsperson Variants of this minifigure were released in 1996 with red pants, and in 1998 with green pants.

Ponytail hair piece is new this year
Tie-front pink top makes its debut this year

Cafe Girl This ice cream-loving Paradisa minifigure spends her time at the Sidewalk Café (6402).

Cabana Girl Surfing is not as easy as it looks—as this minifigure discovers at Cabana Beach (6410).

Standard blue cap is worn by more than 100 minifigures
Windsurf and sunset design

Surfer This cool Paradisa Surfer dude makes a fashion statement with his new torso design—18 other minifigures will copy his look.

Red halter top is worn by four other minifigures

Ambulance Patient
This minifigure won't come to any harm—she's in set 6666 Ambulance.

Cool sunglasses
BRUISED BRICK? I'M HERE TO HELP.

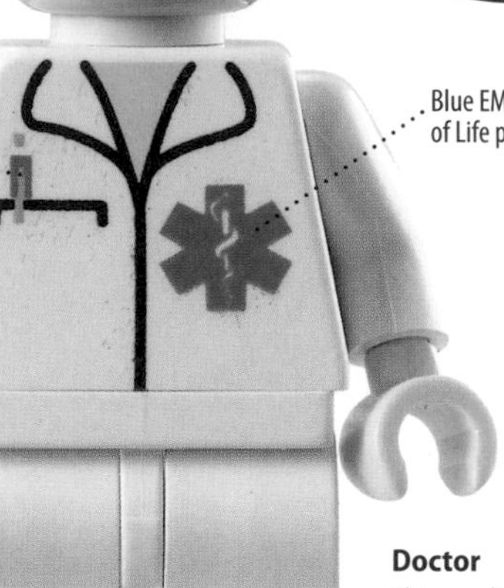
Pen for writing prescriptions
Blue EMT Star of Life pattern

Doctor
This medical minifigure has a fresh look this year thanks to his new crisp white torso and hat.

2004 variant has a new head piece
Exclusive torso

Flight Attendant
This minifigure knows where all the safety exits are and she never has a LEGO hair out of place.

Airport ID
Plane logo

Airport Worker
This minifigure's pristine blue uniform is new this year. He makes an appearance in two sets—Century Skyway (6597) and Jet (1775).

The pilot is sponsored by Octan gas.
Octan

Helicopter Pilot
This daredevil Pilot performs death-defying tricks exclusively in his Stunt Copter (6515).

Only the hair piece is different from the Ambulance Patient

Pizza Lover
This familiar-looking minifigure has stepped out for a slice of pizza in Pizza To Go (6350).

DID YOU KNOW?
The Race subtheme included not only auto racing sets, but also speedboat racing.

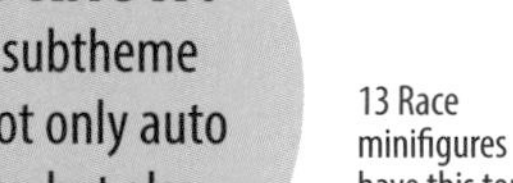
Helmet is decorated with seven stars
Trans blue visor
13 Race minifigures have this torso
TEAM 1
RACING

Race Rival
His torso says he's #1 and he's determined to prove it against his blue-suited rival in Sail N' Fly Marina (6543).

Smiling head piece with eyebrows is new in 1994
Leather jacket torso is also new this year

Leather Jacket Man This cool minifigure is exclusive to Hot Rod Club (6561) in the Race subtheme. The set also features a hot rod workshop, two hot rod cars, and a motorcycle.

This helmet is also worn by seven other minifigures.
It's safety first with this detachable life preserver

Boat Racer A speedboat enthusiast, this minifigure appears in Sail N' Fly Marina (6543) along with two boats and a seaplane.

Blue visor
White helmet piece covers the shoulders
All the Aquanauts wear the same blue suits
I THOUGHT THIS WAS GOING TO BE A POOL PARTY...

Aquanaut Commander This minifigure's job is to drive the submarine. His head with freckles and a red headband with a "C" in the middle is new this year.

1995

ANOTHER LANDMARK year, 1995 saw the 40th anniversary of the LEGO® System building sets. To celebrate, the next big play theme was introduced, Aquazone, along with a new version of Castle. Over in LEGO® Space, Unitron was discontinued after only one year and two sets. However, 1995 was a year with far-ranging effects, sparking a trend for underwater play themes and introducing one iconic bony figure who would appear in almost 50 sets over the next 18 years. Can you guess who he is?

LEGO® AQUAZONE

Adventure lurked beneath the waves in Aquazone, a new play theme set in the depths of the ocean. Aquazone joined Pirates as the first major new play themes to join the core three (Town, Space, and Castle). Six sets were released in this theme in 1995.

DID YOU KNOW?
Aquazone lasted for three exciting years, until it was discontinued in 1998.

Sea green shades
Diving suit

Aquanaut Diver The Diver has a unique head piece with green sunglasses. He might spend all his time underwater, but he still likes to look cool!

AQUANAUTS

The Aquanaut minifigures are undersea miners based at the Neptune Discovery Lab, searching the sea for Hydrolator crystals. Only three Aquanaut minifigures were produced.

Head piece was first seen on the Space Police Chief in 1992.
Black visor

Jock Clouseau Radio expert Jock Clouseau has two variants in 1995—one with flippers and one without.

Torso is exclusive to the 1995 Aquasharks
Black, gloved hands

Aquashark His black diving suit is decorated with a grinning shark logo. The black helmet with shoulder protection is new this year.

LEGO SYSTEM
6115

Shark Scout (6115)
The smallest Aquasharks set, Shark Scout features a vehicle and one minifigure.

AQUASHARKS

Villainous miners, the Aquasharks are out to steal whatever the Aquanauts might dig up. They appear in two sets this year, but only two minifigures were created.

Floppy haired head piece is new this year

Aquashark Diver This minifigure is identical to the other Aquashark, apart from his visor.

LEGO® CASTLE

The Royal Knights arrived this year in five sets, including a castle of their own. This Castle subtheme is best known for introducing the skeleton figure and the first king minifigure to wear an actual crown. The Royal Knights would reign supreme through 1995 and 1996.

Standard smiling head piece
Scale mail pattern on torso
Gray helmet with chin guard

White Knight The Knight drives the King's carriage in set 6044.

Gray Knight This royal protector appears in only one set, Royal Drawbridge (6078).

Helmet with chin guard
Lion's head shield is exclusive to this minifigure
Red helmet with black visor

Red Bowman A variant without a quiver was released in 1996.

Black Knight The royal champion likes to keep his identity secret.

Detachable plume of white feathers
The gold crown makes its debut in 1995
THIS CROWN IS REALLY HEAVY!
New torso with fearsome lion crest
Two variants have blue pants, one has white
Cape

The King Three variants of the King are released in 1995, each with a new torso featuring a lion's head crest.

Blue Knight This minifigure's job is to guard the castle, and his special helmet means that his neck and nose are protected from enemy bowmen.

Gray helmet with neck and nose protectors
Same torso as the Black Knight

Mustache Knight This noble Knight is distinguished by his impressive mustache.

HELLO BONES

The skeleton figure made his first appearance in 1995 in three sets, two from LEGO Castle, and one from LEGO® Pirates. He has appeared in almost 50 more sets to date.

All-white figure
Standard skull pattern
Six ribs on torso
Legs with four-toed feet

Unique torso
Standard female head piece
Black ponytail appears on more than 60 minifigures
Surfboard pattern
Torso appears on nine Town minifigures
Surfer is in set 4151

Pink Sweater Girl Pretty in pink, this minifigure appears in the Girl's Set (4151).

Casual Female This red, white, and blue female is found in the Large FreeStyle Bucket (4152).

Surfer This cool dude wears the standard LEGO surfer outfit—blue pants and a white tank top.

LEGO® FREESTYLE

LEGO Basic took on the name FreeStyle from 1995 to 1998, offering boxes and buckets with basic system bricks and a small number of minifigures. Five sets were released in 1995, including a Girl's Set (4151), which featured five minifigure characters. No other FreeStyle set during its three year run would ever feature more than two minifigures.

Red shirt and blue base

Smiling Boy This happy figure appears in the 41-piece Large Stack'n'Learn (2084).

Dark brown hair
Red shirt with blue dungarees

Dungarees Boy This figure of a young boy appears in 12 LEGO Primo sets between 1995 and 2001.

LEGO® PRIMO™

Aimed at the youngest builders, PRIMO replaced LEGO Baby in 1995. It featured colorful toys intended for children from 6 to 24 months, and single piece figures that were perfect for little hands.

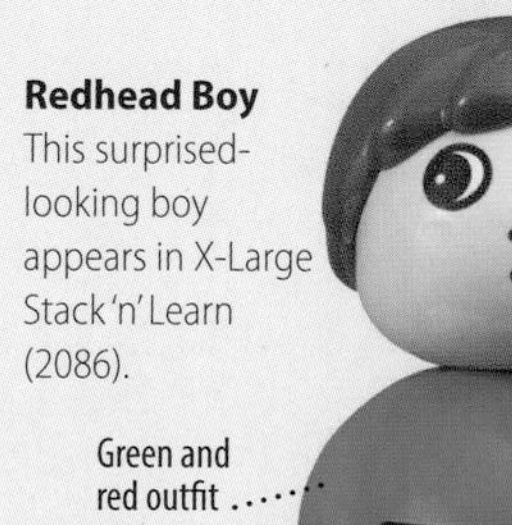

Green and red outfit

Redhead Boy This surprised-looking boy appears in X-Large Stack'n'Learn (2086).

Round base instead of legs

Red Outfit Boy Dressed all in red, this figure appears in the nine-part Medium Stack'n' Learn (2082).

1995

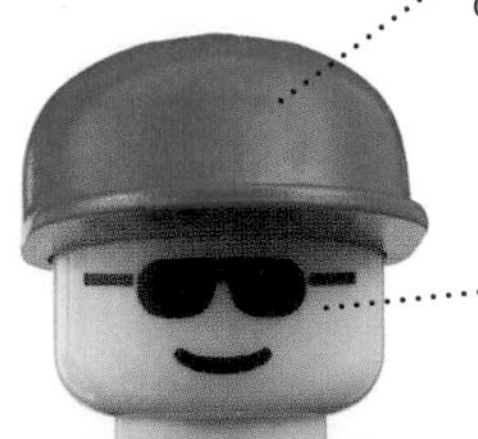

Standard LEGO cap in blue

Popular head piece, used on more than 135 minifigures

Zip-up jacket torso is new this year

F1 Mechanic This specialist minifigure has to repair a broken down Formula 1 car in F1 Hauler (6484). He'd better not get his new torso dirty!

Dumper Driver When dirt needs picking up and taking from one place to another, this minifigure is happy to help.

Dump truck logo proudly displayed on torso

Cool shades

Torso appears on five Coast Guard minifigures

All three Coast Guards in 1995 wear the same red pants.

Street Sweeper It's a dirty job, but this minifigure has to do it. He keeps the LEGO Town clean in Street Sweeper (6649).

Air Rescuer This Coast Guard takes to the skies in his helicopter to rescue minifigures in peril.

Black hair piece used on around 200 minifigures

Torso is new this year

Same head and torso as F1 Mechanic

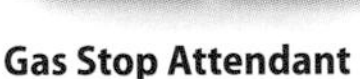

Gas Stop Attendant Any minifigure who visits the Gas Stop Shop (6562) will be served by this helpful guy.

F1 Hauler Driver Also in set 6484, this minifigure drives a special F1 repair truck.

Coast Guard logo

Detachable life preserver

Sea Rescuer This brave Coast Guard rescues minifigures who are in danger at sea.

Maersk Truck Driver Maersk is a real-world company based in Copenhagen, Denmark. This minifigure is exclusive to the two 1995 sets.

This hat piece is only used in this year.

Torso seen only on this minifigure and a 1996 variant

Mission Control This minifigure's job is to coordinate land and sea rescues in Hurricane Harbor (6338).

HEJ, I HAVE JUST DRIVEN FROM DENMARK!

Mærsk logo

LEGO® TOWN

It was a year of excitement and variety for LEGO Town. Hurricane Harbor (6338), the first Coast Guard base set in six years, kept watch over the waves. Two special Mærsk cargo truck sets appeared, but were sold only in Denmark. LEGO Town even went into space with the new Launch Command models.

DID YOU KNOW?
Paradisa sets were the first to feature pink, dark pink, and lime green colors.

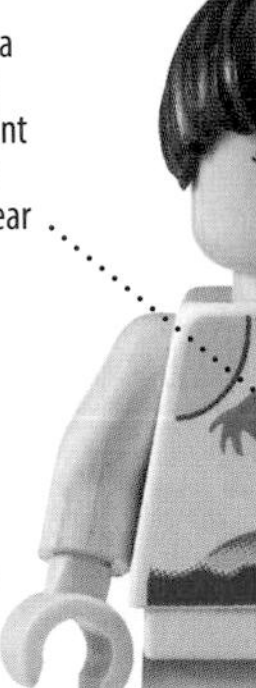

Torso with a sunset and dolphin print tank top is new this year

Dolphin Fan Set 6414 featured a dolphin and a female minifigure who was keen to swim with it.

Dolphin Point (6414) Hungry minifigures can climb the pink stairs to the ice-cream parlor for a treat in this Paradisa set.

PARADISA

Once again, Paradisa was the place to be with the new Dolphin Point set (6414) featuring four minifigures. This elaborate model included a two-story lighthouse complete with lantern and an ice-cream shop.

Scientist Exclusive to Shuttle Launch Pad (6339), the brainy Scientist has two unique parts—his head and his torso.

ID badge

Unique head

Headset to keep in radio contact with the rest of the crew

Same torso as Chopper Pilot

Ground Crew This minifigure is busy in 1995, appearing in three sets, but his feet stay firmly on the ground.

DID YOU KNOW?
The new Launch Command logo would be reused in 1999 in the LEGO Space Port subtheme.

Astronaut Thanks to the hard work of the minifigures on the ground, the Astronaut makes it to space in Moon Walker (6516).

5...4...3...2...1... GET READY FOR BLAST OFF!

It's vital to stay in radio contact with Earth

Gold chrome visor, new this year

New torso, also seen on another astronaut minifigure in 1995

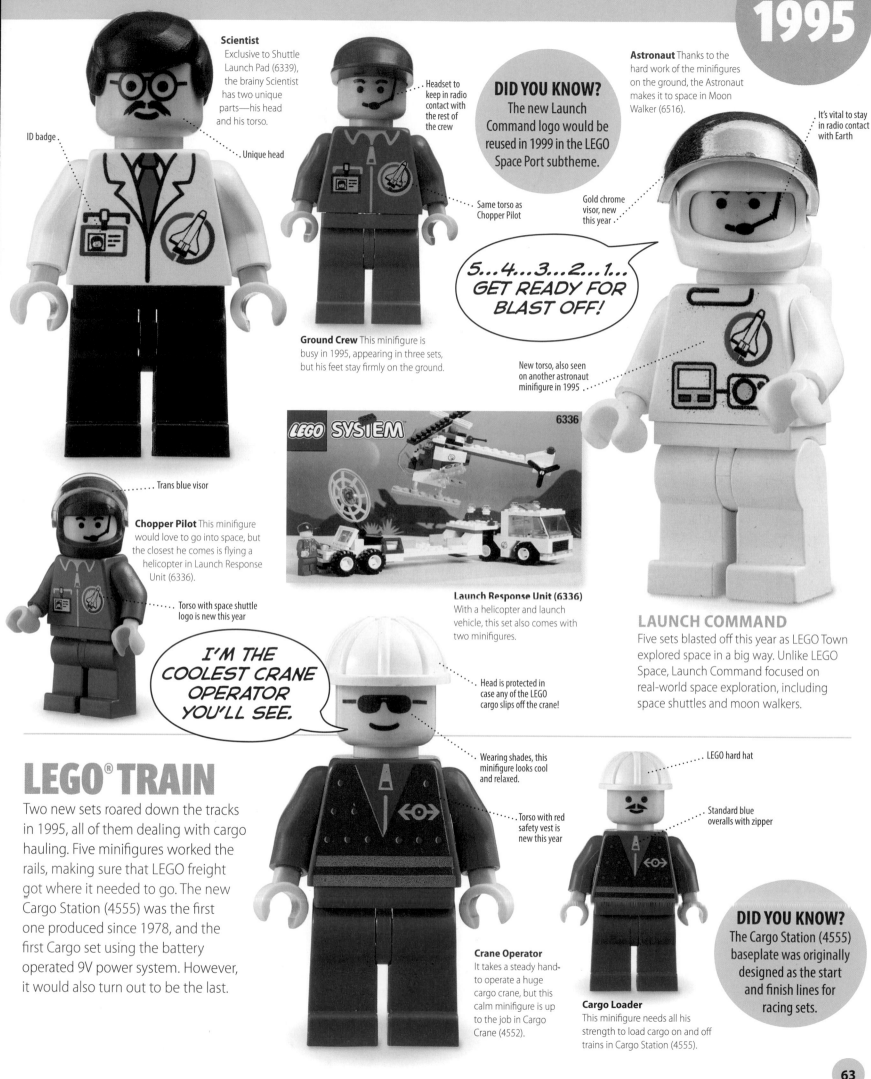

Launch Response Unit (6336) With a helicopter and launch vehicle, this set also comes with two minifigures.

Trans blue visor

Chopper Pilot This minifigure would love to go into space, but the closest he comes is flying a helicopter in Launch Response Unit (6336).

Torso with space shuttle logo is new this year

LAUNCH COMMAND

Five sets blasted off this year as LEGO Town explored space in a big way. Unlike LEGO Space, Launch Command focused on real-world space exploration, including space shuttles and moon walkers.

LEGO® TRAIN

Two new sets roared down the tracks in 1995, all of them dealing with cargo hauling. Five minifigures worked the rails, making sure that LEGO freight got where it needed to go. The new Cargo Station (4555) was the first one produced since 1978, and the first Cargo set using the battery operated 9V power system. However, it would also turn out to be the last.

I'M THE COOLEST CRANE OPERATOR YOU'LL SEE.

Head is protected in case any of the LEGO cargo slips off the crane!

Wearing shades, this minifigure looks cool and relaxed.

Torso with red safety vest is new this year

Crane Operator It takes a steady hand to operate a huge cargo crane, but this calm minifigure is up to the job in Cargo Crane (4552).

LEGO hard hat

Standard blue overalls with zipper

Cargo Loader This minifigure needs all his strength to load cargo on and off trains in Cargo Station (4555).

DID YOU KNOW?
The Cargo Station (4555) baseplate was originally designed as the start and finish lines for racing sets.

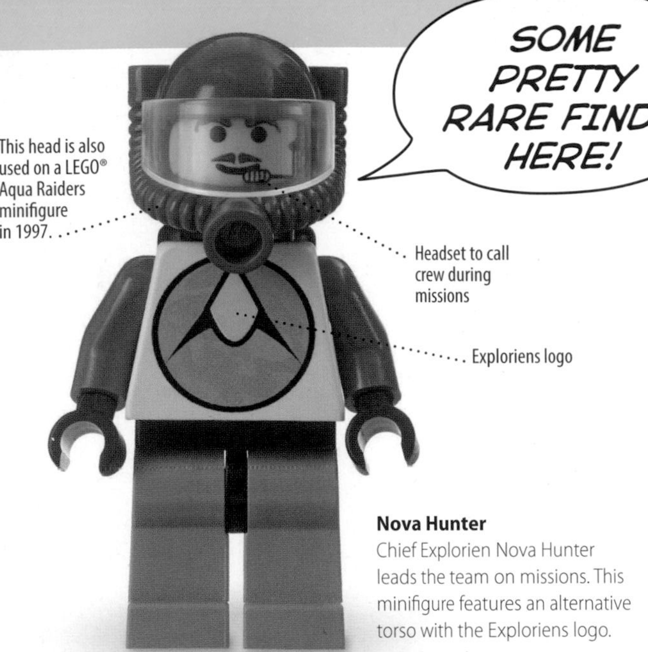
SOME PRETTY RARE FINDS HERE!
This head is also used on a LEGO® Aqua Raiders minifigure in 1997.
Headset to call crew during missions
Exploriens logo

Nova Hunter Chief Explorien Nova Hunter leads the team on missions. This minifigure features an alternative torso with the Exploriens logo.

1996

PERHAPS THE BIGGEST news for LEGO® minifigures this year was the introduction of LEGO.com. For the first time, fans could go online to access information, games, and activities, and also to shop for their favorite minifigures and sets. And there was plenty for LEGO fans to see online this year, as new themes LEGO® Western and LEGO® Time Cruisers were introduced, along with the short-lived Castle Dark Forest and Space Exploriens subthemes. From the distant past to the far future, LEGO building was everywhere in 1996!

LEGO® SPACE

The Exploriens were new space travelers introduced in nine sets in 1996. They searched the galaxy for fossils, accompanied by their robot Ann Droid—both the second robot and second female minifigure in the history of LEGO Space. Operating out of Android Base (6958) as well as the smaller Nebula Outpost (6899), the Exploriens hung up their space helmets in 1996.

Translucent green light stud

Android face print

Armor protects internal mechanics

Ann Droid The only female in the LEGO Exploriens team, Ann Droid features a unique translucent head piece. Her name is a play on the word "android".

Breathing apparatus

Headset printed on face

Hosepipe attached to helmet

Helmet

Explorien This minifigure has an alternative Explorien torso—he's thankful that it has oxygen controls.

LEGO TIME CRUISERS

The first and so far only LEGO theme dealing with time travel, the Time Cruisers Dr. Cyber, his assistant Tim, a robot, and a monkey, traveled back in time on various missions. It lasted two years.

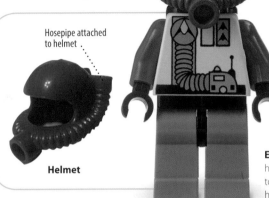

Same translucent green light stud as the LEGO Space Ann Droid minifigure

Wacco This figure's head piece is also seen on Spyrius Droid from LEGO Space in 1994.

Cross-eyed expression is unique
Pencil tied to bow tie
Pocket watch

Dr. Cyber Traveling in time has made Dr. Cyber cross-eyed. Well, he's seen some crazy things!

"T" print on torso for Tim.

Freckles on face

Red Cap Tim Dr. Cyber's assistant, Tim, travels with him on all trips back in time.

Nose print debuted this year but it is rarely used as a feature.

Tim This variant of Tim features a new head, with bangs and a wide-eyed expression.

LEGO® PIRATES

LEGO Pirates underwent a major redesign in 1996, as the Pirates and Islanders were joined by a new faction. The Imperial Armada was out to hunt down the pesky Pirates, but even their Flagship (6280) was no match for the Pirates' dreaded Skull's Eye Schooner (6286).

Plume fits into helmet hole

Silver breastplate guards against attacks

Admiral Head of the Armada flagship, the Admiral minifigure is always seen with his armor plate on—hunting pirates is a risky business.

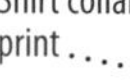

Shirt collar print

Leather belt print

Striped cavalry uniform design

Red Soldier Clad in red, this soldier is the most common minifigure in the sets from the Imperial Armada theme.

Officer This elaborately dressed minifigure wears a triple plume piece, which fits into his hat.

Decorative gold medal

Pirate hat

Silver button print on jacket

Wooden peg-leg

Pirate Captain A clash with the soldiers has cost the Pirate his right leg—he wears a peg-leg instead.

DID YOU KNOW?
The style of the Armada crew is based on Conquistadors from the 1600s.

White Shirt Pirate No pirate would be complete without a bandana accessory. This minifigure's bandana is hiding a bald patch on his head!

Green pirate vest

Anchor tattoo

Pirate The bandana piece is also seen on more than 70 minifigures, including the 2009 Hondo Ohnaka minifigure from the LEGO® *Star Wars*® theme.

LEGO SYSTEM
6280

Armada Flagship (6280) This set comes with a twin-mast ship and three Imperial Armada minifigures.

LEGO® CASTLE

Castle fans ventured into the Dark Forest this year, with three sets produced for this short-lived subtheme. In a reimagining of the Forestmen subtheme from the late 1980s, green-clad bandits hid in the hollow trees of the woods, clashing with Royal Knights, Black Knights, and Dragon Masters. Led by Rob N. Hood, they stole from the rich, but who they gave the treasure to was never clear.

DID YOU KNOW?
LEGO designers rarely add printed noses to minifigures—to keep the graphics as neat and simple as possible.

Stylized mustache and goatee

Forestman This Forestman's plume accessory also comes in black, yellow, blue, and white.

Blue Forestman This Forestman doesn't follow the minifigure crowd—unlike his friends, he has a blue and brown color scheme.

HAND OVER YOUR GOLD BRICKS!

Studded shirt pattern on torso

Red leather belt

Fringed hair pattern

Pouch to carry supplies

Archer This cheery Archer has a new head with choppy bangs—he can't stop smiling about it.

Straggly hair visible under cowl

Drooping mustache

Cloaked Forestman Working in the forest can be dangerous. This Forestman wears a brown cowl to try and blend in.

1996

LEGO WESTERN

It was all about lawmen and outlaws in 1996, with plenty of new pieces and fun for young cowpokes. It was the first LEGO play theme to focus on the Wild West and it lasted well into 1997. In 2013, The LEGO Group returned to the Wild West with LEGO® *The Lone Ranger*™, based on the Disney movie.

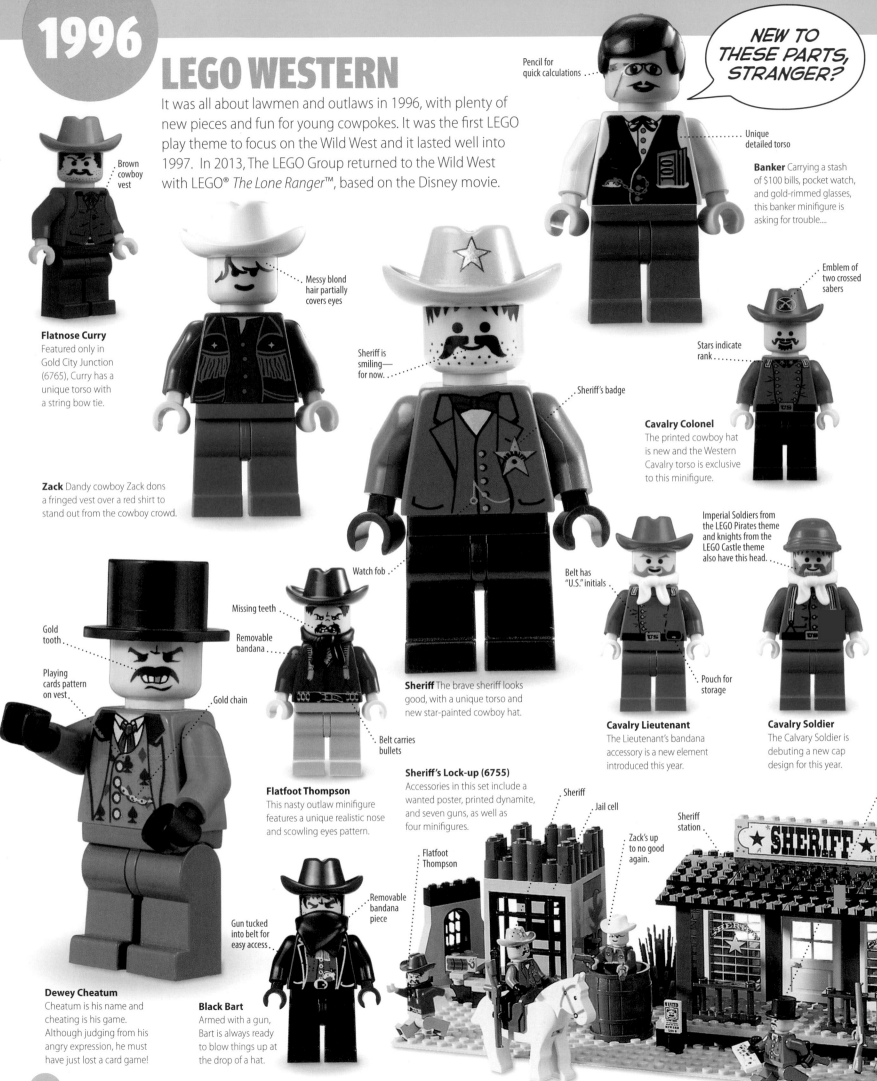

NEW TO THESE PARTS, STRANGER?
Pencil for quick calculations
Unique detailed torso

Banker Carrying a stash of $100 bills, pocket watch, and gold-rimmed glasses, this banker minifigure is asking for trouble....

Brown cowboy vest

Flatnose Curry Featured only in Gold City Junction (6765), Curry has a unique torso with a string bow tie.

Messy blond hair partially covers eyes

Zack Dandy cowboy Zack dons a fringed vest over a red shirt to stand out from the cowboy crowd.

Sheriff is smiling—for now.
Sheriff's badge
Watch fob

Sheriff The brave sheriff looks good, with a unique torso and new star-painted cowboy hat.

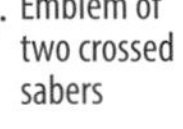

Emblem of two crossed sabers

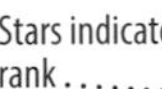

Stars indicate rank

Cavalry Colonel The printed cowboy hat is new and the Western Cavalry torso is exclusive to this minifigure.

Belt has "U.S." initials
Pouch for storage

Cavalry Lieutenant The Lieutenant's bandana accessory is a new element introduced this year.

Imperial Soldiers from the LEGO Pirates theme and knights from the LEGO Castle theme also have this head.

Cavalry Soldier The Calvary Soldier is debuting a new cap design for this year.

Gold tooth
Playing cards pattern on vest
Gold chain

Dewey Cheatum Cheatum is his name and cheating is his game. Although judging from his angry expression, he must have just lost a card game!

Missing teeth
Removable bandana
Belt carries bullets

Flatfoot Thompson This nasty outlaw minifigure features a unique realistic nose and scowling eyes pattern.

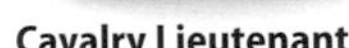

Removable bandana piece
Gun tucked into belt for easy access

Black Bart Armed with a gun, Bart is always ready to blow things up at the drop of a hat.

Sheriff's Lock-up (6755) Accessories in this set include a wanted poster, printed dynamite, and seven guns, as well as four minifigures.

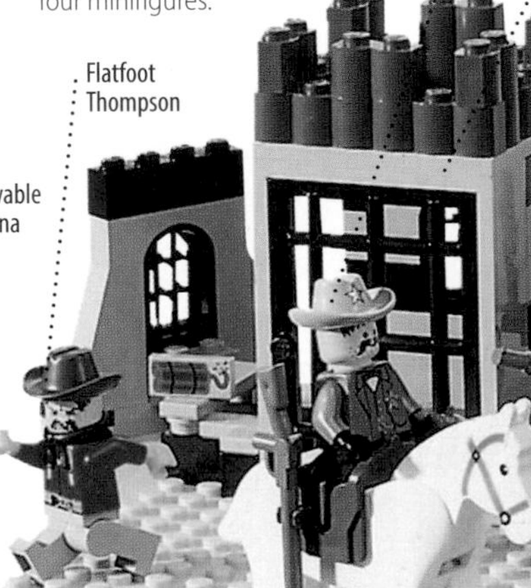

Sheriff
Jail cell
Sheriff station
Zack's up to no good again.
Flatfoot Thompson
SHERIFF

LEGO® TOWN

It was back to the racetrack for LEGO Town, with awesome new sets like Indy Transport (6335), complete with three new minifigures, a truck, and three Formula 1 race cars. The truck transported the cars to the track, where the mechanic minifigures could get them ready for the race.

Jet Pilot This pilot minifigure is ready for some thrills in his star-patterned jumpsuit and helmet.

Black sunglasses

Zippered jumpsuit

RACE
TEAM

Turbo Charger This race car driver minifigure is wearing a new torso, printed with the Octan logo.

Red belt

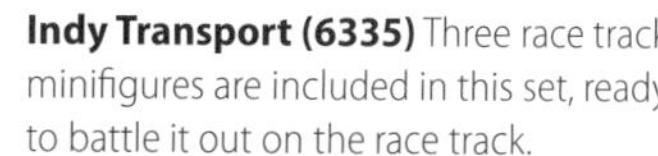

Indy Transport (6335) Three race track minifigures are included in this set, ready to battle it out on the race track.

LEGO SYSTEM
6335
Octan

VELUX PROMOTION

This minifigure was included in the promotional set House with Roof-Windows (1854). The house featured a dining area and a bedroom on the top floor. It also had a slanted roof, which is a rare occurrence on LEGO houses!

VELUX

Velux sticker on torso

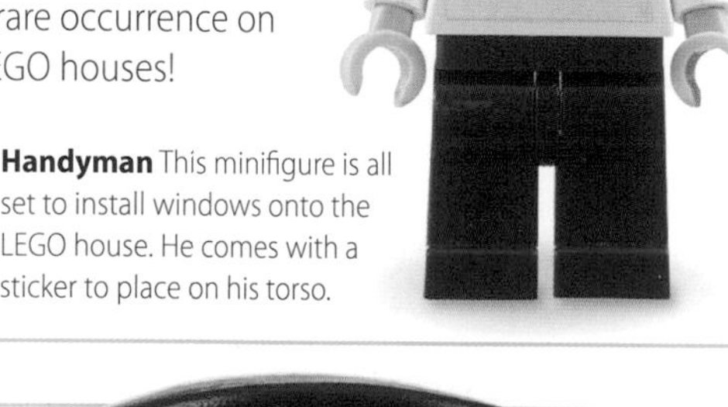

Handyman This minifigure is all set to install windows onto the LEGO house. He comes with a sticker to place on his torso.

NOW BOARDING FOR LEGO TOWN AND DARK FOREST.

Pointed mustache print

Railway logo

Railway Employee
This minifigure's head is also used on the LEGO® *Star Wars*® Biggs Darklighter minifigure released in 1999.

Female ponytail hair piece

Torso with palm tree and horse detail is new for this year

Passenger Although this minifigure is wearing clothes from the LEGO® Paradisa theme, she actually appears in the LEGO Train set Cargo Railway (4559).

DID YOU KNOW?

The Train Station set (2150) was largely based on 1991's Metro Station (4554).

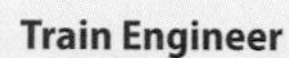

Train Engineer
This important-looking train engineer maintains the tracks for the LEGO DUPLO trains.

Curly mustache

LEGO® TRAIN

Passengers were ready to board the LEGO Train, thanks to a new Train station set (2150) featuring eight minifigures. The station was complete with a waiting room, a snack bar, and a platform for boarding. This was the first train station set in five years and the last until 1999.

LEGO® DUPLO®

This engineer was ready to take little builders to new adventures! After a two year absence, DUPLO Train returned with six sets this year. Both battery-operated trains and push-along trains were available.

DON'T CALL ME CONE HEAD!
Quiver holds arrows
Drooping mustache print
Fleur-de-lis pattern on torso

Helmet Knight A new torso design adorns this minifigure. His conical helmet also has a chin guard.

Cape has a spider printed on the back

Single tooth printed on mouth

Spider emblem

Willa the Witch
This is the first (but not the last) witch minifigure. The sloped skirt piece is printed for the first time.

LEGO CASTLE

Things took a spooky turn with the introduction of Fright Knights, a new Castle subtheme featuring creepy knights led by Basil the Bat Lord. Black dragons, witches, crystal balls, and flying broomsticks figured in the 10 seriously supernatural sets. Fright Knights lasted for two years before disappearing into the shadows.

Bat wings are attached to helmet

Basil the Bat Lord
Ghoulish leader of the Fright Knights, this minifigure appears in sets with and without his cape.

Bat symbol on back of cape

Armor vest

Cape resembles bat wings

Basil's cape

1997

IT WAS ALL ABOUT weird and wild villains this year. Witches, bats, and evil dragons appeared in Fright Knights, the new LEGO® Castle subtheme, while the heroic LEGO® Time Cruisers met their match in the fiendish Time Twisters. Meanwhile, in LEGO® Space, strange aliens from the UFO subtheme battled the robots of Roboforce. For those who preferred more peaceful play, LEGO® Town offered Australian exploration in the Outback subtheme or a trip beneath the sea with the Divers.

Willa the Witch
Knight's plume on helmet
Basil the Bat Lord
Gate can be lowered and raised

Night Lord's Castle (6097)
This spooky castle set comes with seven minifigures, including a black dragon. Scary surprises include a skull that appears inside a crystal ball and a secret rotating wall.

Red Plume Fright Knight This Knight is clad in a new armored torso, also seen on Professor Millennium in 1997, from the LEGO® Time Cruisers theme.

I'M ACTUALLY REALLY SCARED OF BATS.
Halberd
Helmet with neck protector
Bushy beard
Studded armor printed torso
Shield with bat print

Armored Knight
This minifigure is proudly wearing an armored torso introduced this year.

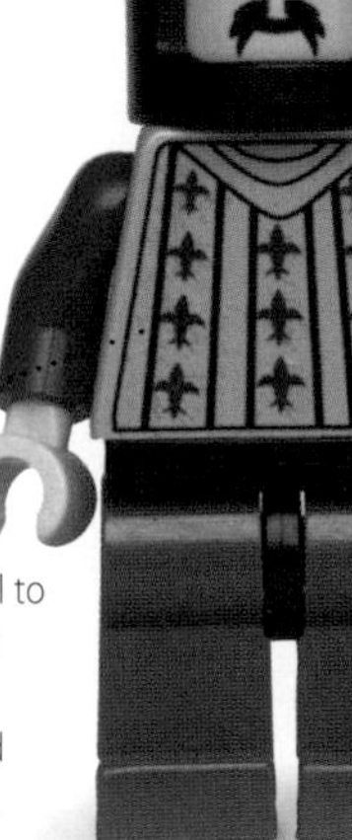
Helmet was first released in 1979
Three minifigures have this torso

Fright Knight Identical to the Helmet Knight apart from the quiver, this minifigure is often found carrying a spear instead.

LEGO® WESTERN

Back for its second year in 1997, this play theme focused almost exclusively on Native Americans. The first Native American minifigures ever produced, they came with never before seen accessories such as the Chief's headdress and hair pieces with feathers, as well as Native American teepees to build.

Feathers worn as part of Native American tradition
Wrinkled forehead
Warpaint printed on face
Bone necklace

Chief There's no doubting that this minifigure is the Chief of the tribe thanks to his impressive headdress.

Removable feathers
Decorative bone chest piece
Downcast eyes
Fringe pattern on legs
Pistol tucked away in belt
Bushy eyebrows

Medicine Man Wearing a new buffalo headdress, this tribe member heals sick tribal minifigures.

Tan Shirt Native American Orange tribal paint distinguishes this minifigure from his tribe's people.

Black Bart This variant of Black Bart is almost identical to the 1996 minifigure, apart from a slightly diffrent head and a white bandana.

Black-tipped feathers
Quiver
Many of the minifigures in this theme have printed noses.
Decorative tribal pattern on legs

Plain Native American Unlike the other Native American minifigures, this tribe member doesn't wear face paint.

Red Shirt Native American The braided hair piece is unique to the LEGO Western theme.

DID YOU KNOW? The quiver accessory has been carried by around 70 minifigures.

LEGO TIME CRUISERS

The second year of Time Cruisers introduced the evil Time Twisters. Professor Millennium and his twin brother, Tony, traveled to the past to loot ancient treasures, pursued by the Time Cruisers. A ghost and a skeleton also came along for the ride as the Time Twisters meddled with history.

I'M STEALING THE PYRAMIDS NEXT!

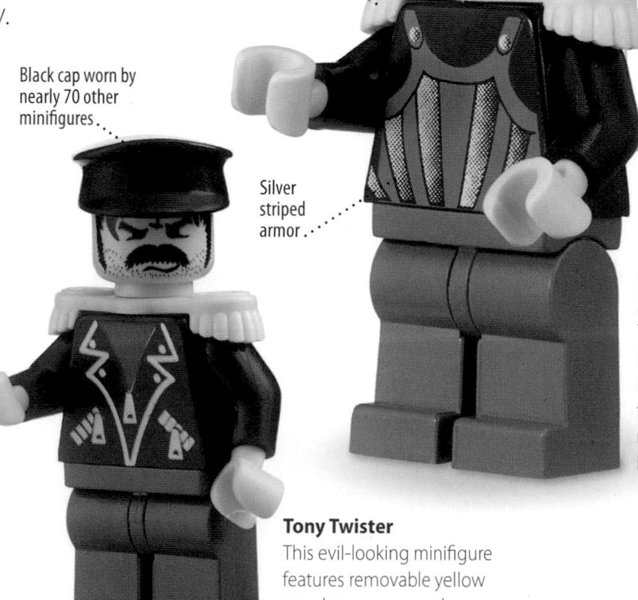
Epaulet
Black cap worn by nearly 70 other minifigures
Silver striped armor

Professor Millennium The evil Professor's torso is also seen on the Fright Knight minifigures in 1997.

Tony Twister This evil-looking minifigure features removable yellow epaulets worn over the torso.

Top hat
Biker-style leather jacket

Skeleton From the Time Cruisers board game, this is the first time a skull head was featured on a regular torso.

Oxygen tubes on helmet
Suit mechanics printed on torso
Green hook replaces left hand

Aquaraider with Hook With a green hook to aid him, this Aquaraider is sure to find some precious minerals on the sea floor.

Aquaraider This young team member bulldozes the ocean floor in Aqua Dozer (2161).

LEGO® AQUAZONE

The Aquaraiders appeared in 1997, with three ships and plans to mine valuable minerals from the sea floor. Although they were part of the Aquazone universe, no Aquanauts or Aquasharks appeared in their sets. This was to be their only year beneath the sea.

Blank head piece
White minifigure legs are new for the ghost this year

Beneath the Ghost

Ghost A long glow-in-the-dark shroud piece covers a standard LEGO minifigure to create the updated iconic ghost.

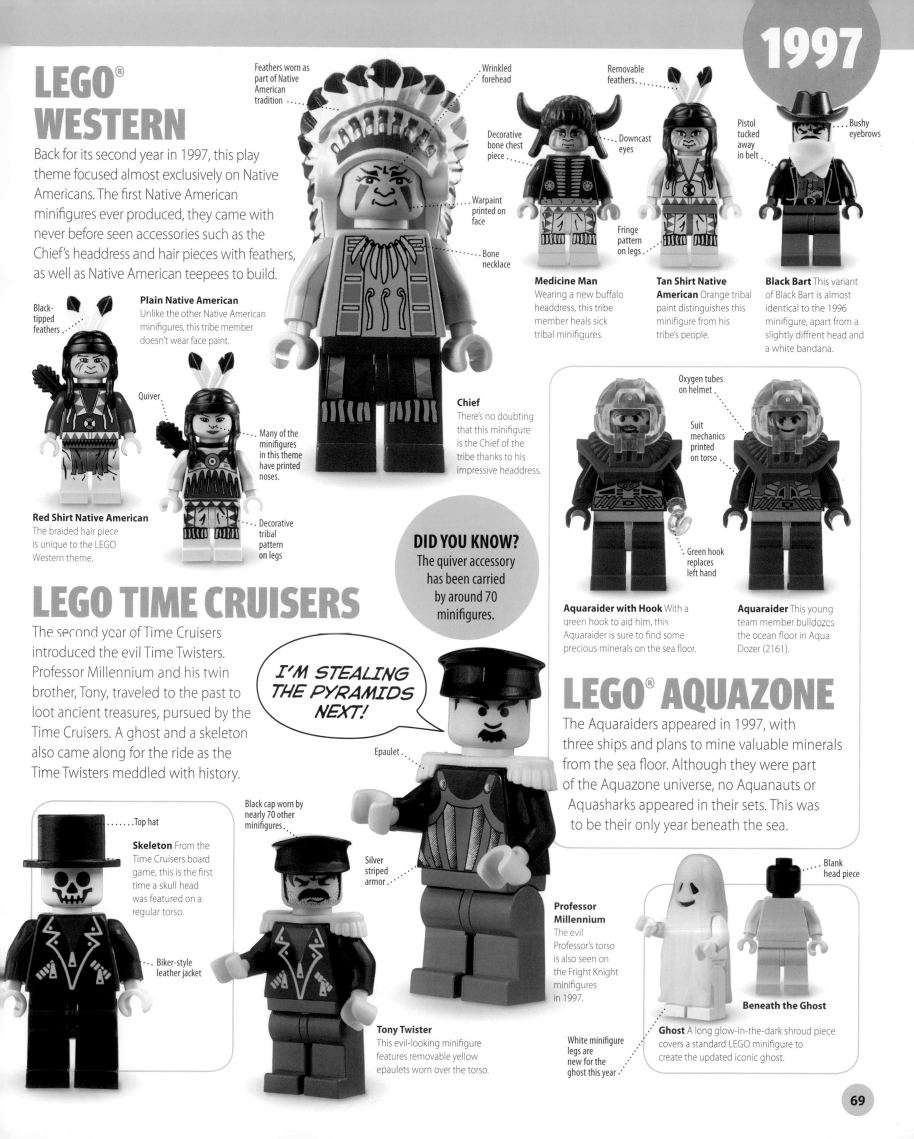

1997

LEGO SPACE

Up to 1997, LEGO Space focused primarily on human astronauts, with a few robots thrown in. This year aliens showed up in a big way in the UFO subtheme, the first characters in what was a long and colorful lineup of LEGO extraterrestrials.

Magnetic crane
Red Alien at the controls
UFO pattern
Laser lights

Alien Avenger (6975) This flying saucer model includes a handle so that it can be spun around, two rotating lasers, and two heat-sensitive stickers, which can be touched to reveal an alien head.

UFO

After launching in 1996 with just a keychain, UFO came back strong with 13 sets this year. This was the first LEGO play theme to feature aliens from outer space as minifigures.

Gray mask

Chest armor also seen on Insectoids, in 1998

Blue Alien Traveling in the Cyber Saucer (6999) makes this alien minifigure green around the gills.

Trans-orange head piece

Red Alien This alien might look like he's smiling, but he definitely doesn't come in peace.

Wire pattern on helmet
Chest armor
Golden wires on legs

Alpha Draconis This alien leader is terrified of his own reflection, so he wears his helmet at all times.

Rectangular visor serves as eyes

Unique torso with intricate circuit detail

Circuit pattern extends to legs

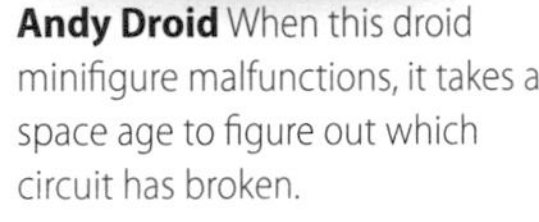

Andy Droid When this droid minifigure malfunctions, it takes a space age to figure out which circuit has broken.

Large, blue eye shield

Golden circuitry on torso

Blue Droid The concept of walking is alien to this droid minifigure—he can usually be seen on his Cyber Blaster (6818).

ROBOFORCE

Fighting for justice in the galaxy, the astronauts of Roboforce pilot big robots equipped for battle or to rescue space explorers.

LEGO SYSTEM
6975

Alien Avenger (6975) This set includes a large flying saucer, two small vehicles, and four minifigures.

Red bandana
ROBO

Roboforce Astronaut Nothing makes this astronaut happier than controlling his Robo Stalker (2153).

Helmet element is also seen on the Exploriens in the Space theme in 1996 and the Rock Raiders in 2000.
ROBO

Astronaut Variant This variation of the Roboforce astronaut isn't as high-tech as his Roboforce pal—he has plain legs.

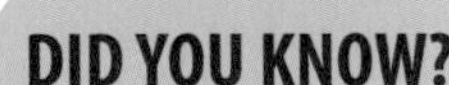

DID YOU KNOW?
Roboforce was only available to buy in the United States.

Head piece also worn by Unitron Chief from the Unitron subtheme in 1994
Roboforce logo
ROBO

Chip Nebula As leader of Roboforce, Chip feels it's only right that he gets to wear super cool silver shades.

LEGO TOWN

Town traveled from the arid desert to the depths of the ocean in 1997, launching two new subthemes—Divers and Outback. The Race and Paradisa subthemes entered their final years, but there was still lots of action with exciting sets such as Crisis News Crew (6553). This year also saw the launch of Town Jr., which had simpler sets for younger builders.

Cap to shield face from sun
Camera-ready face
News channel logo
NOW FOR A BREAKING STORY...

Cameraman This Cameraman captures all the off-road racing action in the outback—he would actually prefer to be in front of the camera.

News Anchor Unfortunately, this News Anchor had a shortlived career, appearing in only one set: Crisis News Crew (6553).

LEGO® ISLAND

"i" for Infomaniac

This promotional minifigure came with the LEGO *Island* video game —the first to feature minifigures. The game was only released in the United States.

Infomaniac The Infomaniac's head is full to bursting with all sorts of information about the LEGO Island—well, he did create it!

Plain green torso

CLASSIC

A total of 48 new Town sets came out this year, as Town minifigures explored the Australian wilderness and traveled the sea, looking for adventure wherever they went.

Person When this guy heard he was going to be included in the Flying Duck (1824) he went quackers!

TOWN JR.

The sirens were blaring as Town Jr. launched with new Fire sets, including the Blaze Brigade (6554) and a Fire Engine (6486). The Town also got a new bank to keep their LEGO money safe (6566) and the police were in hot pursuit of a robber in Roadblock Runners (6549).

PARADISA

Paradisa ended its five-year run this year with the release of four sets, bringing the island vacation to a close. The figures and ponies have not reappeared (so far), and many of the building pieces are rare.

Pretty lace collar

Paradisa Girl
There's never a dull day for this girl—she works at the Fun Fair (6547).

POLICE
Only three police minifigures have worn this police hat ever
Police badge
THAT'S SOME BIG POLICEMAN!

Policeman The robber's definitely not going to get away with this Police minifigure in pursuit in Roadblock Runners (6549).

Bank uniform torso is exclusive to this minifigure

Guard The Townspeople trust this man with their hard-earned dollars in the Bank (6566).

Gray bank uniform vest
ID card

Bank Driver Looking cool in shades, this minifigure drives an armored car full of cash in Bank (6566).

LEGO® SCALA™

The SCALA name returned after 17 years, launching figures for the first time. SCALA figures wore real clothing and had hair made from strands instead of molded plastic. The new SCALA came to an end in 2001.

Molded facial features
Voluminous blonde hair
Cozy bath robe
Posable arms

Andrea Andrea is ready for a day of pampering in the Bathroom (3242).

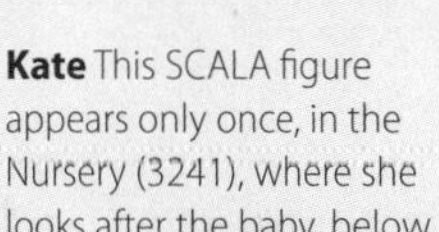
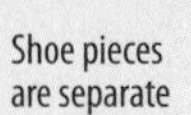
Shoe pieces are separate

Kate This SCALA figure appears only once, in the Nursery (3241), where she looks after the baby, below.

Happy but hungry

Baby
This happy toddler is waiting for her feed. Hurry up, Kate!

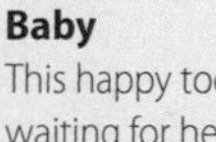
White lace top
Blue floral skirt

Emma This doll has every beauty product at her disposal in the Beauty Studio (3200).

LEGO TOWN CONTINUED

DIVERS

A brand new LEGO Town subtheme, Divers made a splash this year with 12 sets. Unlike Aquazone, Divers was a realistic line, focusing on real-world undersea exploration.

Diving mask element is new this year
DIVER? NO, I ALWAYS DRESS LIKE THIS.
Diving suit
Sleeveless tank top
Sunglasses
Essential life preserver
Divers logo
Cap covers blond hair pattern
LEGO SYSTEM
6441
8-12
Transparent diving mask
Scuba tank element seen for the first time this year
LEGO® Divers' submarine logo
Hair peeks out from under cap
Printed headset for communicating with crew
Pilots wear yellow pants
Real-world diver down flag symbol
Air gauge on diving suit

Diver Equipped with a scuba tank and flippers, this diver is all geared up to explore life under the sea.

Boat Man This minifigure assists the divers in their underwater explorations and he is determined to look cool doing it!

Dinghy Boy He is wearing a life preserver, but it probably won't protect this minifigure against the sharks in Shark Cage Cove (6558).

Submarine Pilot A headset is essential to keep this pilot minifigure up-to-date on any amazing discoveries made by the divers.

Deep Reef Refuge (6441) This underwater lab comes with sea animals and five diver minifigures who long to explore the mysteries of the deep blue sea.

Red Diver Shark attacks are a real risk for the divers, but this minifigure just can't stop smiling.

Blond Diver This minifigure works on a research ship, but he dreams of becoming a diver one day.

Chopper Pilot Four diver minifigures have the same head piece with headset and shaggy brown hair.

Sub Pilot This smiling minifigure operates a submersible in Discovery Station (1782).

DIVER AND SHARK

This happy explorer might not be happy for much longer—he encounters a nasty shark in a promotional set (2871). This minifigure was also used for a restaurant promotion in 1998.

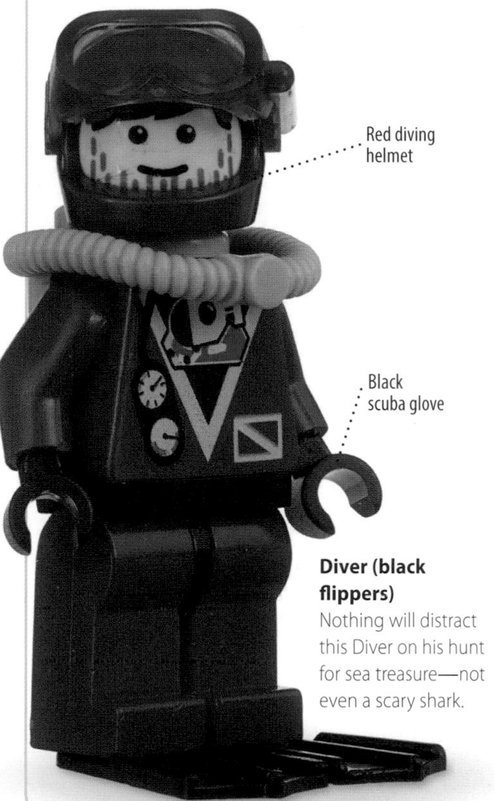
Red diving helmet
Black scuba glove

Diver (black flippers) Nothing will distract this Diver on his hunt for sea treasure—not even a scary shark.

Head piece also seen on Sub Pilot

Pilot This Pilot minifigure has tried his hardest to look different from the Sub Pilot—by wearing black pants.

Life preserver fits over head piece
UM, ARE THOSE REALLY CAVEMEN?

Crew Member This minifigure thinks he might be in the wrong job—he suffers from severe sea sickness!

Headset for communicating with divers

Treasure Pilot Part of a treasure-hunting party, this Pilot assists the divers from a submersible.

Cap keeps him a tiny bit warmer at sea

Crew This cheeky crewman loves to have a gossip with his friends via his headset.

Same head piece as Blond Diver
Red flippers

Treasure Hunter This diver discovers treasure in the Sea Hunter (6555). He still hasn't told his fellow divers....

DID YOU KNOW?

This is the only underwater subtheme to include real-world diver down flags (flags placed on the water to indicate that there is a diver below).

Deep Reef Refuge (6441) The Divers have all they need for their underwater research in this set, which includes a mini-submarine, research station, and five minifigures.

Lights needed under sea
441
Robotic arm
Crew member

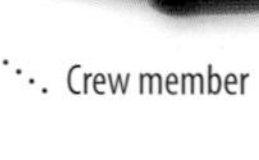

LEGO® DUPLO® DINO

DUPLO Dino combined DUPLO cave people with dinosaurs for junior-aged fun. The dinosaurs and figures roamed the Earth for three years before the subtheme went extinct.

Nose printed on head piece

Caveman This figure is wearing a hide top—they were all the rage back in the day.

Female hair piece
Eyelashes add a feminine touch.

Cavewoman A tooth necklace adorns the torso of this cavewoman. It's not her tooth, but that of a fierce animal!

Freckled nose

Young Boy This freckled boy has the same torso design as his daddy, the caveman.

I'M HARRY, COME FLY WITH ME!
Wool lining to keep warm
Bomber jacket torso is exclusive to Harry Cane.

Harry Cane The brave pilot dons an aviator cap and goggles, both new elements this year.

Egyptian Nemes headdress
Red eyes of the undead
Sewn up mouth
Pharaoh breastplate
Toes printed on leg piece

LEGO ADVENTURERS

LEGO Adventurers took a small group of daring heroes all over the world in search of amazing artifacts. Debuting this year, Adventurers launched with 21 sets, centered on the search for the Re-Gou Ruby in Egypt. Unfortunately, the ruby was protected by the undead Pharaoh Hotep and pursued by unscrupulous treasure hunters.

Pharaoh Hotep This is the first mummy minifigure. It features exclusive head, legs, and torso.

1998

IT WAS A BUSY and rewarding year for LEGO® minifigure fans. LEGO Space fans ran into a swarm of Insectoids, while Ninja snuck into the LEGO® Castle theme. The LEGO® Adventurers headed for Egypt to battle a nasty mummy, the Hydronauts challenged the Stingrays beneath the waves, and LEGO® Technic launched CyberSlam, which featured the first LEGO Technic figures. This was the final year in which a licensed play theme was not part of the assortment, but that was about to change....

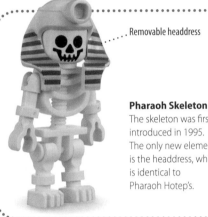

Removable headdress

Pharaoh Skeleton The skeleton was first introduced in 1995. The only new element is the headdress, which is identical to Pharaoh Hotep's.

ADVENTURERS

Johnny Thunder, Pippin Reed, and Professor Lightning were the mainstays of this theme, and appeared again and again in its five year run under various names in various countries. Johnny and Pippin also featured in later LEGO Studios sets.

Pith helmet

Bow tie

Backpack element is new this year

Backpack

Charles Lightning The archaeologist minifigure is wearing a pith helmet, a new element this year.

Helmet identical to Charles Lightning's

Compass

Pen for jotting down notes

Pippin Reed Traveling the world with her friend Johnny Thunder, reporter Pippin takes her trusty compass everywhere.

Buttoned-up fedora hat

Bandana knotted around neck

Johnny Thunder The fearless adventurer minifigure makes his debut in a desert safari jacket and brand-new fedora hat.

GLOBETROTTING ENEMIES

Baron Von Barron works side by side with a villain named Sam Sinister in 1998, but the Baron eventually changes his name to Lord Sam Sinister in time for the Adventurers subtheme Dino Island, in 2000.

LEGO SYSTEM
5988

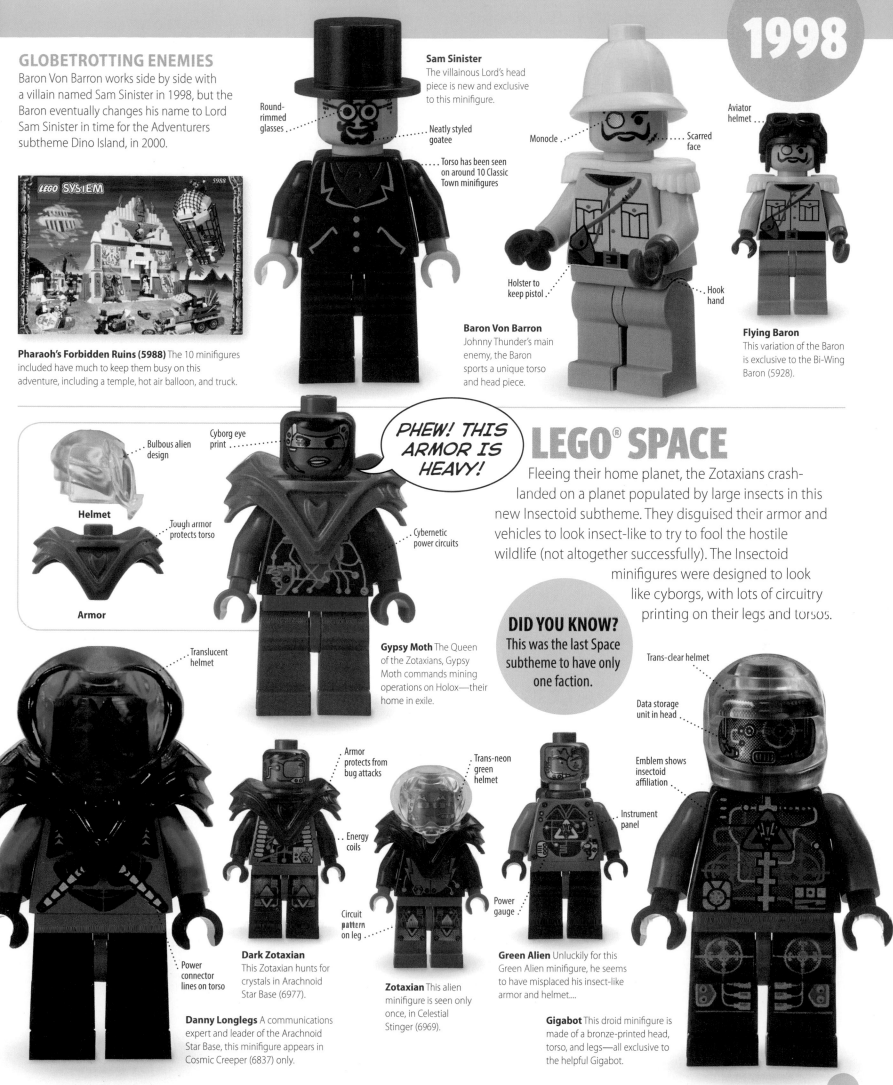

Pharaoh's Forbidden Ruins (5988) The 10 minifigures included have much to keep them busy on this adventure, including a temple, hot air balloon, and truck.

Round-rimmed glasses
Neatly styled goatee
Torso has been seen on around 10 Classic Town minifigures

Sam Sinister
The villainous Lord's head piece is new and exclusive to this minifigure.

Monocle
Scarred face
Holster to keep pistol
Hook hand

Baron Von Barron
Johnny Thunder's main enemy, the Baron sports a unique torso and head piece.

Aviator helmet

Flying Baron
This variation of the Baron is exclusive to the Bi-Wing Baron (5928).

LEGO® SPACE

Fleeing their home planet, the Zotaxians crash-landed on a planet populated by large insects in this new Insectoid subtheme. They disguised their armor and vehicles to look insect-like to try to fool the hostile wildlife (not altogether successfully). The Insectoid minifigures were designed to look like cyborgs, with lots of circuitry printing on their legs and torsos.

Bulbous alien design

Helmet

Tough armor protects torso

Armor

PHEW! THIS ARMOR IS HEAVY!

Cyborg eye print
Cybernetic power circuits

Gypsy Moth The Queen of the Zotaxians, Gypsy Moth commands mining operations on Holox—their home in exile.

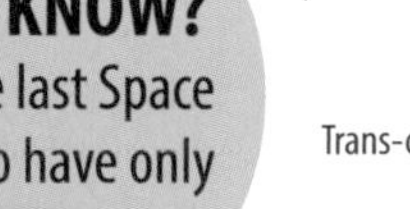

DID YOU KNOW?
This was the last Space subtheme to have only one faction.

Translucent helmet
Power connector lines on torso

Danny Longlegs A communications expert and leader of the Arachnoid Star Base, this minifigure appears in Cosmic Creeper (6837) only.

Armor protects from bug attacks

Energy coils

Dark Zotaxian This Zotaxian hunts for crystals in Arachnoid Star Base (6977).

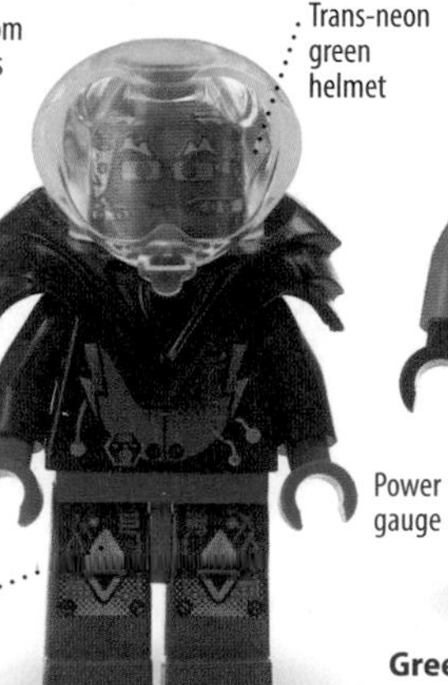
Trans-neon green helmet
Circuit pattern on leg

Zotaxian This alien minifigure is seen only once, in Celestial Stinger (6969).

Instrument panel

Power gauge

Green Alien Unluckily for this Green Alien minifigure, he seems to have misplaced his insect-like armor and helmet....

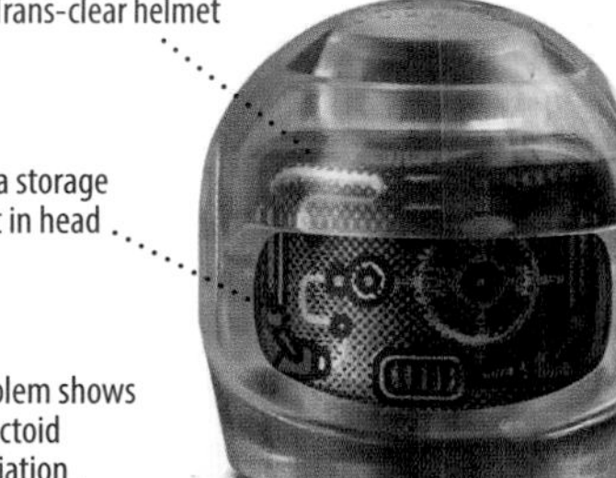

Trans-clear helmet
Data storage unit in head
Emblem shows insectoid affiliation

Gigabot This droid minifigure is made of a bronze-printed head, torso, and legs—all exclusive to the helpful Gigabot.

LEGO CASTLE

LEGO Castle took inspiration from the Far East in 1998 and launched a Ninja subtheme set in feudal Japan. Shogun Gi-Dan and his friend Ito, the gray ninja, battled the bandit Kendo, his henchmen, and the black ninja Bonsai for an ancient treasure. The ninja were in action until 2000.

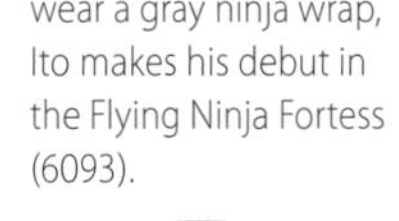

I WEAR THIS TO COSTUME PARTIES.
Sharp eyes on the lookout for trouble
Head wrap hides identity
Protective scale mail armor underneath wrap
Ninja throwing star

Ito The only ninja to wear a gray ninja wrap, Ito makes his debut in the Flying Ninja Fortress (6093).

Bonsai This stealthy ninja wears an all-black ninja wrap so he can hide in the shadows undetected.

DID YOU KNOW?
The Ninja subtheme introduced the samurai helmet, ninja hood, and katana sword elements.

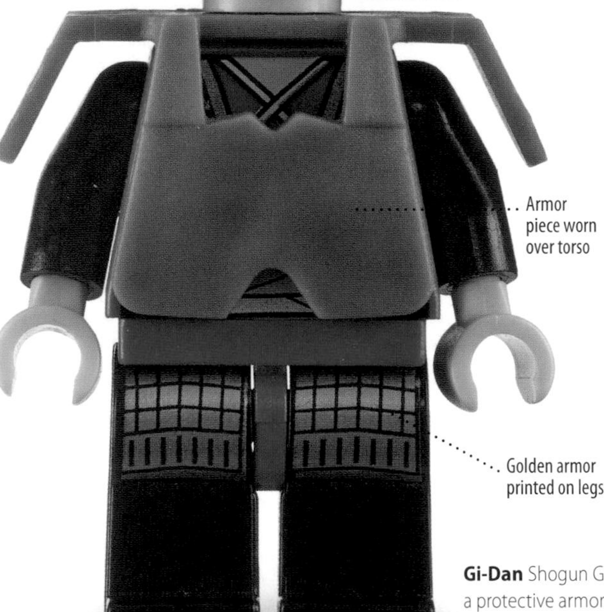
Shogun-style crest fits into helmet slot
White sideburns
Armor piece worn over torso
Golden armor printed on legs

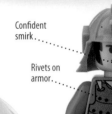

Gi-Dan Shogun Gi-Dan wears a protective armor piece, and guards the Ninja treasures.

LEGO SYSTEM 6093 8-12

Flying Ninja Fortress (6093) With 687 pieces and nine minifigures, this set has three Ninja treasures as well as a number of traps to be discovered.

Confident smirk
Rivets on armor
Samurai-style helmet
Strapped-on armor

Kata This samurai minifigure's armor piece looks shiny and new—probably because he only makes an appearance in one set, the Flying Ninja Fortress (6093).

HEY SHOGUN, SHOW ME YOUR GUN?

Ragged head wrap
Slanted eye patch
Tattered armor

Kendo The robber chief has an exclusive face and torso print.

Thin mustache
Knife tucked under belt
Patchwork on vest
Dojo is not afraid to use his musket.

Robber With his tattered vest, it looks like this robber has come into contact with the ninja warriors recently!

Dojo Underneath his helmet this samurai wears a red bandana—being a warrior can be sweaty work!

LEGO® AQUAZONE

Deep beneath the sea, the Hydronaut miners were locked in battle with the aquatic mutant Stingrays, in what was to be the final Aquazone subtheme. This was the last year of underwater adventures until Alpha Team's Mission Deep Sea in 2002.

Breathing mask printed on face
Black Flippers

Crystal Miner This minifigure is all set for a dive in Hydro Crystallization Station (6199).

Eyes focused on mission at hand

Visor also seen on Aquaraiders from LEGO® Aquazone in 1997

Chrome rebreather

Diving instrument

Red diving gloves

Captain Hank Hydro Leader of the Hydronaut missions, Hank is well respected by the other Hydronauts.

Breathing apparatus under helmet
Electronic gauge

Hip "Muddy" Waters This Hydronaut is an expert at collecting crystals from the depths of the oceans—hence his "Muddy" nickname.

Protective underwater helmet

Mutant fish-like armor

Gills for breathing underwater

Wide, fish-like mouth

Head Piece

Manta Ray The chief of the villainous Stingrays, this minifigure feels most comfortable when he's in charge of the Stingray Stormer (6198).

Pressure valve

Claw-like mutant pattern

Stinger Ray This Stingray villain goes alone to steal crystals in Sea Creeper (6140).

Helmet is unique to the Stingrays

Intense red eyes

Power supply

Raven Ray Despite his high-tech suit and wicked mind, the evil Raven Ray is often captured by the Hydronauts.

LEGO TECHNIC

LEGO Technic released more figures in 1998, with the Cyber Strikers (8257)—twin combat vehicles, each with a figure, and CyberMaster (8483), which included a model with a programmable brick that worked with a software program.

Circuit pattern on torso

Arms are posable

LEGO Technic Man This figure drives a demolition vehicle in Cyber Strikers (8257).

Same side parting as LEGO Technic Man

Molded cyborg pattern on arm

Gray cybernetic leg

CyberMaster Half of CyberMaster's body is robotic and is fitted with wires.

Cyborg eye piece

Cybernetic arm

Energy unit printed on torso

Legs are hinged and posable

Powered Striker This figure competes with LEGO Technic Man in Cyber Strikers (8257).

1998

LEGO® TOWN

This was an exciting year for LEGO Town, with the introduction of two new subthemes—Res-Q and Extreme Team. Res-Q in particular made an impact on future themes, and emergency vehicles are still a popular part of the LEGO City assortment. Finding new ways to play in LEGO Town was by now a tradition.

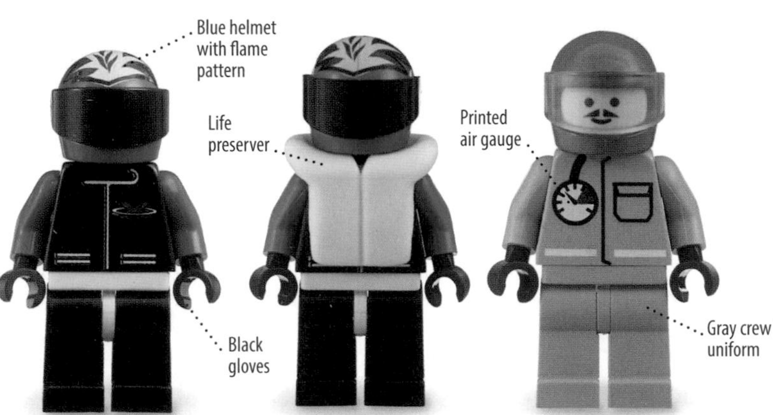
Blue helmet with flame pattern
Life preserver
Printed air gauge
Black gloves
Gray crew uniform

Zipliner This racer rides a zipline to reach his buggy. It's a good thing he's wearing a helmet—he's afraid of heights!

Rafter This daredevil minifigure rafts down rivers for fun. Thankfully, he's waterproof and wearing a life preserver.

Ground Crew Assistant for Team Extreme, this guy prefers to keep his minifigure feet firmly on the ground.

UM, HELLO? I CAN'T SEE!

Movable visor

Double pockets

EXTREME TEAM

Town went extreme with this subtheme, which focused on wild sports such as hang gliding, drag racing, and whitewater rafting. The Extreme Team screeched to a halt after 1999.

Collar strap over zipper
Extreme Team Red X logo

Extreme Racer An action junkie, this minifigure flies a plane in the Daredevil Flight Squad (6582).

Off-road Driver No one has overtaken this Off-road Driver in a race. Yet.

CLASSIC

Popular themes were well represented this year, with a new Truck Stop (6329) and Super Cycle Center (6426) leading the way. Some classic minifigures, such as the Mail Worker, got a new look this year as well.

DID YOU KNOW?
Postal Service is one of the fictional LEGO Town organizations.

The Mail Worker's favorite color is red.

Mail Worker A newly-designed LEGO Post logo adorns this minifigure's torso.

Reflective silver shades
Thick zipper pattern

Biker Bob The head and torso pieces of this speed-loving minifigure are unique—and cool dude Bob knows it!

LEGO® LOCO

One of the highlights of 1998 was the release of LEGO Loco, a town-building video game with some emphasis on trains. These two minifigures were from a promotional Handcar set (2585) given out with the CD-ROM.

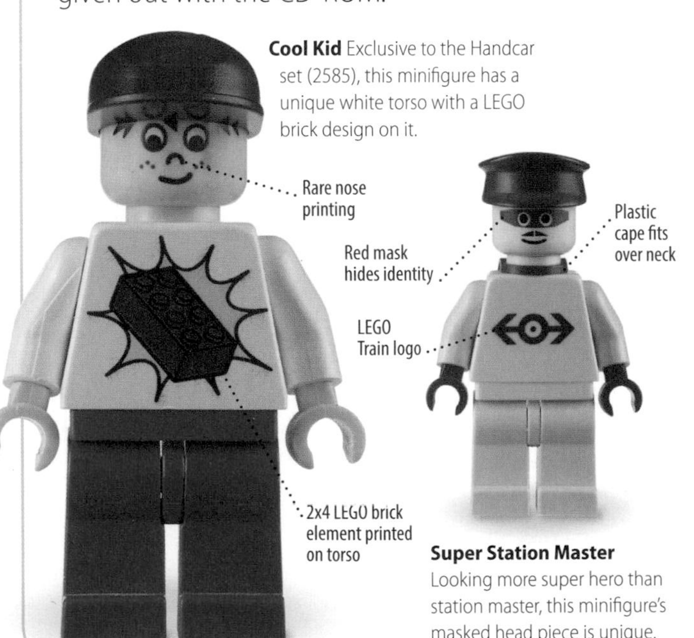
Rare nose printing
2x4 LEGO brick element printed on torso

Cool Kid Exclusive to the Handcar set (2585), this minifigure has a unique white torso with a LEGO brick design on it.

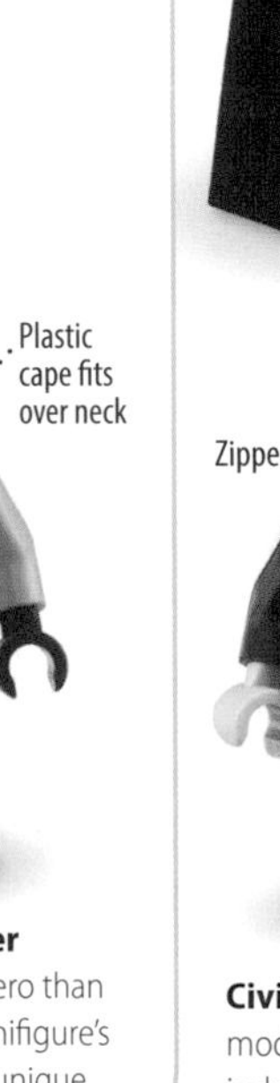
Red mask hides identity
Plastic cape fits over neck
LEGO Train logo

Super Station Master Looking more super hero than station master, this minifigure's masked head piece is unique.

Zipper
Black goggles
Striped shirt under jacket

Civilian This cool dude is modeling a leather bomber jacket, which had been seen for the first time in 1993.

Mechanic Seen only once, in the Truck Stop (6329), this minifigure is an expert in vehicle repair.

RES-Q

Res-Q launched as a new Town subtheme in 1998 with eight sets, the largest being the Emergency Response Center (6479). The line ended in 1999, but the organization continued to come to the rescue in the Studios, Soccer, and Jack Stone themes.

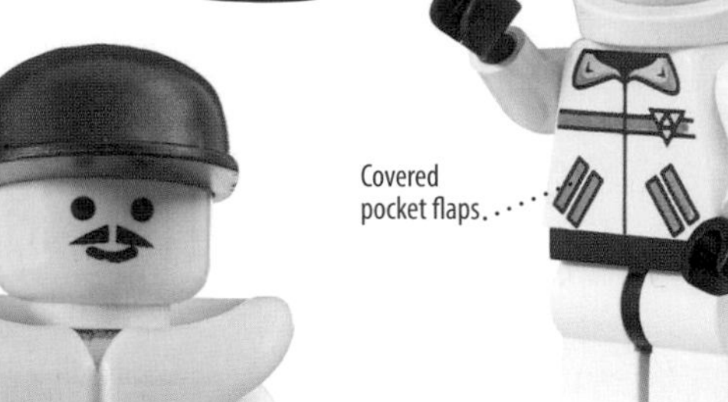

ROGER AND OUT? BUT I'M BOB!
Transparent visor attaches to helmet
Covered pocket flaps

Flat-billed cap

Headset to call for emergency backup

Res-Q logo

Orange stripes visible under life preserver

Res-Q uniform orange stripes

Lifeguard Featuring only in the Res-Q Lifeguard (2962), this helmeted lifeguard keeps minifigures safe at the beach.

Black Cap Rescuer When this guy isn't rescuing minifigures on his speedboat, he's grooming his pointy mustache.

Chopper Rescuer This Res-Q team pilot minifigure often gets hot under his collared jacket.

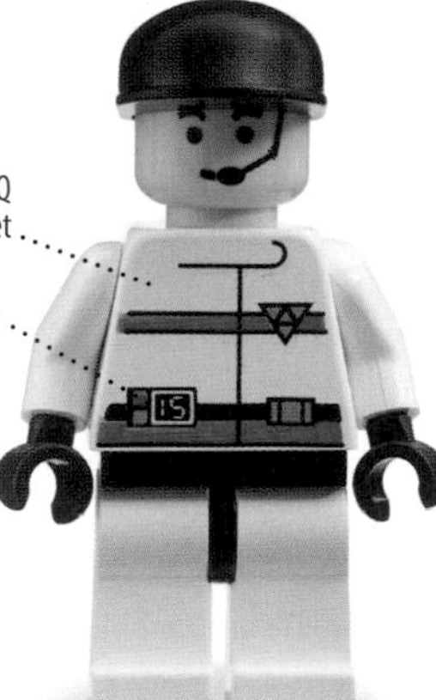

Res-Q jacket
Stopwatch

Response Rescuer This minifigure is part of a big emergency team in the Emergency Response Center (6479).

Res-Q Cruiser (6473) One of the biggest Res-Q sets, Res-Q Cruiser includes two vehicles, two land vehicles, a hoverboat, and three minifigures.

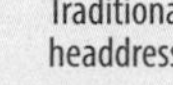

Traditional headdress

Chief Brown Bear The chief is seen in the Native American Village (2438). He has a necklace around his neck.

Native pattern on torso

Village Child Son of Chief Brown Bear, this boy's face, like his father's, is streaked with warpaint.

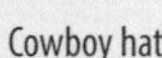

Cowboy hat
Knotted bandana printed on torso

Cowboy From the Western Town (2435), this cowboy stands guard at the frontier town.

LEGO® DUPLO®

Western was a new LEGO DUPLO subtheme launched in 1998 with nine sets, containing 10 new figures. No more sets were ever released for this line.

CARGO CENTER

A new Cargo Center (6330) arrived in LEGO Town in 1998. It included a forklift, a helicopter, two trucks, and five new minifigures. Time for another delivery!

WHY WON'T THEY LET ME DRIVE THE CHOPPER!
Cargo logo
Construction helmet
Green vest over white shirt
Pants match tie

Cargo Staff An expert in handling cargo, this staffer is exclusive to the Cargo Center set (6330).

Forklift Operator This minifigure transports heavy cargo in his only appearance in set 6330.

LEGO® SEASONAL

This festive Santa Claus appeared in the 1998 and 1999 Advent Calendars, and then reappeared in 2010 as part of the Vintage Minifigure Collection.

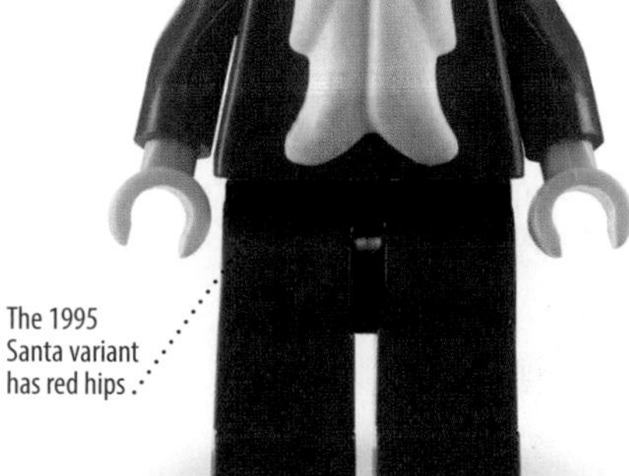

Molded beard piece
The 1995 Santa variant has red hips

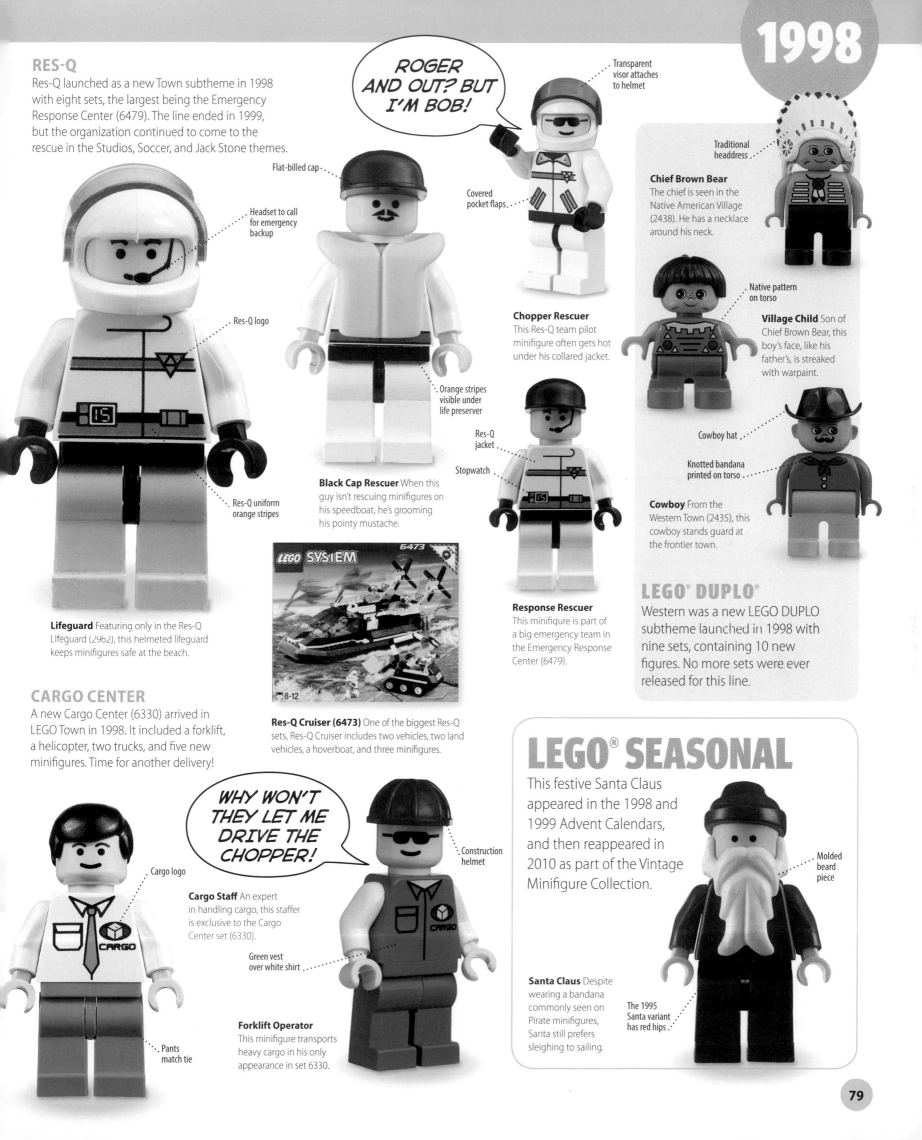

Santa Claus Despite wearing a bandana commonly seen on Pirate minifigures, Santa still prefers sleighing to sailing.

A CUT ABOVE

THE FIRST MINIFIGURES had very simple hairstyles, but as time has passed, hair pieces have gotten more varied and downright crazy! As with hats and other headgear, hair pieces attach to the stud on top of the head piece. Hair can help to identify a character—for example, everyone knows Princess Leia's two buns or Superman's forehead curl. Hair can also reflect the style of a theme, such as the LEGO® EXO-FORCE™ anime-inspired hair pieces. Some hair pieces include facial hair, such as Hagrid's bushy beard, the Caveman's mustache, and many others. Pigtails, wigs, and even mohawks—minifigures have had them all.

Pigtails • 1978 • Doctor • LEGOLAND Town.

Short back and sides • 1979 • Boy • LEGOLAND Town.

Shaggy long hair and beard • 2001 • Rubeus Hagrid • LEGO® Harry Potter™.

Medium-length center part • 2001 • Albus Dumbledore • LEGO Harry Potter.

Flowing, swept back long hair • 2007 • Crown Princess • LEGO Castle.

Severe bob with straight bangs • 2008 • Claw-Dette • LEGO Agents.

Shoulder-length, tousled • 2010 • Caveman • LEGO Minifigures.

Slick bob with gold hairband • 2011 • Egyptian Queen • LEGO Minifigures.

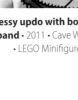

Smooth bun • 2011 • Kimono Girl • LEGO Minifigures.

Messy updo with bone hair band • 2011 • Cave Woman • LEGO Minifigures.

Upswept hair with bun • 2011 • Ice Skater • LEGO Minifigures.

Extra long, straight hair with hairband • 2012 • Hippie • LEGO Minifigures.

Messed-up bed hair • 2012 • Sleepyhead • LEGO Minifigures.

Swept bangs with headphones • 2012 • DJ • LEGO Minifigures.

Judge's wig • 2013 • Judge • LEGO Minifigures.

Combed short hair with gold leaves • 2013 • Roman Emperor • LEGO Minifigures.

Short bob cut, swept bangs • 1983 • Striped Lady • LEGOLAND Town.

Ponytail • 1992 • Female Swimmer • LEGO Paradisa.

Long braids with headband • 1997 • Plain Native American • LEGO Western.

Bun • 1999 • Padmé Naberrie • LEGO® *Star Wars*®.

Side buns • 2000 • Princess Leia • LEGO *Star Wars*.

Short bowl cut • 2001 • Ron Weasley • LEGO Harry Potter.

Combed widow's peak • 2002 • Vampire • LEGO Studios.

Half slicked back, half spiked • 2006 • Two Face • LEGO® Batman™.

Futuristic hair with spikes to the side • 2006 • Hikaru • LEGO EXO-FORCE.

Floppy hair in angular sections • 2006 • Takeshi • LEGO EXO-FORCE.

Floppy, flowing male hair • 2008 • Anakin Skywalker • LEGO® *Star Wars*® Clone Wars™.

Stripy, long head-tails with twin peaks • 2008 • Ahsoka Tano • LEGO *Star Wars* Clone Wars.

Stripy spikes • 2008 • Dr. Inferno • LEGO Agents.

Wavy updo • 2009 • Nightclub Willie Scott • LEGO® *Indiana Jones*™.

Bubble perm • 2010 • Circus Clown • LEGO Minifigures

Mohawk spike • 2011 • Punk Rocker • LEGO Minifigures.

Gelled hair with spitcurl • 2011 • Superman • LEGO® DC Universe™ Super Heroes.

Swept back hair with attached pointy ears • 2011 • Elf • LEGO Minifigures.

High ponytail with pink stripe • 2012 • Skater Girl • LEGO Minifigures.

Long, layered bob • 2012 • Rocker Girl • LEGO Minifigures.

Hair braided with strips of bark • 2013 • Forest Maiden • LEGO Minifigures.

Wavy retro bob • 2013 • Hollywood Starlet • LEGO Minifigures.

Comb-over • 2013 • Grandpa • LEGO Minifigures.

Tangled snakes • 2013 • Medusa • LEGO Minifigures.

Sleek layered hair • 2013 • Trendsetter • LEGO Minifigures.

THIS COULD BE THE START OF SOMETHING EPIC!
Head also used on Luke Skywalker minifigures
Padawan robes
Later variants have tan legs

Padawan Obi-Wan Kenobi This is the first of more than 20 Obi-Wan minifigures. It shows him as a young Jedi apprentice in Episode I.

LEGO *STAR WARS*

It was a great experiment—could sets based on the classic *Star Wars* films and the newest movie, Episode I *The Phantom Menace* be a hit? Could a licensed play theme bring in legions of new fans for LEGO building? The answer to both was a resounding yes, producing one of the greatest success stories in the LEGO Group's history. And it's still going strong over a decade later!

Pulled-back hair piece and head piece are exclusive to Qui-Gon

Qui-Gon Jinn Appearing in four sets in 1999 alone, the LEGO version of the doomed Jedi Master has lasted much longer than the movie version!

1999

THE WORLD OF LEGO® minifigures changed forever in 1999, with the release of the first LEGO® *Star Wars*® sets. It was the first licensed theme ever produced by the LEGO Group and would prove to be a massive success, spawning LEGO video games, animated shorts, books, and more in years to come. Other big news this year included the opening of LEGOLAND® California in Carlsbad, CA and the release of the LEGO® Rock Raiders, LEGO® Adventurers: Jungle, and LEGO® DUPLO® Winnie the Pooh™ themes.

Long hair piece with top braid also seen on Padmé's daughter Princess Leia
Torso is unique to this variant
Standard black pants

Padmé Naberrie The Queen of Naboo is in disguise as a handmaiden. Padmé wasn't seen in her royal robes until 2012.

Head piece also used on a female soccer player in the Soccer theme in 2001

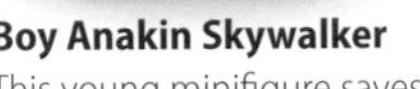

Boy Anakin Skywalker This young minifigure saves the galaxy in one set, Naboo Fighter (7141).

Gray helmet and matching goggles
This variant appears in two sets in 1999—Anakin's Podracer (7131) and Mos Espa (7171).

Boy Anakin Skywalker variant The only difference between the two 1999 Anakin variants is the helmet color.

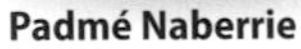

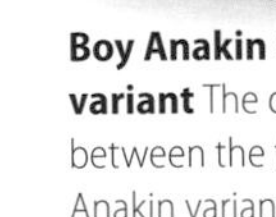

Head piece also used on a Gungan soldier in 2001
Jar Jar's clothing is simple
Dark gray legs can be seen on more than 45 minifigures

Jar Jar Binks Jar Jar's amphibious Gungan head was the first to be developed specially for a minifigure. His untidy torso is also unique.

EPISODE I

The first LEGO *Star Wars* subtheme was *Star Wars:* Episode I *The Phantom Menace*, with eight sets and all-new minifigures. Many of the models and minifigures would be revised and updated in later years.

Maul's Zabrak horns are missing from this version
Unique torso

Darth Maul The first version of the Sith apprentice featured a regular head piece with unique facial tattoos.

LEGO SYSTEM
7151
STAR WARS
SITH INFILTRATOR

Sith Infiltrator (7151) Darth Maul's Sith Infiltrator stealth ship, known as the *Scimitar*, was released in 1999, and then updated in 2007 and 2011.

DROIDS AND PODRACERS

The famous Boonta Eve Classic podracing scene came to life with figures of Anakin's rival drivers and a Pit Droid. The first Battle Droid also debuted this year.

Gasgano wears the same helmet and goggles as Anakin Skywalker

Gasgano Only appearing in one set, this rare podracing figure has unique head and torso pieces.

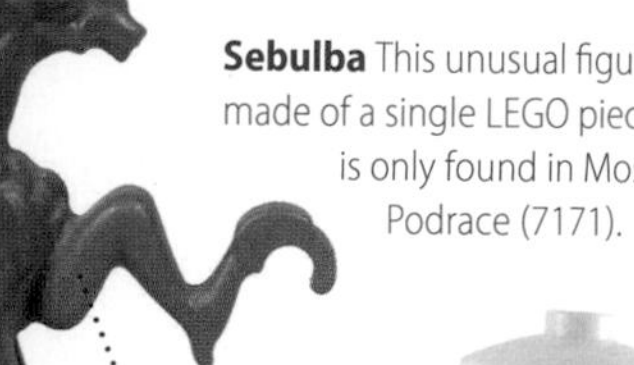

Sebulba This unusual figure is made of a single LEGO piece and is only found in Mos Espa Podrace (7171).

Later versions had more detail and colors

Yellow photoreceptor

Pit Droid Three Pit Droid variants were released in 2009, ready to fix any malfunctions. This version belongs to Anakin Skywalker.

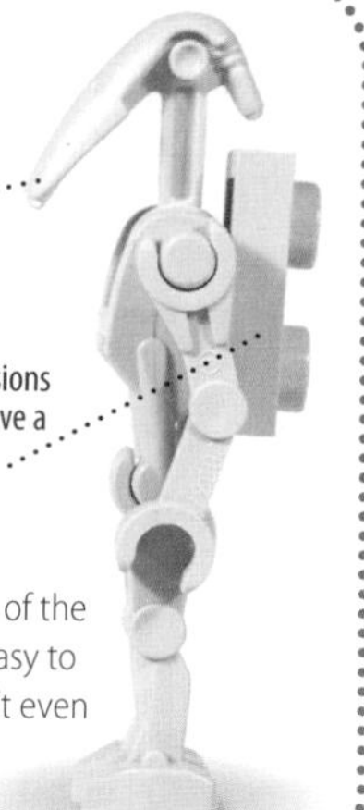

Head piece specially created for the battle droids

Later versions do not have a backpack

Battle Droid The first version of the Battle Droid is easy to defeat—he can't even hold a blaster properly!

Hair piece also seen on Draco Malfoy from the LEGO® Harry Potter™ theme

Unique torso with simple white tunic

Tan leggings

Young Luke Skywalker The future Jedi's early life as a Tatooine farmboy is the inspiration for his first LEGO minifigure.

EPISODES IV, V, AND VI

The first five classic LEGO *Star Wars* sets also came out this year, with minifigures of favorite characters such as Luke Skywalker, Darth Vader, and Obi-Wan Kenobi and models of the X-wing and TIE fighter.

Head piece also seen on more than 15 pirate minifigures

Rebel Technician The tan uniform is worn only by this hard working minifigure and a Rebel Engineer in 2000.

2011 version has a buckle detail on the belt

Obi-Wan "Ben" Kenobi This older version of the exiled Jedi Knight has a unique head and torso and is exclusive to the Landspeeder (7110).

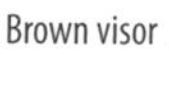

Brown visor

Torso is unique to this variant

Hoth Rebel Trooper Warmly dressed for the ice planet Hoth, this rebel minifigure appears in Snowspeeder (7130).

Rebel pilot helmet

Dak Ralter Also in set 7130, this rebel pilot mans the snowspeeder's guns for Luke Skywalker, who flies the craft.

Rebel g-suit worn by 12 minifigures

Helmet is exclusive to four Luke pilot variants

Luke Skywalker Pilot Tatooine is a distant memory for this minifigure as he makes his debut as a rebel pilot in two sets this year.

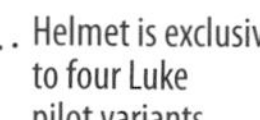

Unique torso—the back is plain khaki

Camouflage Luke This minifigure is designed to blend in on the forest moon of Endor, but his chin dimple and cybernetic hand reveal his identity.

ASTROMECH DROIDS

The most famous astromech droid of all is R2-D2. The first LEGO version of this iconic character was released this year and at least one version of him has been produced every year since.

R2-D2 Each of Artoo's three parts were created specially for his minifigure and then refined on later versions.

R2-D2's legs are joined to his body with LEGO Technic pins

Head piece pattern is slightly different from R2.

R5-D4 This red astromech droid uses the same torso design as R2, but has red printing instead of blue.

Helmet is exclusive to Biggs

Biggs wears the same suit as his friend Luke Skywalker.

Biggs Darklighter This minifigure was killed in the rebels' attack on the first Death Star so he only appears in one set—X-Wing Fighter (7140).

Imperial Scout Trooper Wearing lighter armor than a regular stormtrooper, this minifigure often undertakes dangerous solo missions.

Unique torso

Darth Vader Although many parts of this minifigure have since been updated, the helmet has remained the same since its debut in 1999.

Vader has a scarred gray head piece underneath his helmet

Standard LEGO cloak completes the Sith lord's look

Scout helmet fits over head so that only the black visor shows

AAARRRGH WHERE'S THE BRAKE?!!!

Scout Trooper in Action The Scout Trooper usually comes with a specialist helmet and rides a speeder bike.

G-suit is worn by X- and Y-wing pilots.

Dutch Vander This brave rebel minifigure flies a Y-wing fighter in set 7150, but he perishes in the Battle of Yavin.

1999

LEGO® TOWN

LEGO Town continued to be a core theme in 1999, with new Space Port and Coast Guard sets hitting the shelves. Following the success of Launch Command and Divers in previous years, Town continued to expand its reach, introducing its own versions of other popular themes such as classic Space.

Popular head piece, seen on more than 20 minifigures

Pristine white lab coat

Scientist Featuring an updated torso, this variant of the Scientist is exclusive to a single 1999 set—Test Shuttle (3067).

Space Port logo

Same head, hat, and torso as other variant

Scientist Variant Wearing black pants, instead of white, this Scientist variant appears in three sets in 1999.

Shuttle Security Guard This serious minifigure patrols the Space Port in his helicopter, checking that everything is in order.

Head piece seen on more than 10 other minifigures

Exclusive torso with ID badge, Space Port logo, and Security insignia

The first variant has a construction helmet, the second a white cap, and a third has a red cap.

Ground Controller Variant Three very similar variants of the Ground Controller minifigure are released in 1999. The only differences are their hats!

Torso is exclusive to three Ground Controller variants

Ground Controller Exclusive to Mission Control (6456), this minifigure is the vital link between Earth and the astronauts out in space.

Standard red pants

Black visor is attached to white fire helmet

Air pressure gauge

Fireman with Breathing Apparatus This Fireman has an identical head, torso, and legs to the Fire Mechanic released in 1994, but he has a specialist helmet, breathing apparatus, and air tanks.

SPACE PORT

Space Port was the successor to 1995's Launch Command and it featured more sets and a greater variety of vehicles and minifigures than the previous theme. Minifigures included astronauts, scientists, and ground crew.

Head piece also used on the Aquanaut Jock Clouseau in 1995

Jet pack previously seen in the 1991 Blacktron II space theme

Torso is new this year

Satellite Repair Guy This repair man has a tough job to do—he has to fix a satellite in space! He's got his space suit and jet pack on, but where has his wrench floated off to?

Gold visor is down to protect the Moon Explorer's eyes from the sun's rays

Helmet first seen on the Aquazone Hydronauts in 1998

Same head and torso as the Satellite Repair Guy

Moon Explorer This intrepid minifigure travels all the way to the moon and explores it in his Lunar Rover (6463).

Female Astronaut The only female astronaut in the lineup has a unique new torso featuring the Space Port logo and breathing pipes.

Female head piece with radio set is new this year

White helmet is also used on the Moon Explorer

LEGO® TOWN JR. AND CITY CENTER

LEGO Town Jr. was phased out in 1999 and was replaced by City Center. The sets continued to feature more simplified building for younger fans and included Coast Guard, Fire, and Police models.

IT'S A GOOD JOB MY LIPSTICK IS WATERPROOF!

Detachable life preserver

Another variant has a ponytail instead of a cap

LEGO SYSTEM
5-10
6435
CITY

Coast Guard HQ (6435) This set includes six minifigures, a speedboat, small boat, helicopter, beach buggy, and trike.

THAT'S NO CRIMINAL, IT'S A TUNA FISH!

New torso is unique to this minifigure

Coast Guard logo

ID badge

Coast Guard Chief The Chief is in charge of all the Coast Guard minifigures. During a mission, he has to think quickly and tell everyone else what to do.

Headset ensures that the Coast Guard can radio for back up if he needs it

Female Coast Guard One of two female minifigures in Coast Guard HQ (6435), this variant does her job at sea, while the other variant rides to the rescue on land using an all-terrain trike.

Rapid Response If the Coast Guard needs to travel a short distance, fast, this Rapid Response minifigure uses a small motor-powered inflatable boat.

Head piece with blue sunglasses is new this year

Standard Coast Guard torso with white arms

Beach Patrol Appearing in his own set, Beach Buggy (6437), this Coast Guard patrols the beach checking for sharks or swimmers in distress.

CLASSIC

Special licensed minifigures also appeared this year, including a Shell Oil worker and a Boston Red Sox baseball player, which was available only through a promotion at Fenway Park (the Red Sox's home stadium).

Red helmet with black visor

Exclusive Shell logo

The torso is the only new element.

Shell Oil Worker This minifigure appears in two sets this year—one from Town, Dragster (1250) and one from City Center, Shell Service Station (1256).

RED SOX

Standard LEGO baseball cap

All white uniform with Red Sox logo

Red Sox Baseball Player This promotional minifigure has a unique torso in white with the official Red Sox logo on the front.

DID YOU KNOW? There has been at least one LEGOLAND® Town, LEGO Town, or LEGO® City set released every year since 1978.

Torso used on four Mechanic minifigure variants

Mechanic One of five minifigures in Roadside Repair (6434), the Mechanic can fix any vehicle in record time.

McDonald's Worker LEGO McDonald's Restaurant (3438) was only available in the United States via the LEGO online store.

Standard red LEGO cap

Unique torso with the McDonald's logo

Matching red pants complete the uniform

NO SLIMY SPACE SLUG IS GOING TO STOP ME!

LEGO ROCK RAIDERS

In 1999, a crack team of space miner minifigures found themselves trapped on an alien world. The good news was that there were energy crystals to mine, but the bad news was that there were some pretty nasty monsters there, too. This first visit to the LEGO underground had an impressive multimedia life with a video game and in-box comics, as well as traditional sets.

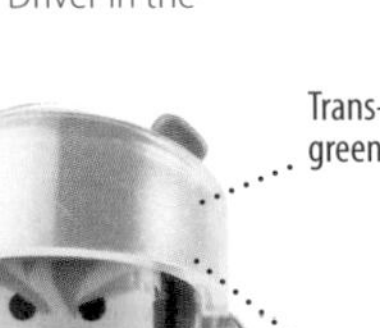

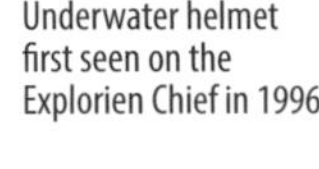

Underwater helmet first seen on the Explorien Chief in 1996

Torso is new and unique to Jet

Jet The only female Rock Raider has a new head piece with red lips, blonde hair, and a headset. It is exclusive to the 1999 and 2000 variants of Jet.

Axel Appearing in four sets in 1999, Axel has a new head piece that is exclusive to his two variants and a 2001 Boat Driver in the Studios theme.

Trans-neon green visor

In 2000, Axel wears a black visor instead.

New torso with coveralls and goggles printing

LEGO SYSTEM
ROCK RAIDERS
4930
6-10

Rock Raiders (4930) This set features Axel, Sparks, Docs, Bandit, and Jet, plus a rock for them to raid for crystals.

Head piece is new this year and only seen on two Studios Cameramen minifigures in 2000 and 2001.

Torso is exclusive to three variants of Docs

Docs This miner minifigure has an unusual look—he wears his glasses on his forehead and a black bandana knotted around his neck.

DID YOU KNOW?

The construction helmet has been worn by around 130 minifigures since 1978.

Bandana keeps the sweat out of Bandit's eyes when he's mining

Torso with red sweater and coveralls is unique to this minifigure

Standard issue blue pants

Bandit This tough minifigure has a unique head with angry brown eyebrows, a bushy beard and mustache, and a cool blue bandana. Don't mess with him!

Goggles were first introduced in 1998

Head piece is new this year

Sparks is the miners' mechanic, so he always keeps a wrench handy.

Sparks Unlike his mining colleagues, Sparks' torso is not exclusive to him. In fact, his torso can also be seen on a 2001 female minifigure from the Town theme.

LEGO® SCALA™ DOLLS

This year the SCALA line continued its focus on the SCALA dolls, which were larger than minifigures with many accessories. Eight were released in 1999.

Spotted halter top with jeans and extra accessories

Marie
Vivacious Marie appears in four sets between 1998 and 2001. This casually dressed version is from Marie in her Studio (3142).

FIRST LEGO® LEAGUE

Every year since 1998, the LEGO Group and the non-profit organization FIRST have held the *FIRST* LEGO League global tournament. In it, teams of elementary and middle school students use LEGO® MINDSTORMS® technology to build a working robot and solve a problem involving minifigures in a real-world situation. This minifigure was a giveaway to school teams of up to ten children, participating in the 1999 season.

Head piece is new this year, but not exclusive

Exclusive torso

***FIRST* LEGO League Minifigure**
Given to each team member, the minifigure features the name and location of the participating school on the back of the torso.

LEGO ADVENTURERS

Johnny Thunder and the Adventurers team were back for their second year. This time they were heading to the South American jungle in search of the mysterious sundisc, and many new minifigures and new pieces took part in this quest. The Adventurers were determined to obtain the artifact from the powerful Achu before villains Señor Palomar and Rudo Villano. Of course, Johnny won in the end!

New, unique head piece

Gabarros A new character this year, the South American sailor uses his local knowledge to help both Señor Palomar and Johnny Thunder find the sundisc.

Villano wears a black version of Johnny Thunder's hat.

Backpack

Villano has two pistols tucked into his belt

Rudo Villano Another new arrival for this year, Rudo (also known as Max in the UK) has a new, exclusive scruffy torso and scarred head. He also has a variant without a backpack.

Elaborate feathered headdress is detachable

Head piece has two gray stripes printed on it

Cape has tribal pattern printed on the back

Unique tribal markings on torso and legs

Achu This mystical minifigure guards an ancient treasure and he's not about to give it up! Every piece is new and unique to Achu.

New head piece also used on a 2003 LEGO Sports NBA player

Classic white LEGO cowboy hat

Backpack clips around neck

CURSES! I FORGOT MY SUNSCREEN!

Torso with white jacket and brown vest is unique to Señor Palomar

Señor Palomar New for this year, Señor Palomar appears in Spider's Secret (5936). In this set he has a backpack, but in two others released this year he does not.

LEGO® DUPLO® PAST AND PRESENT

LEGO DUPLO continued to entertain in 1999. DUPLO Dino entered what seemed to be its final year, until a revival in 2007 brought it back. DUPLO Construction was also big this year.

Smiling face with stubble detail

Construction Worker This figure was hard at work in 1999, appearing ten times in five sets. He seems pretty happy though.

Fur bib printed on torso

Cave Baby This cute prehistoric baby appears with three other figures in Dinosaurs Fun Forest (2821).

Jungle Surprise (1271) Inside a small Jungle temple lies a sundisc waiting to be discovered by a minifigure.

LEGO
Jungle Surprise
1271
6-10
Cont: 24 pcs/pzs/pcs

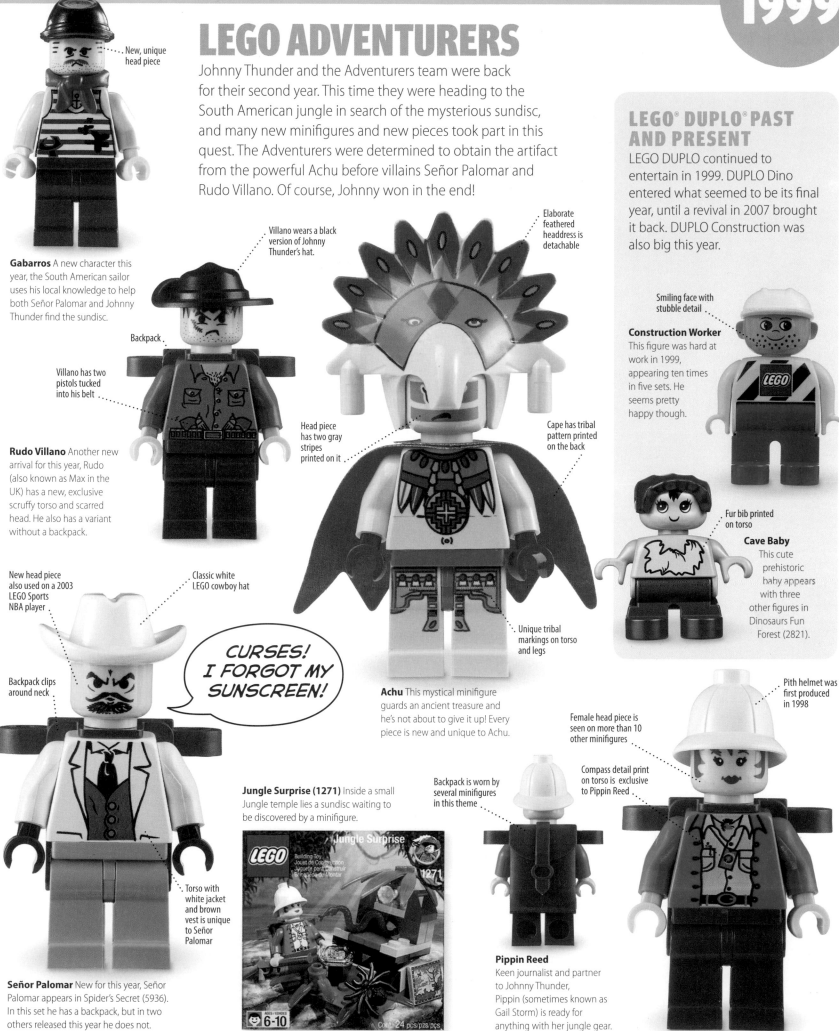

Backpack is worn by several minifigures in this theme

Pippin Reed Keen journalist and partner to Johnny Thunder, Pippin (sometimes known as Gail Storm) is ready for anything with her jungle gear.

Pith helmet was first produced in 1998

Female head piece is seen on more than 10 other minifigures

Compass detail print on torso is exclusive to Pippin Reed

2000s

LEGO® *Star Wars®* was just the start of licensed play themes. Other film-based characters soon followed, from student wizard Harry Potter, to the web-slinging Spider-Man. The first minifigures based on real-world celebrities led to another design revolution, with the advent of realistic skin tones for licensed LEGO themes. The minifigures of the new millennium grew extra faces on the backs of their heads, threw basketballs, shrank down on shorter legs, landed on Mars, and even dabbled in some movie-making of their own!

SAVE! AND A BEAUTY, IF I SAY SO MYSELF!
Different national flag stickers are supplied. This minifigure wears the German flag.
Black gloves—the ball won't slip through his fingers.

Black Team Goalkeeper
This black-capped minifigure is the goalkeeper from the Black Team Bus (3404). Like all team bus goalies, he has a plain green torso.

2000

PICKING THE BIGGEST LEGO® event of 2000 is no easy task. Was it the release of some of the most famous and iconic LEGO® *Star Wars®* sets ever? How about exciting new subthemes for LEGO® Adventurers and LEGO® Castle? Or the snowy action of the LEGO® Arctic subtheme? Could it be the amazing success of LEGO® Soccer (known as LEGO® Football in Europe), which went on to launch dozens more LEGO® Sports sets? One thing is beyond any doubt, 2000 was a year when excitement and sheer fun ruled—and what's more, it held the promise of an incredible decade to come!

LEGO SOCCER

The LEGO Group scored in the world of sports in 2000 with the launch of the first LEGO Soccer sets (the LEGO Sports brand would not be used until 2003). These were a surprise hit, spawning future sets for basketball, hockey, and extreme sports. Soccer player minifigures were designed to be personalized, so they could play for different teams and countries.

Hair piece introduced in 1979 is still in style for many LEGO soccer players!

German flag sticker on front torso

Black Team Player With a change of sticker, this minifigure could play for any one of five teams in the Black Team Bus (3404).

TEAM BUS SETS

To play, teams must first get to the stadium! Five team bus sets were brought out in 2000, including an Americas Team transport and buses for Red, Blue, and Black teams. Each included six minifigures and a soccer ball.

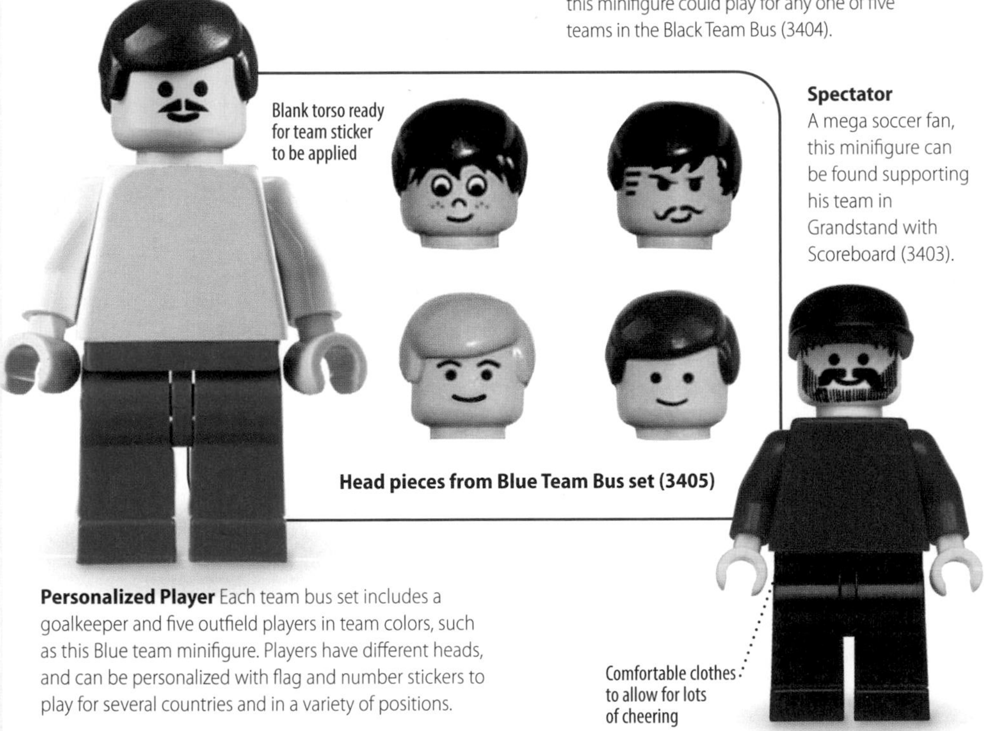
Blank torso ready for team sticker to be applied
Comfortable clothes to allow for lots of cheering

Head pieces from Blue Team Bus set (3405)

Spectator
A mega soccer fan, this minifigure can be found supporting his team in Grandstand with Scoreboard (3403).

Personalized Player Each team bus set includes a goalkeeper and five outfield players in team colors, such as this Blue team minifigure. Players have different heads, and can be personalized with flag and number stickers to play for several countries and in a variety of positions.

LEGO
3405

Blue Team Bus (3405) This set contains the bus elements, six minifigures, and sticker sheets with a choice of national flags for their front torsos and numbers for their backs.

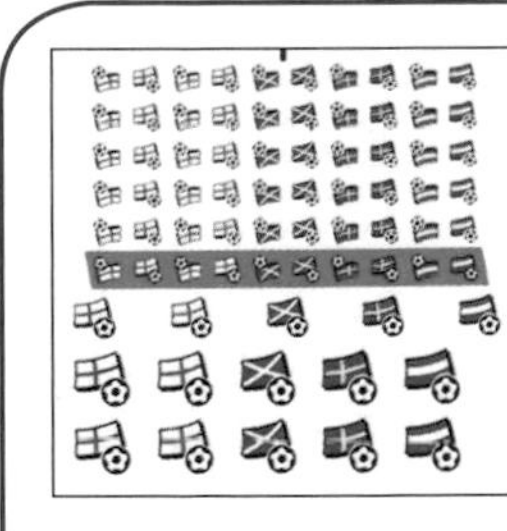

Flag stickers (above)
Number stickers (right)

SOCCER SETS

The most popular Soccer set was the Championship Challenge (3409), which featured 10 outfield players, two goalkeepers, and a field of play. Mounted on flexible stands, minifigures could flick the ball. The set was such a hit that it inspired a sequel, Championship Challenge II (3420), in 2002.

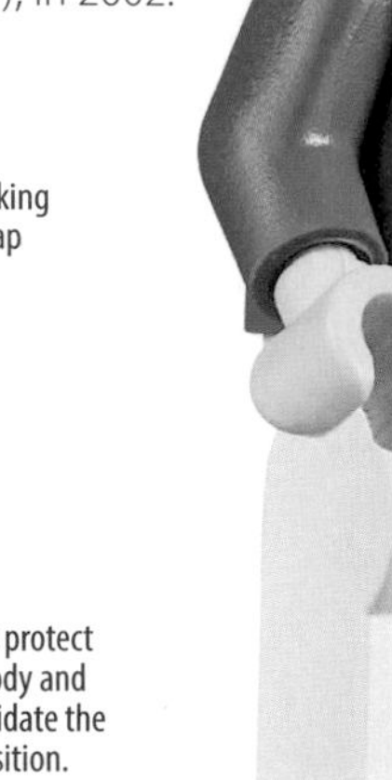

Green and White Team Player In the Field Expander set (3410), players wear the same jersey but they have different numbers on their backs.

He shoots, he scores—and he looks pretty pleased with himself!

Straggly hair peeking out from under cap

Stubbly face

Studs protect his body and intimidate the opposition.

Angry Goalie This aggressive-looking goalie appears only in the Championship Challenge set (3409).

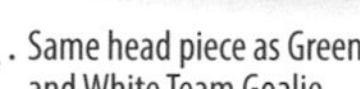

Same head piece as Green and White Team Goalie

Studded jersey saves him from bruises when he's saving goals.

Blue Goalie The Goal Keeper set (3413) comes with a blue variant of the angry goalie. A stick and turntable arrangement allows him to move around the goal to make some agile saves.

SHOOT 'N' SCORE

This small set featured two minifigures—a soccer player and a goalie. It was ideal for young builders who wanted to practice shots on goal before moving on to actual competition.

Soccer Legend
French soccer superstar Zinedine Zidane got his own minifigure in the Shoot 'n' Score with Zidane set (3401). Magnifique!

New head with intense, smoldering expression

Sideburns are printed on head and hair piece is separate.

Adidas sponsor logo printed on legs

LEGO ADVENTURERS

The Adventurers faced prehistoric peril this year in LEGO® Dino Island, the third subtheme in the series. Fourteen sets were released, but most contained fewer than 100 pieces, making this the second-smallest subtheme in Adventurers history—but not in popularity!

DID YOU KNOW? LEGOLAND® California features a ride based on the LEGO Adventurers theme.

Aviator helmet and goggles

Pippin Reed Also known as Gail Storm, this fearless female hunts down flying reptiles in her Island Chopper (5935). She carries a rifle, and a shovel!

Shady, wide brimmed hat

Another variant has brown hips instead of black.

Mr. Cunningham He may be a minifigure master of disguise, but Mr. Cunningham can't even hide the pot belly printed on his new torso.

LEGO
5955

All-Terrain Trapper (5955) The three minifigures in this set include the evil villains' leader, Baron Von Barron.

Hair piece worn by more than 120 minifigures in black

Pursed lips—she's concentrating!

Belt has lots of pouches to hide things in.

Alexia Sinister The sister of Baron Von Barron, Alexia is always scheming to steal treasure. The Baron himself used the name "Sam Sinister" in some sets this year.

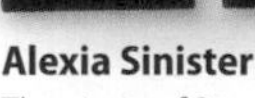

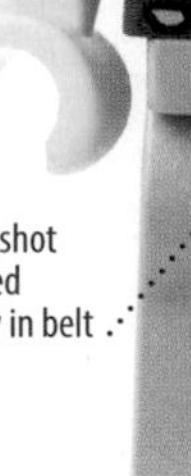

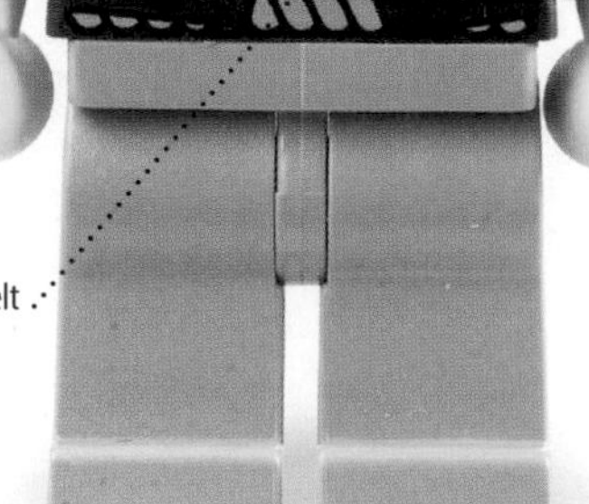

Mike This minifigure likes to partner with other Dino Island heroes. He's a mean aim with his trusty slingshot!

Brown cavalry cap

The Dino Island sun has given him freckles.

Exclusive torso design

Slingshot tucked away in belt

Ninja crest appears on three minifigures' helmets

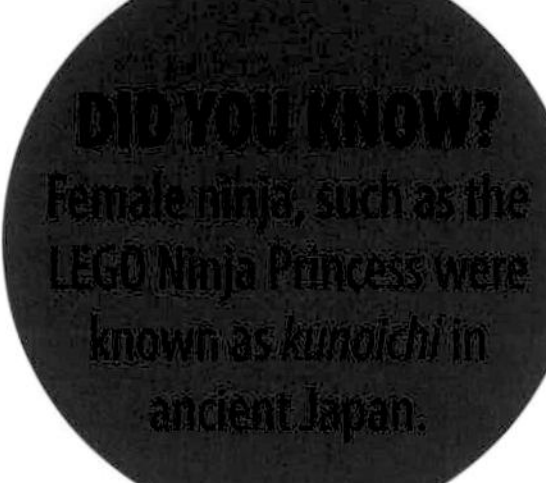
DID YOU KNOW?
Female ninja, such as the LEGO Ninja Princess were known as *kunoichi* in ancient Japan.

WATCH US DISAPPEAR BEFORE YOUR EYES!

Ninja Princess
Only the second female to appear in the LEGO Ninja subtheme, this warrior minifigure fights alongside her male companion.

Long eyelashes reveal female identity

Ninja hides a shuriken and dagger in her robes

NINJA

Only three LEGO Ninja sets were released this year, none of them building sets. Instea, they were known as Mini Heroes Collections (3344, 3345, and 3346), and contained just minifigures, display bases, and collector cards.

Classic Green Ninja
Dressed for stealth in his robe and head wrap, this Ninja's identity remains hidden.

Red bandana printed on head under helmet

Protective metallic scale-mail worn under robe

Samurai dragon robe and dagger printed on torso

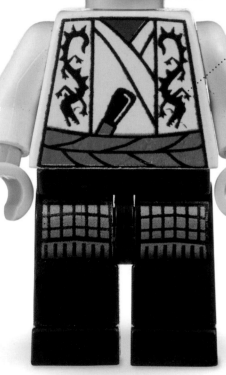

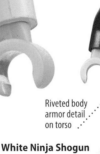

Long mustache indicates older age

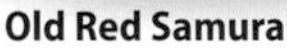

Riveted body armor detail on torso

White Ninja Shogun
This fierce ancient warrior minifigure is equipped with metallic leg armor and golden antler-like helmet crest in set 3346.

Old Red Samurai
An experienced warrior, this venerable minifigure fights alongside a younger Red Samurai in the Mini Heroes Collection set (3345).

LEGO CASTLE

This year saw the end of the LEGO® Ninja subtheme. The Ninja would slip quietly into the shadows until 2011, when the concept would return with LEGO® Ninjago (although one Ninja would briefly sneak back in 2009 as a Vintage Minifigure). LEGO Castle continued, however, returning to medieval Europe with the first Knights' Kingdom subtheme. This line focused on the battle between King Leo's knights and Cedric the Bull's raiders. The two kings were locked in a ferocious feud over the future of the minifigure kingdom.

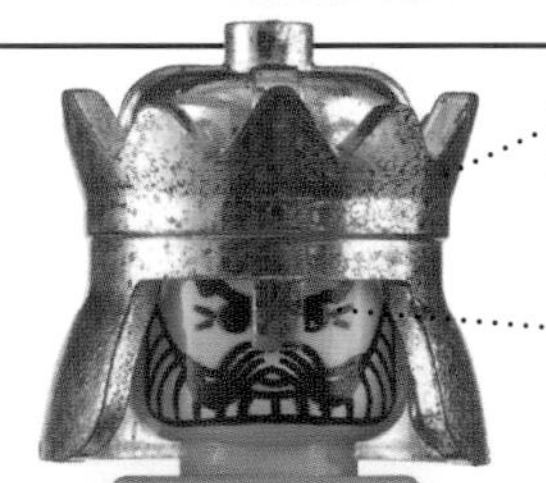

Crown and helmet are one piece.

Aged, lined face—he has reigned for a long time.

Torso features King Leo's lion head shield.

King Leo This regal minifigure of King Leo is the central character in Knights' Kingdom and appears in all five sets.

Hinged visor can be raised and lowered.

Elegant, close-fitting armor in gold and silver

Princess Storm
King Leo's brave daughter is the first female knight minifigure in the LEGO Castle theme.

LEGO
6098

King Leo's Castle (6098) This set comes with seven minifigures, including King Leo, Queen Leonora, and Princess Storm, and a creepy skeleton figure, too.

Queen Leonora
This majestic minifigure of King Leo's wife has a printed sloped piece instead of legs. She is part of King Leo's Castle (6098).

Headdress based on medieval hennin

Outer red robe printed across torso and skirt

Keys to the castle safely attached to chain belt.

LEGO® KNIGHTS' KINGDOM

King Leo lived in the first medieval-style LEGO castle made since 1995, which was also the first to come with a complete royal family. Cedric had no castle, so he and his Bulls made it their mission to knock down Leo's using ax carts, catapults, cannons, and battering rams.

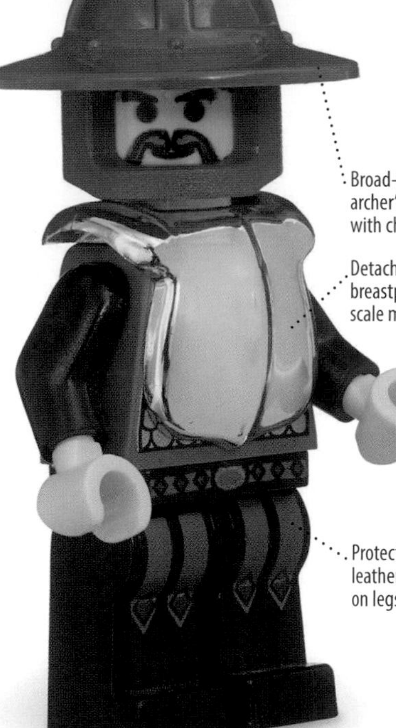
Broad-brimmed archer's helmet with chin guard
Detachable breastplate over scale mail torso.
Protective leather straps on legs

John of Mayne Richard's partner wears unique metallic armor in the Dungeon set (4817).

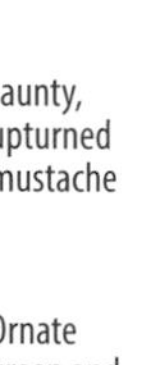
Quiver attaches at back
Jaunty, upturned mustache
Ornate green and silver belt
Armor print extends to legs

Archer Richard The heroic Richard aims to defend King Leo's kingdom alone in the Defense Archer set (4801).

Red plume fits into hole on visor

HAS ANYONE SEEN THE OIL CAN?

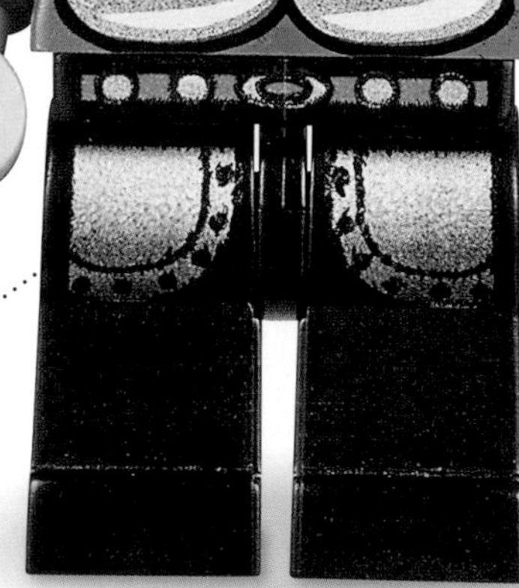
Knights' Kingdom plate armor printed on legs

Richard the Strong Richard is the best and bravest among King Leo's knights. He features in the Royal Joust set (6095).

Unique head has angry, scowling face
Red gloves make him stand out from his men

Cedric the Bull Like his namesake animal, this minifigure is always ready to charge! He leads his band of robbers in their constant attacks on King Leo's castle.

Horns clip to helmet via a dragon's mouth crest.
Cheek guards protect his face (and hide his unkempt hair)
Brown leather scale mail torso pattern

Gilbert the Bad Gilbert has an eye (just the one) for designing foul war machines, like the giant slingshot in the Catapult Crusher set (6032).

LEGO
7-12
6096

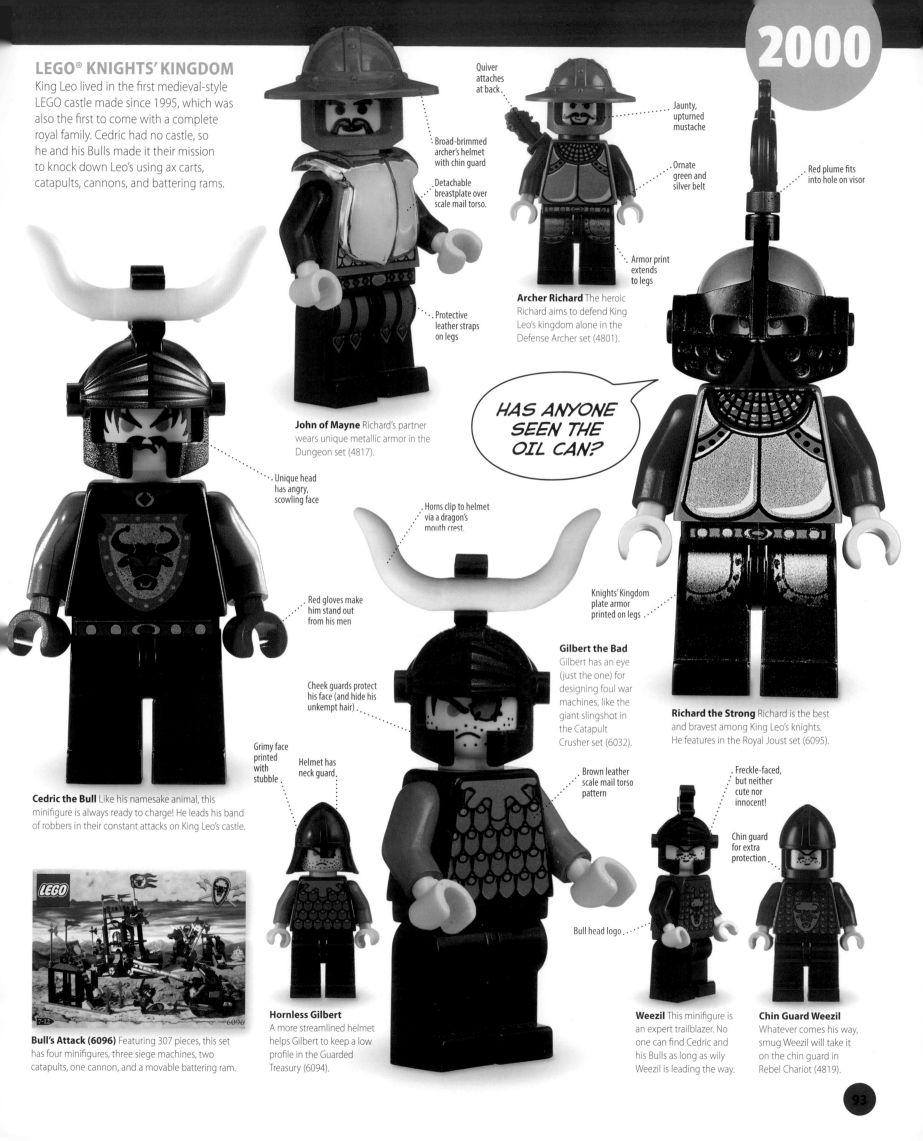

Bull's Attack (6096) Featuring 307 pieces, this set has four minifigures, three siege machines, two catapults, one cannon, and a movable battering ram.

Grimy face printed with stubble
Helmet has neck guard

Hornless Gilbert A more streamlined helmet helps Gilbert to keep a low profile in the Guarded Treasury (6094).

Freckle-faced, but neither cute nor innocent!
Chin guard for extra protection
Bull head logo

Weezil This minifigure is an expert trailblazer. No one can find Cedric and his Bulls as long as wily Weezil is leading the way.

Chin Guard Weezil Whatever comes his way, smug Weezil will take it on the chin guard in Rebel Chariot (4819).

2000

LEGO® TOWN

LEGO Town headed due north in 2000, with the Arctic subtheme creating a short, sharp blizzard of activity. But while things were ice cold in some places, they were red hot in others. LEGO Race burned up the race track, Space Port headed for the Red Planet, and there were new Fire Fighters sets. A year of variety indeed!

Scorpion motif on torso

Wrench A mechanic and a racer, Wrench appears in Grip 'n' Go Challenge (6713) released this year.

Safety helmet fitted with breathing hose

THAT'S NOT THE ENGINE ROARING—IT'S ME!

Smirk—Chip is confident he will win!

He loves tigers, so chose one as his race motif

Chip Driving through flame obstacles won't send Chip into minifigure meltdown in Turbo Tiger (6519). His protective race suit and helmet will save him.

Flame pattern on helmet
YOU COULD SAY I'M QUITE A SNAPPY DRESSER!
Crocodile motif—she's snappy around the track
Gloves help her keep a firm grip on the wheel.

Lucky Clad in her favorite color, Lucky is all set to try her racing luck in Green Buggy (1284).

RACE

The Race subtheme made its final pitstop this year, with 13 sets that included new driver and pit crew minifigures and vehicles such as buggies, dragsters, and monster trucks. A new line, Racers, would begin revving up in 2001.

SPACE PORT

This year's only Space Port set was the last ever. Mars Mission (3059) included instructions for building multiple models using the pieces in the box, each being given a one, two, or three brick symbol to indicate the level of difficulty.

Gold chrome visor
Headset for communication
Space port logo on torso

Astronaut This space traveler is the only minifigure in the Mars Mission set.

LEGO
RACE
MOTOR
6616

Rocket Dragster (6616) This set includes a long, aerodynamic yellow racer and a Chip minifigure.

Traditional Lego® face print

CLASSIC

In spite of a trend toward detail, the pre-1989 classic minifigure still made an appearance now and then. This happy fellow remains, to many, the iconic symbol of the LEGO minifigure.

T
Telekom logo supplied as a sticker

Telekom Cyclist This minifigure is included in set 1199—a promotional set for the Tour de France cycle race. He bears the logo of the German telecommunications company Telekom.

LEGO TOWN JR. AND CITY CENTER

Only three sets came out for LEGO Town Jr. this year as the subtheme was phased out in favor of a new one—City Center. The largest Town Jr. set was Busy City (3058), released as part of a Master Builders line, with instructions for how to build several different models of vehicles.

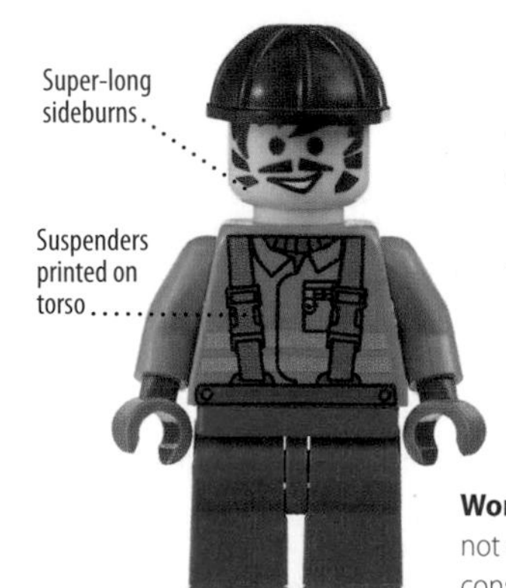

Super-long sideburns
Suspenders printed on torso

Workman Fred A builder, if not exactly a Master Builder, this construction worker is seen in sets 1296 and 3351.

DID YOU KNOW?
So far, around 170 minifigures have worn the white long-billed cap.
Badges on uniform
Walkie-talkie to pass on orders
Patterned red belt

Fireman Like all Firemen released in 2000, this City Center minifigure wears a new gray uniform.

ARCTIC

Brrrrr! Brave explorers headed to the freezing Arctic in this Town subtheme, which lasted for a year. They were hunting for meteorites that had fallen to Earth with alien life trapped inside. Ten sets came out, featuring realistic snow vehicles and the first ever polar bear figures to appear in a LEGO set.

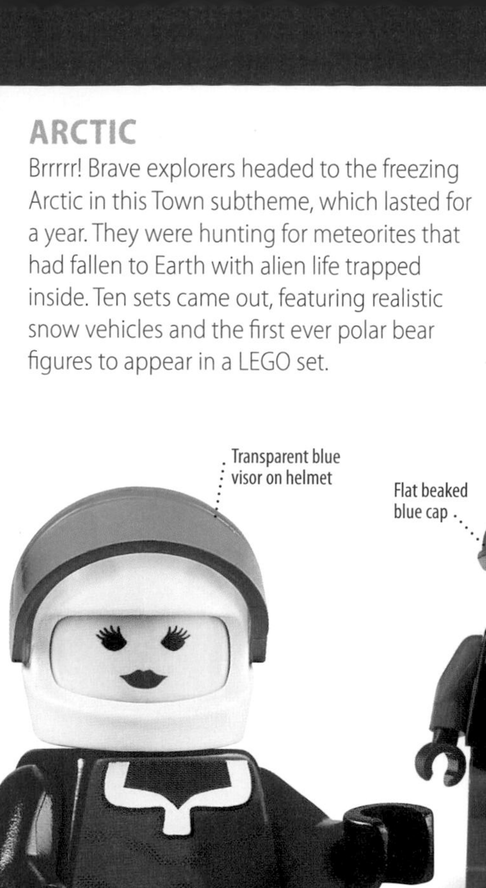

Transparent blue visor on helmet
Polar bear image for Arctic theme

Sleeping bag A backpack holds the sleeping bag.

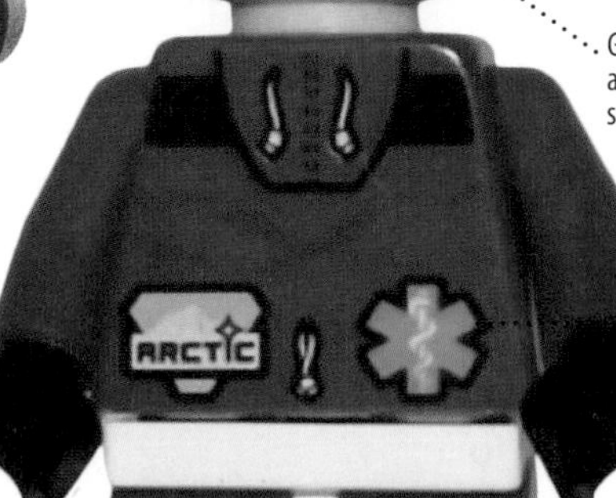

Blue goggles shield his eyes from snow glare.
ARCTIC
Face printed with dark ski-goggles pattern
Gray beard and eyebrows suggest age
"Star of life" is symbol of emergency medical services

Cosmo This Captain Ross lookalike is actually another explorer from the Arctic theme.

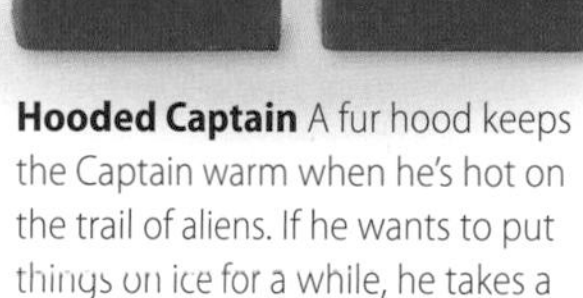

Flat beaked blue cap

Captain Ross The minifigure Captain wears a plain blue cap when he's chilling out in the Mobile Outpost (6520).

Hooded Captain A fur hood keeps the Captain warm when he's hot on the trail of aliens. If he wants to put things on ice for a while, he takes a nap in his insulated sleeping bag.

Red Medic Dealing with colds, frostbite, and polar bear bites are all part of this minifigure's job. He appears only in the Polar Base set (6575).

Crystal Aput Rescue helicopter pilot Crystal makes sure the the Red Medic always drops in where he's needed. Like him, she wears a red snow suit.

Although he is hatless, Scooter sometimes wears a green cap.

Large Arctic logo in center of torso

Pull cords tighten jacket neck to keep snow out.

Hood fits over head piece and torso

Scooter Explorer Scooter is a minifigure on a mission. He's hunting down an alien spider in the Arctic Expedition set (6573).

Hooded Scooter Scooter is ready to face chillier challenges in his snug hoodie. The subtheme was the first to feature fur-lined hood pieces.

LEGO® BELVILLE™ FAIRY TALES

LEGO BELVILLE continued its flight through fairyland in 2000, delighting fans with five sets featuring good fairies, royal coaches, palaces, and other classic fairy tale elements.

Silver moon pattern
Pink floral pattern on white figure

Fairy Tales The LEGO BELVILLE Fairy figures came with optional fabric fairy wing attachments and plastic bow ties.

Minifigure comes with no hair piece
FIRST
LEGO
Y2K
Y2K represents the year 2000

Y2K To mark the new millenium, a minifigure called Y2K was released for FLL members to use in their builds.

FIRST LEGO® LEAGUE

In its second year, *FIRST* LEGO League challenged its teams and their robots to complete tasks such as rescuing a trapped scientist and retrieving crates of rock before a volcano erupted. It was the final year in which no actual set was produced for FLL tournaments.

LEGO *STAR WARS*

The Force was strong with LEGO *Star Wars* fans this year, as some of the most famous characters in the epic saga— Han Solo, Princess Leia, Emperor Palpatine, Boba Fett, C-3PO, and Chewbacca—became minifigures for the first time. Although only three sets were released in 2000, they included the first *Millennium Falcon* and the first X-wing fighter.

I'VE ALWAYS BEEN A BIT OF A REBEL.

Specially created braided buns hair piece

Flowing senatorial gown printed on torso

Silver belt symbolises Alderaan royalty

Princess Leia Feisty Princess Leia Organa's first minifigure is dressed in her senatorial robes and features her famous bun hairstyle.

Trademark lopsided grin on head piece

"Han style" black vest and light shirt

Legs printed with gun belt holster pattern

Han Solo This is one of three minifigure variants of lovable pilot Han Solo released in 2000. He wears the casual, open-necked shirt and vest *Star Wars* fans know so well.

Unique head piece has hair that flows down his chest and back

Bowcaster ammunition bandolier

Chewbacca
Though he is taller than humans, this Wookiee hero minifigure is standard size. The specially designed Chewie head piece sits on a torso also used for two Ewok minifigures.

Audiosensors on either side of head

Plain pearl gold legs unique to C-3PO

C-3PO A new head mold was cast for C-3PO's minifigure, which debuted in the *Millenium Falcon* set (7190).

TIME FOR A FACIAL.

Angry, distorted face print unique to this minifigure

Sith robes printed on torso

Black cloth cape

DID YOU KNOW?
The LEGO *Star Wars* theme was the first licensed property in 40 years.

Emperor Palpatine The evil Lord of the Sith has a suitably scary, wrinkled face for his first appearance in the LEGO *Star Wars* theme. His minifigure features the same hood piece as the Darth Maul minifigure from 1999.

Helmet covers black head piece with no face

Rocket power for quick getaways

All in One
Boba's detailed helmet and jetpack are one piece.

Mandalorian body armor printed on gray torso

Boba Fett This is the original minifigure of the Mandalorian bounty hunter.

Uniform printed on torso is unique to the Security Officer

Cap has been worn by many minifigures, such as Stan Shunpike's purple version in LEGO® Harry Potter™.

Naboo Security Officer
The smiling Security Officer minifigure keeps the peace on Naboo, aided by his green Flash Speeder craft from set 7124.

LEGO® STUDIOS

Fans got a chance to make their own movies this year with the LEGO Studios Steven Spielberg MovieMaker set (1349). This innovative item came with a stop-motion camera and editing software, and included a recreation of a scene from *The Lost World: Jurassic Park*.

Shades protect his eyes from the glare of studio lights.

Grip This guy brings a bit of bare-armed muscle to the set. He'll lift or shift anything the film crew needs him to.

Padded gloves for carrying heavy equipment

Utility belt holds screwdriver for dismantling props

Stylish white bandana

Pen for jotting down notes

Like all crew members, she wears an ID badge.

Female Assistant The cameraman's assistant uses her wireless headset to keep tabs on the shoot at all times.

Practical orange vest

Beard and glasses like those worn by Steven Spielberg

Director Looks familiar? This minifigure is based on filmmaker Steven Spielberg. He features in 11 sets, including Explosion Studio (1352).

Same face design as Doc from the Rock Raiders theme

Cameraman's emblem

Cameraman The Cameraman is always right at the center of the on-set action, tracking, panning, and zooming. That's how he rolls!

CREW

Along with the director and cameraman, the LEGO Studios set featured a grip, an assistant, a stunt man, and a fireman in case things got a bit heated on the movie lot. A camera track with camera provided more realistic fun.

CAST

The actors in this set played Adventurers Johnny Thunder and Pippin Reed in an exciting scene where they flee from a rampaging dinosaur. They were the first of a number of actors to grace the LEGO Studios' big screen.

Crop top under open jacket

Actress This glammed-up minifigure is the star in the Steven Spielberg MovieMaker set (1349).

Tumbling tresses

Compass for checking directions

Red bandana protects against harsh winds

Playing Pippin Our leading lady is playing adventurer Pippin Reed in the Dino Head Attack (1354). She's changed her clothes, but not her makeup!

Protective gloves also provide grip

Pilot The wily Pilot is part of a single set (1349) this year. This minifigure plays the part of an extra.

Stuntman When there are dangerous stunts to be done, this highly trained (and highly insured) minifigure steps in.

Same legs, torso, and head as the Pilot

LEGO® ROCK RAIDERS

The Rock Raiders' adventures came to an end this year. The four sets produced were all promotional models. Some Rock Raider minifigures were also released as part of a LEGO Mini Heroes Collection set (3347).

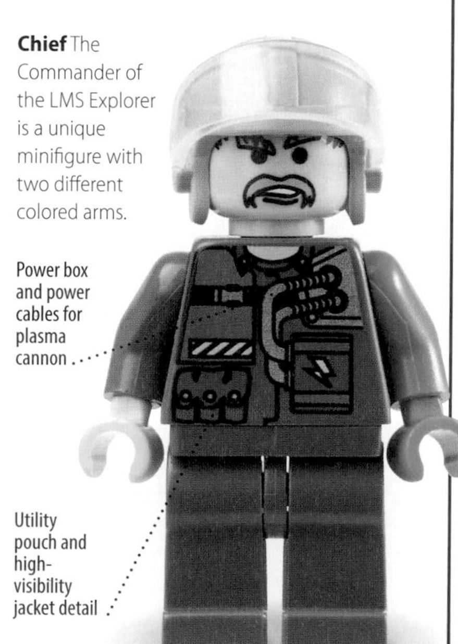

Chief The Commander of the LMS Explorer is a unique minifigure with two different colored arms.

Power box and power cables for plasma cannon

Utility pouch and high-visibility jacket detail

Classic grin • Male Person • 1978 • LEGOLAND Town.

Beard, mustache, and eye patch • Captain Redbeard • 1989 • LEGO Pirates.

Full lips • Female Pirate • 1989 • LEGO Pirates.

Mustache and stubble • Blue Pirate • 1989 • LEGO Pirates.

Headset and eyebrows • Space Police Chief • 1992 • LEGO Space.

Orange face paint and nose • Tan Shirt Native American • 1997 • LEGO Western.

Glow-in-the-dark shroud • Ghost • 1997 • LEGO Castle.

Droid head with large eye shield • Blue Droid • 1997 • LEGO Space.

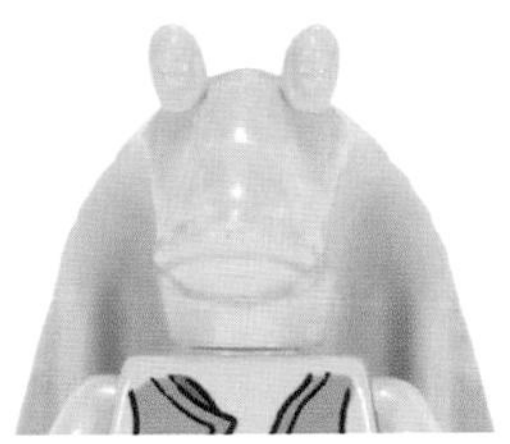
Modified Gungan head • Jar Jar Binks • 1999 • LEGO® *Star Wars®*.

Modified Wookiee head • Chewbacca • 2000 • LEGO *Star Wars*.

HEADS UP, EVERYONE!

Werewolf mask • Werewolf • 2002 • LEGO Studios.

Grimacing face with zippered head extension • Frankenstein's Monster • 2002.• LEGO Studios.

THE BASIC DESIGN of the standard minifigure head—a rounded piece with a stud on top—has not changed since the early years. The first heads always smiled, but in 1989, LEGO® Pirates introduced new face prints that included beards, eyepatches, and a range of different facial expressions. The launch of licensed themes in 1999 saw a massive innovation—specially molded heads created for less human-like characters, and soon many non-licensed themes introduced these too. The reversible head was introduced in 2001, which allowed a minifigure to change his or her expression when they felt like it.

Open-mouthed modified alien head • Kranxx • 2009 • LEGO Space.

Bug-eyed modified head with tongue • Squidman • 2009 • LEGO Space.

Modified minotaur head with horns • Minotaur • 2012 • LEGO Minifigures.

Gray zombie face • Zombie Bride • 2012 • LEGO Monster Fighters.

Freckles • Vendor • 1992 • LEGO Paradisa.

Cool shades • Pool Guy • 1992 • LEGO Paradisa.

Pretty eyelashes and lips • Surfer Girl • 1992 • LEGO Paradisa.

Printed droid head • Spyrius Droid • 1994 • LEGO Space.

Cross-eyed, glasses, and facial hair • Dr. Cyber • 1996 • LEGO Time Cruisers.

Glow-in-the-dark head • Professor Snape • 2001 • LEGO® Harry Potter™.

First reversible head • Professor Quirrel • 2001 • LEGO Harry Potter.

Huge grin • Flex • 2001 • LEGO Alpha Team.

Purple eyeshadow and glasses • Cam Attaway • 2001 • LEGO Alpha Team.

Modified Yoda head • Yoda • 2002 • LEGO *Star Wars*.

Red Spider-Man mask with silver web pattern • Spider-Man • 2002 • LEGO® Spider-Man™.

Skin-colored head with thin mustache • Lando Calrissian • 2003 • LEGO *Star Wars*.

Skin-colored head with large eyes • Mary Jane Watson • 2004 • LEGO Spider-Man.

Evil black skull head • Super Ice Drone • 2004 • LEGO Alpha Team.

Modified, soft rubber Kel Dor head • Plo Koon • 2008 • LEGO® *Star Wars*® Clone Wars™.

Blue head with purple lips and Twi'lek tentacles • Aayla Secura • 2010 • LEGO *Star Wars*.

White face with green eyebrows and wide smile • The Joker • 2012 • LEGO® DC Universe™ Super Heroes.

Half-purple and scarred face • Two-Face • 2012 • LEGO DC Universe Super Heroes.

Block-shaped head with large blue eyes • Clockwork Robot • 2012 • LEGO Minifigures.

Green face with spiked tiara • Lady Liberty • 2012 • LEGO Minifigures.

Modified snake head with fangs • Lizaru • 2012 • LEGO Ninjago.

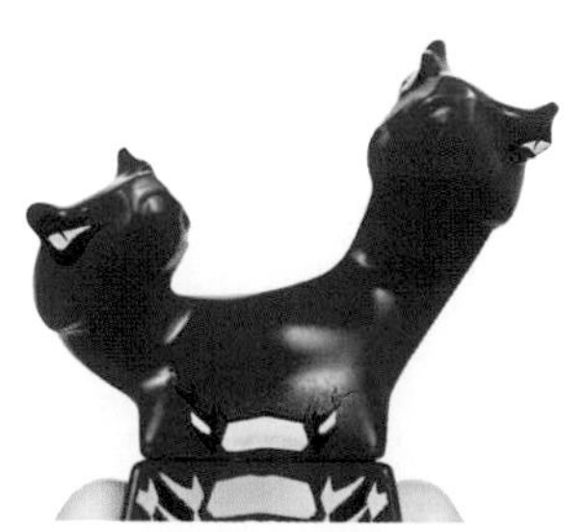
Two-headed modified snake head • Fangdam • 2012 • LEGO Ninjago.

Lion head mask with crown pattern • Laval • 2013 • LEGO Legends of Chima.

Eagle mask with gold tiara • Eris • 2013 • LEGO Legends of Chima.

Modified Turtle head with bandana • Raphael • 2013 • LEGO® Teenage Mutant Ninja. Turtles™.

The Sorting Hat replaces Harry's iconic hair piece.
Starry wizard's robe is unique to the LEGO Harry Potter theme

Harry the Boy Wizard New pupil Harry wears a standard Hogwarts torso and the first of two versions of the Sorting Hat.

2001

SUPER-SPIES, SORCERERS, and space aliens helped to make 2001 a magical year for LEGO® fans! Two major themes, LEGO® Harry Potter™ and the non-minifigure based BIONICLE®, launched in 2001, but that was only the beginning. Exciting LEGO System themes such as LEGO® Alpha Team and LEGO® Life on Mars also joined the lineup. Aspiring movie-makers had a lot of LEGO® Studios sets to choose from, while younger builders could enjoy LEGO® DUPLO® Bob the Builder™ and the new Jack Stone models. LEGO building was bigger and better than ever in 2001!

LEGO HARRY POTTER

LEGO Harry Potter was the second major licensed theme after LEGO® *Star Wars*®, premiering with 11 sets and 30 new minifigures based on the *Harry Potter and the Sorcerer's Stone* movie. Also appearing were the first sets of Hogwarts Castle (4709) and the Hogwarts Express (4708), which would both prove so popular that several updates would be issued over the next few years.

Trademark lightning-shaped scar
Gryffindor uniform

Harry Potter™ A new, violet variant of the cloth robe was introduced specially for the theme. Harry wears the colorful robe in three sets.

THE WIZARD AND HIS FRIENDS

Fans just couldn't get enough of Harry and his friends. The theme's first year saw no less than four variants of Harry, three of Hermione Granger, and three of Ron Weasley.

Gryffindor crest

Hermione Granger™ All Gryffindor minifigures, including Hermione, wear the scarlet and gold uniform in years one and two. Their torsos and legs are identical.

Hogwarts school crest

Wizard Girl This Hermione minifigure is not yet in Gryffindor so she wears a school crest on her torso piece instead of a Gryffindor one.

Bowl-shaped hair piece in Earth orange

Ron Weasley™ The first six Ron minifigures feature this quirky grinning face, with eyebrows colored to match his hair piece.

Face printed with arrogant sneer

Draco Malfoy™ This is the first of eight Draco Malfoy minifigures. As a member of Slytherin, his uniform bears the green and silver snake crest of his house.

Yellow hands and face were used for all Harry minifigures until 2004

Casual Harry This is one of more than 20 different Harry minifigures. He wears these casual clothes to board the Hogwarts Express (4708).

Unique knitted sweater pattern

Casual Hermione Hermione has changed into a casual but stylish blue sweater and jeans for the Diagon Alley Shops (4723).

Redhead Ron's face has exclusive freckle pattern
Standard Hogwarts robe

Casual Ron Ron's robe keeps him warm when he's relaxing in the common room in Gryffindor House (4722).

Shaggy beard and hair are one piece
Super-sized legs are unposable
Extra-long torso piece gives Hagrid his half-giant height

Rubeus Hagrid™ There are three variants of Hogwarts' half-giant gamekeeper. Each one stands a whole head taller than his minifigure friends.

CASTLE RESIDENTS

Not all LEGO Harry Potter minifigures are human—or even alive! Peeves was the first LEGO ghost to be built from standard minifigure parts, the silver knight was a statue in Hogwarts Castle, and the Chess Queen was a minifigure-sized chess piece guarding the Sorcerer's Stone.

Face printed onto a light gray standard LEGO head
Ghostly markings of jacket and shirt

Peeves the Poltergeist
This gray-bodied minifigure appears in two LEGO sets (4705 and 4079).

Shiny silver crown

Faceless head is a cylindrical LEGO brick

Chess Queen
Harry and Ron come up against this ghastly game piece in The Chamber of the Winged Keys (4704).

A spooky gray face lurks under the two-piece helmet.

Silver Knights
The warrior statue minifigure holds a large LEGO sword and stands guard at Hogwarts Castle (4709).

HOGWARTS PROFESSORS

Both Albus Dumbledore™ and Professor Snape™ appear for the first time in this year. Professor Quirrell was the first of several Defense Against the Dark Arts teacher minifigures, but he appears in only one set.

DID YOU KNOW?
Three other versions of the Hogwarts Express were released—two in 2004 and one in 2010.

Face printed with sarcastically raised eyebrow

Glowing complexion

Professor Snape
The Potions Master is the first minifigure to have a glow-in-the-dark head.

Long purple frock coat with pocket details

Plain black cloth robe

Albus Dumbledore™
The first minifigure of the Hogwarts headmaster has detailed purple robes and purple wizarding cloak.

Ornate details on robes can be seen if beard is removed

Hair and beard are two separate removable pieces

Legs printed with wizarding gadgets

Evil face
Voldemort's features are printed on the reverse of the head.

Unique purple turban hides a hideous secret
Purple jacket and scarf match color of exotic turban

Professor Quirrell™ The Professor Quirrell minifigure is the first to have a special double-sided head. Turn it around and Lord Voldemort's face is revealed!

2001

LEGO® SPACE

LEGO Space traveled to the Red Planet for the first time with the Life on Mars subtheme, which focused on astronauts exploring Mars and encountering a friendly species of alien. Adventures revolved around the humans helping the good Martians stop a planned rebellion by a bad Martian. Life on Mars lasted for only one year and its sets would be the last in the Space theme until 2007.

Chrome visor

Wired up to his heart monitor, Mac never misses a beat.

Special unit Mac's exclusive torso is printed with the heart-monitoring unit he has to wear in space.

Black gloves

Large helmet and breathing apparatus cover torso detail

Mac The captain of the Solar Explorer may look relaxed and laid back, but make no mistake—Mac runs a tight ship! His minifigure only appears in the Solar Explorer (7315).

DID YOU KNOW?
LEGO Life on Mars is the only subtheme where humans and aliens coexist peacefully.

Communication headset
Same torso design as BB in different colors

Crew Member This minifigure's head piece is used by 10 minifigures in total, including divers and ground control crew.

LEGO
MARS
SOLAR EXPLORER
7-12
7315
Cont. 242 pcs/pzs/pcs

Solar Explorer (7315) This set features the largest astronaut's vehicle, which acts as the space base, and three minifigures.

LEGO® JACK STONE

Jack Stone focused on hero Jack saving the day in various guises. The figures were "mid-figs", mid-sized figures that could not be taken apart.

Helmet worn when piloting rescue boat
Torso printed with rescue overalls

Res Q Worker This figure shows Jack Stone in his role as an intrepid rescuer at the Aqua Super Station (4610).

BB's Helmet BB's headgear has two studs on the back, which allow him to attach to space vehicles, so he can "hover" above the ground.

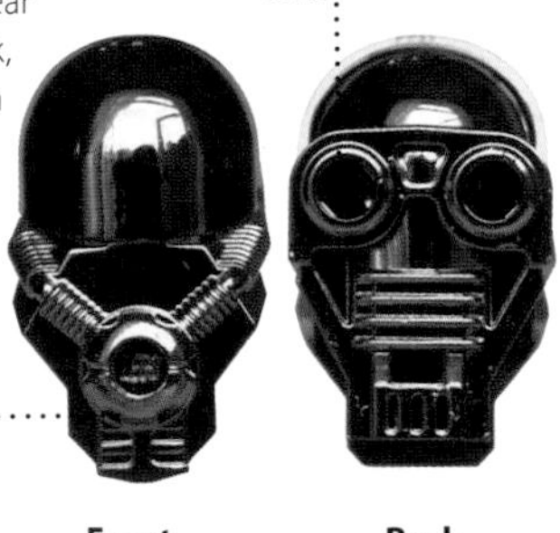

Studs
Breathing apparatus
Front
Back

Simple face detail with messy orange hair

BB Mac's co-pilot in the Solar Explorer is very young and very keen. He wears the same helmet as his hero Mac over his unique, tousle-haired head.

Blue space suit matches Crew Member's
Full chrome blue visor

Astronauts' Assistant The only difference between this minifigure and the Crew Member is the size of his visor.

Doc Ailing astronauts can rely on this dedicated doctor to fix them up. His minifigure appears in two sets (7315 and 7312).

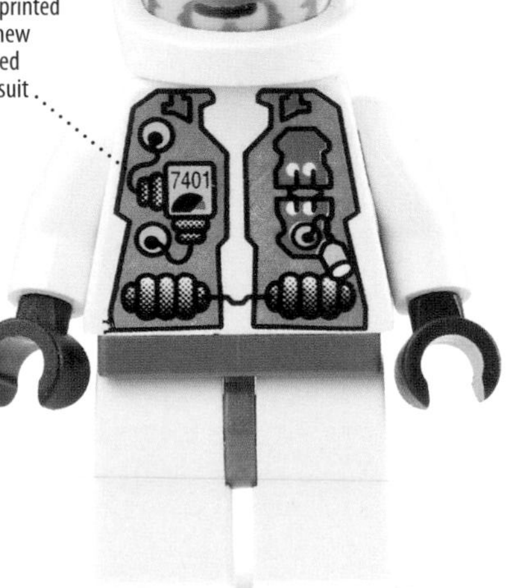

Chrome visor is worn by many astronauts in the LEGO® Space sets
Gray eyebrow beard show h mature medi
Torso printed with new detailed spacesuit
7401

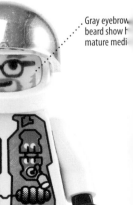

MARTIAN COLONY

All named after stars, the Martians used an air pump and tube transport system to get around. They had more armed vehicles than the astronauts, so it's lucky they were friendly!

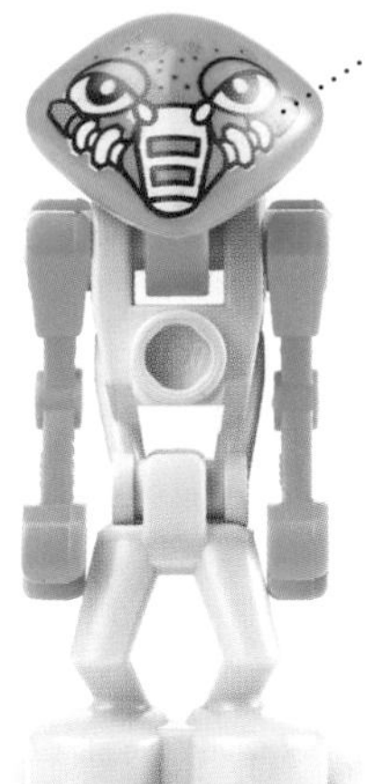
Air tube mask printed on martian head

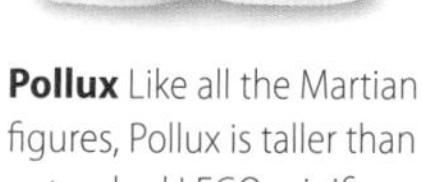

Pollux Like all the Martian figures, Pollux is taller than a standard LEGO minifigure.

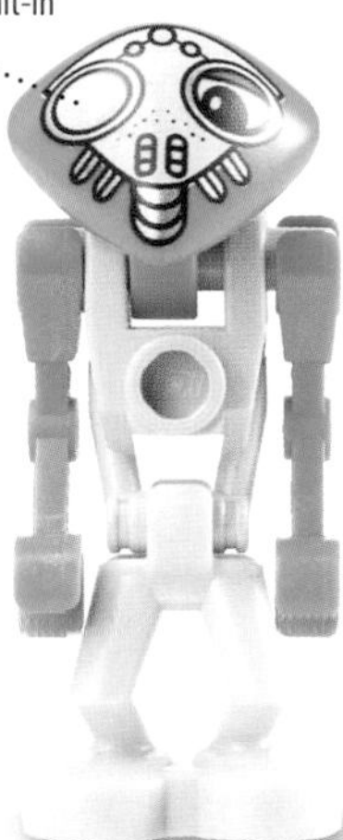
Mask has built-in eye patch

Canopus Digging for meteors is this Martian's mission in the Excavation Searcher (7316).

Lime freckle pattern
Torso design indicates leader status
Angled legs are only used for Martians

Riegel This Martian may be green in color, but he has years of experience at leading his people. He's also the General of the Aero Tube Hangar (7317), a Biodium mining outpost on Mars.

Orange freckles

Doctor's white attire

Antares Just like a human doctor, Martian medic Antares wears clean, clinical white.

Medium green skin shade

Arcturus The shade of green on this red-eyed Martian spy figure is unique to him among the colony.

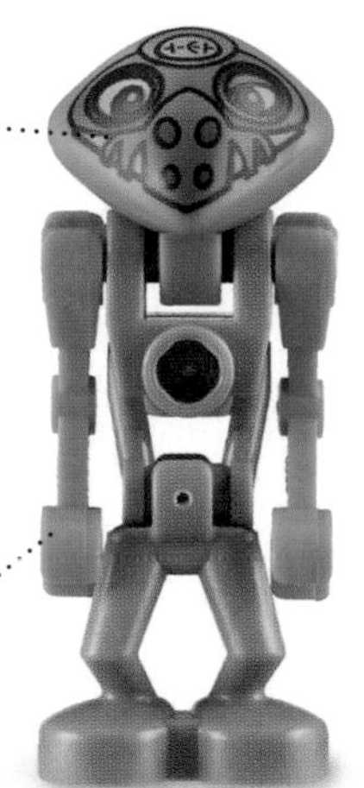
Unique mask pattern
Dark turquoise mechanical arm

Mizar Mizar's full-cover mask hints that working at the Aero Tube Hangar is a risky business.

Blue and silver Martian pilot mask

Centauri Martians, such as Centauri, have torsos and arms like *Star Wars*® Battle Droids, but in bright colors.

Plain head suits clear-thinking character

Vega This serious scientist doesn't want to wear a protective mask. It might disrupt his thinking process!

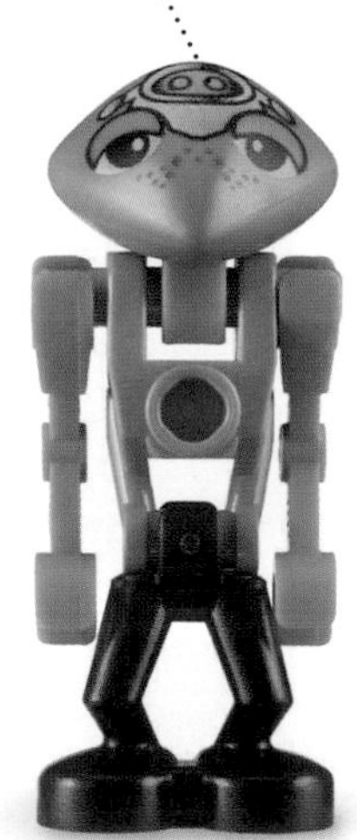
Same head piece as Antares

Black-legged Martian The Martians' Jet Scooter is driven by this nameless but fearless speedster.

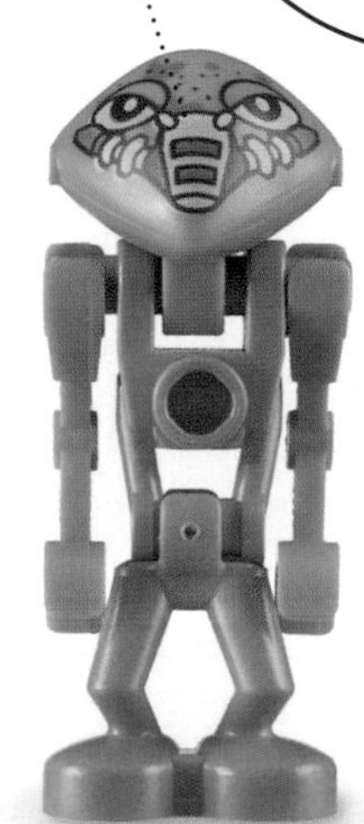
Mask with mouth cover

Orange-legged Martian This masked Martian mans the controls of the Worker Robot (7302).

MY JUMPSUIT IS OUT OF THIS WORLD!

Martian mascara gives a wide-eyed look
Legs, arms, and torso same as male Martians

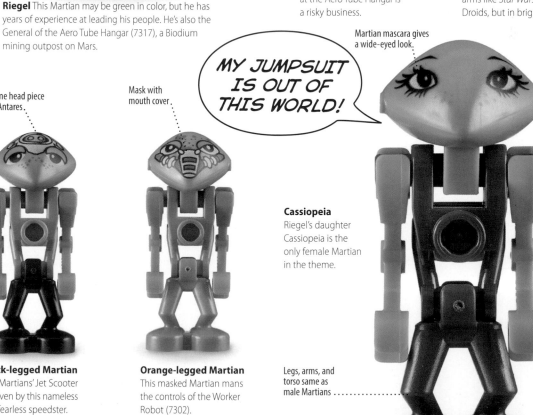

Cassiopeia Riegel's daughter Cassiopeia is the only female Martian in the theme.

LEGO ALPHA TEAM

Super-spies took on a malevolent mind-manipulator in the first LEGO secret agent theme—Alpha Team. Evil Ogel sought to transform the population into Skeleton Drones using mind control orbs. The seven agents of Alpha Team battled him on land, sea, and in the air in six new sets, featuring nine new minifigures. Alpha Team and Ogel would be back for rematches in 2002 and 2004.

Unique new head piece

Alpha Team logo on necklace

Utility belt holds mechanic's tools

Cam Attaway Alpha Team's mechanic wears her purple glasses for the first and only time in the Alpha Team ATV (6774).

HEY, THAT'S SUPPOSED TO BE A SECRET!

Headset for communicating with the team

Utility belt worn over buttoned jacket

Dash Justice At the first sign of trouble, team leader Dash will be there in a flash! Brave Dash pilots his helicopter in the Alpha Team Helicopter (6773).

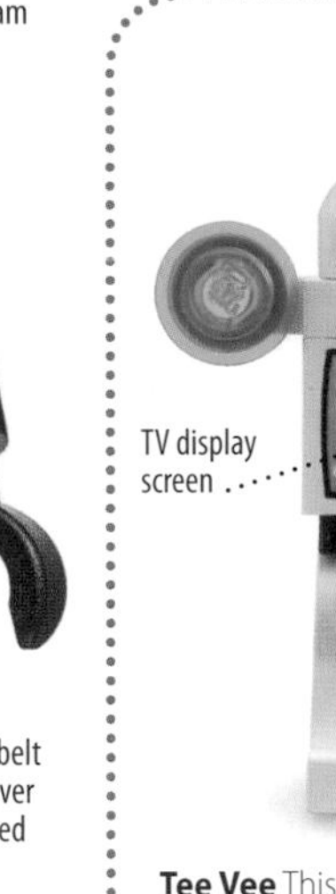

Black levers instead of head piece

TV display screen

Tee Vee This first variant of Alpha Team's communications robot is fully programmed and switched on—as you'd expect of a TV set on minifigure legs!

Explosives fixed to vest

Mouth clenched in concentration

Crunch Working for Alpha Team is a real blast for Crunch. He's the team's dedicated explosives expert.

Purple hair is unique to 2001 and 2002 variants.

Three pockets on utility belt

Radia One of only two female minifigures on the team, clever Radia has a mind as bright as the lasers she works with.

Aviator-style protective helmet

Pockets on legs for tools

Flex No problem is too knotty for Flex, Alpha Team's ropes expert. He's just happy to be on the team... delighted in fact!

DID YOU KNOW?
"Ogel" is LEGO spelled backward—he represents the opposite of LEGO fun and play.

LEGO
Alpha Team
6776

Ogel Control Center (6776) This set saw Ogel's first minifigure appearance. He was protected by two Minion Commanders.

DIDN'T SEE THAT EVIL ORB COMING!

Skeleton head

Epaulets only appear on first variant

Minion Commander A mindless drone with a head of bone, this minifigure is the first variant of Ogel's minions.

Movable chrome gold visor

Menacing red eye

Elaborate shoulder armor

Protective armor clips over torso

Ogel The Alpha Team's foe appears in his first variant with plain black legs and torso. His armored shoulder protection is so bulky it partly covers his scowl.

LEGO® *STAR WARS*®

It was another year of firsts for LEGO *Star Wars*, with the debuts of two classic characters from Episodes IV, V, and VI: the crimson-clad Royal Guard and the iconic Stormtrooper. But they were not the only *Star Wars* rookies. Watto, from *Star Wars:* Episode I *The Phantom Menace*, made his first appearance in his very own set—Watto's Junkyard (7186).

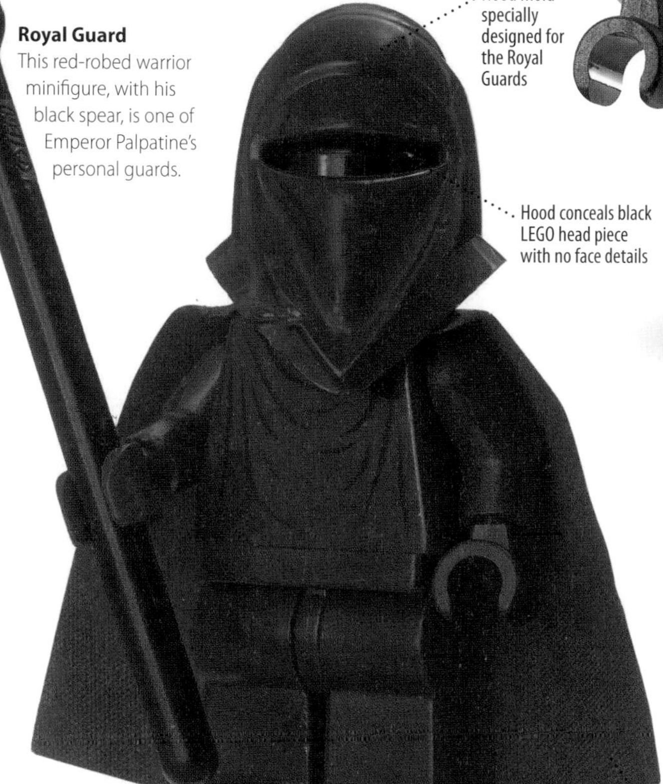
Hood mold specially designed for the Royal Guards
Hood conceals black LEGO head piece with no face details
Red cloth cape unique to *Star Wars* Royal Guards

Royal Guard This red-robed warrior minifigure, with his black spear, is one of Emperor Palpatine's personal guards.

Ventilated space helmet

Utility belt with blaster power cell reserves

Stormtrooper This year saw the debut of the original Stormtrooper minifigure. There would be many future variants.

Imperial TIE emblem on helmet
Special black armor with life support system

TIE Pilot The original variant of the Imperial Pilot flies the much feared TIE Fighter (7146).

Simple black uniform with belt

Imperial Pilot This minifigure pilots Emperor Palpatine's Shuttle (7166). Later variants are much less cheerful!

LEGO
7166
STAR WARS
IMPERIAL SHUTTLE

Imperial Shuttle (7166) Palpatine's infamous space ship was introduced in 2001 along with four minifigures including two Royal Guards.

Plain head, wings and torso fit over standard LEGO torso

Watto Appearing only in Watto's Junkyard (7186), this minifigure variant of the winged Toydarian junkyard dealer is both unique and rare.

LEGO® SOCCER

The Women's Team, a brand new set in the LEGO Soccer theme, was released in conjunction with the Women's European Soccer Championships, this year held in Germany. No new pieces were used, but it scored a memorable first nevertheless: a women's team had never before appeared in a LEGO Soccer set.

Having a team hairstyle gives players a sense of solidarity.
LET'S GET IT IN THE LEGO NET!
Plain blue Women's Team jersey

Blonde Player Women are said to be good at multitasking, but this girl has one aim—putting the ball in the back of the net! She's playing with her teammates for the first time in the Women's Team (3416) and they're going for goal.

Ponytail detail on hair piece
Country flag sticker can be stuck here.

Black-haired Player This defender is ready to tackle anything—or anyone—the opposition might throw at her.

Spending hours outdoors has given her freckles.

Brunette Player It takes more than 90 minutes to win a match. This minifigure trains for hours every day in her yellow team bib.

Same cap worn by male goalkeepers

Goalie The Goalie, with smiling LEGO face, looks more carefree than her pals. She's a safe pair of hands and she knows it!

2001

LEGO STUDIOS

Fans had gone wild for the LEGO Studios Steven Spielberg MovieMaker set in 2000. To follow up on its success, 14 more sets were released this year, all designed to be part of LEGO fans' homemade films. Two of the sets were based on the making of the *Jurassic Park III* movie, with LEGO® Adventurers Johnny Thunder and Pippin Reed taking the place of the real stars.

Aviator's cap with padded ear flaps

Stubble adds to tough-guy image.

Padded jacket protects him from scrapes

Stunt Man The Stunt Man Catapult (1356) includes a launcher to propel this fearless minifigure over a wall of fire.

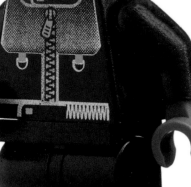

LEGO
STUDIOS
JURASSIC PARK III
1370

Raptor Rumble Studio (1370) As part of the Studios Jurassic Park III theme, this set includes Johnny Thunder, Pippin Reed, and a cameraman, as well as two raptors and a pteranodon.

Cap shades her face so the sun doesn't melt her makeup

Backpack clips onto the back of torso

Compass worn on safari shirt

Pippin Reed This one of many variants of the Pippin Reed minifigure is ready for some dino-dodging action in the Raptor Rumble Studio (1370).

LEGO® TOWN

It turned out to be an unusually quiet year for the usually bustling LEGO Town. Only three sets were released: two promotional Airport models (1100 and 2718) and a reissue of 1992's Gas N'Wash (6472).

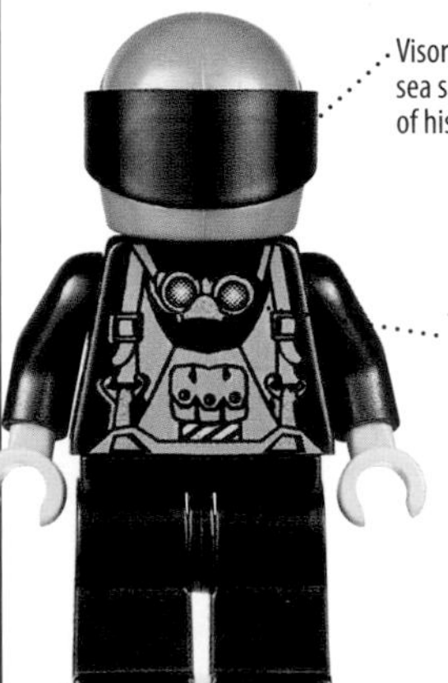

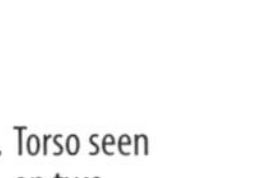

Visor keeps sea spray out of his eyes.

Torso seen on two minifigures in 1999 to 2000, in the Rock Raiders theme

Pockets and wrench detail hidden under life preserver

Town Worker Also part of the Sky Pirates (1100), this minifigure stays afloat, with or without a boat, in her life preserver.

Boat Driver In full protective gear, this minifigure is happy to fly or sail in the face of danger in the Sky Pirates (1100).

Sky Pirates (1100) This promotional set includes two minifigures, an airplane, a dock, a speed boat, and a white shark.

LEGO
1100
Specially made for Airline Companies

LEGO® TIME TEACHING CLOCK

Young fans could now learn to tell the time with a buildable clock. It came with a minifigure whose collection of hats included a chef's hat for meal times, a baseball cap for play times, and a ghost mask for bedtimes!

Wizard's hat shows that it's time for learning

Pocket to hold tools for mending the clock

Clock Man This minifigure always has time for LEGO fans. Designed to fit on top of a working clock, he only appears this year. He has a standard LEGO head and blue legs.

QUICKY

Quicky the bunny is the cute mascot of Nesquik®, Nestlé's popular flavored milk drink. His minifigure, which appeared in three promotional sets under the LEGO Studios banner, was designed to show an actor portraying Quicky for a movie.

Rabbit mask fits over a white head piece
"N" for Nestlé

Quicky The torso, head, and bunny mask are exclusive to this minifigure.

GRRR! DON'T YOU KNOW WHO I AM?
Hat with turned up side brim
Long, striped sideburns grown for the role
Tattered jacket and vest from a 1999 role as a Ninja robber

Mustachioed Actor Determined to stay in character, this minifigure grimly maintains a fierce scowl. He appears in his own Actor 3 set (4065), playing the role of a robber.

Casual outfit can be swapped for a costume

Actress This red-haired minifigure appears in her own Studios themed polybag set (4062).

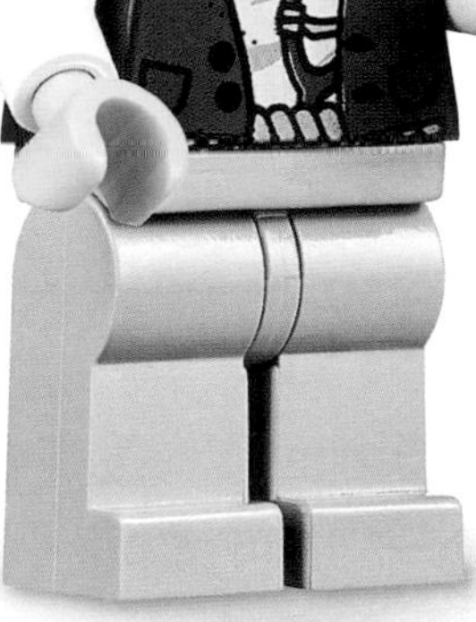
A slingshot is a key part of an explorer's costume

Actor Always camera ready, the actor has the same head as Mike from the Adventurers theme, in 2002.

DID YOU KNOW?
Movies made using LEGO elements in stop-motion are called "Brickfilms."

Headset for communicating with crew
ID badge

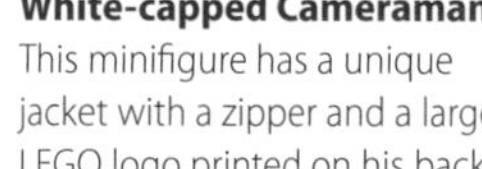

White-capped Cameraman This minifigure has a unique jacket with a zipper and a large LEGO logo printed on his back.

Pen for taking notes

Female Assistant The reverse of this minifigure's torso features a large movie clapboard.

Screwdriver close to hand

Grip This versatile technician minifigure has three variants, and he appears in three sets.

Camera crew ID card
Pen clipped inside pocket

Red-capped Cameraman The Cameraman has the same head piece as Docs from the Rock Raiders theme in 1999.

LEGO® DUPLO®

LEGO DUPLO was on a roll in 2001. The new sets released included six *Winnie the Pooh*™ sets and six for the new *Bob the Builder* line, which would last for eight years.

Coveralls have heart-shaped buttons: she loves her job!

Female DUPLO Figure This unique figure has red hair—and a green thumb! She tends the flowers in the Growing Garden (3088) from the LEGO DUPLO Town theme.

LEGO DUPLO BOB THE BUILDER™

This popular figure from the self-titled British television series made his debut in his own subtheme this year. Can he fix it? Yes, he can!

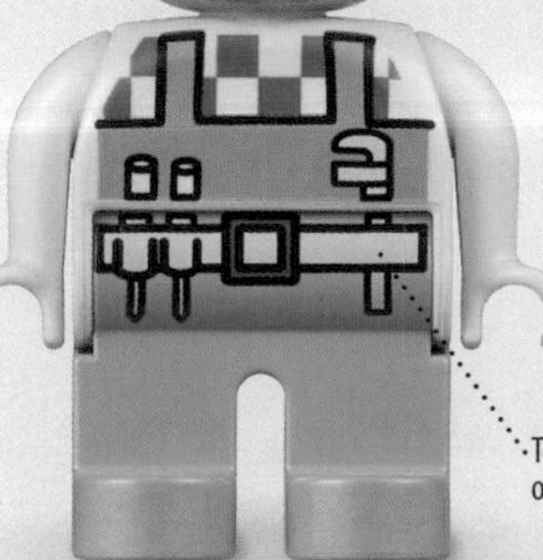
Tool belt and overalls

Bob This handy man never goes anywhere without his trusty tool belt and hard hat.

MY UNIT IS ME, MYSELF, AND I.

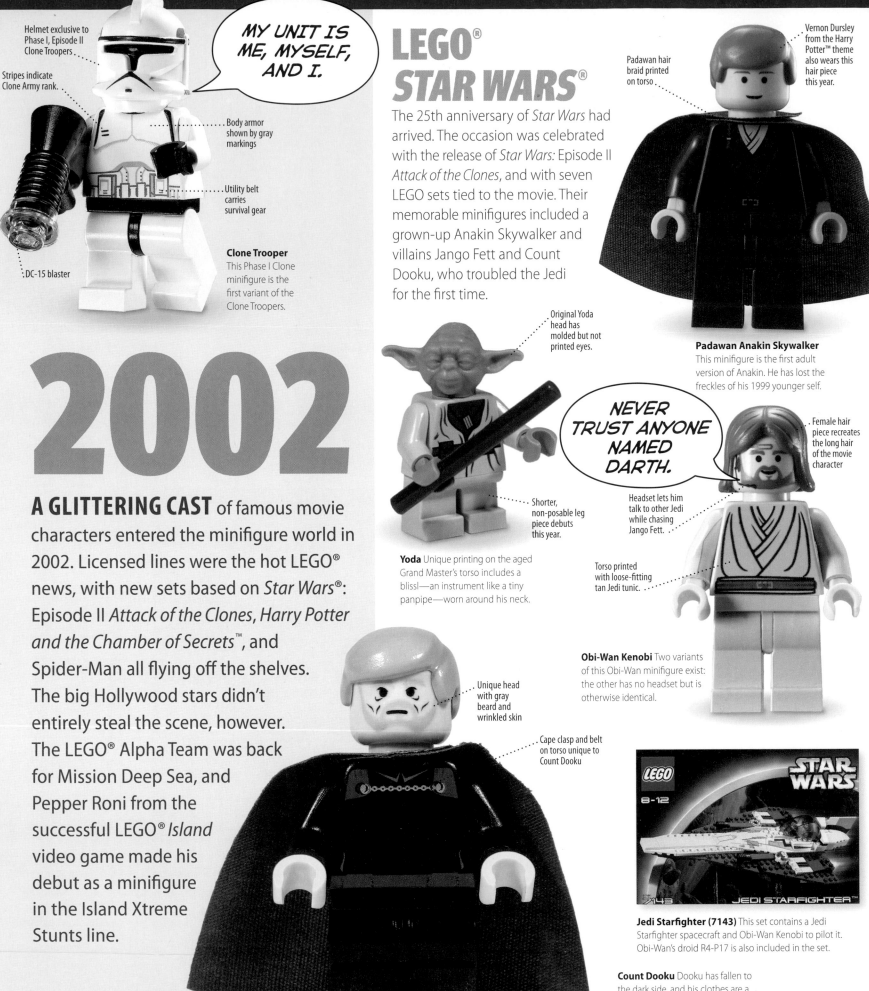

Helmet exclusive to Phase I, Episode II Clone Troopers
Stripes indicate Clone Army rank.
Body armor shown by gray markings
Utility belt carries survival gear
DC-15 blaster

Clone Trooper This Phase I Clone minifigure is the first variant of the Clone Troopers.

2002

A GLITTERING CAST of famous movie characters entered the minifigure world in 2002. Licensed lines were the hot LEGO® news, with new sets based on *Star Wars*®: Episode II *Attack of the Clones*, *Harry Potter and the Chamber of Secrets*™, and Spider-Man all flying off the shelves. The big Hollywood stars didn't entirely steal the scene, however. The LEGO® Alpha Team was back for Mission Deep Sea, and Pepper Roni from the successful LEGO® *Island* video game made his debut as a minifigure in the Island Xtreme Stunts line.

LEGO® STAR WARS®

The 25th anniversary of *Star Wars* had arrived. The occasion was celebrated with the release of *Star Wars:* Episode II *Attack of the Clones*, and with seven LEGO sets tied to the movie. Their memorable minifigures included a grown-up Anakin Skywalker and villains Jango Fett and Count Dooku, who troubled the Jedi for the first time.

Padawan hair braid printed on torso
Vernon Dursley from the Harry Potter™ theme also wears this hair piece this year.

Padawan Anakin Skywalker This minifigure is the first adult version of Anakin. He has lost the freckles of his 1999 younger self.

Original Yoda head has molded but not printed eyes.

Shorter, non-posable leg piece debuts this year.

Yoda Unique printing on the aged Grand Master's torso includes a blissl—an instrument like a tiny panpipe—worn around his neck.

NEVER TRUST ANYONE NAMED DARTH.

Female hair piece recreates the long hair of the movie character

Headset lets him talk to other Jedi while chasing Jango Fett.

Torso printed with loose-fitting tan Jedi tunic.

Obi-Wan Kenobi Two variants of this Obi-Wan minifigure exist: the other has no headset but is otherwise identical.

Unique head with gray beard and wrinkled skin
Cape clasp and belt on torso unique to Count Dooku

LEGO
STAR WARS
8-12
7143
JEDI STARFIGHTER™

Jedi Starfighter (7143) This set contains a Jedi Starfighter spacecraft and Obi-Wan Kenobi to pilot it. Obi-Wan's droid R4-P17 is also included in the set.

Count Dooku Dooku has fallen to the dark side, and his clothes are a little on the dark side too—they are all black or brown. His minifigure came with Jedi Duel (7103).

IF ONLY THERE WERE MORE OF ME...
J-12 jetpack and helmet are one piece
Boba's face is a childish version of Jango's.
Custom-made blasters are actually LEGO revolvers
Short LEGO legs are unposable.

Young Boba Fett Yoda and this child variant of Jango's clone son are the first minifigures to feature the short LEGO legs.

Jango Fett A minifigure mercenary and bounty hunter, Jango appears in set 7153. His head is plain black on one side with a stubbly face and balaclava outline on the other side.

BATTLE DROIDS

Although the Separatist Battle Droids had appeared as LEGO figures before, this was the first year for Super Battle Droids and Droidekas. The Clone Wars were about to get a lot tougher!

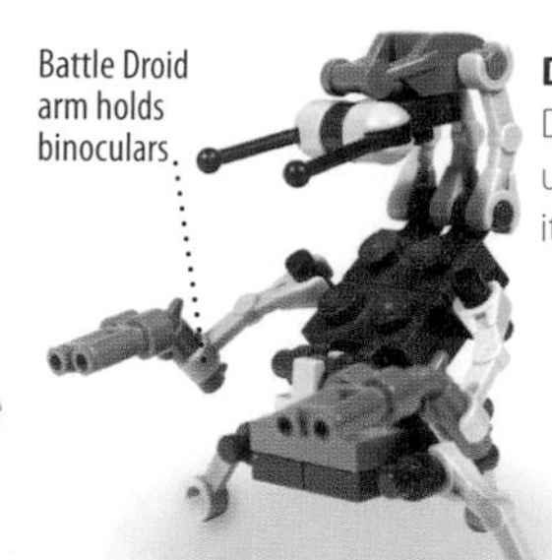
Battle Droid arm holds binoculars

Droideka This heavy Destroyer Droid is made up of 26 pieces, including its weapons.

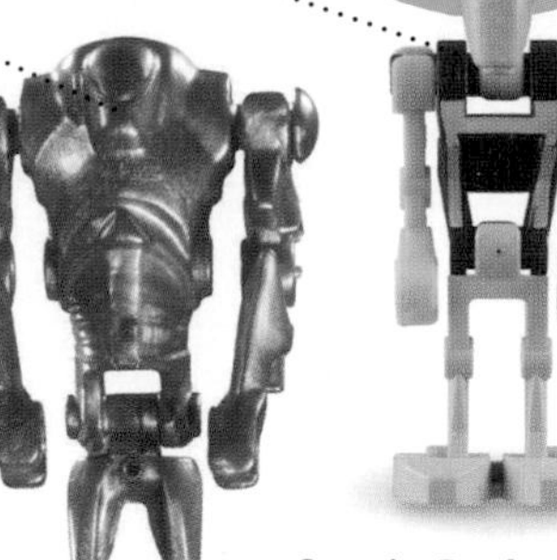
Head is molded as part of torso.
Head clips on to shoulder section of torso

Super Battle Droid Towering over ordinary Battle Droids, this imposing figure boasts all-new parts in a unique metal blue color.

Security Battle Droid A red torso identifies this Battle Droid as one of a few advanced enough to act as prison guards.

Veil worn by Zam when she is posing as a human

Unique torso and hips with specialized equipment and armor

Zam Wesell Like Jango, Zam is a bounty hunter. Unlike him, she is also a Clawdite shapeshifter, so her minifigure head has both a human face and a reptilian Clawdite one.

Mask and goggles offer protection from sun and sand
Humidifer to make dry air easier to breathe

Tusken Raider This mysterious minifigure moves through deserts in his sand-colored shroud and crossed utility belt.

LEGO® SPIDER-MAN™

The web-head swung into the LEGO lineup for the first time, as a subtheme of LEGO® Studios. The Spider-Man Action Studio (1376) featured the first Spider-Man and Peter Parker minifigures, and Green Goblin (1374) included the Green Goblin and Mary Jane. Fans could now drop Spidey into a variety of sticky situations in their own stop-motion movies.

Removable neck bracket goes here.
Spider-Man's classic hero costume with spider logo
Red gloves ensure that Spidey's body is fully protected.

Spider-Man The first ever version of Spider-Man features an exclusive neck bracket, which allows him to "stick" to walls.

DID YOU KNOW?
LEGO Spider-Man minifigures are the most popular characters to feature in fan films.

Features not printed on mask

Green Goblin Mask

Green Goblin Spidey's archenemy, Norman Osborn, hides his identity under a grotesque mask. Sadly, his minifigure face isn't much prettier. Armor is printed on his legs and torso.

Peter's trademark glasses
Zipper jacket print on torso

Peter Parker Spider-Man's alter ego has a two-sided head—one with glasses, one without.

Chinese design on torso

Two-sided head piece: happy and scared

Mary Jane Watson Peter's red-haired love interest is dressed for a trip to the carnival in the Green Goblin set (1374).

LEGO® EXPLORE® BOB THE BUILDER™

LEGO DUPLO became known as LEGO Explore in 2002 to 2003. In this theme, Bob and his crew returned with five sets in 2002. The one new character was Spud, a mischievous scarecrow who always wants to help, yet somehow makes things worse.

No hair piece
Scarf is also printed on the back

Spud This scarecrow doesn't want to scare anyone, he just wants to make friends!

Head is not detachable

Tool belt worn over blue jumpsuit

Wendy Bob's good friend Wendy is a builder herself, and wears a utility belt with tools on her waist.

2002

LEGO® HARRY POTTER™

The boy wizard returned for a second magical year in 2002. This time, the sets focused not just on Hogwarts, but on other places in Harry's world too, such as the family house of Harry's Muggle relatives, the Dursleys. Ten sets were released based on the second movie, *Harry Potter and the Chamber of Secrets*™, with three more based on the first movie, *Harry Potter and the Sorcerer's Stone*™.

SORCERER'S STONE

The new *Harry Potter and the Sorcerer's Stone*™ sets introduced two new species: goblins and trolls. Goblins would return in 2011.

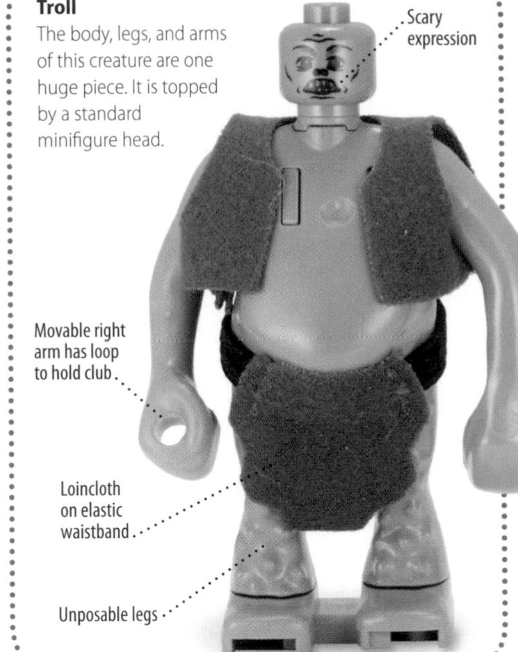

Scary expression
Movable right arm has loop to hold club
Loincloth on elastic waistband
Unposable legs

Troll The body, legs, and arms of this creature are one huge piece. It is topped by a standard minifigure head.

Specially molded head
Bank teller's uniform

Goblin This short-legged minifigure is an employee in Gringotts Bank (4714).

Casual zippered plaid jacket

Ron Weasley™ This is the last minifigure of Ron to feature a yellow head and the only variant released in 2002.

Cute freckles
Gryffindor crest

Ginny Weasley™ As a first-year student at Hogwarts, Ginny gets her first minifigure. It is her only variant to feature a yellow head.

CHAMBER OF SECRETS

The 2002 LEGO Harry Potter sets had several new minifigures, including Dobby the house-elf, Professor McGonagall, Professor Lockhart, Tom Riddle, Lucius Malfoy, and Madam Hooch, plus three new variants of Harry.

DID YOU KNOW? Professor McGonagall is the only LEGO Harry Potter minifigure to wear a green wizard's hat.

Gilderoy Lockhart™ The ornately printed torso and light-pink hips and legs are unique to this minifigure.

Groomed blond hair
Carefully chosen pink outfit

Elaborate gold design on vest

Green Lockhart This stylish variant of the professor is seen in two LEGO Harry Potter sets in this year (4733 and HPG01—a promotional release in Hong Kong).

Pilot's goggles

Madam Hooch™ The gray striped robe is unique to this variant of the Hogwarts flying instructor.

Green wizard's hat
Spell book
Face has wrinkle printing

Professor McGonagall™ This strict professor's printed sloped piece was seen in two sets released this year (4729 and HPG04—a promotional set).

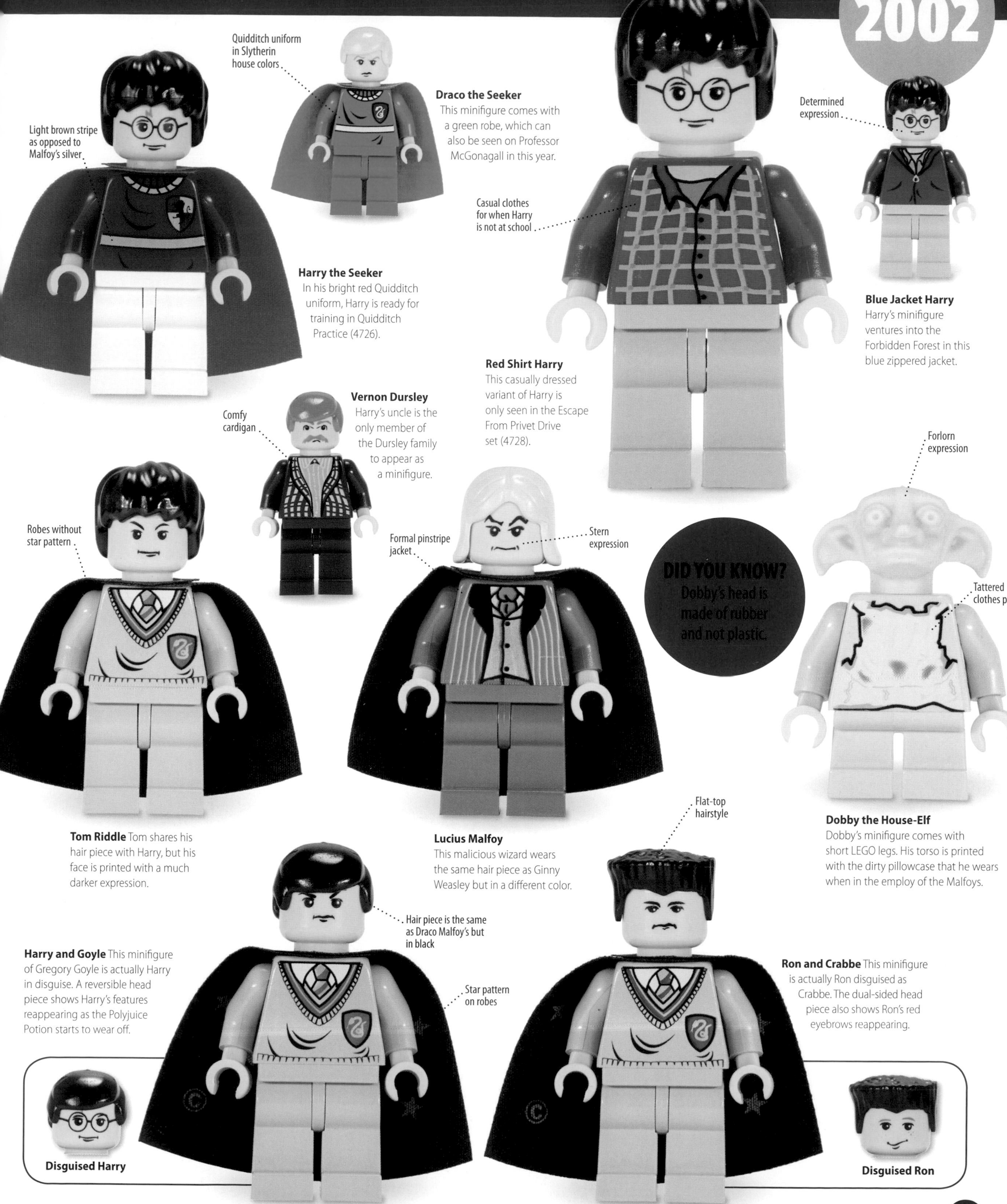
2002
Quidditch uniform in Slytherin house colors
Light brown stripe as opposed to Malfoy's silver
Draco the Seeker This minifigure comes with a green robe, which can also be seen on Professor McGonagall in this year.
Determined expression
Casual clothes for when Harry is not at school
Harry the Seeker In his bright red Quidditch uniform, Harry is ready for training in Quidditch Practice (4726).
Blue Jacket Harry Harry's minifigure ventures into the Forbidden Forest in this blue zippered jacket.
Red Shirt Harry This casually dressed variant of Harry is only seen in the Escape From Privet Drive set (4728).
Vernon Dursley Harry's uncle is the only member of the Dursley family to appear as a minifigure.
Comfy cardigan
Forlorn expression
Robes without star pattern
Formal pinstripe jacket
Stern expression
DID YOU KNOW? Dobby's head is made of rubber and not plastic.
Tattered clothes print
Flat-top hairstyle
Tom Riddle Tom shares his hair piece with Harry, but his face is printed with a much darker expression.
Lucius Malfoy This malicious wizard wears the same hair piece as Ginny Weasley but in a different color.
Dobby the House-Elf Dobby's minifigure comes with short LEGO legs. His torso is printed with the dirty pillowcase that he wears when in the employ of the Malfoys.
Hair piece is the same as Draco Malfoy's but in black
Harry and Goyle This minifigure of Gregory Goyle is actually Harry in disguise. A reversible head piece shows Harry's features reappearing as the Polyjuice Potion starts to wear off.
Star pattern on robes
Ron and Crabbe This minifigure is actually Ron disguised as Crabbe. The dual-sided head piece also shows Ron's red eyebrows reappearing.
Disguised Harry
Disguised Ron

2002

LEGO ALPHA TEAM

Ogel took his evil beneath the waves in the second year of Alpha Team, entitled Mission Deep Sea. His plan: use his orbs to mutate sea creatures into monstrous slaves. It took all of Alpha Team's skill, and some awesome underwater vehicles, to put a stop to this foul plan.

Helmet with diving mask
Oxygen tubes
Detachable flippers

Dash Justice With a determined, steely look in his eyes, this minifigure is looking forward to taking on the evil Ogel.

SEA SAVIORS

All of Alpha Team was back in 2002, with new undersea gear and high-tech weaponry. Sixteen new sets came out this year, many of them featuring mutant sea creatures.

Stubble

Crunch Explosives expert Crunch has been underwater for so long, he just hasn't found the time to shave.

Communication unit for talking to the team

Pockets for storing equipment

Radia The 2002 version of Radia has purple hair and the 2004 version has black hair—she gets bored easily!

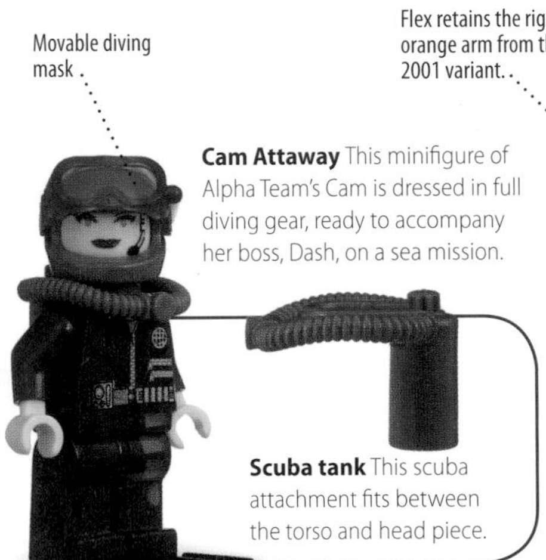
Movable diving mask

Cam Attaway This minifigure of Alpha Team's Cam is dressed in full diving gear, ready to accompany her boss, Dash, on a sea mission.

Scuba tank This scuba attachment fits between the torso and head piece.

Flex retains the right orange arm from the 2001 variant.
Huge smile

Flex Scuba-diving Flex is happiest working the Sub-Surface Scooter (set 4791), as can be seen from his huge grin.

LEGO Alpha Team logo
Vital diving equipment

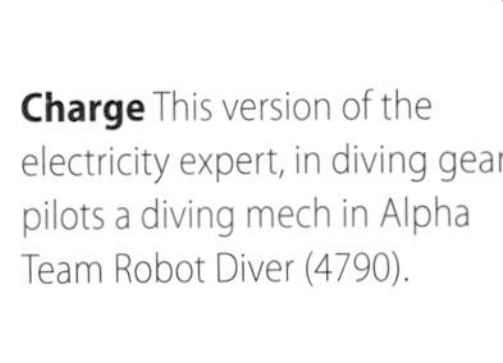

Charge This version of the electricity expert, in diving gear, pilots a diving mech in Alpha Team Robot Diver (4790).

SEA VILLAINS

Ogel returned with modified versions of his skeleton drones and orbs, plus new underwater vehicles and sea creatures at his command. But it wasn't enough to win!

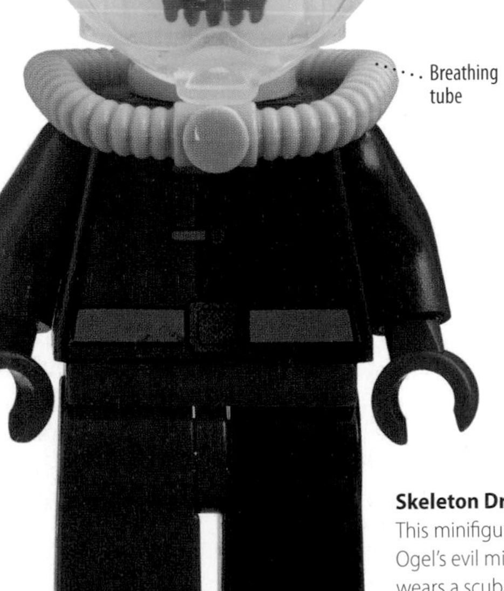
Skeleton face markings
Breathing tube

Skeleton Drone This minifigure of Ogel's evil minion wears a scuba tank and helmet to carry out his deadly underwater mission.

Armor with shoulder protection
Red hook

Ogel The criminal mastermind's left hand has been replaced with a red hook after he lost it in an earlier confrontation with the Alpha Team. He doesn't look very happy about it!

Bubble-shaped, trans-neon green helmet
Red and black uniform is the same as the 2001 version

Commander The medal print on the torso of this minifigure indicates that he is the appointed commander of the Skeleton Drones.

LEGO
Alpha Team
4797
MISSION DEEP SEA

Ogel Mutant Killer Whale (4797) This underwater set comes with one Skeleton Drone minifigure.

LEGO® SOCCER

Soccer was king for the third year, with sets tied to the 2002 FIFA World Cup™ and a new version of the LEGO Championship Challenge (3420). The Grand Championship Cup (3425) was the largest Soccer set ever released, with 22 minifigures, and would be the last LEGO Soccer stadium set for four years.

JE JOUE AU FOOT. ALLEZ LES BLEUS!
Rooster logo on jersey
French Football Federation logo

French Soccer Player This player sports the French team colors of blue, red, and white. His legs display the Adidas logo.

New style v-neck football shirt

Goalie Appearing in a promotional set (4453), the Goalie always looks mean to scare the opposition.

Mustache print

Red Stripe Defender From the Defender 3 set (4448), this Defender minifigure makes sure the Goalie doesn't have to work too hard.

V-neck football strip

Black Stripe Defender From the Defender 1 set (4443), this minifigure shares the same head piece as many other players.

Neatly combed hair

Silver Coca-Cola Player This player takes it easy on the field—he doesn't want to get his uniform dirty!

Pearl-gold strip

Gold Coca-Cola Player This minifigure tries to be aggressive during the match—but he's a nice guy off the field.

SOCCER WORLD CUP

The 2002 FIFA World Cup™ in Japan and South Korea was sponsored by Coca-Cola. A number of small sets with soccer player minifigures with Coca-Cola logos were released as a tie-in.

LEGO® CASTLE

This was a relatively quiet year for LEGO Castle—only two sets were released. Black Falcon's Fortress (10039) was a re-release of a 1986 set, and Blacksmith Shop (3739) was a fan-designed model available only through the LEGO Shop At Home website. These would be the last Castle sets until 2004.

Shiny scale mail
Ruby necklace
Perfect princess curls

Blacksmith There are two things that this minifigure takes great pride in: the armor he makes and his mustache.

Maiden This minifigure works at the Blacksmith Shop (3739) with the Blacksmith. She keeps the keys to the shop, as the Blacksmith is always losing them!

DID YOU KNOW? The Blacksmith Shop was released as a "My Own Creation" set, since it was fan-designed.

LEGO® SPACE

These two promotional minifigures hold a special place in LEGO history. Following their appearance at the World Space Congress, images of them were launched into space on the NASA Mars Exploration Rovers *Spirit* and *Opportunity* in 2003.

Classic LEGO® helmet with chrome visor

Biff Starling It's not obvious, but this minifigure is nervous—he's hoping he doesn't meet any Blacktron astronauts on his misson.

Torso pattern exclusive to these two minifigures
Gold ribbing

Sandy Moondust This space robot or "astrobot" shares a torso with only one other minifigure—her space colleague, Biff Starling.

2002

LEGO® STUDIOS

The monsters came out to howl in 2002, as LEGO Studios unleashed four horror movie sets. The Mummy, the Vampire, the Monster, and the Werewolf were all there—along with directors, cameramen, and actors and actresses to be the "victims." It was all good film fun, and also the first time there had ever been a Vampire minifigure.

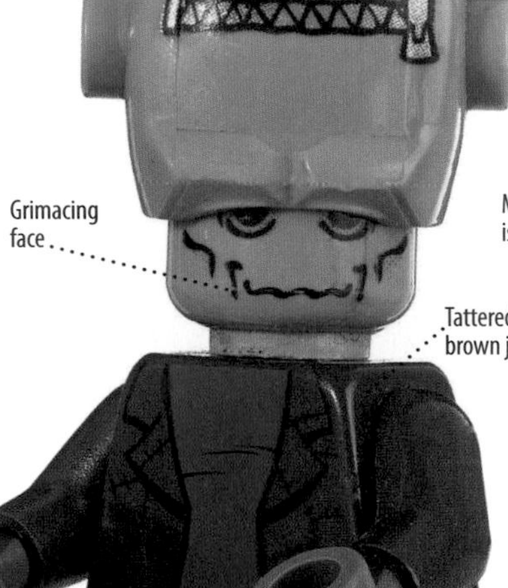

Back of head piece is also zippered
Grimacing face
Tattered brown jacket

Frankenstein's Monster The head gear on this minifigure is an extension of the monster's forehead. The zipper keeps the contents of his head from spilling out!

Manic grin is sinister
Stethoscope pattern

Mad Scientist This mad minifigure works in the Scary Laboratory (1382). He has a double-sided head —with glasses and without glasses.

Hefty mask fits over head piece
Ripped shirt

Werewolf Exclusive to Werewolf Ambush (1380), this isn't really a werewolf—it's a minifigure actor dressed in a werewolf mask for a scary movie.

Headdress is exclusive to this minifigure, but is similar to the ones from the Adventurers theme in 1998
Lips stitched up
Bandage pattern extends to legs

Mummy This bandaged mummy minifigure is part of only one set—Curse of the Pharaoh (1383).

Hair piece is new this year. It's also seen on Wolverine from the Marvel Super Heroes theme in 2012.
White, lifeless hands

Vampire This scary Vampire is thirsty for minifigure blood! Turn his head around to see his mouth open, ready for a bite.

The Hunchback only has one tooth remaining
White rope keeps shirt in place

Hunchback Carrying a basket on his back, the poor Hunchback has a uniquely grotesque torso and head piece.

LEGO® RACERS

LEGO Racers spun off from Town Race in 2001. This year brought Drome Racers, a subtheme that featured an extensive story and multiple minifigure characters. Centering on a vast indoor racing arena called the Drome, it featured six teams racing for glory. Each instruction booklet included a Drome Racers comic.

I WAS BORN TO WIN!

Horned, black and yellow design

Nitro Flash Driver This control freak minifigure isn't happy—his race car is remote controlled, in RC-Nitro Flash (4589).

Seven stars pattern on helmet
Right arm different color from left

Scorcher Although his torso says "4," this minifigure always comes 1st in the Hot Scorcher set (4584).

Race jacket pattern new for this year

Red Duel Racer This racer takes on Orange Driver in Dual Racers (4587).

Finish flag on helmet

Orange Driver The mustached driver is so confident he'll finish the race, he has a checkered flag printed on his helmet.

Striped green helmet to look like a snake
Jacket pattern with straps

Storming Cobra From the Storming Cobra set (4596), this racer minifigure drives a green racing car over a ramp—just for fun.

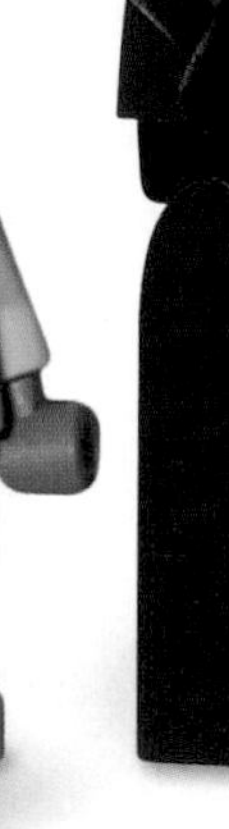

Monobrow and stubble on face

Nitro Driver This racer drives the Nitro Pulverizer vehicle (4585), which can be combined with the car from Hot Scorcher (4584) to form a dragster.

LEGO® *ISLAND XTREME STUNTS*

Based on the successful LEGO *Island* and LEGO *Island 2* video games, the new theme Xtreme Stunts introduced pizza delivery guy and ace skateboarder Pepper Roni and his enemy, the Brickster, in minifigure form. The sets combined skateboard, boat, and all-terrain vehicle (ATV) stunts with Pepper's efforts to keep LEGO Island safe. After 2002, the theme only featured three promotional sets.

Surfer dudes love a flowery pattern
Cool sunglasses with silver rim
WANT YOUR PIZZA WITH A SIDE OF KICKFLIPS?
Pizza pattern on torso
Knee pads protect from falls

Snap Lockitt The flowery pattern on Snap's torso fits in well with the lifeguard's laidback nature.

Pepper Roni A skateboard expert, Pepper Roni keeps the Island safe from criminals. He is also a pizza delivery boy.

STUNT MANIACS

Pepper was joined by all his friends from the PC game, including Sky Lane and Snap Lockitt. This theme used a bracket and bar system to allow the minifigures to perform their stunts, similar to the LEGO® Gravity Games™ stunt sticks introduced in 2003.

Standard police cap
White mustache
Stylish red vest and bow tie
Infomaniac's 1999 variant has black pants

Infomaniac
The creator of LEGO Island has a reverse italicized "i" logo on his torso for his name. He appears only in one set this year—Xtreme Tower (6740).

Tube top with string ties
Bar attaches to stud on neck bracket

Neck bracket A bar fits into the stud on the back of the neck bracket so that Sky can do her daring skateboard stunts.

Sky Lane Pepper Roni's daring friend often helps him fight criminals. She wears a neck bracket while performing stunts.

LEGO
ISLAND XTREME STUNTS
6740

Xtreme Tower (6740) The largest set released this year from this theme, it includes six minifigures, the Xtreme Tower, a helicopter, and a skateboard.

DID YOU KNOW?
A lucky few LEGO Group employees carry customized minifigures with their names on them instead of business cards.

MISCHIEF-MAKERS

The Brickster has a very simple plan: take LEGO Island apart by stealing every brick in the place, with the help of his henchmen. Fortunately, Pepper is around to stop him!

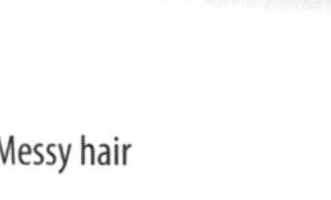

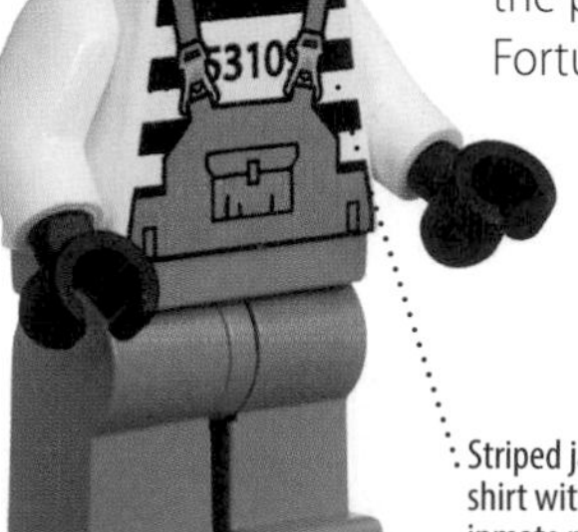

Messy hair
Striped jail shirt with inmate number

Young Henchman
This Henchman minifigure isn't as confused as Old Henchman—yet.

Black bandana
Confused expression
Gray goatee

Old Henchman Acting as Brickster's sidekick just gets more confusing with each day that passes....

STICK 'EM UP AND GIMME ALL THE BRICKS YOU HAVE.
Green eyes seen through glasses
Jail stripes pattern common on all three con men
23768
Prison number
Blue glove on left hand

Brickster LEGO *Island Xtreme Stunts'* main villain is always scheming to escape from jail and steal bricks from other buildings on the Island.

I'M GOING TO BLOW THIS CASE WIDE OPEN!

Gray beard
New torso complete with rumpled shirt and gold badge

Police Chief Late nights working a case in the Police HQ (7035) has added wrinkles to the Police Chief's minifigure head.

2003

THE LEGO® MINIFIGURE celebrated its 25th birthday in grand style. After decades of only yellow minifigures, the iconic characters got a major redesign as natural skin tones were introduced. Minifigures of popular NBA players, such as Kobe Bryant, were the first to receive this more realistic treatment. Other licensed minifigures from LEGO® *Star Wars*®, LEGO® *Indiana Jones*™, and LEGO *Spider-Man*™ would soon follow suit. 2003 also saw big changes in LEGO® Town, LEGO® Sports expanded to include a wider range of sports, including LEGO® Soccer, and the most ambitious LEGO® Adventurers line ever was released.

LEGO® WORLD CITY

LEGO Town became LEGO World City in 2003, and the emphasis was on action. Police and Fire sets dominated, with Trains still playing a role, while Construction and Airport took a back seat for a short while. World City would last for two years, before being replaced by LEGO® City.

Knitted cap
Wicked smile revealing a gold tooth

Torso with inmate number is new and unique to this minifigure
50380

Jail Prisoner Unfortunately for this jailbird, he was arrested and has been locked up in the Police HQ (7035).

POLICE

The World City Police featured in six sets in 2003, including a new Police HQ (7035) and a Surveillance Truck (7034). Only two of the sets contained criminal minifigures.

I SPEND ALL DAY STUCK IN TRAFFIC.
Wireless radio
Golden buttons on collar

Highway Patrol Officer This minifigure works with the Highway Patrol and Undercover team—nothing gets past his minifigure eyes.

Police Officer A smiling Policeman is always reassuring. This one is from the Police HQ (7035).

Silver sunglasses for flying in sunny skies

Police Pilot The Police Pilot fights crime from the skies, and he looks cool doing it, with new silver shades and a leather jacket.

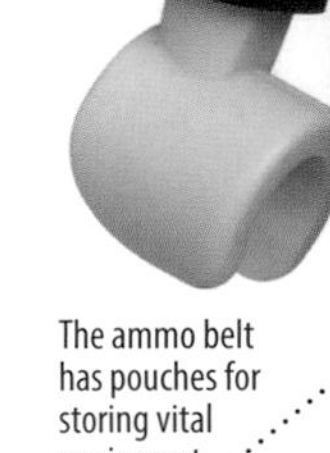
Scowling head piece is new this year

Bike Patrolman It looks like the Bike Patrolman has spotted some minifigures speeding!

He has the same smiling head as the Police Officer.
Patrolman torso is new this year
Radio to call for backup
The ammo belt has pouches for storing vital equipment.

Capped Patrolman This Patrolman is smiling for a reason—not only does he appear in World City set Squad Car (7030), he also gets to help Spider-Man chase a thief in Spider-Man's First Chase (4850).

Same head as the Jail Prisoner
Raised eyebrow looks menacing

Car Bandit The crafty Car Bandit tries to make a quick getaway with stolen money, gold, and jewels in Armored Car Action (7033).

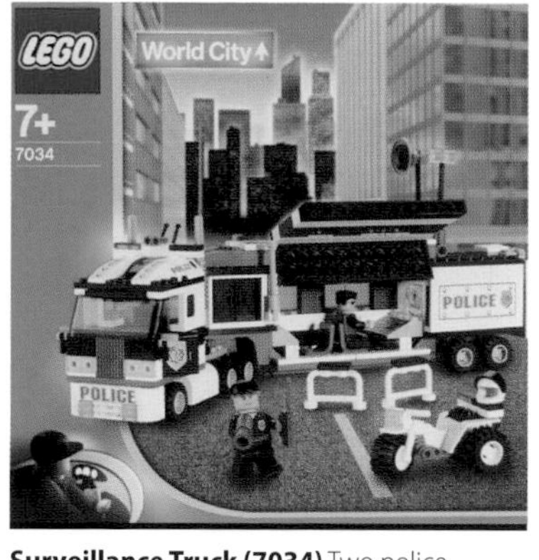
LEGO
World City
7+
7034
POLICE

Surveillance Truck (7034) Two police minifigures man this truck, which includes a semi-trailer complete with work station, plus a trike for speedy missions.

Tinted glasses protect the eyes

Utility belt with radio

Printed torso Underneath his vest, the new torso of the Security Guard has a gold badge and utility belt.

Security Guard The blue bulletproof vest protects the Security Guard's minifigure torso from any attacks.

FIRE

The World City Fire team hit the waves in a new Fire Command Craft (7046). The theme included the fire chief minifigure in a rescue boat and two firefighters on board to battle blazes on the high seas.

Orange flotation vest

Circular saw to cut through hulls and rescue trapped crews

Smiling Firefighter Exclusive to set 7046, the Firefighter wears his flotation vest and uniform with pride.

It's safety first with this white helmet

Radio keeps him in touch with main craft

Reflective stripe pattern under vest

Firefighter This Firefighter is fearless, but he's also sensible— while on rescue missions at sea he always wears a flotation vest.

DID YOU KNOW? The deck of the ship in Fire Command Craft (7046) can be lifted to access a command center.

New head with brown beard
New firefighter's badge
Hot drink to revive rescuees

Fireboat Captain Captaining the Fireboat can be stressful—but this minifigure always has a smile on his new head piece.

Radio antenna

Captain's cabin

Water hose pipe for tackling big blazes

Rescue boat hose

Fire Command Craft (7046) A fire-fighting ship fitted with three hoses, a rescue boat, and three firefighting minifigures featured in this set.

2003 LEGO TOWN CONTINUED

COAST GUARD

The only Coast Guard sets released in a span of 10 years, Coast Watch HQ (7047) and Hovercraft Hideout (7045) featured plenty of World City action as the heroes confronted smugglers for the first time.

Blades rotate on pivot
Intake ports move chopper forward
Cockpit seats two minifigures
Floating pads allow landing and take off from water
CW-7044

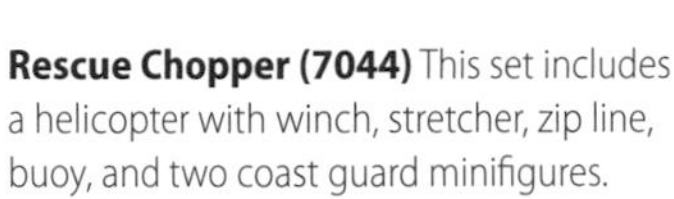

Rescue Chopper (7044) This set includes a helicopter with winch, stretcher, zip line, buoy, and two coast guard minifigures.

Protective helmet with black visor
Black clip element from helicopter
Orange sunglasses
Zip line handle
New torso with LEGO® Coast Guard emblem
Orange Coast Guard full-body uniform
New head complete with high cheekbones and chin dimple
Air pressure gauge
Flipper for swimming to the rescue

Pilot Minifigure pilot to the rescue! No emergency is too big for this coast guard, in Rescue Chopper (7044).

Co-Pilot The Co-Pilot wears orange sunglasses to match his uniform—well, he thinks he looks cool.

Buggy Driver This minifigure spends his days on the beach—not building sand castles, but patrolling it, in Dune Patrol (7042).

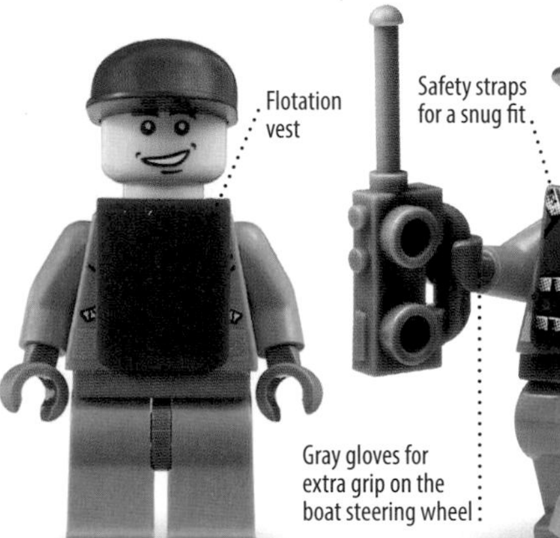
Flotation vest
Safety straps for a snug fit
Gray gloves for extra grip on the boat steering wheel

Hair piece also seen on Charge from the LEGO® Alpha Team subtheme in 2001
Serious head piece is new this year

Power Boat Driver
The Power Boat driver doesn't take any risks when on a mission—he dons a cap and flotation vest in set 7047.

New Boat Driver The Boat Driver is very happy indeed—he's the only minifigure to wear this new stickered flotation vest, exclusive to set 7047.

Coast Guard
Coast guarding is a serious business—as you can tell from this minifigure's pursed lips.

LUCKILY FOR ME, PLASTIC FLOATS.
Silver sunglasses shield eyes from sun's reflection on the water
Zippered pockets keep out water

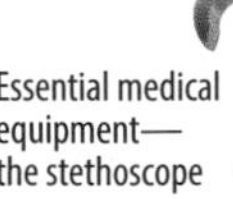
Spectacles
Essential medical equipment—the stethoscope

LEGO
World City
8+
7047

Coast Watch HQ (7047) This set comes with a platform, radar dish, speedboat, helicopter, and four minifigures.

DID YOU KNOW?
Approximately 12 minifigures are produced every second.

Coast Watch Crew
Part of the Coast Guard crew, this minifigure constantly monitors the coast for criminal activity.

Coast Guard Doctor
The Doctor might have the same hair piece as the Mad Scientist from the LEGO Studios theme (in 2002), but minifigure patients can rest assured that he's not crazy.

WE'LL BE IN BILLUND BY MORNING!
Scar mark hints at a troubled past
Printed facial expression exclusive to this minifigure
New torso with roll neck sweater and blue jacket.
Goofy expression
Stolen money
Golden airlines badge
Detailed eyelash pattern
Pilot blazer pattern on torso
Legs are non-movable
I WISH I WAS AT HOME WITH MY LEGO BRICKS!
Square glasses
Button-down shirt
Orange train ticket
A transparent version of this hat appears as a jellyfish in the LEGO® Harry Potter™ theme in 2005.
First appearance of this head piece with curly mustache
Pot belly indicates the chef enjoys his job
Flat, gelled hair gives a professional look.
BE COOL. DON'T BLOW MY COVER.
Dark glasses keep identity hidden
Slick suitcase full of secret documents
Tailored suit
Necklace has golden pendant
Tapered jacket print
Heavy luggage to heave onto the train

Hovercraft Pilot If you had to chase the silly Smuggler you would look this angry, too. The Pilot is exclusive to the Hovercraft Hideout (7045).

Smuggler
The Smuggler had better watch out—he has one angry Hovercraft Pilot after him, in set 7045.

Pilot Dressed in a uniform, which is exclusive to this minifigure, the airlines Pilot can't wait to take to the skies.

Passenger
A female minifigure passenger accompanies little Timmy on the plane.

Timmy With freckled face and baseball cap, young Timmy is excited—he's about to board a plane for the first time.

AIRLINE EXCLUSIVE SETS

Multiple versions of the promotional Passenger Plane set were released in 2003 to 2004, each identical except for a sticker pack inside, unique to individual airlines.

CITY FOLK

It wasn't all high adventure in World City. Minifigures were still traveling by train, going through Grand Central Station on their way to their destinations.

Commuter
The commuter minifigure is wearing a new blazer—he'd love to shout about it, but he can't—he's a minifigure.

Undercover Cop
Dark hair, dark glasses, and a dark suit ensure that this minifigure cop blends into the background when he's on the lookout for crooks and thieves.

Passenger Boarding the High Speed Train (4511) is quite an occasion for this minifigure—she's wearing a brand new jacket and her special red lipstick.

Chef In between serving the passengers at Grand Central Station (4513), the Chef likes to create his own wacky recipes.

2003

LEGO SPORTS

LEGO Sports was a new theme for 2003, incorporating LEGO Soccer with extreme sports and basketball. But this meant more than just designing new sets, it required the redesign of the minifigure for basketball. The addition of the stunt stick to the Gravity Games sets meant that minifigures could be played with in a whole new way!

Helmet with check pattern is new this year

CHECK OUT MY GNARLY GOGGLES.

Race number is a sticker

Light gray gloves

Big Air Snowboarder This minifigure has the same head piece as Madam Hooch from the LEGO Harry Potter theme, but she prefers snowboards to broomsticks.

LEGO
SPORTS
3537

Skateboard Vert Park Challenge (3537) The Gravity Games Sports subtheme includes a skateboarders' park with two skater minifigures.

Transparent blue goggles

Wide smile seen through helmet

Plain torso under stickered vest attachment

Grinning Snowboarder With a cheeky wink, this gnarly boarder performs twists and turns as he races against the Goatee Snowboarder.

GRAVITY GAMES

The LEGO® Gravity Games™ sets featured special stunt sticks that could be attached to the minifigures to allow them to do mid-air stunts. Vertical ramps also made for even more excitement.

Stylish trimmed goatee

Goatee Snowboarder This goatee-sporting minifigure is only found in the Snowboard Boarder Cross Race (3538).

Even super-cool snowboarders need gloves to keep warm!

Helmet first seen in the 2002 Racers theme

Tough Snowboarder This snowboarder looks tough, but he still likes to protect his minifigure skin from the sun's glare with colored sunscreen.

DID YOU KNOW? LEGO Gravity Games is based on the real-world multi-sport event of the same name, held from 1999 to 2006.

Helmet seen on more than 325 other minifigures

Gray Snowboarder Being up against the Tough Snowbarder doesn't scare this minifigure—he has years of experience on the slopes.

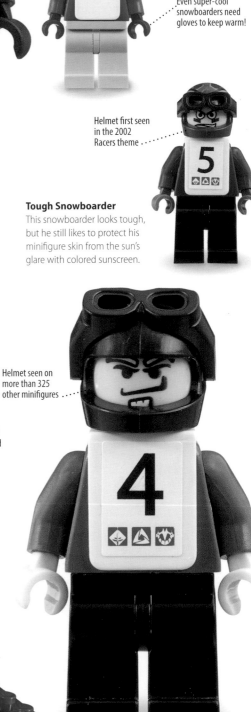

The course features jumps and drops

Snowboard features red minifigure outline

Snowboard Boarder Cross Race (3538) In this set, two minifigures race to the finish line at the bottom of the snowy and tricky competition course.

LEGO GRAVITY GAMES PROMOTIONAL SETS

Half of the LEGO Gravity Games sets were promotions for companies including Duracell, something that continued into 2004. Each set featured a minifigure and stunt stick.

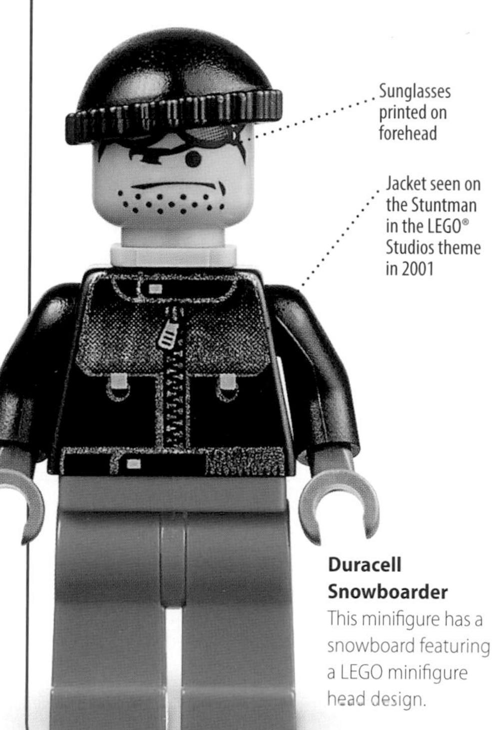
Sunglasses printed on forehead
Jacket seen on the Stuntman in the LEGO® Studios theme in 2001

Duracell Snowboarder This minifigure has a snowboard featuring a LEGO minifigure head design.

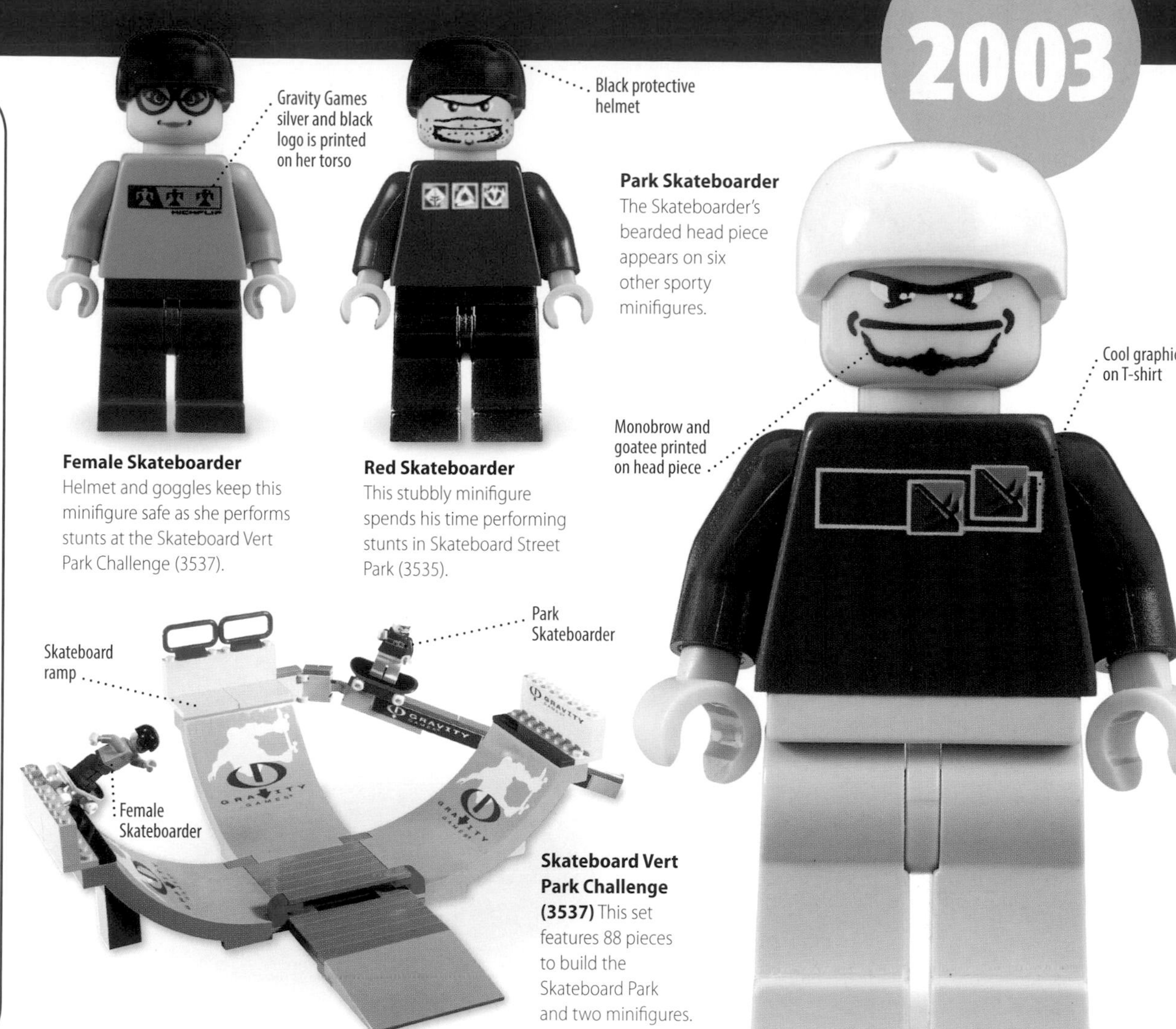
Gravity Games silver and black logo is printed on her torso
Black protective helmet
Cool graphics on T-shirt
Monobrow and goatee printed on head piece
Skateboard ramp
Park Skateboarder
Female Skateboarder

Female Skateboarder Helmet and goggles keep this minifigure safe as she performs stunts at the Skateboard Vert Park Challenge (3537).

Red Skateboarder This stubbly minifigure spends his time performing stunts in Skateboard Street Park (3535).

Park Skateboarder The Skateboarder's bearded head piece appears on six other sporty minifigures.

Skateboard Vert Park Challenge (3537) This set features 88 pieces to build the Skateboard Park and two minifigures.

No hair piece because hair is cut very short

Kobe Bryant The Los Angeles Lakers' most famous player has a minifigure that features his famous wide smile.

Memphis Grizzlies jersey

Pau Gasol The Memphis rookie's smiling face has eyebrows printed in a different color than his hair.

Blue uniform of NBA All-Star Game East team
Arms modified to hold basketball

East NBA player Springing off to shoot some hoops is sure to make this minifigure player's team happy.

NBA BASKETBALL

NBA Basketball minifigures were the first to feature realistic skin tones—because they were also the first minifigures to be based on real people. Those not representing famous players remained yellow, but they all underwent a radical redesign with springs built into their legs, and arms and hands specially constructed to hold, throw, and slam dunk the ball.

West NBA player Minifigures in red uniforms play for NBA All-Star Game West team.

Long mustache
NBA logo and player number printed on torso
Springs to "jump" and shoot

STREET BASKETBALL

These street basketballers have the same design as their NBA counterparts. Sets came with four minifigures and lever action for slam dunking.

Orange sunglasses can be put on to take away any glare

Street Player Come rain or sunshine, this player is always ready to play some b-ball.

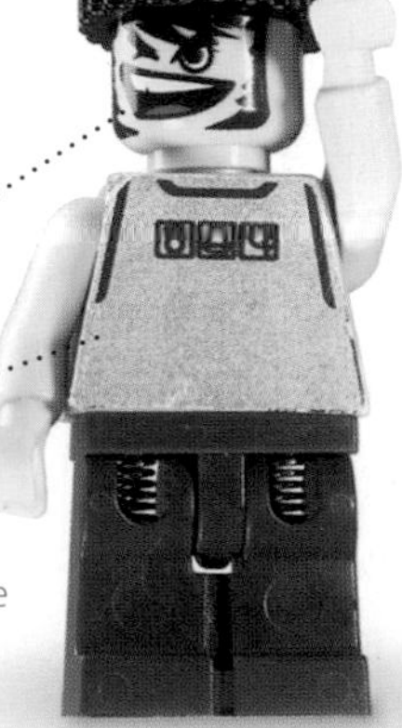
Long black hair sideburns
New torso with textured jersey pattern

Basket Shooter The gray-clad minifigure is from the Street Ball 2 vs. 2 set (3431).

2003

LEGO *STAR WARS*

It was a year almost as huge as Jabba the Hutt himself, as the first Jabba's Palace (4480) was released. New minifigures included Princess Leia in her slave outfit, Lando Calrissian, and Greedo, plus a figure of Jabba, of course.

I'M SO RARE THERE'S A BOUNTY ON MY HEAD!

Boba Fett This unique variant of the bounty hunter—in set 10123—is the first minifigure to have printed arms.

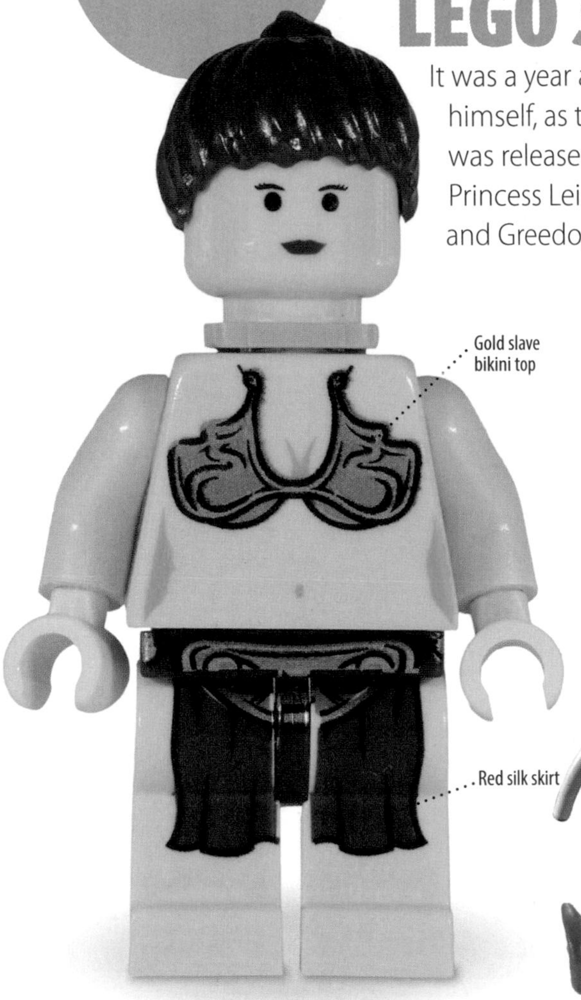

Green Mandalorian armor

Armored knee pads

Blaster

Gold slave bikini top

Red silk skirt

Princess Leia The Alderaan Princess minifigure is dressed in her famous gold bikini, which she wore when enslaved by Jabba the Hutt.

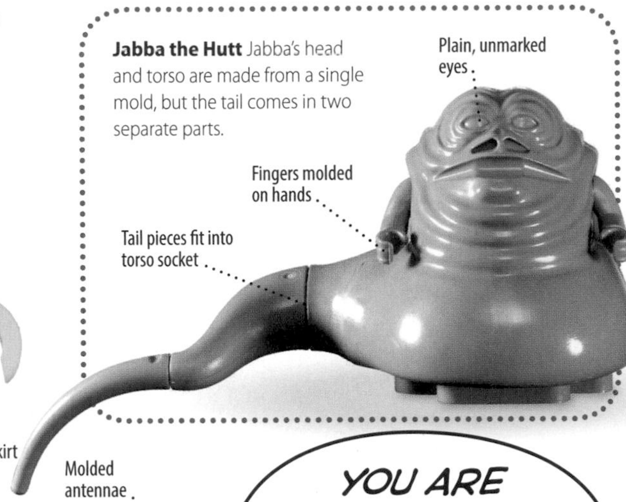

Jabba the Hutt Jabba's head and torso are made from a single mold, but the tail comes in two separate parts.

Plain, unmarked eyes

Fingers molded on hands

Tail pieces fit into torso socket

YOU ARE NOT THE DROID I AM LOOKING FOR.

Breathing filters

Oxygen-filled rebreather pack

Commanders wear orange pauldrons.

Black glove

Printed belt holds blaster ammo

Sandtrooper
To aid breathing in the extreme desert climate, this minifigure wears a rebreather pack.

Molded antennae

Elongated snout

Arms with painted tan stripes

Brown hips and sand blue legs are unique to Greedo.

Greedo A bumpy head mold was designed specially for Greedo. His large eyes are fitted with light reflectors.

DID YOU KNOW?
Boba Fett from Cloud City (10123) is one of the rarest and most collectible minifigures.

Cloud City (10123) In this set, which features seven minifigures, the villainous Darth Vader has trapped Han Solo in carbonite. The Lando minifigure tries to rescue the Han Solo minifigure.

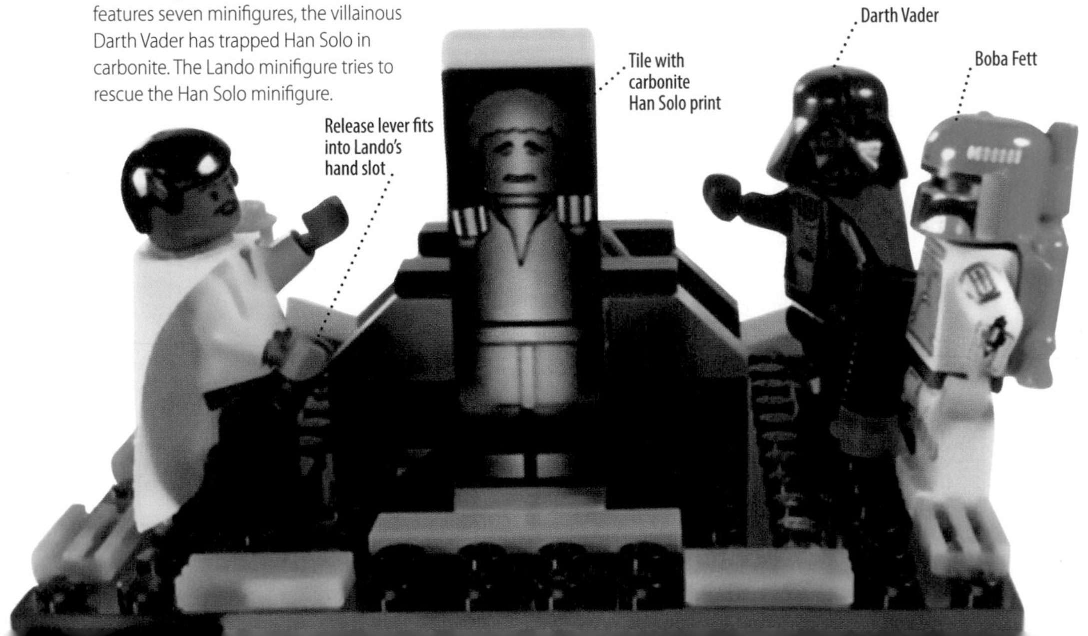

Release lever fits into Lando's hand slot

Tile with carbonite Han Solo print

Darth Vader

Boba Fett

Lando Calrissian
Lando's brown head piece is the first flesh-colored minifigure head for the *Star Wars* theme.

Shirt with dark blue collar

Dual-colored cape is blue outside and yellow inside

Blaster made from megaphone piece

LEGO SPIDER-MAN

The second year of the LEGO Spider-Man theme moved away from LEGO Studios, with three sets based on the first Spider-Man movie. Major new minifigures introduced were the Green Goblin's alter ego, Norman Osborn, as well as Peter Parker in his wrestling costume. The theme was discontinued in 2004 but would return in 2012.

I'M JUST NOT SURE GREEN IS MY COLOR.

Determined expression

Double-faced The other side of Osborn's dual face shows a scared expression.

Norman Osborn This shirtless, yellow-torsoed minifigure represents Norman Osborn before his transformation into the Green Goblin in The Origins (4851).

I'M YOUR FRIENDLY NEIGHBORHOOD SPIDER-MAN

New balaclava print covers mouth and nose

Spider-Man's wondrous web

New faded spider and web print on torso

White gloves

Wrestling Peter For his fight against Bone Saw McGraw, Parker fashions this costume, which is only found in Spider-Man's First Chase (4850).

New torso with polo shirt and jacket
Eyes printed with green eyeshadow
New white and pink torso

Peter Parker A studious-looking Parker is off on a school trip to the science lab in The Origins (4851). Watch out for spiders, Peter....

Mary Jane Appearing only in The Final Showdown (4852) Peter Parker's minifigure love interest features an exclusive torso piece.

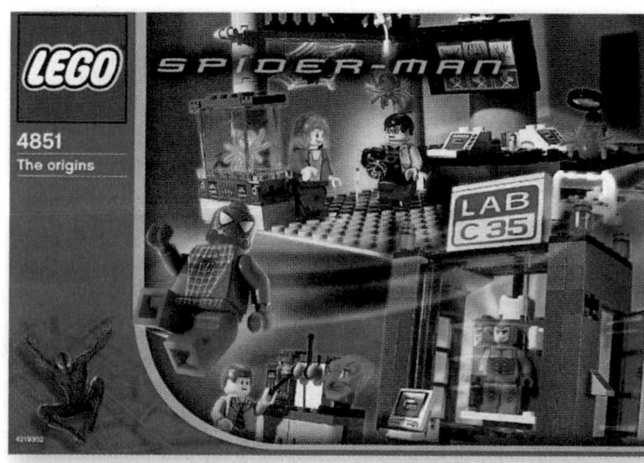

LEGO
SPIDER-MAN
4851
The origins
LAB
C35

The Origins (4851) This set features the lab where Peter Parker was bitten by a radioactive spider. It includes six minifigures.

LEGO® RACERS

This year saw the release of the second Williams F1 Racer set, a 1:27 scale racecar with a driver. The set was based on the well-known British racing team, and followed Ferrari and Lamborghini as Racers licenses. This was the last Williams F1 set and minifigure produced.

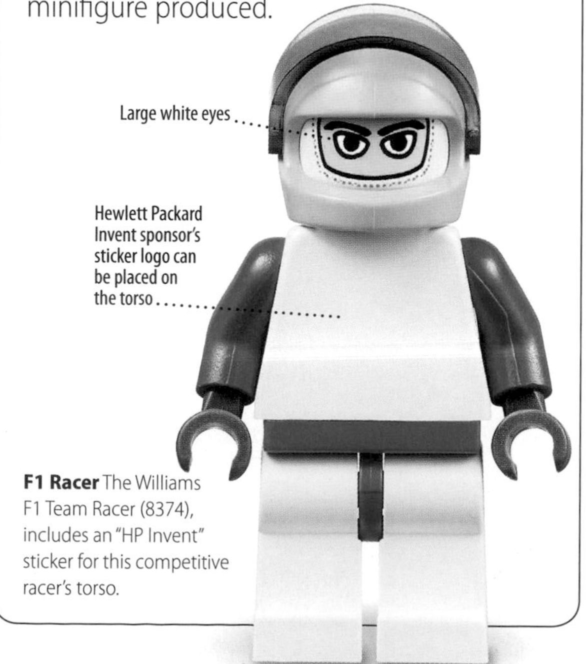

Large white eyes
Hewlett Packard Invent sponsor's sticker logo can be placed on the torso

F1 Racer The Williams F1 Team Racer (8374), includes an "HP Invent" sticker for this competitive racer's torso.

LEGO® EXPLORE® LITTLE ROBOTS™

The Little Robots from the BBC children's series was a LEGO Explore theme for two years, starting in 2003. Five sets were released featuring Tiny, Noisy, and the team.

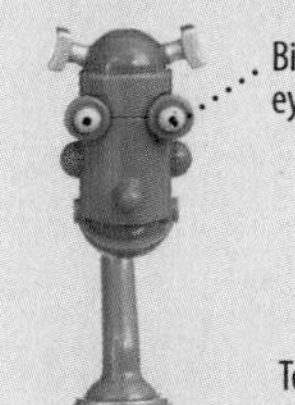

Big, bulging eyes

Stretchy This junk-loving robot has wheels instead of legs and a thin tube-like neck.

Red shoulder pads

Torso has switch pattern

Sporty Stretchy is assisted in the Junk Yard by this beefy robot, with a green, red, and gold body.

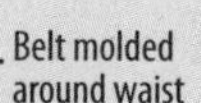

Belt molded around waist

Tiny Specially molded hands help this little robot hold the Day and Night lever in the Junk Yard.

Prominent black nose for sniffing

Messy Tiny's green and golden robot-dog pet from the Tiny and Friends set (7441) is always running away.

Trumpet-like face

Noisy Noisy by name, and noisy by nature. This figure has a trumpet for a nose and he blows it to scare Tiny.

ARE YOU READY FOR AN ADVENTURE?

LEGO ADVENTURERS

LEGO® Orient Expedition was the last Adventurers subtheme, released with 15 sets and three promotional minifigure sets. The brave adventurers set off on a daring quest to recover the Golden Dragon of Marco Polo. In addition to having the most detailed storyline of any Adventurers line, the sets also came with pieces of a board game that could be assembled and played.

Desert outfit for his Orient adventure

Gun fixed under belt

Johnny Thunder A new version of the adventurer minifigure returns with a new head with side-burns and a chin dimple.

Wide brim hat

Exploring Johnny Dressed to explore the cold Himalayas, Johnny's bangs and sideburns are still visible under his hat.

New torso with fur-lined jacket

Tile of map of the Himalayas

Revolver for protection

Head gear also seen on Professor Karkaroff and Victor Krum from the Harry Potter™ theme in 2005, but in black

New head with red lips

Red woolen scarf

New and exclusive torso with fur-lined jacket

Black gloves

Pippin Reed Brave Pippin scares off a yeti in Yeti's Hideout (7412) and manages to get her minifigure hands on a jewel!

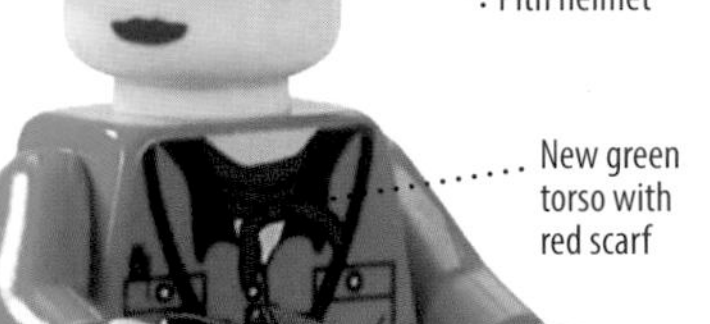

Pith helmet

New green torso with red scarf

Reporter Pippin This version of Pippin appears in Elephant Caravan (7414), where the race is on against Lord Sinister—who will get to the treasure first?

ADVENTURERS

Many favorite characters were back for 2003, including Johnny Thunder and Pippin Reed. Their thrilling journey would take them through India and China and even to Mount Everest.

Aviator glasses keep the sand out of Pippin's eyes

Compass hangs around her neck

Desert Pippin If any minifigure can find the Golden Dragon, Pippin Reed can, in the Dragon Fortress (7419).

Dr. Kilroy The brilliant scientist Dr. Kilroy, also known as Dr. Lightning, sure is a snappy dresser in Scorpion Palace (7418).

White, wispy beard

Paisley pattern on vest

FRIENDS AND ALLIES

Three new faces joined the team: Babloo, from India; Sherpa guide Sangye Dorje; and Jing Lee, the only newcomer who became a permanent part of the group.

DID YOU KNOW? The LEGO Orient Expedition subtheme introduced the scimitar, elephant, and sherpa hat elements.

Identical head gear to Pippin Reed

Ax to cut through slippery ice

Sherpa Sangye Dorje The young mountain guide knows that snow shoes are essential wear when traveling to the Temple of Mount Everest (7417).

Red sash tied around waist

Backpack filled with supplies

Snow shoes attach to legs

Red turban

New torso with blue vest and yellow embroidery pattern

Babloo Seen only in the Elephant Caravan (7414), Babloo fights off the the bad guys with his scimitar.

Ponytail hair piece

New torso with Chinese shirt print

Jing Lee Martial arts is this minifigure's expertise—those baddies had better watch out!

Rifle to hunt yeti
New, fur-lined hat
Sleeveless fur jacket
Scimitar is just like Babloo's
KNIFE TO MEET YOU JOHNNY THUNDER...
Bushy gray beard
Top hat worn by many minifigures, including the Circus Ringmaster from the LEGO® Minifigures theme in 2010
Monocle over eye
Revolver fits into hand
Patterned shield
New torso with dagger tucked inside sash
Holster pattern on torso
New head with fu manchu-style mustache and cheekbones
Dragon emblem on staff
Chinese Emperor pattern
New cape with high collar and pointed tails
LEGO
ORIENT EXPEDITION
7419
Helmet disconnect clasp
NASA logo
Basil the Bat Lord from LEGO® Castle wears this head gear in 1997, but in black
Inverted radar dish piece with Asian print used as a Chinese hat
Turban covers printed messy hair
Sinister orange eyes
Armor from LEGO® Ninja Castle subtheme
New armor print on torso
Oval shield
Arrow molded on crossbow

UP TO NO GOOD

Four evil villains confronted the Adventurers: perennial nemesis Lord Sinister, fiendish Emperor Chang Wu, ruthless Maharaja Lallu, and crooked yeti hunter Ngan Pa.

Ngan Pa This greedy yeti hunter makes life difficult for the Adventurers. He has an exclusive torso piece and carries a very big rifle, which he's not afraid to use....

Maharaja Lallu The ruthless Indian tyrant looks ready to fight Dr. Kilroy and his team. His patterned shield isn't for decoration, however—it's for protection!

Emperor Chang Wu Exclusive to the Dragon Fortress (7419), this black caped minifigure looks truly terrifying!

Lord Sam Sinister A hook for his left arm and a battle-scarred face give this minifigure a menacing new look.

Dragon Fortress (7419) This Orient Expedition was the final set released in the theme, and contains nine minifigures.

Apollo Astronaut A NASA space suit is vital for this minifigure's out of world experiences.

LEGO® DISCOVERY

LEGO Discovery was a one-year theme focusing on real-life space flight. Only one of the six sets featured minifigures: The Lunar Lander (10029). The other sets were replicas of NASA spacecraft.

Statue's head piece

Henchman This minifigure guards the Scorpion Palace (7418) day and night. His minifigure legs hurt!

Dragon Fortress Statue If the adventurers want to get into the Dragon Fortress (7419), they'll have to get past this scary statue first.

Dragon Fortress Guard Chang Wu's fortress is protected by his minifigure guards wielding crossbows.

GOOD VS. BAD

HEROES, IT IS SAID, are measured by the villains they battle. If that's the case, LEGO® minifigure heroes have nothing to worry about, for they have faced some of the most formidable villains in the history of toys. From the Black Falcon knights and the Space Police's most wanted aliens, to Captain Brickbeard and Lord Vampyre, all the way up to infamous types such as Lord Garmadon and Cragger, the roster of minifigure evildoers is long and colorful. Fortunately, for every bad guy there is a brave hero or heroine ready to fight for justice!

Castle They look peaceful enough now, but the Crusaders and the Black Falcons fought against each other for eight years.

LEGO Monster Fighters Finally, Major Quinton Steele has got his hands on a moonstone. But with the Werewolf in hot pursuit, he had better run as fast as his minifigure legs can carry him!

LEGO Ninjago If anyone can take on the evil Lord Garmadon and win, it's the Ultimate Spinjitzu Master, Lloyd Garmadon!

LEGO Space Police III The Space Police work hard to protect the minifigure public from hardened alien criminals such as leader of the Space Biker Gang, Kranxx.

LEGO Agents Agent Trace isn't intimidated by Fire Arm's massive gun—but she is offended by his flat-top hair piece.

LEGO Monster Fighters Lord Vampyre plans to inflict darkness upon the world. His archenemy Dr. Rodney Rathbone does all he can to stop him.

LEGO Pirates Captain Redbeard sails the seas in search of treasure, trying to avoid Governor Broadside and his Imperial Officers.

LEGO Atlantis Ace Speedman searches for the lost city of Atlantis, but this Shark Warrior isn't going to give it up easily.

LEGO Agents Agent Chase has to stop Dr. Inferno—not only does he plan to take over the world, but his hair piece is a crime against fashion.

LEGO Alien Conquest The Aliens landed on Earth to collect brainpower from humans, but come up against the Alien Defense Unit Sergeant and his team.

LEGO Legends of Chima
Cragger and Prince of the Lion Tribe Laval used to be best friends. But once Cragger discovers the power of CHI, it signals the end of their friendship and of Chima's Age of Peace.

LEGO Legends of Chima
Determined to ensure CHI is distributed fairly, laidback Gorilla Grizzam better watch out for wicked Wilhurt!

Castle When the Crusaders aren't battling the Black Falcons, they have to contend with the Forestmen.

LEGO Ninjago
Spitta goes after Sensei Wu with his mace. He's in for a shock when he discovers that the wise Sensei is a Spinjitzu Master.

LEGO City
The sneaky crook gets up to mischief in LEGO City, but the Policeman always manages to catch him.

LEGO Atlantis Even though the mighty Portal Emperor is in front of him greedily guarding sunken treasure, Lance Spears doesn't look perturbed.

I CAN'T FAIL THIS TIME... CAN I?
Ogel has one red eye, and one black.
Black, mechanical shoulder pads
Blue hook replaces red one on 2002 version.

Ogel The minifigure's only design change since 2002 is the color of his hook. Now, Ogel feels ready for his final battle against Alpha Team.

Transparent blue bubble helmet
New silver outline around scarab logo
Black and red torso and legs
Ogel's Ice Orbs can freeze anything.

Super Ice Drone The black skull head piece with white printing and red eyes is unique.

Ogel Minion This skeleton minifigure has a new helmet to stop him from freezing himself!

OGEL AND HIS MINIONS

Ogel's plan is to freeze the world with the help of his skeleton drones and ice orbs. Thanks to his powerful Mind Control Orbs, the skeletons follow the evil minifigure's orders without hesitation.

2004

2004 SAW THE COMEBACK of some old favorites, as LEGO® Alpha Team and LEGO® DUPLO® returned. LEGO® Harry Potter™ and BIONICLE® also remained strong. LEGO® Spider-Man™ swung back into action as *Spider-Man 2* arrived in movie theaters. Ferrari sets were released for the first time and LEGO® *Star Wars*® continued to flourish with the launch of iconic classic sets and sets from the expanded universe.

LEGO ALPHA TEAM

After a year's absence, Alpha Team returned to stop evil Ogel in Mission: Deep Freeze. With a new logo, redesigned minifigures, and three new minifigure heroes—Zed, Diamond Tooth, and Arrow—it was a new team for a new era.

GOOD THING I WORE MY THERMAL UNDERWEAR!

Dash keeps his brown, flat-top hair piece in 2004.

New head piece features black sunglasses and a grimacing expression.

New, triangular Alpha Team logo

New uniform with blue sleeve and silver zipper details.

Dash Alpha Team leader Dash has a completely new look in 2004.

ALPHA TEAM

Changes to the team this year included agents Cam and Crunch being replaced by Arrow and Diamond Tooth, special agent Zed appearing in his Blizzard Blaster, and Tee-Vee's first appearance in an android form.

Sports-style helmet
Goatee beard
Different logo on torso than the rest of the team

Zed This special agent minifigure appears in only one set—Blizzard Blaster (4770).

Orb-collecting crane
Tee-Vee
Thermo blaster
Ogel Minion
Arrow drives a snow scooter, one of two in the set.

Mobile Command Center (4746) Alpha Team's mobile base is ideal for traveling over frozen terrain.

Bandana printed on head piece
Special magnifying lens
Arrow's team color is yellow.

Diamond Tooth New for 2004, Diamond Tooth is the mining expert for Alpha Team and he pilots the Tundra Tracker (4744).

Arrow Alpha Team's new mechanic has the same torso as Diamond, apart from his right arm.

Ogel's Mountain Fortress (4748) Ogel's skull-shaped base is defended by two skeleton drones, along with Ogel in his Sky Spider vehicle.

THIS IS BASE TO ARROW, DO YOU COPY?
Red robot eyes
Team color is turquoise
Magnifying glass

Previous versions had purple hair, not black.

Flex and Charge have the same uniform in different colors.

Radia The only female minifigure on the team in 2004, Radia is a laser expert.

Flex Alpha Team's rope expert is also famous for his hilarious jokes.

Red safety harness printed on torso and legs

Charge The team's electricity expert appears in all three Alpha Team series, but has a brand new uniform in 2004.

Tee-Vee Alpha Team's communications expert has appeared in three very different guises—a TV with legs, an underwater vehicle, and now, finally, an android minifigure.

Hoth Princess Leia This variant features Leia's iconic bun hairstyle. In 2011 the rebel leader has braids instead.

NEXT TIME, I'M DRIVING!

Print details on torso include the rebel leader's insignia
Flesh colored hands—the 2011 variant has white hands

LEGO *STAR WARS*

2004 saw the release of a number of classic *Star Wars* sets, including a new version of the *Millennium Falcon* (4504). This version of the ship featured both Han Solo and Princess Leia in their Hoth outfits from *Star Wars:* Episode V *The Empire Strikes Back*.

Printed fur trimmed hood—Han's 2011 variant comes with detachable hood.
Furry hood protects Han in a chilly blizzard.
Han's handy electrobinoculars hang from a strap.

Hoth Han Solo The rebel pilot is dressed warmly for the icy conditions on Hoth.

Hoth Han Solo Variant This rare yellow variant featured in a promotional version of set 4504 with all-yellow minifigures.

Large sensor dish
Chewbacca and Han sit in the cockpit of the promotional set, featuring yellow minifigures.

***Millennium Falcon* (4504)** The ship's triangular shaped panels can be pulled open on their hinges to reveal all the action inside.

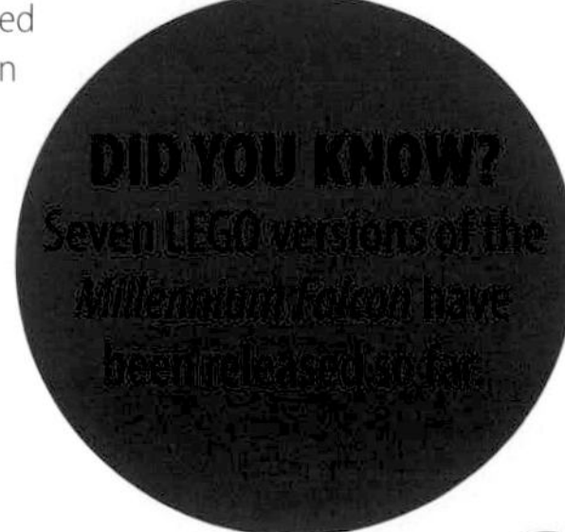

DID YOU KNOW? Seven LEGO versions of the *Millennium Falcon* have been released so far.

LEGO HARRY POTTER

Harry Potter and the Prisoner of Azkaban™ got the LEGO treatment in 2004. Sets included new versions of Hogwarts Castle (4757), Hagrid's Hut (4754), and the Hogwarts Express (4758), along with several models depicting key scenes from the film. There were nine new sets in total, plus the first mini-set—the Knight Bus (4755). In this year, all the minifigures, except Professor Snape, were also remade with the new flesh tones.

Harry Potter has a flesh-colored head for the first time.

Harry's tie and sweater are printed with the Gryffindor house colors.

Third-Year Harry Potter Three minifigures of Harry in his Gryffindor uniform were released this year. Each has the same head, torso, and legs, but two have robes.

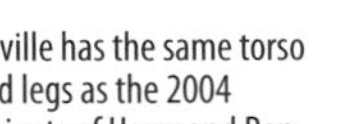

Draco Malfoy Harry's archenemy is dressed all in green, ready to do battle on the Quidditch pitch.

Slytherin house crest

A 2010 variant of the minifigure has white pants instead of green.

Ron has his trademark red hair piece

All the 2004 Harry Potter minifigures have the same head piece

Flesh-colored version of 2001 head

Casual Ron Weasley Ron's torso with striped sweater and open shirt is unique to two Hogwarts Express sets released in 2004.

Casual Harry Potter Three casually dressed Harry Potter minifigures were released in 2004. The others feature a different torso or legs.

Time-Turner Hermione Granger Hermione has a unique detail on her Gryffindor uniform—a magical Time-Turner. A robed variant was also released.

DID YOU KNOW?
2004 saw the release of the first and only motorized version of the Hogwarts Express train (10132).

STUDENTS

This year brought new versions of Harry Potter, Hermione Granger, Draco Malfoy, Ron Weasley, and Neville Longbottom. Harry actually appeared in six different incarnations, although many of the variations were very minor.

Neville has the same torso and legs as the 2004 variants of Harry and Ron.

Neville Longbottom™ Harry's friend Neville appears as a minifigure for the first time. His unique head piece wears a nervous expression in the set Professor Lupin's Classroom (4752).

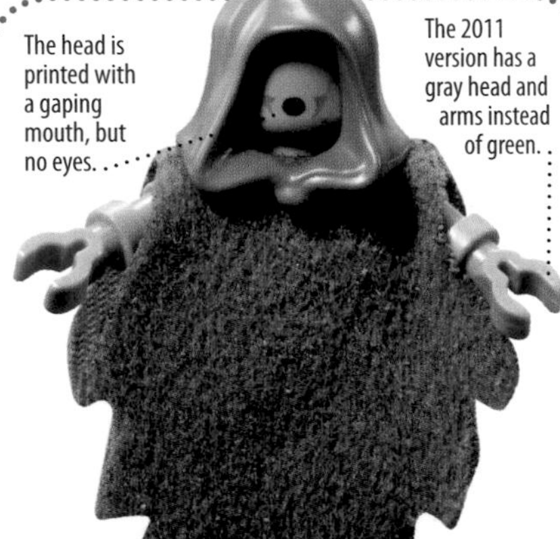

The head is printed with a gaping mouth, but no eyes.

The 2011 version has a gray head and arms instead of green.

Tattered gray robe and hood

Dementor The first version of the spooky Azkaban guard was released in four sets. It comes with a LEGO dish piece that can be attached to the base to keep it upright.

OTHER CHARACTERS

Major and minor characters from the film debuted as minifigures in 2004, including Sirius Black, Peter Pettigrew, and Knight Bus driver Stan Shunpike. Black made his only two appearances in this year.

Stan's head and torso are unique to the Knight Bus (4755).

Ticket machine

Knight Bus Driver Stan Shunpike is a special minifigure—the first to be made almost entirely from purple pieces.

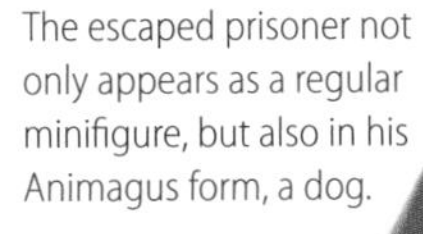

Sirius has the same hair piece as Professor Snape.

Sirius Black™ The escaped prisoner not only appears as a regular minifigure, but also in his Animagus form, a dog.

Tattered uniform of Azkaban Prison

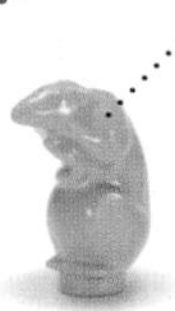

Peter Pettigrew™ Peter Pettigrew appears as both a minifigure and his Animagus form—Ron's pet rat, Scabbers.

The rat stands in an upright position on its back legs—a clue to its concealed wizard form.

Torso and head are unique to the Shrieking Shack (4756)

Crossbow

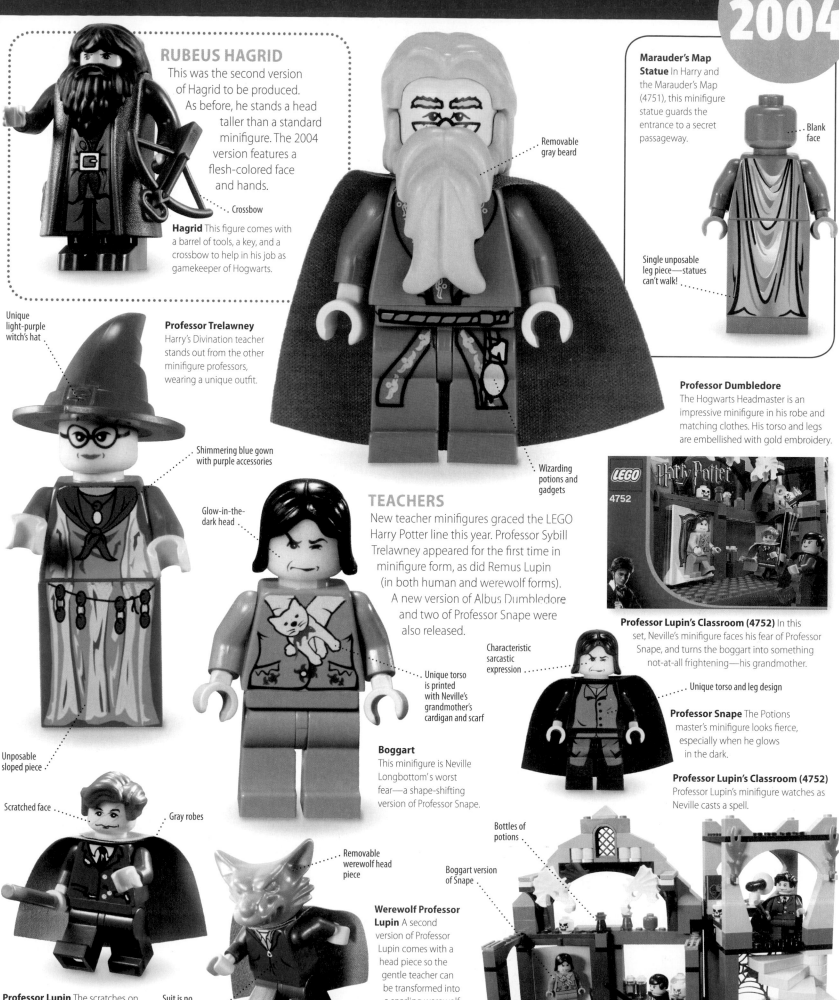

RUBEUS HAGRID

This was the second version of Hagrid to be produced. As before, he stands a head taller than a standard minifigure. The 2004 version features a flesh-colored face and hands.

Hagrid This figure comes with a barrel of tools, a key, and a crossbow to help in his job as gamekeeper of Hogwarts.

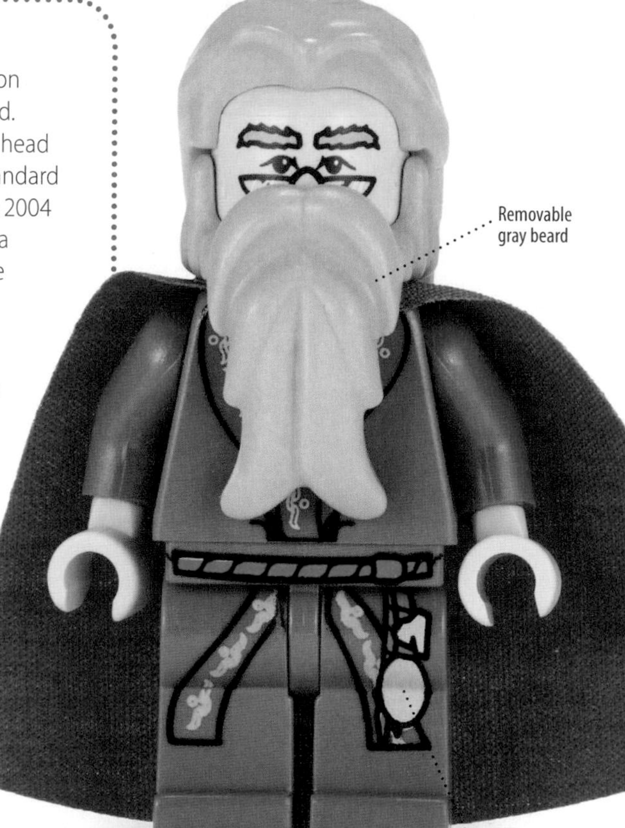
Removable gray beard
Wizarding potions and gadgets

Professor Dumbledore The Hogwarts Headmaster is an impressive minifigure in his robe and matching clothes. His torso and legs are embellished with gold embroidery.

Blank face
Single unposable leg piece—statues can't walk!

Marauder's Map Statue In Harry and the Marauder's Map (4751), this minifigure statue guards the entrance to a secret passageway.

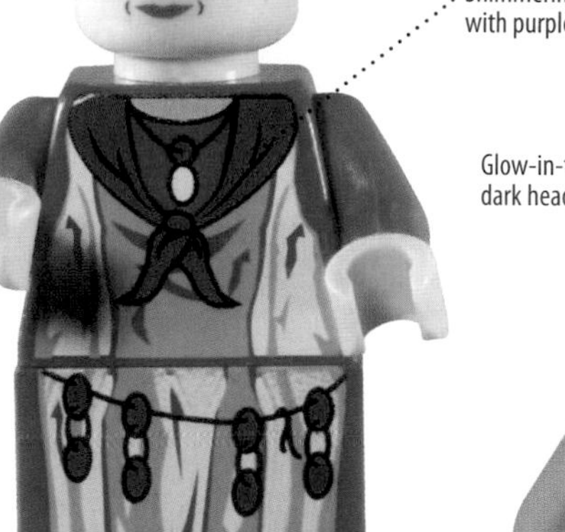
Unique light-purple witch's hat
Shimmering blue gown with purple accessories
Unposable sloped piece

Professor Trelawney Harry's Divination teacher stands out from the other minifigure professors, wearing a unique outfit.

TEACHERS

New teacher minifigures graced the LEGO Harry Potter line this year. Professor Sybill Trelawney appeared for the first time in minifigure form, as did Remus Lupin (in both human and werewolf forms). A new version of Albus Dumbledore and two of Professor Snape were also released.

Glow-in-the-dark head
Unique torso is printed with Neville's grandmother's cardigan and scarf

Boggart This minifigure is Neville Longbottom's worst fear—a shape-shifting version of Professor Snape.

LEGO
Harry Potter
4752

Professor Lupin's Classroom (4752) In this set, Neville's minifigure faces his fear of Professor Snape, and turns the boggart into something not-at-all frightening—his grandmother.

Characteristic sarcastic expression
Unique torso and leg design

Professor Snape The Potions master's minifigure looks fierce, especially when he glows in the dark.

Scratched face
Gray robes

Professor Lupin The scratches on his face and his tattered suit hint at this minifigure's secret. A full moon would reveal it....

Removable werewolf head piece
Suit is no longer tattered

Werewolf Professor Lupin A second version of Professor Lupin comes with a head piece so the gentle teacher can be transformed into a snarling werewolf.

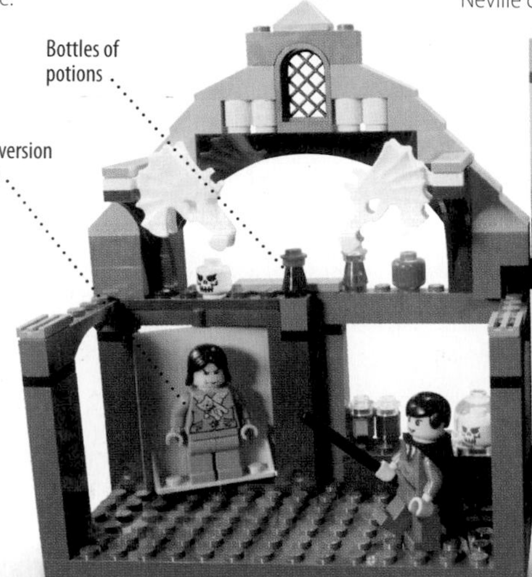

Bottles of potions
Boggart version of Snape

Professor Lupin's Classroom (4752) Professor Lupin's minifigure watches as Neville casts a spell.

2004

LEGO® WORLD CITY

Ten years after its first release, the classic Century Skyway set (6597) was re-released in 2004. The twelve minifigures that came with the new set had minimal changes from their original 1994 versions.

Hat and head pieces are unchanged

The tie on the previous version was black

Pilot The LEGO pilot has a slightly updated torso with a new red tie and revised silver plane logo.

Freckled face

Airport Worker This minifigure has the same silver plane logo as the pilot and a new ID badge.

The passenger is casually dressed.

Passenger The 2004 version has a new head, featuring eyebrows and a wide smile.

LEGO® FERRARI

LEGO Ferrari was introduced as a subtheme of LEGO® Racers in 2004, with minifigures of pit crew members and real-life Formula 1 drivers Michael Schumacher and Rubens Barrichello. Four System sets were released this year, as well as Ferrari-based LEGO® Technic sets. The LEGO Ferrari relationship would prove to be a long-lasting one.

Removable helmet

F1 Ferrari Pit Crew Member Underneath his helmet, the minifigure wears a red balaclava. The head piece was also used in 2003 for Spider-Man.

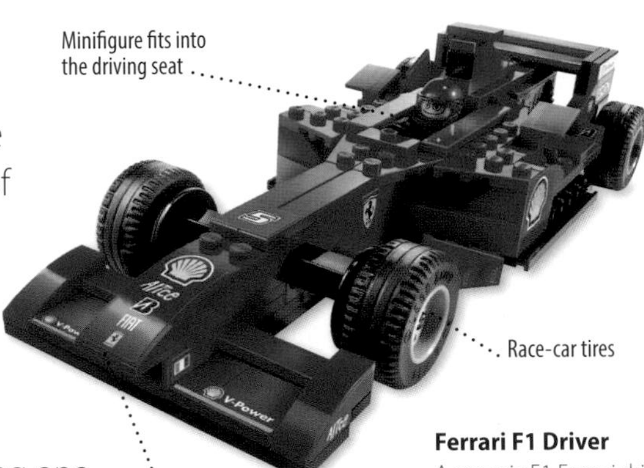

Minifigure fits into the driving seat

Race-car tires

Famous Ferrari red

Ferrari F1 Driver A generic F1 Ferrari driver appears in set 8362. The LEGO car is 1:24 scale model of an actual Ferrari race car.

DID YOU KNOW? The first LEGO sets to feature Ferrari cars were promotional items released in 1997.

Mechanic In 2004, this minifigure appeared in a second LEGO DUPLO Ferrari set complete with pit stop and fuel truck.

Racer The racer minifigure appeared in his race car in both Duplo Ferrari sets released in 2004.

Simpler race-car design for younger fans

LEGO® DUPLO® FERRARI

Little builders had the chance to race to the finish line with this LEGO DUPLO Ville (formerly known as DUPLO Town) Ferrari F1. It came with a minifigure driver, podium, and silver trophy.

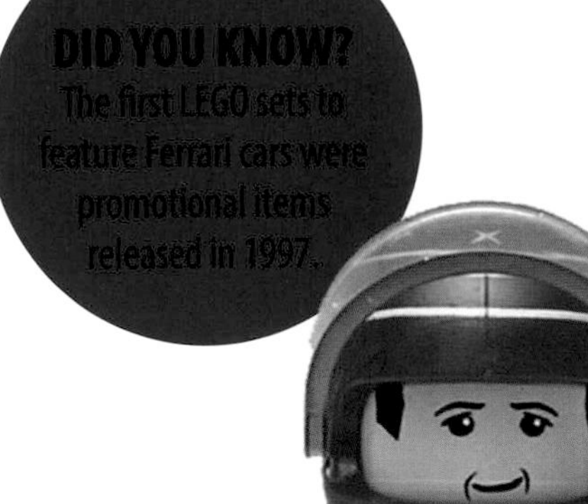

I'M RUBENS... HE'S MICHAEL!

M. Schumacher
R. Barrichello

Unique pattern printed on the top of the helmet

Unique head piece resembles real-life driver

Famous Ferrari stallion logo

Sponsors' logos

Driver's name is printed on torso.

German flag represents driver's nationality

Brazilian flag represents driver's nationality

M. Schumacher This minifigure's unique head piece is designed to closely resemble race-car driver Michael Schumacher.

R. Barrichello The LEGO designers add many real-life details including authentic facial features and helmet design.

LEGO® CASTLE

The second LEGO Castle subtheme to be called Knights' Kingdom appeared this year, both as a subtheme and as buildable action figures. The evil Vladek and his army of Shadow Knights battled the forces of King Mathias and his four brave knights, Rascus, Danju, Jayko, and Santis. Seven sets were released in this first year of the line.

Underneath his helmet, Jayko is smiling

Jayko The youngest of the four knights, Jayko is often known as "the Rookie." His main color, medium blue, is new.

Removable armor

Rascus The four knights have detachable, printed armor, with plain torsos underneath.

Underneath his helmet, Rascus has a goatee beard.
Variant with printed torso instead of armor

Rascus (Without Armor) Rascus is a great warrior and he is famous for his agility and flexibility.

Gold crown first seen on Royal Knights in 1995
Crown covers the sides of the head, and the nose
Mathias' symbols are a crown and a lion.

King Mathias Appearing in two sets this year, King Mathias rules his kingdom, Morcia, with wisdom and nobility.

Danju's hair is dark tan, underneath his helmet

Danju The oldest of King Mathias' four knights, Danju is also the wisest. His dark purple color is also new this year.

Santis wears dark gray gloves.

Santis
This knight is famous for his great strength. Santis was also released as a larger action figure, along with six other Knights Kingdom characters.

Medieval helmet protects face
Angry expression
Red breastplate with scorpion symbol

Shadow Knight
Vladek's loyal Shadow Knight minifigures help him carry out his evil schemes.

The evil minifigure wears black armor with red details.

Vladek
Leader of the Shadow Knights, the wicked Vladek kidnaps King Mathias and tries to take his place as ruler.

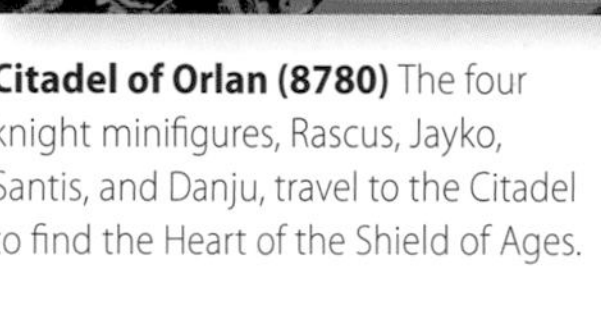

LEGO
Knights' Kingdom
7+
8780

Citadel of Orlan (8780) The four knight minifigures, Rascus, Jayko, Santis, and Danju, travel to the Citadel to find the Heart of the Shield of Ages.

The Guardian wields a transparent lime-green spear.
Rascus climbs the Citadel
Santis
A Shadow Knight plans to stop Rascus and Santis.

Citadel of Orlan (8780) This set includes the variant of Rascus without detachable armor—it's so he can easily climb up the Citadel wall.

Detachable gray beard
The Guardian does not have a hat or hair piece—just printed hair.
Brown torso and legs with gray details

The Guardian
This wise old minifigure protects the Heart of the Shield of Ages in the Citadel of Orlan. He will only give it to those who are worthy.

2004

Escaping jewel thief
HEY, COME BACK HERE WITH THAT!
DIAMONDS
VARICK ST.
Web line
City rat
Pretty patterned sweater
M.J. is skin-colored in 2004.
Aunt May is the only minifigure with this light gray ponytail.
Head piece is unchanged
Unimpressed expression
Scruffy collar and tie
New web design in 2004
Flat-top hair piece
Casual vest over zippered jacket
This blue suit can also be seen on Bruce Wayne in 2006.
Spider-Man's costume is also a darker blue in 2004.
Casual blue pants
Hand piece

Spider-Man's Street Chase (4853) Spider-Man tries to stop two jewel thieves in this set—can he catch them?

Mary Jane Watson Like Peter Parker, M.J. gets a new outfit. Her facial features are also updated.

DID YOU KNOW? 2004 included the first appearances of J. Jonah Jameson and Harry Osborn as minifigures.

LEGO SPIDER-MAN

LEGO Spider-Man returned in 2004 as *Spider-Man 2* hit movie theaters. This time, Aunt May, Mary Jane, and the other minifigures featured skin-colored faces and hands. The line included five new sets and 17 minifigures, including four different versions of Dr. Octopus. This was the final year of the Spider-Man play theme until 2012, when it returned as part of the LEGO® Marvel Super Heroes theme.

Aunt May Peter Parker's Aunt May's minifigure is unique to Doc Ock's Bank Robbery (4854).

J. Jonah Jameson It might be Peter Parker's boss' first appearance but his black flat-top hair piece can be found on more than 20 other minifigures.

Spider-Man The wall-crawler keeps the same head seen on his 2002 and 2003 versions, but has an updated web design on his torso and legs.

Peter Parker Not only does Spider-Man's alter ego have a slight image makeover in 2004, he also has a skin-colored head for the first time.

SPIDER-MAN AND FRIENDS

This was the third time Spider-Man had appeared in minifigure form. Along with the webbed wonder, the 2004 sets showcased all the major characters including Aunt May, Peter Parker, Harry Osborn, J. Jonah Jameson, and Mary Jane Watson. The new Peter Parker figure was more casually dressed than previous versions and he was not wearing glasses.

Harry Osborn Peter Parker's best friend has two minifigures in 2004: one wearing a blue suit (above) and the other wearing a gray pinstripe suit.

Gravity Games torso first seen in 2003
Vented helmet
Gravity Games torso with white and silver logos

Street Hockey Player with Glasses The two minifigures appear in set 3579 along with a small Street Hockey arena and two goals.

Red Street Hockey Player These minifigures are designed for a one-on-one game, involving two players.

STREET HOCKEY

This Street Hockey set (3579) featured two minifigures on movable bases controlled by levers. One seemed to be much more confident of winning than the other!

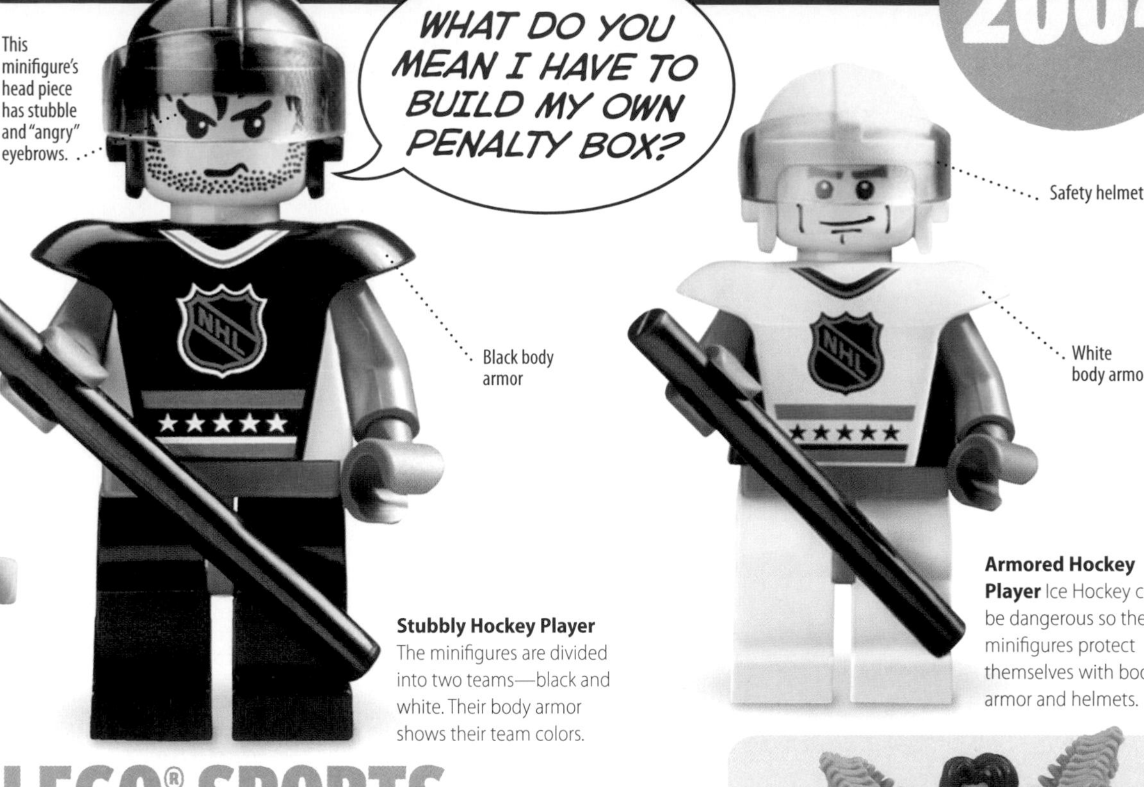
This minifigure's head piece has stubble and "angry" eyebrows.
WHAT DO YOU MEAN I HAVE TO BUILD MY OWN PENALTY BOX?
Safety helmet
Black body armor
White body armor

Stubbly Hockey Player The minifigures are divided into two teams—black and white. Their body armor shows their team colors.

Armored Hockey Player Ice Hockey can be dangerous so the minifigures protect themselves with body armor and helmets.

LEGO® SPORTS

The Hockey subtheme of Sports first appeared in 2003, but there were no minifigures—just brick-built players. In 2004 one set featured minifigures, NHL Championship Challenge (3578). There were eight ice hockey players, each with a different face. They were attached to movable bases, controlled by levers and designed for a two-player game.

Doc Ock uses his tentacle arms to crush his foes

Dr. Octopus Thanks to his grabber arms, Dr. Octopus is slightly more complex than the other 4+ figures.

Bendable tentacles
I GIVE GREAT HUGS!
A special neck clip attaches Doc Ock's robotic arms to his minifigure.
Green suit

Doc Ock: Frowning Due to his unique design, Doc Ock has 26 parts. The average minifigure has four to six parts.

DR. OCTOPUS

The villainous Doc Ock came in four versions in 2004: frowning, smiling, angry, and in his Fusion Lab outfit.

LEGO SPIDER-MAN 2 4855

Spider-Man's Train Rescue (4855) Spider-Man battles Doc Ock on top of a subway train. The set also features minifigures of J. Jonah Jameson and a subway train conductor.

Peter Parker Unlike traditional minifigures, the 4+ versions have molded noses.

Spider-Man The 4+ figure has similar costume detailing to the regular minifigure.

SPIDER-MAN™ 4+

LEGO® Spider-Man™ was the only licensed theme in the 4+ line, which was first introduced in 2003. At two inches (10 cm) tall, the figures were larger than minifigures, with little or no building required—perfect for little hands.

Breathing apparatus
Air tanks
Protective visor
Fire extinguisher
THIS YEAR WAS SMOKING HOT!

Heroic Firefighter
This firefighter looks every bit the rugged hero, with a dimpled chin and determined expression.

2005

IT WAS A YEAR full of new play themes and new innovations for the LEGO Group. LEGO® City (the successor to LEGO® Town and World City), LEGO® Dino Attack, LEGO® Power Racers, and LEGO® Tiny Turbos all made their first appearances. The LEGO® Factory initiative allowed fans to design sets for other fans to order. Sets based on *Star Wars*®: Episode III *Revenge of the Sith* and *Harry Potter and the Goblet of Fire*™ helped fans bring the movies to life. Minifigure star power was also on display in new LEGO® *Star Wars*® video games and mini-movies.

LEGO CITY

LEGO City took over from World City this year, and immediately began expanding the scope of the play theme by adding construction to the traditional police and fire sets. LEGO City gave builders the chance to play in the "real world," with minifigures representing both everyday heroes and the regular folks who keep a city running.

FIRE

The LEGO City Fire minifigures were on the job in 2005, with a new Fire Station (7240), Fire Truck (7239), Fire Helicopter (7238), and Fire Car (7241). To the rescue!

Flame on badge

Radio

Happy Firefighter
With a cheerful smile, this minifigure is always happy to help his fellow citizens.

White helmet
Reflective stripes

Cool Firefighter
Appearing on Day 1 of the 2005 City Advent Calendar has given this minifigure a confidence boost!

Signal paddle
Stylish blue tie
Working flashlight

Flashlight Cop
This police officer has a light-up flashlight to shed some light at crime scenes.

Traffic Cop
His angry scowl suggests that this cop is not to be messed with!

SOUND THE ALARM! SOMEONE DRANK MY COFFEE!

New torso features a red tie, updated from last year's blue tie (seen on Flashlight Cop).

Stern Policeman
This Policeman shares the same head as the chess piece version of Jayko from Knights' Kingdom in 2005.

POLICE

The LEGO City Police Force made its first appearance in two years with four new sets, including a Police Station (7237). With only a few exceptions, the theme would virtually disappear until 2008.

Knitted cap
Gold tooth
Inmate number
New head with dark blue shades
Leather jacket

Prison Inmate With an arched eyebrow and a menacing grin, this new minifigure looks like trouble!

Police Biker
This minifigure comes with a new torso, designed to look like a leather jacket.

DID YOU KNOW?
Police dogs made their debut in LEGO City sets this year.

Torso featuring the Octan logo

Gas Station Worker Wearing blue coveralls printed with the famous Octan logo makes this Gas Station Worker proud.

Standard head

Businessman In a tailored black suit with formal shirt and tie, this minifigure looks serious!

CITY LIFE

Along with Police, Fire, and Construction, 2005 saw a new Community Workers minifigure set, a LEGO City Advent Calendar, and one Airport set—the Desert Biplane complete with pilot.

Aviator cap first seen in the LEGO® Adventurers theme in 1998

Only two minifigures have this torso

Desert Biplane Pilot This Pilot minifigure pilot looks a bit disgruntled. Could it be the fact that his torso isn't unique? It is also seen on Lucius Malfoy from the LEGO® Harry Potter™ theme in 2003.

LEGO City workers love red caps.

Radio for communicating with colleagues

Sleeveless Man This dude's head was first seen in the LEGO Adventurers theme in 2003.

Specs appeal

Male Worker In a casual suit, this guy looks happy and relaxed on his way to work!

Stubble

Torso with coverall print is new for this year

Crane Operator Bright orange coveralls mean that this construction worker is easy to see on the construction site.

Red helmet with visor

Life preserver

Speedboat Driver Under the life vest is a new torso, with a jacket pattern featuring the Octan logo.

Doctor with Glasses Wearing a sleek, side buttoned lab coat with stethoscope, this doctor looks caring and sophisticated.

Square glasses

Stethoscope

Six-point Star of Life symbol

Doctor This doctor wears a new buttoned shirt featuring the blue EMT Star of Life emblem.

HOSPITAL

The first Hospital-themed model in 17 years appeared in 2005, with a promotional Paramedic set offered in the Czech Republic and at LEGOLAND® Windsor, UK. A new torso design with the Star of Life symbol also made an appearance this year.

Diver Girl All ready to dive beneath the LEGO ocean waves, this minifigure wears a floral bathing suit and black flippers, and carries air tanks on her back.

Cool shades

Flippers

DID YOU KNOW? These were the first construction-themed sets in five years.

Chef's hat

Head appears on one other minifigure—another chef!

Pizza Chef This cheerful pizza chef has a large curly mustache and a huge grin.

Ponytail hair piece

Pearl necklace

Red lipstick

Office Worker This stylish minifigure loves accessorizing—her pearl necklace is a personal favorite.

Construction Site (7243) This set includes a large crane, a dump truck, a rock crusher with a conveyor belt, and three minifigures to operate all the machinery.

LEGO
CITY
5+
7243
298
WARNING: CHOKING HAZARD

Construction helmet

Formal shirt and tie

Foreman As the head of the team, the foreman must look the part—he wears a shirt and tie under his jacket.

New vest design

Reflective stripes

Worker with Shovel This minifigure has a new torso, featuring an orange vest over a blue shirt.

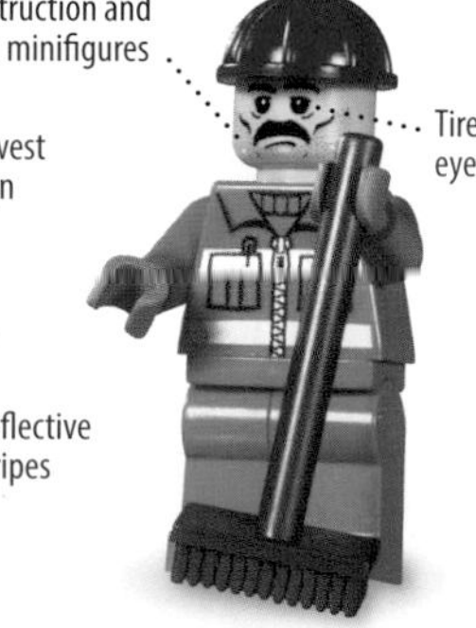

Head only seen on Construction and Train minifigures

Tired eyes

Worker with Broom Construction workers work hard all day, so it's no wonder this minifigure looks tired!

CONSTRUCTION

LEGO City was on the move, and the minifigure Construction workers helped it grow. The foreman minifigure kept an eye on the workers as they operated heavy machinery and started another new building.

BIONICLE®

BIONICLE went from being just buildable action figures to an actual play theme in 2005, with sets based on the Toa Hordikas' fight against the Visorak spiders. Figures had no articulation but all their deadly details were captured in plastic.

Rhotuka wind spinner

Toa Hordika Matau The Toa of Air wields two sharp fang blades that can slice through webs and cables with ease.

Ice spinner creates ice and can freeze objects

Toa Hordika Nuju This figure is completely white, reflecting that he is the Toa of Ice. When he rubs his Hordika Teeth tools together it creates an ultrasonic hum.

Fin barbs can be used for underwater climbing

Toa Hordika Nokama All in blue, this figure is the Toa of Water. She can create anything from Water—from a stream to a tidal wave.

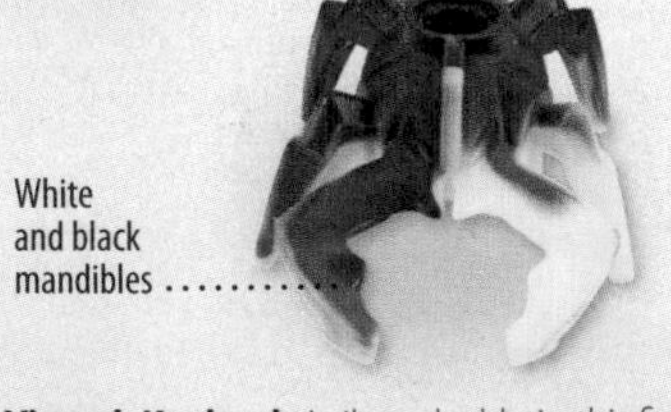
White and black mandibles

Visorak Keelerak Agile and athletic, this figure has large mandibles and razor-sharp legs.

Black and white color distribution varies randomly on all Visoraks.

Visorak Boggarak This figure's mandibles are both white. It can emit sonic waves which turn enemies into stone or gas.

Digger This Digger minifigure features the new torso, with red harness and field glasses pattern.

Face with stubble and a red headband
Utility belt
A steady hand even in the face of danger

DID YOU KNOW?
LEGO Dino Attack was released in Europe as Dino 2010 with some changes to the sets and story.

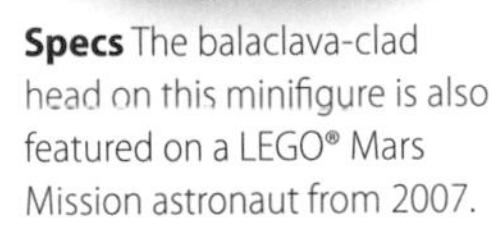
Balaclava

Specs The balaclava-clad head on this minifigure is also featured on a LEGO® Mars Mission astronaut from 2007.

Field glasses

Viper with Field Glasses The torso print is the same as Digger's, but the field glasses are gray.

Battle scar
Ammunition belt
Lethal knife
Vest holds various tools and a book

Viper with Weapons Viper's vest holds many weapons to fight the war against the dinosaurs.

Specs with Tools Specs' new torso features lime green-handled tools and a red book detail.

LEGO DINO ATTACK

Dangerous dinosaurs go on a rampage and only the Dino team can stop them in this new theme. Each set included a Dino team vehicle and a mutant dinosaur. Minifigures featured new heads, and new torsos with equipment or weapons printed on them for each character.

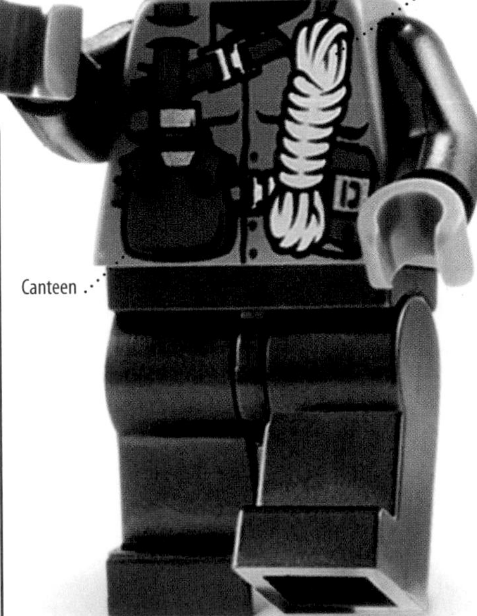
GOOD THING DINOS ARE LOUSY AT HIDE AND SEEK!
Camouflage pattern
Rope
Canteen

Shadow This minifigure's new head is specially camouflaged for creeping up on the dinosaurs undetected.

DE BOUWSTEEN

De Bouwsteen minifigure The back of the minifigure features the LEGO logo.

DUTCH TREAT

This minifigure was produced with special permission from the LEGO Group, and only 1000 were ever released. The extremely rare minifigures were accompanied by a certificate and given out to members of De Bouwsteen, a group of Dutch adult fans of LEGO (AFOLs), at LEGO World Netherlands in 2005.

LEGO® VIKINGS

Courageous Scandinavian warriors battled mythological monsters in five exciting LEGO Vikings sets in this new theme. Minifigures featured many new torsos and heads, as well as a new small, white barb piece used as the horns for the helmets. Vikings would be replaced by the new Castle line in 2007.

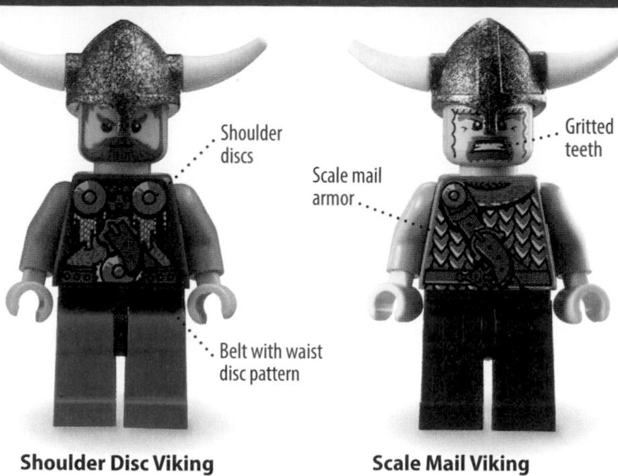
Shoulder discs
Belt with waist disc pattern
Scale mail armor
Gritted teeth

Shoulder Disc Viking Unfortunately for this Viking, his new shoulder discs won't stay shiny for long.

Scale Mail Viking Despite a new torso with scale mail resembling the scales of a fish or a reptile, this Viking still seems angry!

LEGO
VIKINGS
7019

Viking Fortress (7019) This set includes six viking warriors who must defend their fortress from the dreaded Fafnir Dragon.

New style of helmet with side holes
Barbarian armor new this year

Barbarian Armor Viking Barbarian-style armor really helps this Viking to channel his inner rage.

Dimple

Handsome Viking This Viking has a rugged charm and is one of the few Viking minifigures to have a happy expression.

White barb used as horn
Armor breastplate

Stern Viking Featuring the new speckled armor breastplate, this Viking is ready to defend his village from fearsome monsters.

Ax attached to leather belt

Ax Viking This new torso features a deadly ax—watch out Fafnir dragon!

Thick sword for serious fighting
Studded collar
Leather belt
Patterned round shield

Serious Viking This minifigure is included in only one set, Viking Fortress (7019), in which the vikings fight the Fafnir Dragon.

Golden helmet reflects his status
White beard and sideburns
Black cape

Viking King As leader of the Vikings, it's only right that the caped Viking King is regally dressed in red.

DID YOU KNOW?
Most of the monsters in the Vikings sets came from Norse myths.

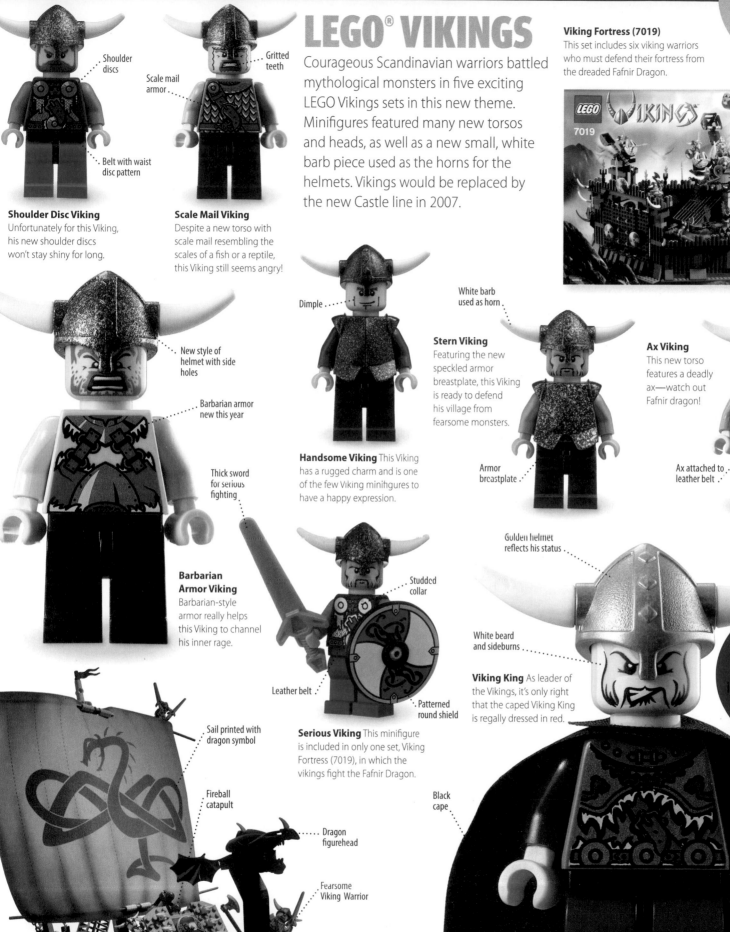

Sail printed with dragon symbol
Fireball catapult
Dragon figurehead
Fearsome Viking Warrior
Cage prison

Viking Ship Challenges the Midgard Serpent (7018) This set features the first galley made by the LEGO Group and is the first set to include a sea serpent model. It features the Viking King minifigure and six Viking warriors.

2005

LEGO *STAR WARS*

Star Wars®: Episode III *Revenge of the Sith* dominated the LEGO assortment in 2005, with 13 sets devoted to the new movie. As well as several new minifigures, light-up lightsabers were added to many sets. Anakin Skywalker's transformation to Darth Vader provided the climax to the three prequels and a compelling LEGO set.

Head button turns lightsaber on and off

THEY PUT THE "LIGHT" IN LIGHTSABER!

Gray tunic

Brown Jedi robe

Light-up Lightsaber Mace Windu This Mace Windu minifigure is pretty special—he is wielding a purple light-up lightsaber—the only minifigure to do so.

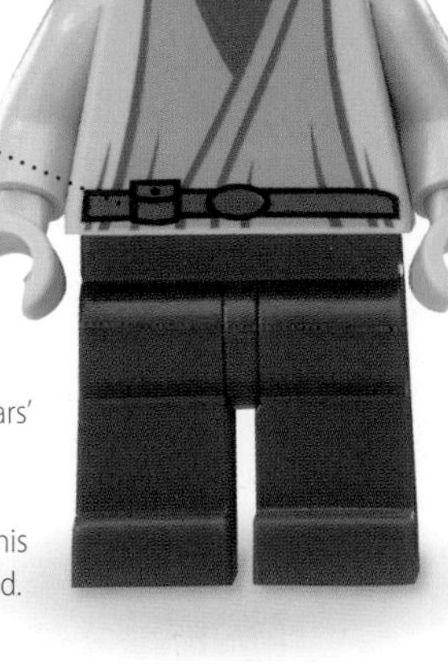

Owen's weary face with its gray eyebrows and stubble is unique to his minifigure.
Utility belt with pouch

Owen Lars The uncle and guardian of Luke Skywalker, Owen Lars' minifigure wears a simple desert robe and tunic to show his farming background.

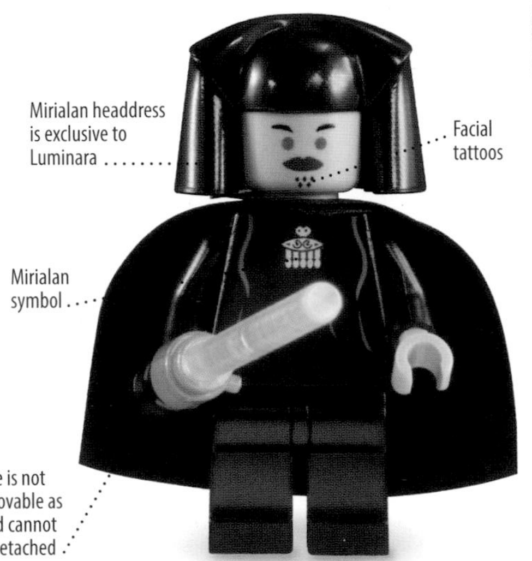

Mirialan headdress is exclusive to Luminara
Facial tattoos
Mirialan symbol
Cape is not removable as head cannot be detached

Luminara Unduli This skilled Jedi Master has a unique head piece with facial tattoos that represent her physical accomplishments.

LEGO
STAR WARS
7+
7257
282

Ultimate Lightsaber Duel (7257) This set is based on the duel between Anakin Skywalker and Obi-Wan Kenobi on Mustafar. It is the only set to include the light-up lightsaber versions of Anakin and Obi-Wan.

JEDI AND MORE

2005 saw the first appearance of Jedi Mace Windu and Luminara Unduli in minifigure form, plus Owen Lars and a Wookiee warrior. There was also a new version of Obi-Wan Kenobi.

Orange eyes glow with mischief
Specially fitted cloak for short-legged minifigures
Ion blaster

Jawa This shady character hides under a large hood element. It's perfect for snooping around and carrying out dodgy droid deals.

Lightsaber and minifigure are one complete assembly
Molded hood
TEACHING ANAKIN SEEMED LIKE A GOOD IDEA AT THE TIME...

Obi-Wan Kenobi This new variant of Obi-Wan features a light-up lightsaber. He appears in Ultimate Lightsaber Duel (7257) where he must fight his former apprentice, Anakin Skywalker.

Bandolier
Clan emblem

Wookiee Warrior A gold helmet is joined to a unique molded head piece in this Wookiee minifigure.

DROIDS FOR SALE

2005 was a profitable year in droid sales for the Jawas! Newly released figures of R1-G4, GNK, and Treadwell Droids were ready to be salvaged from scrap and sold on.

Printed control panel
White mechanical legs

R5-D4 The Jawas hope to make a profit selling this astromech droid figure in the Sandcrawler (10144).

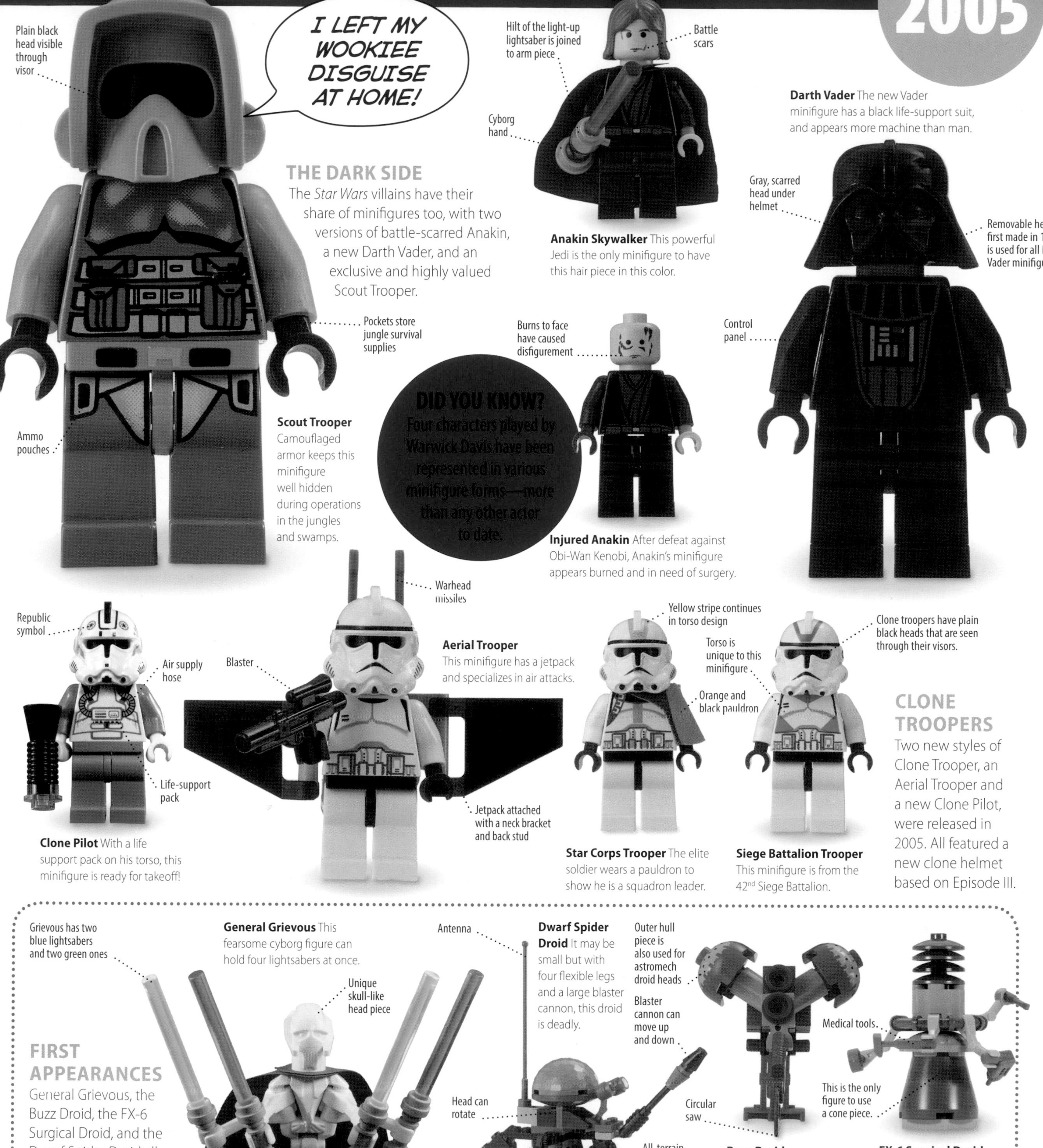
I LEFT MY WOOKIEE DISGUISE AT HOME!
Plain black head visible through visor
Pockets store jungle survival supplies
Ammo pouches
Hilt of the light-up lightsaber is joined to arm piece
Battle scars
Cyborg hand
Gray, scarred head under helmet
Removable helmet first made in 1999 is used for all Darth Vader minifigures.
Control panel
Burns to face have caused disfigurement
Warhead missiles
Republic symbol
Air supply hose
Life-support pack
Blaster
Jetpack attached with a neck bracket and back stud
Yellow stripe continues in torso design
Torso is unique to this minifigure
Orange and black pauldron
Clone troopers have plain black heads that are seen through their visors.
Grievous has two blue lightsabers and two green ones
Unique skull-like head piece
Cape is gray on one side and red on the other
Antenna
Head can rotate
All-terrain legs
Outer hull piece is also used for astromech droid heads
Blaster cannon can move up and down
Circular saw
Medical tools
This is the only figure to use a cone piece.

THE DARK SIDE

The *Star Wars* villains have their share of minifigures too, with two versions of battle-scarred Anakin, a new Darth Vader, and an exclusive and highly valued Scout Trooper.

Scout Trooper Camouflaged armor keeps this minifigure well hidden during operations in the jungles and swamps.

Anakin Skywalker This powerful Jedi is the only minifigure to have this hair piece in this color.

Darth Vader The new Vader minifigure has a black life-support suit, and appears more machine than man.

DID YOU KNOW? Four characters played by Warwick Davis have been represented in various minifigure forms—more than any other actor to date.

Injured Anakin After defeat against Obi-Wan Kenobi, Anakin's minifigure appears burned and in need of surgery.

Clone Pilot With a life support pack on his torso, this minifigure is ready for takeoff!

Aerial Trooper This minifigure has a jetpack and specializes in air attacks.

Star Corps Trooper The elite soldier wears a pauldron to show he is a squadron leader.

Siege Battalion Trooper This minifigure is from the 42nd Siege Battalion.

CLONE TROOPERS

Two new styles of Clone Trooper, an Aerial Trooper and a new Clone Pilot, were released in 2005. All featured a new clone helmet based on Episode III.

FIRST APPEARANCES

General Grievous, the Buzz Droid, the FX-6 Surgical Droid, and the Dwarf Spider Droid all made their debuts in LEGO form in 2005. This was the only appearance of the Spider Droid's blue variant.

General Grievous This fearsome cyborg figure can hold four lightsabers at once.

Dwarf Spider Droid It may be small but with four flexible legs and a large blaster cannon, this droid is deadly.

Buzz Droid This dangerous Separatist droid attaches itself to starships with its legs, and destroys them with a circular saw.

FX-6 Surgical Droid The medical droid plays an important role during the operation to keep Darth Vader alive, by encasing him in his suit.

Deadly sword
Monkey emblem
The bear's ferocious teeth are visible
Danju wields his sword with skill
Wolf emblem
Each of the knights' visors is slightly different in design.
Hawk emblem
RUN OUTSIDE AND PLAY, BOYS!
Head is also used on the Jing Lee the Wanderer minifigure from the LEGO Adventurers theme in 2003.
Sloped piece
Same armor as the 2004 Jayko knight minifigure
Black ponytail hair piece
Evil skull face
Golden crown
King Mathias proudly wears the lion emblem on his armor.
Vladek is an expert sword fighter.
Beneath the helmet is a scowling face.
Royal staff
Chrome gold crown
Black fabric cape
Hip hairstyle
Belt with star fastening
Flower in hair
Aqua skirt
Battle ax
Scorpion emblem
New silver-speckled black armor

Sir Rascus In combat Rascus is agile and flexible, just like the monkey emblem on his shield and armor.

Sir Santis A new shield and breastplate features a bear, reflecting Santis' strength and fortitude.

Sir Danju The wise Danju's emblem is a wolf, printed on his new armor breastplate and his shield.

Sir Jayko Although he is the youngest of the knights, Jayko is powerful and fast. The new hawk emblem design reflects this.

White Chess Queen This minifigure is one of the queens from the Knights' Kingdom chess set.

LEGO® CASTLE

LEGO® Knights' Kingdom returned for its second year in 2005, with seven sets. Both the story—King Mathias and four brave knights versus Vladek and his Shadow Knights—and the majority of the minifigures remained largely the same as in 2004. The new minifigures released for this theme were part of a chess set.

Black Chess Queen This sinister, skeleton-faced minifigure is a chess piece.

Scorpion Prison Cave (8876) This set contains five minifigures, including the captured Sir Danju and the brave Sir Jayko, who quests to rescue his friend.

King Mathias There's a minor change to the King Mathias minifigure this year—his arm color has changed from blue-violet to plain blue.

Dark Lord The new Vladek minifigure now features a red breastplate with an image of a scorpion.

Black Chess King Chess minifigures were only released as part of the chess set (G678).

LEGO® CLIKITS™

LEGO CLIKITS was an arts and crafts line aimed at girls that allowed them to create room decorations, gifts, and accessories. Only three CLIKITS figures were released and each one came in a separate set.

Star With the name Star, it's no surprise that this figure came in a set (7535) with lots of star pieces.

Daisy This figure was included in set 7534 with pieces designed to make jewelry.

Shadow Knight Vladek's army is made up of fierce fighters such as this one.

Elite Shadow Knight This variant shares the same head piece as Vladek.

LEGO HARRY POTTER

The LEGO Harry Potter play theme focused on *Harry Potter and the Goblet of Fire™* in 2005, with four new sets. Three of the four sets dealt with the three deadly tasks from the Triwizard Tournament. Three new versions of Harry appeared this year, and new minifigures included Viktor Krum, Professor Karkaroff, and Mad-Eye Moody.

Bowl-cut hair

Ron Weasley This minifigure's head is reversible—turn it around to see Ron sleeping!

Torn uniform

"POTTER" is printed in large letters on the back of torso piece

Harry Potter™ This is one of three Harry Potter minifigures released for *Harry Potter and the Goblet of Fire*. Each one wears a different outfit suitable for the trials Harry must face. This minifigure wears the first of the three outfits (featured in set 4767).

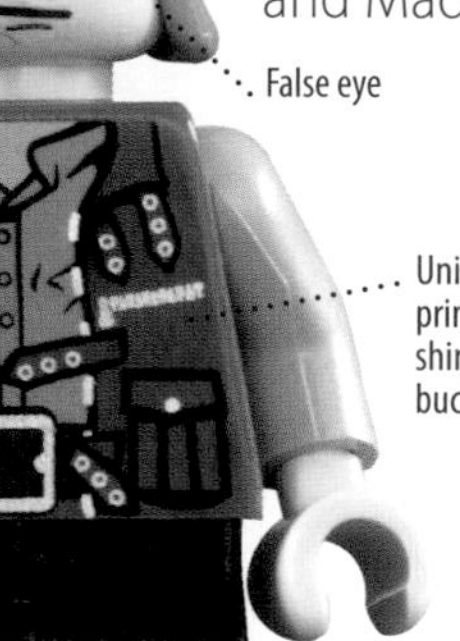

False eye

Unique torso printed with a shirt and a buckled jacket

Mad-Eye Moody With his scarred face and false eye, this minifigure's head piece is unique.

All versions of Dumbledore have the same beard

Professor Dumbledore In this variant, the headmaster wears blue dress robes.

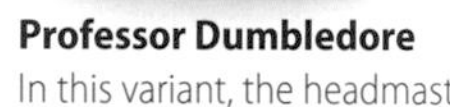

Same uniform as the 2004 minifigure

Hermione Granger This minifigure has a reversible head. The other side shows her in an enchanted sleep.

Whiskery facial markings

Rat-like teeth

Gloved, replacement hand

Wormtail This minifigure's unique head shows signs of his Animagus form—a rat.

Minifigure also comes with a human head piece

Durmstrang crest

Shark Head Viktor This minifigure shows Viktor Krum when he is half-shark, half-human.

DID YOU KNOW? In set 4767, LEGO designers created an egg with a magnetic piece on one side. Harry has a magnetic handle so he can hold it.

Head glows in the dark

Face now has smaller nostrils and eyes changed from red to clear

Lord Voldemort This is the first actual minifigure of Lord Voldemort. Prior to this he featured only as a face on one side of Professor Quirrell's head.

Large fur-like hat

Fur-lined Jacket with toggle fastenings

Viktor Krum This torso piece is identical to Igor Karkaroff's, but Victor's younger-looking face makes it easy to distinguish between the two.

Igor Karkaroff The scowling face with goatee is unique to this minifigure.

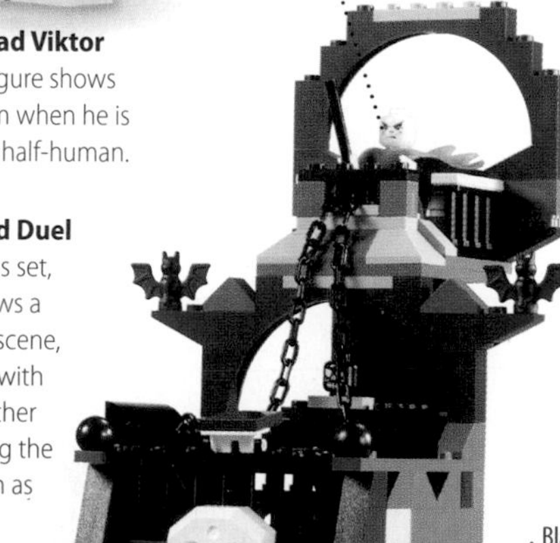

Lord Voldemort

Wormtail

Graveyard Duel (4766) This set, which shows a graveyard scene, also came with ideas for other builds using the bricks, such as this one.

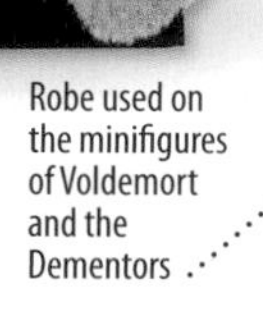

Black skeleton is unique to this set

Death Eater

Black Death Eater mask

Robe used on the minifigures of Voldemort and the Dementors

Death Eater This Death Eater resembles Lucius Malfoy and has a reversible head.

Merperson This Merperson's unique head, torso, and tail are not found on any other minifigure.

Hair piece also used for Poison Ivy from LEGO® Batman™

The first LEGO merperson tail

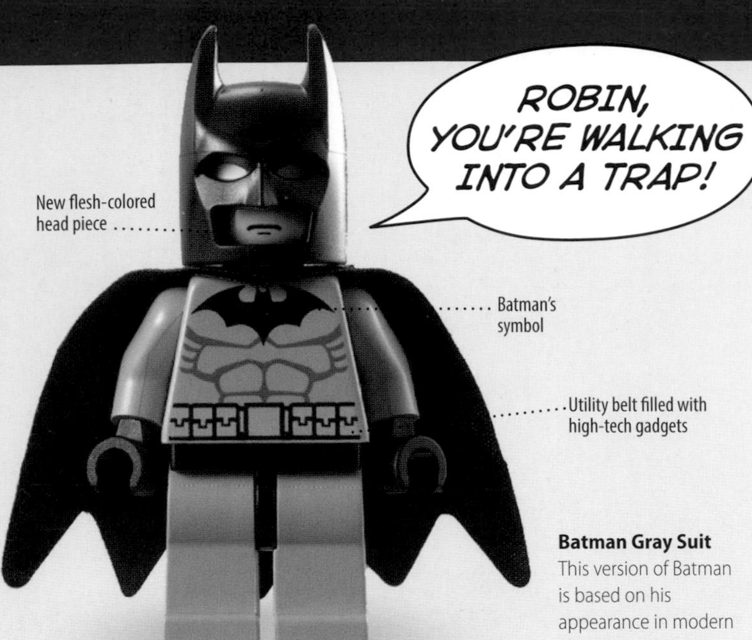

ROBIN, YOU'RE WALKING INTO A TRAP!
New flesh-colored head piece
Batman's symbol
Utility belt filled with high-tech gadgets

Batman Gray Suit This version of Batman is based on his appearance in modern comics and cartoons.

2006

A CAPED CRUSADER, a powerful Airbender, a yellow sponge from beneath the sea, brave young warriors in mighty battle mechs—these were just some of the new LEGO® minifigure "faces" to appear in 2006. Building on its success with *Star Wars*®, LEGO play themes embraced pop culture by welcoming some of the hottest licenses around. Lines such as LEGO® EXO-FORCE™ and LEGO® Aqua Raiders would also provide the adventure and role play LEGO fans craved, while new soccer sets revived LEGO® Sports.

LEGO® BATMAN™

LEGO fans and comic fans both had reason to cheer when the new LEGO Batman theme premiered in 2006. The Dark Knight appeared with some of his best friends and his worst enemies in six sets (a seventh, the Ultimate Batmobile set featured no minifigures). Many of the minifigures also appeared in three magnet collections.

Wavy hair piece

New torso this year with 'R' symbol and yellow utility belt

Robin The minifigure of Batman's ally is based on the third Robin from the comics, Tim Drake. He was the first to wear long pants instead of shorts.

DID YOU KNOW?
Batman's "blank" eyes are created by printing a white band across the minifigure's forehead.

New head piece with mustache and laughter lines

Alfred is always impeccably dressed

Alfred Bruce Wayne's loyal butler, Alfred, wears a new torso this year, with suit jacket, gray vest, and blue bow tie.

New masked head
Nightwing symbol

Nightwing After retiring as Robin, Dick Grayson became Nightwing. His hair piece is also seen on Hitomi, from the LEGO EXO-FORCE theme.

Unique feline mask

Silver shades visible underneath mask

Dual-sided head

Catwoman This jet black catsuit, new this year, allows Catwoman to remain undetected during her nocturnal criminal activities.

THE BATMAN FAMILY

Two versions of the Batman minifigure, plus Robin, Alfred the butler, Nightwing, and Batman's alter ego Bruce Wayne are featured in the 2006 sets.

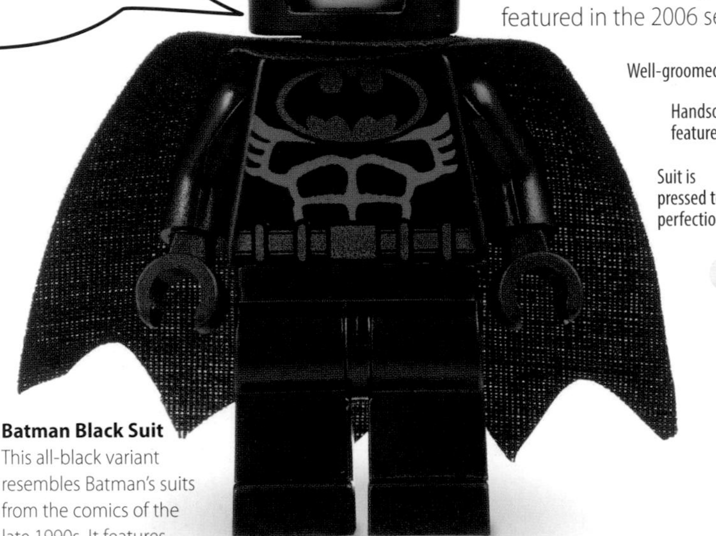

I'D WIPE THAT SMILE OFF YOUR FACE, RIDDLER, IF YOU WEREN'T PLASTIC!

Batman Black Suit This all-black variant resembles Batman's suits from the comics of the late 1990s. It features gold torso details.

Well-groomed hair

Handsome features

Suit is pressed to perfection

Bruce Wayne The Caped Crusader's civilian torso was first seen in 2004 on Harry Osborn from the LEGO® Spider-Man™ theme.

Arkham Asylum Guard This black cap features on a variety of minifigures, from police and pilots, to soccer players and stunt men.

Wry smile

Arkham Asylum Guard with Glasses The psychiatrists and doctors at the asylum try to turn the patients into upstanding minifigures, but the guards know it'll never work!

Smirk

Orange sunglasses

Torso features badge and radio

I DESERVE A BOOK OF MY OWN, AND IF I DON'T GET IT...

The Joker This Joker minifigure featured in a limited edition box set, given away at the 2008 San Diego Comic Con, as well as in set 7782.

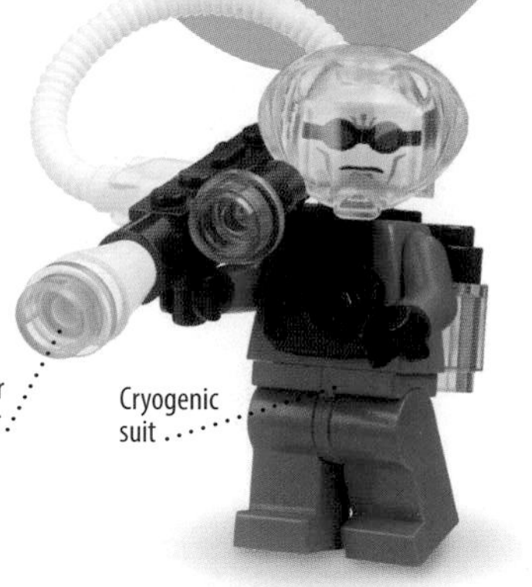

Crazy hair

Permanent grin

The Joker Calling Card

Freezer blaster

Cryogenic suit

Mr. Freeze This cool character's clear bubble helmet was first seen on minifigures from the LEGO® Insectoids theme in 1998.

DID YOU KNOW? A LEGO Batman promotional comic book was published this year.

Teeth of a predator

Unique reptilian torso

Killer Croc The scaly skinned menace has the appearance and the strength of a crocodile.

Top hat is a favorite with minifigure villains

Short LEGO legs

The Penguin This dapper crook wears a tuxedo, with a vest and bow tie, and a monocle over one eye.

Joker Venom popsicle

The Joker's Henchman This goon's purple torso shows that he is the Joker's henchman.

Same torso as his boss

Mr. Freeze's Henchman Working for such a cold hearted-boss isn't easy—no wonder he looks angry!

First time a hair piece is printed

Acid damage

Two-Face's black and white suit reflects his split personality.

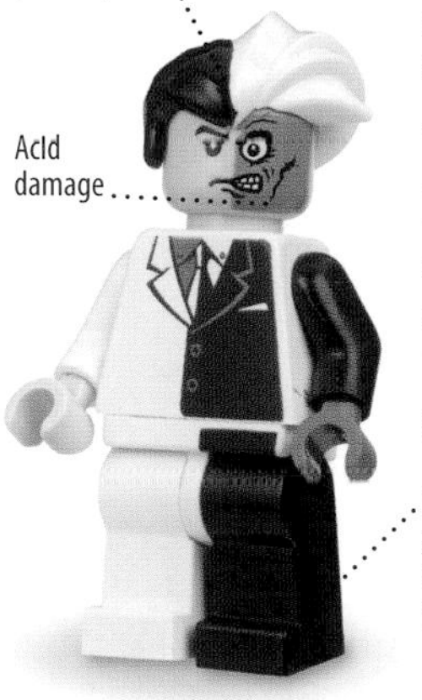

Two-Face This criminal has all new elements that are unique to him. His head is regular on one side, but purple and scarred on the other, with a large exposed eye.

THE VILLAINS

Most of Batman's minifigure archenemies surfaced in 2006, either individually in sets or together in Arkham Asylum (7785). The Joker, Penguin, Two-Face, and Killer Croc all had their own vehicles in the assortment.

Torso pattern resembles the leaves of a plant

Poison Ivy This female villain has a brand new, unique head with green lips and red eyebrows.

Pointed black hat made originally for LEGO® Castle witches and wizards

Scythe

The Scarecrow This sinister red-eyed minifigure has a translucent head that glows in the dark. His torso has printed stitching and a rope belt.

Knitted cap

Two-Face's Henchman This hired stooge has a black and white torso design that reflects his employer's split personality.

Question mark emblem

Green jumpsuit

The Riddler Nothing makes The Riddler happier than leaving complex clues to his crimes for Batman to solve. This year the Riddler has a new head with purple mask detail.

Arkham Asylum (7785) Some of Gotham's most dangerous criminals are included in this set. It features prison cells, an asylum van, and a bedsheet rope to aid escapees.

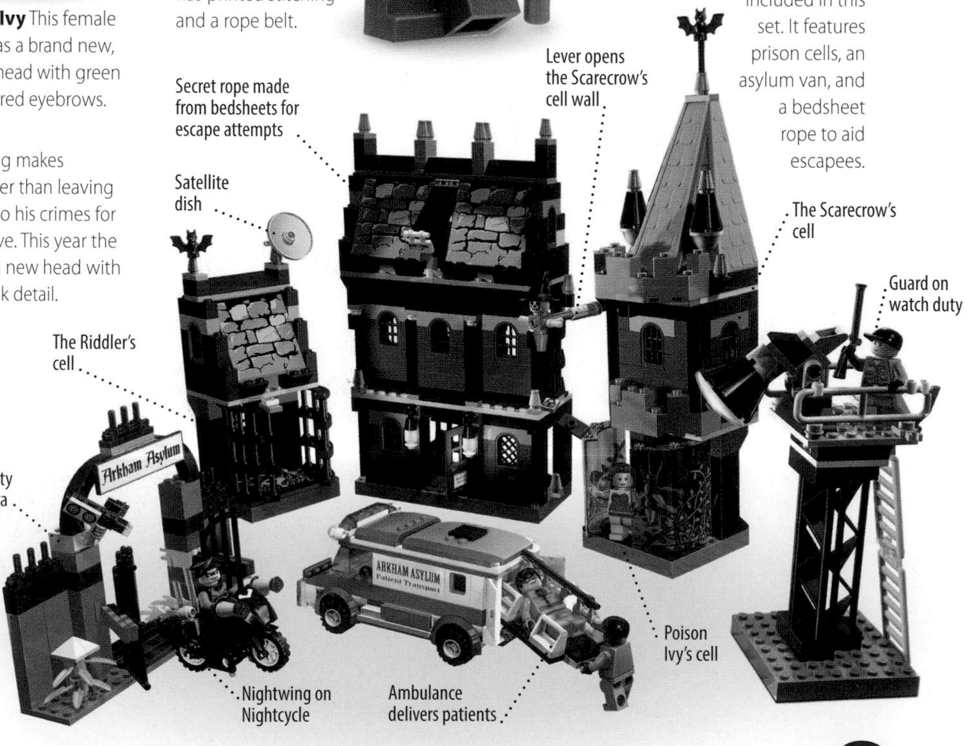

Secret rope made from bedsheets for escape attempts

Lever opens the Scarecrow's cell wall

Satellite dish

The Scarecrow's cell

Guard on watch duty

The Riddler's cell

Security camera

Arkham Asylum

Nightwing on Nightcycle

Ambulance delivers patients

Poison Ivy's cell

LEGO EXO-FORCE

LEGO minifigures met Japanese manga in this exciting new line. Daring young fighters in massive mechs challenged the might of an army of evil robots with their equally massive mechs in 16 sets. The human minifigures featured new torsos and new, swept back hair pieces, as well as anime-inspired facial designs.

New angular, swept back hair piece
New torso with EXO-FORCE uniform
Orange visor
Determined expression
New torso with orange suit and gray armor print
Japanese symbol detail
Utility belt
CAN SOMEONE LOAN ME A CAN OPENER SO I CAN GET OUT OF THIS THING?
This piece is actually a Knight's Kingdom sword
Fiber-optic cable
EMP pincer
Takeshi
Rotating laser canon
Armor from Stealth Hunter is light so the machine is agile
Scar
Intense expression
Red headband
Uplink equipment

Ha-Ya-To As the joker of the team, Ha-Ya-To always has a wry smile—even in the face of danger.

Keiken The leader of the EXO-FORCE team is the eldest and most experienced. Turn his head around to reveal his fighting face.

Hikaru The serious Hikaru has a new, angular, swept sideways hair piece and dual-sided head with an orange visor.

Tank Gunner This EXO-FORCE soldier is a mechanic, a guard, and anything else the team needs.

Mountain Warrior This mighty battle machine can be created by combining the Grand Titan (7701), which features an EMP pincer and a rotating laser cannon, and the Stealth Hunter (7700), which comes with a laser rifle and electro sword. It has space for a minifigure pilot.

Takeshi This minifigure has a new torso design with a dark gray armor breastplate over a red suit.

Purple Hair Ryo The technical expert of the team, there's nothing Ryo can't fix or invent!

DID YOU KNOW?
Every 2006 LEGO EXO-FORCE set features a light-up brick called a "power core."

Sinister red eye

Red-eyed Iron Drone A red axle placed inside its head makes the robot's eyes appear red.

Claw

Devastator These cold and calculating robots have terrifying mechanical claws.

Blue Devastator This figure pilots the Fire Vulture battle machine (7703).

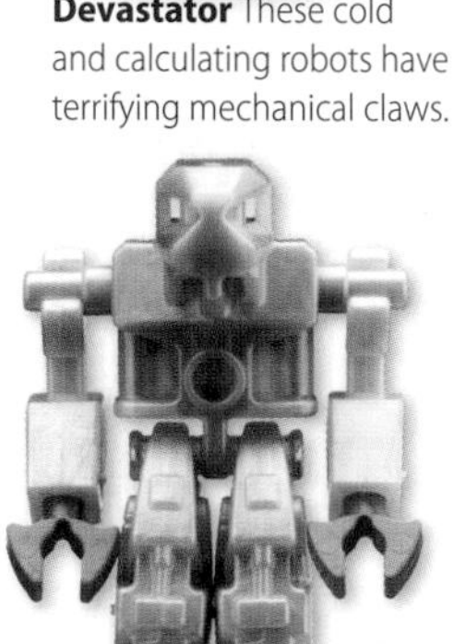

Red Devastator Thunder Fury (7702) is this robot's battle machine.

Green Devastator This robot flies the Sonic Phantom aircraft (7704).

Iron Drone The drone figures are the strongest robots, but are less intelligent than the Devastators.

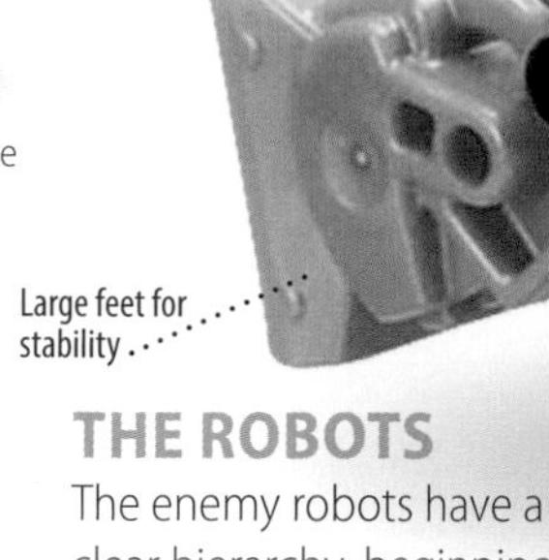
Meca One has many clones
Blaster
Large feet for stability
Devastator head piece
Devastator arms
Spear gun piece

Meca One This cunning golden figure is the leader of the robots.

Mini Venom Walker The legs of this robot are actually pieces normally used as spear guns.

THE ROBOTS

The enemy robots have a clear hierarchy, beginning with the Iron Drone figures and moving up to the three different colors of Devastator and finally to the golden leader, Meca One.

Small holes on edges to reflect the texture of a sponge
Goofy expression
Square pants

SpongeBob SquarePants This minifigure has a unique head piece printed with SpongeBob's face, which fits over a plain yellow torso.

DID YOU KNOW? Plankton also appears in a tiny, single cylinder brick form this year.

Flesh-colored torso with red spots and navel
Legs printed with lime shorts with purple flowers

Patrick Star SpongeBob's dopey best friend Patrick has a unique, cone-shaped head piece.

High-waisted blue pants
Short LEGO legs

Mr. Krabs The owner of the Krusty Krab restaurant has a unique molded head piece and eyes on stalks.

Unique features
Shirt collar pattern

Squidward Tentacles SpongeBob's grumpy neighbor has a regular head piece that is printed with a big nose and large yellow and red eyes.

Small lever
Sticker with Plankton's features

PLANKTON!

This large version of Plankton is made from three round bricks, covered by a sticker. This was the only figure in Build-A-Bob (3826). The set references the TV episode in which Plankton takes over Bob's mind.

LEGO® SPONGEBOB SQUAREPANTS™

Who lives in a LEGO set under the sea? SpongeBob SquarePants! Three sets appeared this year, featuring minifigures of all the major characters. The SpongeBob theme earned a reputation for having many interesting elements and variations of minifigures over the years.

2006

LEGO® AVATAR™ THE LAST AIRBENDER™

Avatar™, based on the popular animated Nickelodeon series *Avatar: The Last Airbender*, was a one-year theme in 2006. Two sets were released, featuring six new minifigures. Aang is the only minifigure to appear in both sets and, like the others in the theme, he features manga-style eyes.

NO, I DON'T KNOW WHAT I'M SMILING ABOUT EITHER.
Master Airbender Tattoo
Bright yellow torso
Orange poncho
New brown legs with yellow patches on the thighs

Aang As the last Airbender, Aang must try to save the world but as his smile suggests, he would rather have fun than fight the Fire Nation!

Strap holds a boomerang on his back
Smirk
Blue robes

Sokka Katara's warrior brother, Sokka is brave and loyal. His unique torso has a printed strap detail.

Classic Castle helmet but in a new color
Armor breastplate

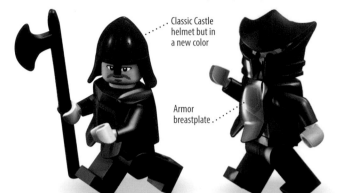

Fire Nation Soldier Serving fiery Prince Zuko is no joke—this soldier is the only minifigure with this new, serious head.

Firebender This scary looking minifigure has the power to control fire. He has a new head piece with a skull-like mask.

Loop of hair
Dark blue robe with white trim

Katara This minifigure has a brand new, unique head that features loops of hair that drape over her face.

New head has ponytail on the back
Scar
Fireproof armor pattern is unique to the Zuko minifigure.

Prince Zuko The exiled heir to the Fire Nation throne has quarrelled with his father. The scar on his face was caused by his father's fire during a duel.

Fire Nation Ship (3829) This mighty ship features five minifigures, Prince Zuko's tower, a removable prison beneath the deck, and a catapult.

Air Temple (3828) This set is of Aang's air temple, as depicted on the television series. It includes Aang, Sokka, Momo, a Firebender, and a Fire Nation soldier.

In the tower there is a trap door leading to the gateway area below.

Aang's air glider

Sokka

Firebender with helmet

Momo the flying lemur

Aang defends the temple using his powers.

Transparent radar dish air shield

DID YOU KNOW?
With only two set releases, Avatar has the fewest number of sets of any LEGO play theme.

LEGO
CITY
5-12
7903

Rescue Helicopter (7903) This set features a helicopter with rotating blades and includes a stretcher and a working winch to airlift patients to safety.

Flying Doctor This air ambulance doctor has a new torso with a jacket pattern that includes a radio, zippers, and the EMT Star of Life logo.

Radio

Zipper

Star of Life logo

EXO-FORCE™ torso

Astronaut This minifigure shares its torso with Ha-Ya-To and Hikaru from the LEGO EXO-FORCE play theme.

FIRST LEGO® LEAGUE

The 2006 *FIRST* LEGO® League challenge was Nano Quest, focusing on applications of nanotechnology. Two of these astronaut minifigures were included with the Nano Quest (9763), acting as passengers in the set's Space Elevator.

LEGO® TECHNIC

This minifigure is unusual as it was included in an educational LEGO Technic set—Science and Technology Base Set (9632). The set came with 25 booklets with building directions for 12 different models.

Black ponytail hair piece

Pretty orange flower pattern

Floral Shirt Girl Minifigures aren't usually featured in LEGO Technic sets, but this Girl seems very happy about it!

LEGO® CITY

When there was an emergency, the LEGO City Emergency Medical team was on the job in 2006. Doctors and air ambulance pilots made up just some of the minifigures released with four Emergency sets. Also in 2006, the LEGO® Train subtheme converted to remote control, with two sets featuring seven minifigures.

Silver shades

Tools in pocket

Construction Worker New coveralls with a handy pocket for storing essential tools has made this construction worker's day.

Doctor with Radio With a new torso featuring pens and a stethoscope, this Doctor is ready to help the ailing citizens of LEGO City.

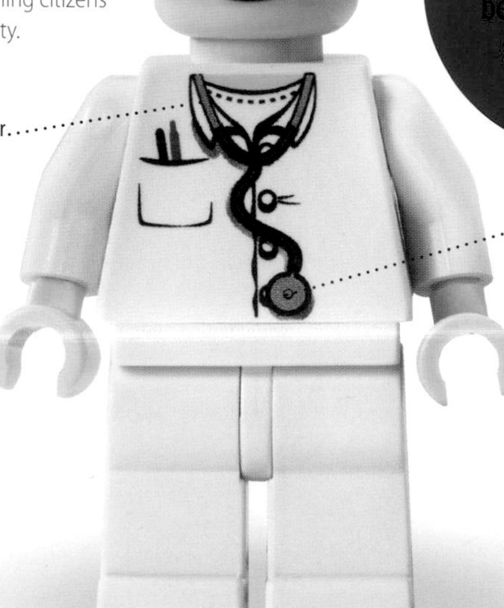

Open collar

Stethoscope

DID YOU KNOW? Hospital (7892) would be the last Hospital set released for six years.

Helmet with visor

Emergency equipment

Air Ambulance Doctor Being part of the air ambulance is a fast-paced, action-packed job, but this minifigure keeps a cool head at all times.

Glasses

The conductor wears his uniform with pride.

Train logo

Conductor Charlie This friendly conductor really enjoys helping passengers.

Hard hat

Reflective strips

Shovel

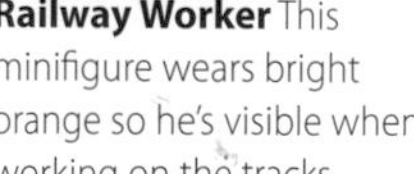

Railway Worker This minifigure wears bright orange so he's visible when working on the tracks.

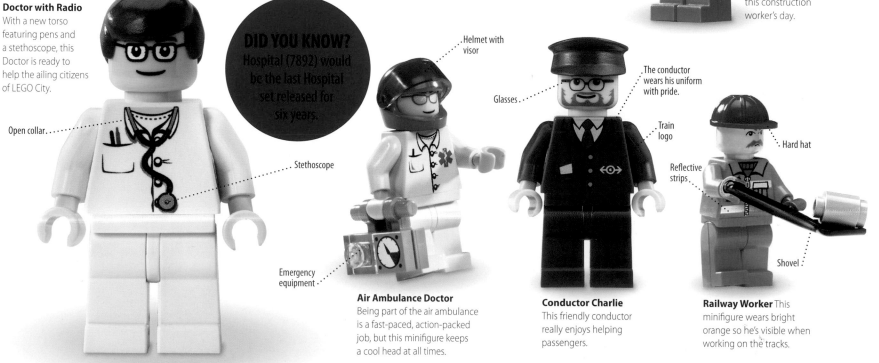

2006

LEGO® CASTLE

LEGO Knights' Kingdom continued the story of the heroic knights of Morcia and their battle against the evil Vladek. The struggle shifted to the mighty Mistlands Tower, and King Jayko was promoted to the throne from his previous rank of knight. Apart from Lord Vladek and King Jayko, all the other characters were new for 2006, including two noble heroes, Sir Kentis and Sir Adric.

Sir Kentis This loyal knight has a new dark green sturdy armor breastplate with a silver chain mail pattern.

Speckled gray helmet worn in 2004 in purple by the knight Danju.

Chain mail pattern

Striking red armor.

Helmet has also been worn in red by the knight Santis in 2004.

Sir Adric Raring to defend King Jayko in battle, Sir Adric just needs to make sure he can see out of his chunky helmet first!

Bushy eyebrows meet in the middle
Evil sneer on face

Dracus The warlord of the evil Rogue Knights, this menacing minifigure stands out in his yellow pants and sleeves.

Fierce facial expression for battle

Bronze studs

Royal Knight uses the same head and armor as Sir Adric.

Karzon Vladek's wicked weapons master is very proud of his bronze armor and likes to show it off with plenty of bad-tempered shouting.

PHEW! GOOD THING I HAVE A FAN IN HERE!

Helmet with fixed face grille

Royal Knight Wearing bright red armor, with silver chain mail and stud pattern, this knight is on the lookout for trouble!

Pointed helmet with nose guard
Silver studs
Leg protection

Good Knight This noble minifigure wears an armor breastplate that features silver studs and chain mail.

LEGO
KNIGHTS' KINGDOM
7-14
8823

Mistlands Tower (8823) King Jayko and his brave knights defend their tower from Vladek in this rare Knights' Kingdom set.

Little of Vladek's face is visible under visor.

Scorpion emblem

CAN SOMEONE HELP ME GET THIS HELMET OFF? PLEASE?

Bright red cape

Lord Vladek The evil knight now wears a black armor breastplate, embellished with a large silver scorpion.

Gray beard fades to white at edges
Hawk symbol
Black cape

King Jayko This royal minifigure has a new pearl gold armor breastplate. It features a silver and black hawk pattern.

LEGO® FERRARI

Four more LEGO® Racers Ferrari sets sped toward the finish line this year. Along with a new version of driver Felipe Massa and a number of pit crew members, this year's lineup included announcers, cameramen, and a race official. A Fuel Filler minifigure was also introduced, wearing modern protective gear.

TV
Press
Checkered pattern

Cameraman Capturing all the race action with his camera, this minifigure wears a stickered vest to show that he's a member of the press.

Charismatic smile
Blue jacket with zipper and pockets

Commentator Keeping race fans up to speed with everything that happens on the track, this is the first appearance of a race commentator minifigure in the Ferrari Racers theme.

Silver shades

Race Engineer This engineer is a new addition to the Ferrari team. He gets the best performance from the vehicle and the driver during the race.

HAS ANYONE SEEN THE CAR KEYS?

Head piece also used for the 2004 Rubens Barrichello minifigure
Torso with Ferrari and sponsors' logos
Suit
Unique torso with name

Felipe Massa This new minifigure represents the real-life racing driver, Felipe Massa. A torso sticker shows his name and the Brazilian flag.

Fuel Filler A helmet with a gold visor to represent the protective clothing used in F1 adorns the Fuel Filler's head.

Race Official Making sure the rules are adhered to, this Race Official is a new addition to the Ferrari Racers sets.

DID YOU KNOW?
Five new minifigure characters make their first appearances in the 2006 LEGO Racers sets.

Ferrari Finish Line (8672)
This set features two Ferrari racing cars, ten minifigures, and great accessories such as checkered flags, pit crew tools, and even a silver trophy.

The winners' flags
Commentator
Cameraman
ITALIAN GRAND PRIX
Hi-tech computer systems and monitors
Pit crew tools
Pit crew member

Piraka Hakann
With intense red eyes and sharp, pointed teeth, this figure's appearance is as scary as his personality!

Figure has moving parts

Mechanical claw

BIONICLE®

The BIONICLE invasion of the world of play themes continued as the heroic Toa Inika and the villainous Piraka appeared in figure form. Four sets were released this year, featuring a total of 12 new figures. All of these featured an assortment of new elements.

Deadly weapon
Lime colored eyes

Toa Inika Hahli
This figure's mechanical arms, torso, and heavy-treaded legs make her a fearsome warrior in battle.

2006

LEGO® *STAR WARS*®

2006 saw the return of some well-loved minifigures, as well as some new ones. The Bespin Security Guard, Dengar, and Ten Numb all made their debuts this year. Luke Skywalker, Princess Leia, Han Solo, and Lando Calrissian returned in the all-new Jabba's Sail Barge (6210).

Green lightsaber
Skin-colored hand. On the 2010 variant it's black.
Jedi robe pattern

Jedi Knight Luke Variants of this minifigure all have the same legs and torso with black Jedi robes.

Face printed with lines to reflect his Sullustan features
Life-support pack

Ten Numb Ten is a Sullustan minifigure. He is exclusive to the B-Wing Starfighter (6208).

Helmet with face guard is unique
Vibro-ax
Brown tunic and gold armor

Lando Calrissian
Disguised as a skiff guard on Jabba's Sail Barge, Lando intends to help his friends.

In LEGO *Star Wars* only Leia wears this hair piece.

Prior to 2011, all variants and versions of Leia used this face.

Chain can be attached to collar

WHO ARE YOU CALLING A SLAVE GIRL?

Tiny gold bikini top doesn't cover up very much

Miniscule skirt and gold bikini briefs

The 2003 variant was yellow.

Slave Princess Leia The proud Princess Leia is forced to be Jabba the Hutt's scantily-clad slave, but Jabba underestimates her—to his peril!

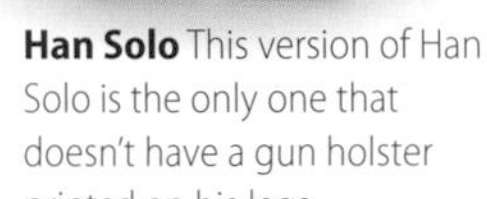

The torso on the 2010 variant has creases on the shirt

Han Solo This version of Han Solo is the only one that doesn't have a gun holster printed on his legs.

Arms printed with red marking to show rank of sergeant
Torso has gold trim and the guards' emblem
Relby-K23 blaster pistol

Bespin Security Guard
This is the only minifigure to have the standard head piece in reddish brown.

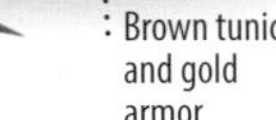

Sail
Boba Fett
Gamorrean Guard
Lando Calrissian
Drive thrust
Luke Skywalker
Han Solo
R2-D2
Jabba the Hutt holding Princess Leia's chain

Jabba's Sail Barge (6210)
This set comes with eight minifigures. The sides of the barge open to reveal Jabba's throne room, prison, and kitchen.

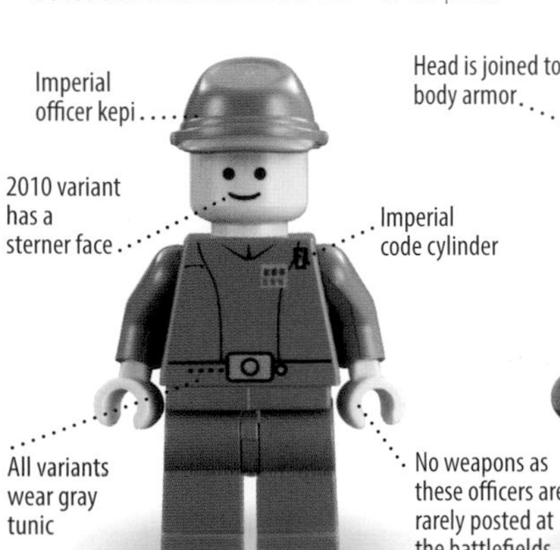

Imperial officer kepi
2010 variant has a sterner face
Imperial code cylinder
All variants wear gray tunic
No weapons as these officers are rarely posted at the battlefields

Imperial Officer This minifigure is a high-ranking soldier in the Emperor's huge army.

Deadly vibro-ax
Head is joined to body armor

Gamorrean Guard
This boar-like creature has a new modified head with snout and tusks.

Since suffering a head injury Dengar always wears a bandage

Ninja wrap also seen in the Ninjago theme in 2011

Torso pattern unique to this minifigure

Dengar This bounty hunter is hired by Darth Vader to capture the *Millennium Falcon*.

DRINK ANYONE?

R2-D2 is forced to be a servant on Jabba the Hutt's Sail Barge, and so this variant comes complete with two drinks and a serving tray attachment.

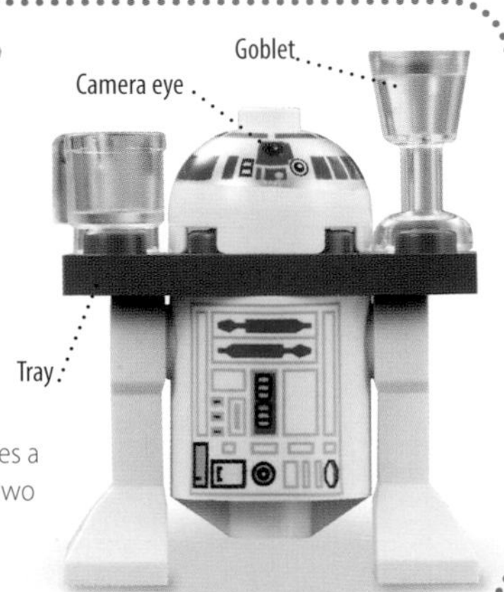

Goblet
Camera eye
Tray

R2-D2 This little droid comprises a head piece, a body piece, and two leg pieces that are joined to its body with LEGO Technic pins.

LEGO SPORTS

Three new LEGO Soccer sets premiered in 2006, including the Grand Soccer Stadium (3569) with 14 minifigures! Six more soccer player minifigures came in the other two sets, Street Soccer (3570), and Soccer Target Practice (3568). This was the last year for the Soccer theme.

Cap

Torso sticker with Adidas logo

Blue Striker Gooooooal! This sharp-shooting minifigure appears in Soccer Target Practice (3568).

DID YOU KNOW?
2006 sets included Adidas® mini soccer balls, and some minifigures had Adidas logos on them.

LEGO® VIKINGS

In 2006 the LEGO Vikings Chess Set was released, as well as two Vikings sets. This included the Army of Vikings with Heavy Artillery Wagon (7020), which came with seven minifigures—the most included in any Vikings set.

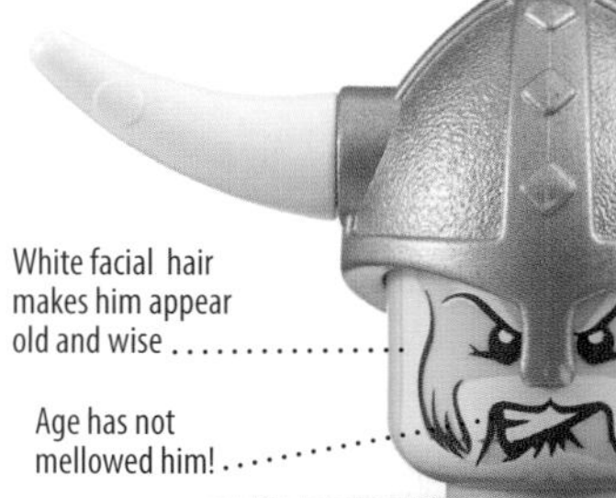

White facial hair makes him appear old and wise

Age has not mellowed him!

DO I LOOK LIKE I WANT TO PLAY CHESS?

Red Chess King The Viking chess pieces have the same torso pattern as the Fantasy Era dwarf minifigures from the Castle theme in 2008.

LEGO
VIKINGS
7-14
7020

Army of Vikings with Heavy Artillery Wagon (7020) This set features seven Viking minifigures and an Artillery Wagon equipped with firing missiles.

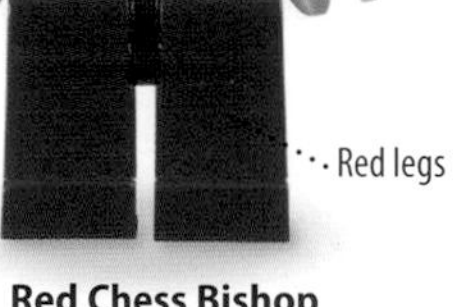

Chess may be a game but these minifigures take it seriously!

Horns are glued to helmet

On the chessboard he holds a sword in each hand

Red legs

Red Chess Bishop So that the chess minifigures did not get mixed up, some of the pieces were stuck together with glue.

Gray hair piece

Gray sloping piece for skirt

Blue Chess Queen The blue and red queens in the Viking chess set are the only ones that have happy expressions. They must be winning....

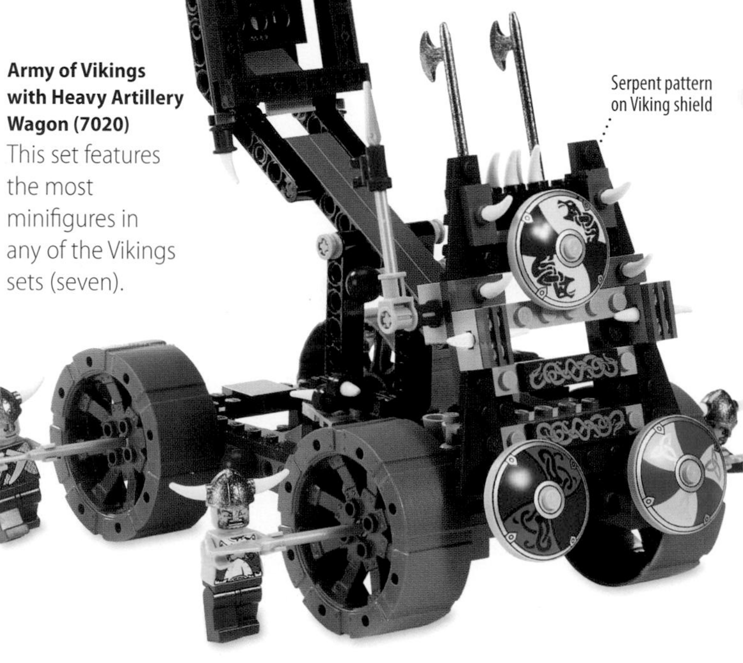

Catapult

Serpent pattern on Viking shield

Leader of the Viking Warriors

Army of Vikings with Heavy Artillery Wagon (7020) This set features the most minifigures in any of the Vikings sets (seven).

Black and silver speckled halberd

Silver shoulder discs

Viking Warrior This Viking Warrior is angry—very angry. He's ready to head into battle with his fellow Vikings in set 7020.

ON THE MOVE!

THERE'S ONE THING you can say about LEGO® minifigures: they never stand still! Over the years, minifigures have ridden just about every kind of vehicle you can imagine, from skateboards and snowboards to motorcycles and airplanes. Animals have helped get them from place to place too, including elephants, horses, and even ostriches. But whatever they use, whether it is wheeled, winged, or on four feet, minifigures travel all over the LEGO world looking for adventure!

Jetpack Featuring twin handles, this gadget is essential for the Blacktron II Commander's adventures.

POLICE
POLICE

Motorcycle The Policeman's motorcycle lets him zoom through the traffic to the scene of the crime. He can even attach his radio!

Scooter This happy little boy loves rolling along on his push-scooter.

Fairy wings The dainty wings are on a bracket around the Fairy's neck.

Spinner The Green Ninja minifigure swirls up a tornado. A unique green crown fits on top of the spinner.

Skateboard The minifigure's feet clip onto the skateboard's studs.

49

Roller skates Roller Derby Girl zips along on her detachable black wheels.

Speedor Worriz the Wolf's Speedor wheel is strong, powerful, and fast.

Elephant and cart Pippin the reporter enjoys the bumpy but scenic route from the cart as Babloo encourages his elephant on!

Windsurfing
The windsurfing minifigure clings on tightly to the boom. Life's a breeze, if he can keep his balance!

Horse This faithful steed is made from two LEGO pieces.

Skis Fix the studs on the skis to the Skier's feet and off he zooms.

Snowboard
This minifigure's snowboard is weighted to keep him upright and moving down the slope of his set, Snowboard Boarder Cross Race (3538).

SPALDING
NBA

Spring-loaded legs
In 2003, spring-loaded legs and special new arms were created, allowing this NBA Basketball player to slam dunk the ball.

Bicycle This bright red bicycle is the perfect transport for riding around town taking pictures.

Flippers These flippers are essential for exploring the depths of the ocean.

Ice Skates Wearing these detachable skates, the Ice Skater performs dazzling moves on the ice.

Broomstick Every witch knows that brooms are the best way to travel.

COME ON IN. THE WATER'S FULL OF SHARKS!
Scuba tank
Weight belt
Spear guns doubled as legs for the 2006 LEGO® EXO-FORCE™ Mini Venom Walker

Aqua Raider Diver The divers are armed with spear guns to fend off savage sea creatures.

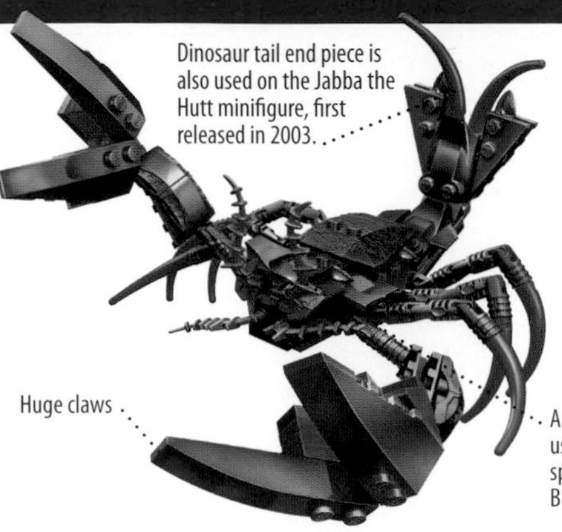

2007

THE EXCITEMENT was building in 2007 as the LEGO Group helped to celebrate the 30th anniversary of *Star Wars*® with a host of new sets and a special 14-carat gold C-3PO minifigure. Harry Potter™ returned in one set, his last until 2010. Meanwhile, new LEGO play themes took center stage, including the undersea LEGO® Aqua Raiders, the out-of-this-world LEGO® Mars Mission, and the fantasy-themed LEGO® Castle. LEGO® Modular Buildings made their first appearance, giving experienced builders the chance to assemble realistic buildings in scale to their minifigure residents.

Mechanical robot arm

Dinosaur tail end piece is also used on the Jabba the Hutt minifigure, first released in 2003.

Lobster Strike (7772) A fearsome giant lobster, an underwater exploration rover to defeat it, and two minifigures are included in this set.

Huge claws

Antennae also used as Barraki spines in BIONICLE® sets.

Spinning drill for collecting underwater crystals

LEGO AQUA RAIDERS

Aqua Raiders plunged beneath the ocean waves in 2007 in seven sets. Unlike previous underwater teams, the Aqua Raiders don't fight other minifigures, but search for treasure along the sea floor. They need to watch out, though—dangerous sea creatures stand between them and their prizes!

DID YOU KNOW? All the Aqua Raiders' head pieces have appeared in previous themes.

Translucent blue diving mask

Knit hat has kept more than 80 minifigures warm, including robbers and farmers.

Aqua Raiders trident logo

Black flippers debuted in the 1995 LEGO® Aquazone theme

Aqua Raider Diver All the Aqua Raiders minifigures wear identical zippered diving suits—new for 2007.

Zippered diving suit

Deep Sea Diver The divers' helmets feature the new distinctive blue trident logo on top.

Hatted Diver After a long day seeking treasure in the depths of the ocean, this minifigure dons a knit hat to keep warm.

Zippered black mask and red eyes

Bulging muscles and scars

Bane This mighty minifigure only ever appears in one set, The Bat-Tank: The Riddler and Bane's Hideout (7787). He gets a redesign in 2012 and switches to a black suit.

Unique torso with yellow utility belt

Dark Blue Knight Batman receives a makeover with a dark blue mask, cape, hips, and hands.

LEGO® BATMAN™

Two sets appeared in 2007, featuring a new dark blue costume for the Caped Crusader. Only one new character was released—the muscle-bound Bane.

Same facial expression as 2007 Aqua Raider Diver

Air pressure regulator

THIS SUIT IS TOO TIGHT!

Angry Spaceman Space travel is no picnic, but this grumpy minifigure is proud to wear the Classic Space logo on his suit.

Sunglasses to protect eyes from dust storms

Communication system

Spaceman The explorers wear standard helmets, but with gold visors—new for 2007.

LEGO® SPACE

2007 saw the first new LEGO Space theme in six years: LEGO Mars Mission. Considered a sequel of sorts to 2001's LEGO® Life on Mars, it differed by making the alien figures a menacing, rather than peaceful, force. Eight sets were released in 2007, featuring astronauts with new torsos and glow-in-the-dark aliens.

Orange sunglasses peek out from under helmet

Miner The astronauts pilot vehicles equipped with drills, claws, and saws for mining precious crystals on Mars.

Same head piece as 2006 LEGO® Sports players

Space Explorer All the Mars Mission minifigures' head pieces have been used in previous years and themes.

ALIEN INVADERS

The mysterious alien figures have traveled from deep within the cosmos to Mars to seek energy crystals to power their sinister technology.

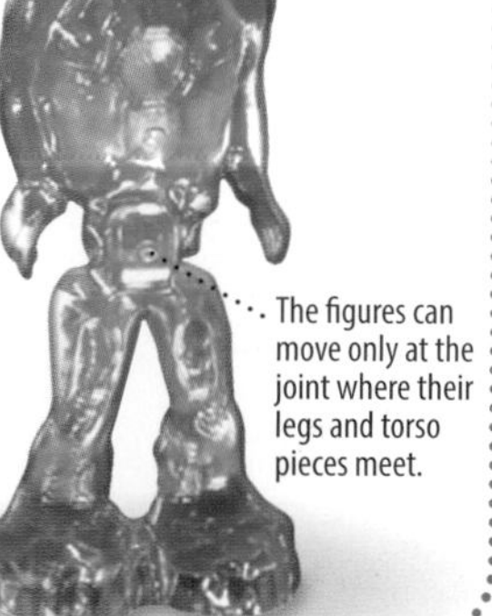

The figures can move only at the joint where their legs and torso pieces meet.

Alien The alien figures are made of two unique transparent green, glow-in-the-dark parts—legs and torso.

Specially molded head piece

Movable legs

Kalmah This fearsome figure may be small, but he strikes fear into the hearts of his Toa Mahri foes.

BIONICLE®

The final year of the miniature BIONICLE theme featured three sets and 11 new figures of the warring Toa Mahri and the Barraki. The sets included both vehicles and Rahi beasts for transporting the figures.

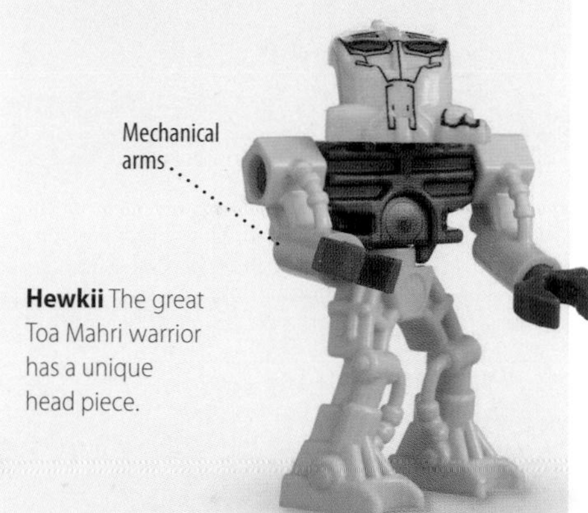

Mechanical arms

Hewkii The great Toa Mahri warrior has a unique head piece.

Large weapon

Powerful jaws with protosteel teeth

Pridak The leader of the evil Barraki is all set to ambush the Toa Mahri.

BIONICLE
8-16
8926

Toa Undersea Attack (8926) This set comes with three miniature Toa Mahri and three Barraki figures, as well as a working missile blaster.

2007

Gold crown-trimmed corset
New dark blue sloped skirt

Crown Princess
Daughter of the Crown King, this fair maiden's smiling face suggests she is safe from the evil Skeleton Warriors. For now....

CROWN KNIGHTS

Led by the brave Crown King, the Crown Knights are made up of foot soldiers and horsemen. They have new torsos with armor breastplate printing and appeared in every 2007 Castle set.

I MAY BE A PLASTIC KING, BUT DON'T CALL ME A RULER!

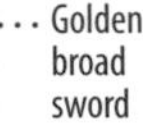

Metallic sword
Helmet is metallic silver for the first time this year.
Scale mail with crown detail

Scared Crown Knight
He is one of the only minifigures in the Castle theme with a dual-sided head. Turn his head around to see his calmer side.

Chrome gold crown
Golden broad sword
Dark blue cloth cape

Crown King with Cape Ruler of the Crown Knights, the caped Crown King has new pearl gold armor to protect him in battle.

LEGO CASTLE

The new LEGO Castle series featured human Crown Knights battling against a scary Skeleton Army led by an evil wizard. This popular theme, referred to as "Fantasy Era" by LEGO fans to distinguish it from Classic Castle sets, lasted for three years. Seven sets were released this year, along with a Castle Chess Set (852001) and Tic Tac Toe game (852132).

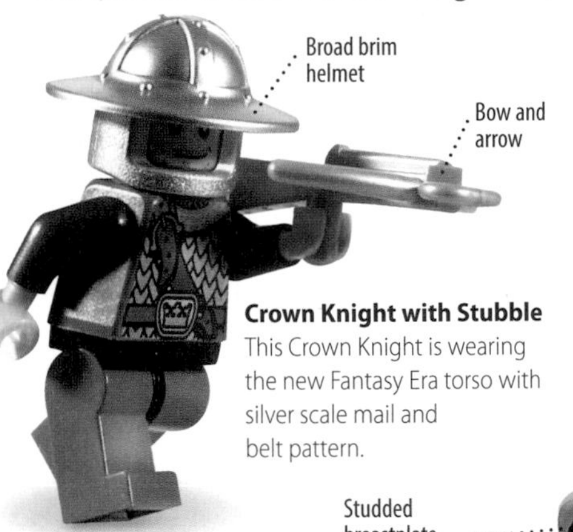
Broad brim helmet
Bow and arrow

Crown Knight with Stubble
This Crown Knight is wearing the new Fantasy Era torso with silver scale mail and belt pattern.

Shield with printed crown emblem

Crown Knight with Visor
The Crown Knight's standard helmet and pointed visor is metallic silver for the first time this year.

Castle helmet with neck protector

Spear

Scar-faced Crown Knight
A battle scar across his lip distinguishes this Knight from the other Crown Knights.

Hood
New torso with scale mail and belt detail

Crown Bishop
From the Fantasy Era Chess Set, the Crown Bishop is hoping his angry expression will scare the Skeleton Army.

Grille helmet
Studded breastplate

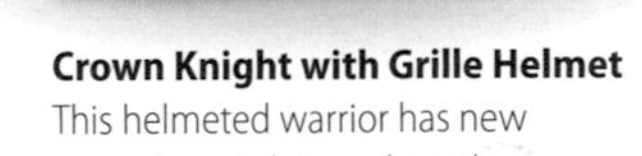

Crown Knight with Grille Helmet
This helmeted warrior has new armor breastplate and pearl gray leg protection.

Quiver of arrows

Crown Knight with Quiver
This is the first year the Knight's broad brim helmet appears in metallic silver.

Chest strap

Scared Crown Knight
Maybe this scared Crown Knight has just spotted an evil Skeleton?

Crown emblem

Battling Crown Knight
This Knight has a sword and he's not afraid to use it!

SKELETON WARRIORS

The standard Fantasy Era Skeleton is black instead of white. Its body and limbs have also been redesigned to hold poses.

Evil scowl

Black Skeleton The Black Skeleton's vertical grip arms are also used for many LEGO® *Star Wars*® droid minifigures.

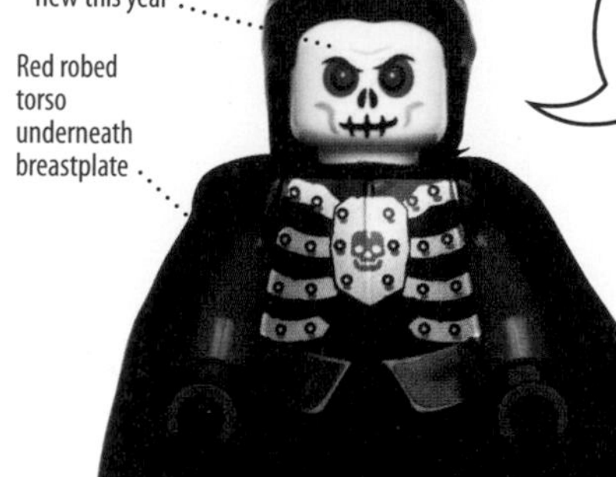
Skull head is new this year
Red robed torso underneath breastplate
IF YOU LOOKED LIKE THIS, YOU'D BE CRANKY TOO.

Evil Queen The red-headed Evil Queen wears a new armor breastplate, with a silver-studded ribcage pattern and skeleton head detail.

THE SKELETON ARMY

The evil wizard's army consists of Skeleton warriors who ride skeleton horses. Other sinister minifigures, such as the Evil Queen and Evil Bishop, appear only in the Fantasy Era Chess Set.

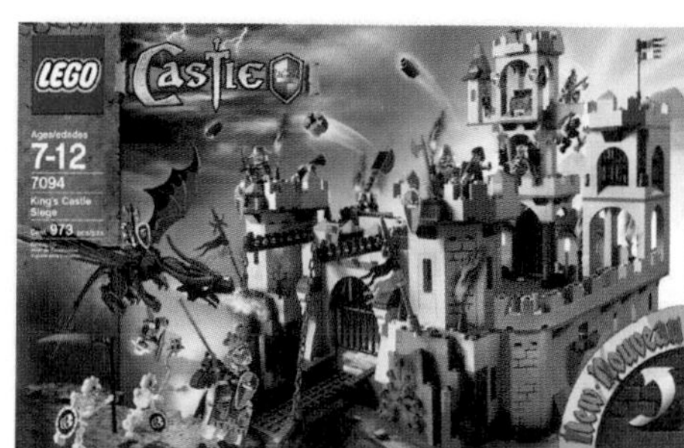
LEGO
Castle
7-12
7094

King's Castle Siege (7094) The castle is under attack! As well as a castle, this set includes ten minifigures and a frightening, fire-breathing dragon.

Double-headed ax

Skeleton Warrior shield

Skeleton Warrior
This warrior's speckled armor was first seen on the Vikings minifigures in 2005.

DID YOU KNOW?

Crossbows, swords, and lances made their first appearance in the Castle theme.

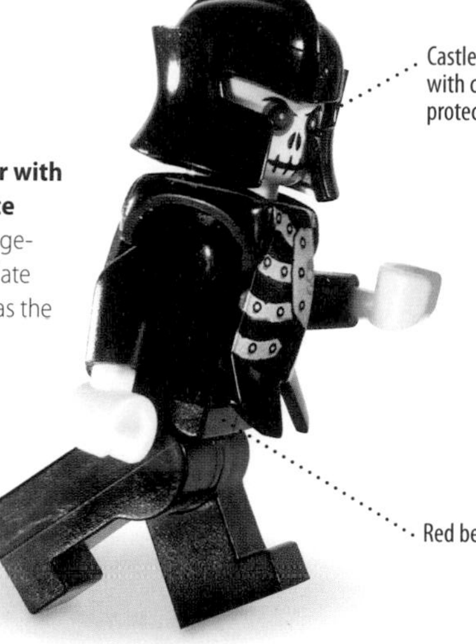
Castle helmet with cheek protection
Red belt

Skeleton Warrior with Black Breastplate
This warrior's ribcage-patterned breastplate detail is the same as the Evil Queen's.

Evil Wizard His hat and legs are exclusive, but the Wizard's head is similar to Ogel's in the Alpha Team theme.

Evil red eye

Wizard hat with printed skull and lightning bolts

Staff with lightning bolts

Charms for sorcery

IF THIS DOESN'T WORK OUT, I'LL BE AN ELECTRICIAN.

Skeleton Tower Can you defeat the wizard and save the Crown Princess? The spooky Skeleton Tower (7093) comes with two Skeleton Warriors, a Crown Knight, the Crown Princess, and the Evil Wizard.

Evil Wizard standing guard
A captive Crown Princess
Hanging skeleton prison
Lightning bolts to warn intruders
Only the bravest Knights make it past this sharp-toothed bridge!
Turn crank to raise and lower skull jaw bridge

LEGO® DUPLO® FARM

This happy farm girl and farm boy were part of 2007's LEGO DUPLO Ville Farm set. Like other DUPLO figures, they have detailed designs and posable arms and legs.

Baseball cap

Farm Boy With his practical coveralls and cap, this boy is ready for a day of hard work on the farm.

Hair kept out of face with a ponytail

Jeans are a must when working on the farm

Farm Girl Mucking out the horse stables is just all in a day's work for this farm girl.

2007

LEGO® HARRY POTTER™

2007 saw the release of one set in the LEGO Harry Potter theme, the third version of Hogwarts Castle (5378), from *Harry Potter and the Order of the Phoenix*™. Nine minifigures came with the set, including Harry Potter in a new school uniform and new versions of Hermione Granger, Draco Malfoy, Professor Snape, and a Death Eater.

Ornate silver mask

Death Eater This version of the Death Eater is exclusive to set 5378.

Smart school tie

Molded hair

Harry Potter™ Harry's tie is printed with the colors of his house—scarlet and gold for Gryffindor.

Green and silver tie—the colors representing Slytherin house

Neat b hair

Draco Malfoy™ This new Draco minifigure has a sneering expression printed on his face.

Double-sided sleeping/smiling head
Gryffindor uniform

Hermione Granger This version of Hermione is unique to set 5378, but the individual parts have been used in other sets.

Frowning expression

Professor Snape Like the Hermione minifigure, this version of Professor Snape is also unique to set 5378.

DID YOU KNOW? The mandrake plants from Hogwarts Castle (5378) included their very own unique minifigure heads.

The castle's interior has hidden items for Harry and his friends to find.
Owl perched in alcove

Hogwarts Castle (5378) This version of the famous castle was the only LEGO model released for *Harry Potter and the Order of the Phoenix.*

Pink blush to match pink suit
Stern mouth
Cat brooch

Professor Dolores Umbridge™ This is the first and only appearance of the Umbridge minifigure, in Hogwarts Castle (5378), although her hair is seen on a worker minifigure in the Modular Green Grocer (10185).

This head is also used for the Rubens Barichello minifigure from 2004.

Ferrari red legs and torso

F. Massa With a new torso and new standard helmet, Massa is ready to burn some rubber.

LEGO® FERRARI

The Ferrari 248 F1 Team roared into action in 2007 in a new set for the LEGO® Racers subtheme. It included eight minifigures: a new variant of Felipe Massa, the minifigure debut of Kimi Raikkonen, two crew members, three engineers, and a record keeper. A second edition of this set contained different race cars and a Michael Schumacher minifigure in place of Raikkonen.

Sponsor logo

K. Raikkonen There's no doubting that this minifigure is Raikkonen. It has the champion driver's head, and his name spelled out on his torso.

LEGO® MODULAR BUILDINGS

Modular Buildings sets were launched this year, giving minifigures the most realistic and detailed street scenes yet to hang out in. The first was Café Corner (10182), part of the Advanced Models theme, which features more challenging models. This was followed by Market Street (10190), a LEGO® Factory exclusive created by talented fan Eric Brok. Each set came with three very busy minifigures.

Male Worker This worker's torso is mostly featured on LEGO City minifigures.

Green coveralls

Neat ponytail

Office Worker This business-like minifigure is dressed appropriately for a day at the office.

Blue jacket

City Worker This man's hair piece was also used for the LEGO Harry Potter Mad-Eye Moody minifigure.

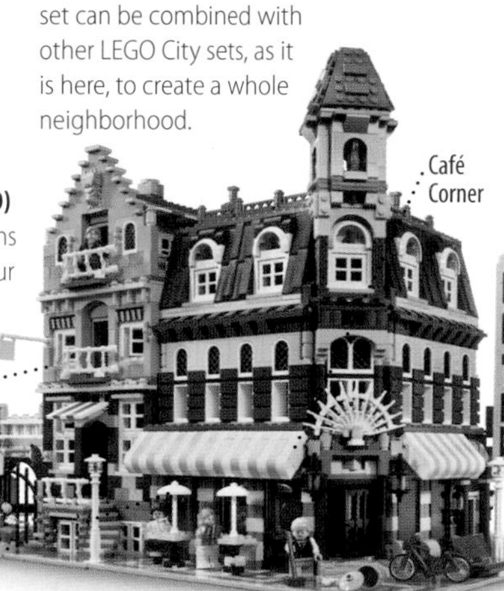
HOTEL

Café Corner (10182) This modular construction set can be combined with other LEGO City sets, as it is here, to create a whole neighborhood.

Café Corner

Market Street (10190) This modular set contains a market place and a four story townhouse, plus three minifigures.

Market Street

Café tables with umbrellas

NOW, WHERE DID I PUT MY GLOVES?

Angular, sideways-swept hair, seen on EXO-FORCE minifigures and LEGO DC's Nightwing minifigure

Super Goalie The Super Goalie's hair piece is usually enough to distract the opposition.

LEGO® SPORTS

This exclusive Goalie minifigure was part of a promotional set given out free with the purchase of some types of Adidas sneakers. It also included a golden soccer ball and a stand for the figure. The minifigure came with flat, gloved "goalie hands" with Adidas goalie glove pattern stickers, which he could hold in his minifigure hands.

LEGO® EXO-FORCE™

LEGO EXO-FORCE returned for a second year in 2007 with 11 new sets. Inspired by Japanese manga and animation, the theme featured a team of human pilots battling against the cunning robot army for control of their mountain home. Most LEGO EXO-FORCE sets were battle machines that both sides created to try to win the war.

I'M ONE OF A KIND...BUT THAT'S OBVIOUS, RIGHT?

Hair piece is also used for LEGO Sports Goalie minifigure

New reversible head. Turn it around to see her angry expression

Hitomi The granddaughter of Sensei Keiken, this is courageous Hitomi's first and only appearance in minifigure form, in Fight for the Golden Tower (8107).

New gold amulet-patterned armor torso

DID YOU KNOW?

Something, or someone, has made Hiraku angry!

Hiraku Brave pilot Hiraku has a new blue, wing-patterned torso.

Bright red angular hair

New gold and violet flight suit torso

Ha-Ya-To Ha-Ya-To's specialty is flying, which explains his windswept hair.

LEGO
EXO-FORCE
7-14
8107

Fight for the Golden Tower (8107) Spinning blades, swords, missiles, and a trapdoor all feature in this set, as well as Hitomi and Devastator minifigures.

LEGO® *STAR WARS*®

2007 brought the 30th anniversary of *Star Wars* and new excitement to the LEGO *Star Wars* play theme. There were new sets taken from all six of the movies, new and exclusive minifigures, a special commemorative 30th anniversary C-3PO minifigure, and the release of one of the largest LEGO *Star Wars* sets to date!

Tousled hair

GUESS WHAT I'M GOING TO BE WHEN I GROW UP?

Freckled face

Short LEGO legs

Anakin Skywalker The third representation of Anakin as a young child, this version features a new head and torso.

All-blue uniform

Silver buckle

Gun, in case of enemy attack

Republic Pilot Wearing a Republic Pilot uniform, it's clear that this pilot is on the Jedi's side.

Light blue lightsaber

Hood with cape

Obi-Wan Kenobi This young version of the Jedi Padawan is exclusive to the Republic Cruiser set (7665).

Republic Cruiser (7655) Jump aboard the famous red starship to help save the galaxy. This is the only set to include the R2-R7 minifigure.

LEGO
STAR WARS
Ages/edades
9-14
7665
Republic Cruiser
919
LIMITED EDITION
EDITION LIMITEE
NOUVEAU!
R2-R7
NEW!
EXCLUSIVE
R2-R7

EPISODE I

One of the highlights of the new Episode I LEGO sets was the new version of Anakin Skywalker, the first to feature short LEGO legs. Short LEGO legs had been introduced to minifigures in 2002, three years after the last young Anakin minifigure.

Green lightsaber

Jedi robe first seen in 2005

Qui-Gon Jinn The wise Jedi Master has a new head with mustache, beard, and chin dimple.

DROIDEKA

This is the second version of a Droideka released. Its brick-built style means it is not considered a standard minifigure. This Droideka features larger pieces than the 2002 version.

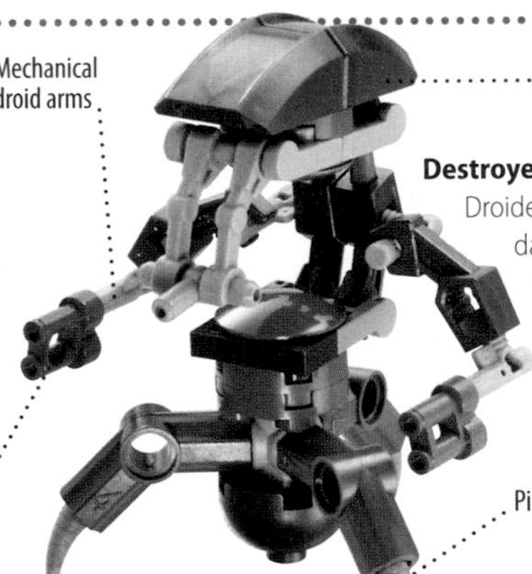

Mechanical droid arms

Sloped head

Binocular piece used as guns

Pincer-like legs

Destroyer Droid Droidekas look dangerous, but they are actually flimsy, slow, and a bit stupid!

General Grievous The cyborg general is without his cape in this version, but he is still just as dangerous!

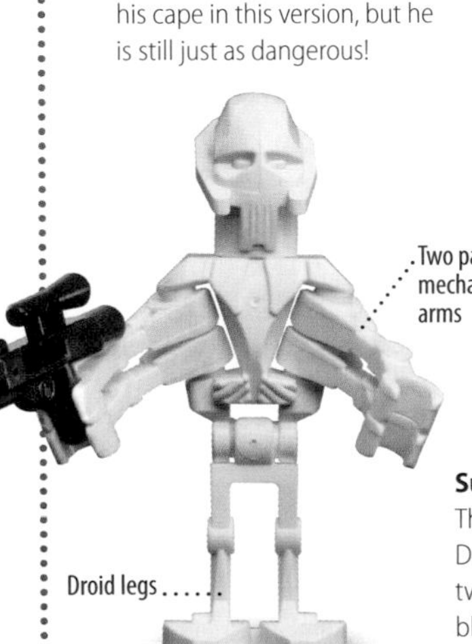

Two pairs of mechanical arms

Droid legs

Strong, bulky body

Mechanical arm

Super Battle Droid The Super Battle Droid figure comes in two colors—metal blue and dark gray.

EPISODE III

Four new sets for *Star Wars:* Episode III *Revenge of the Sith* were released this year, featuring a new Specialist Clone Trooper minifigure as well as Battle Droid and Super Battle Droid figures.

Red markings

Clone troopers are always ready for battle

Shock Trooper Every Clone trooper is created from the DNA of bounty hunter Jango Fett, but this minifigure has a unique helmet and torso.

Matte gray lightsaber hilt. 2007 variant is silver

Back of specially designed head has more sensory tentacles

Tentacles

Unique torso with Jedi robes and silver belt detail

Kit Fisto Jedi General Kit Fisto is the first LEGO *Star Wars* minifigure to have a head made from soft rubber rather than ABS plastic. Plo Koon and Yoda would soon follow suit.

BEING A JEDI WREAKS HAVOC WITH YOUR LOOKS.
Lines under eyes
Layered shirt
Main sensor
Forward floodlight
The set comes with a 311-page instruction booklet

Obi-Wan Kenobi Obi Wan's minifigure is older and wiser, with a furrowed brow and gray hair.

The *Millennium Falcon* This Ultimate Collector Series *Millennium Falcon* (10179) is built out of a whopping 5,195 pieces!

EPIC SET

One of the most sought-after LEGO *Star Wars* sets is also the biggest ever made—the Ultimate *Millennium Falcon* (10179). It featured five minifigures of classic characters—Luke, Han, Leia, Obi-Wan, and Chewbacca.

Smirking expression
Vest and open shirt

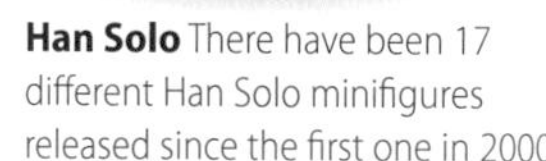

Han Solo There have been 17 different Han Solo minifigures released since the first one in 2000.

Side buns
Leia is wearing red lipstick

Princess Leia A flesh-toned Princess Leia is dressed in her all-white senator's uniform.

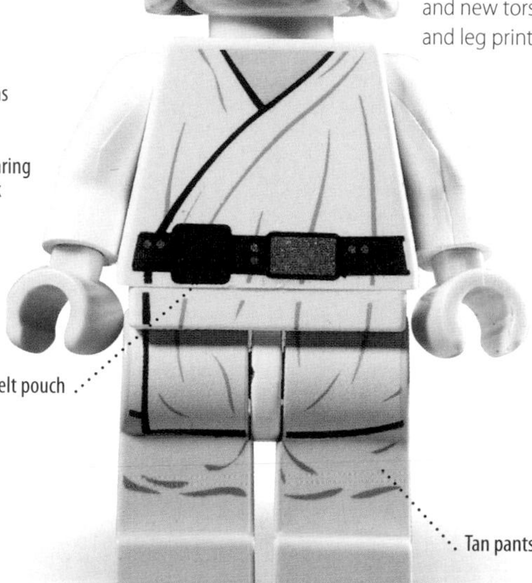
Belt pouch
Tan pants

Tatooine Luke Skywalker An update of a 1999 variant, Luke now has longer hair, skin-colored head and hands, and new torso and leg printing.

R2 SAYS HE INTENDS TO STAY 29 FOREVER.
Only 10,000 limited edition C-3POs were made

C-3PO To celebrate 30 years of *Star Wars*, the LEGO Group created this limited edition chrome gold painted C-3PO. No LEGO *Star Wars* collection is complete without it!

New torso, with black shadow armor design, is exclusive to this minifigure

Shadow Trooper This shady Shadow Trooper has been specially designed for undercover work, with advanced armor that contains magnetic plates.

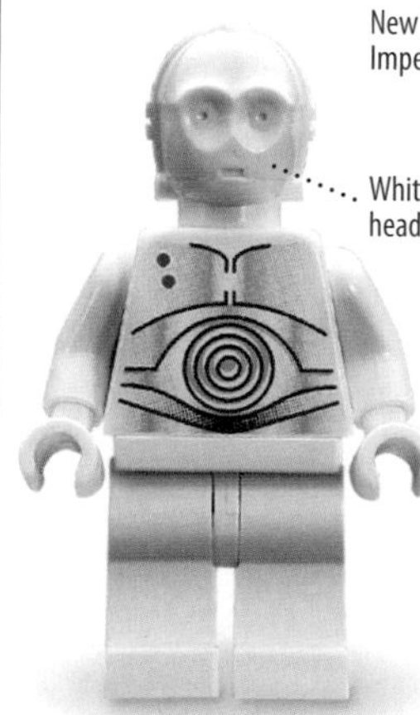
White C-3PO head

K-3PO Exclusive to the limited edition Hoth Rebel Base (7666), this minifigure is highly collectible.

New helmet with red Imperial symbols
Torso with breathing equipment detail is new this year

AT-AT Driver This clone driver pilots an All-Terrain Armored Transport (AT-AT).

Pilot helmet
Officer torso first introduced in 2005

General Veers The stern Imperial Officer Veers makes his debut this year.

Snow gear for fighting on the ice planet Hoth
Backpack for equipment

Hoth Rebel This is the second version of this character, and features a new flesh head.

EPISODE IV, V, AND VI

A handful of brand new LEGO *Star Wars* minifigures appeared this year, including the Shadow Stormtrooper, K-3PO, and General Veers. Since 2007, the K-3PO minifigure has not appeared again, making it a valued collectible.

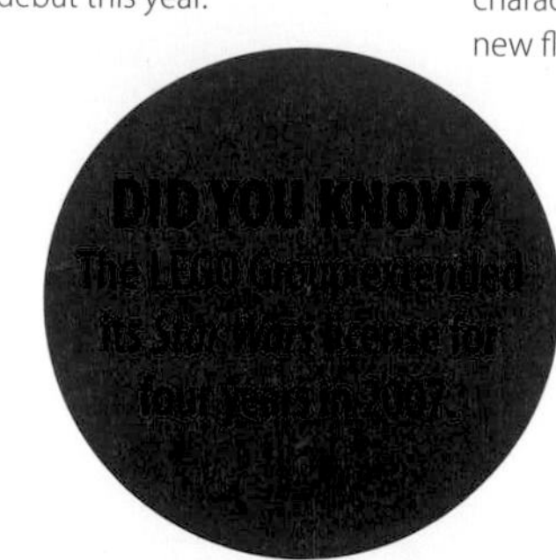
DID YOU KNOW?

Service Station Worker He might have the same torso as the Train Passenger, but his silver shades and visor helmet set this minifigure apart.

Classic Space logo

Service with a smile

Chef whites

Chef This cheerful chef is a promotional minifigure, and wears classic chef whites and a chef's hat.

This loudhailer has featured in many sets, from Batman to *Star Wars*.

Construction Worker With his bright orange jacket and megaphone, this worker is both seen and heard on the building site.

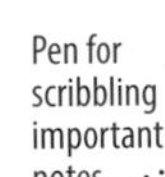

I HELPED TO BUILD THIS CITY!

Hard hat

Safety stripes

Pen for scribbling important notes

Orange coveralls

Construction Manager This construction worker is ready for a hard day's work on the building site, helping to make the LEGO City bigger and better!

Flat-top hair

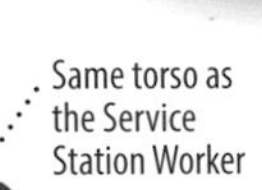

Same torso as the Service Station Worker

Train Passenger This citizen is waiting for the train to arrive to take him on a tour of the City.

LEGO® CITY

Adventure had no limit in the 2007 LEGO City sets. From the Fire Station (7945) and Harbor (7994) to the busy Train Station (7997) and airport (7894), LEGO City was a bustling place to be. The vast majority of minifigures introduced this year used new combinations of existing elements to make nonetheless compelling new characters.

Sea Firefighter Equipped with a helmet, life preserver, and fire extinguisher, this dedicated Firefighter is ready to fight against fire!

Firefighter helmet

Life preserver

Powerful fire extinguisher

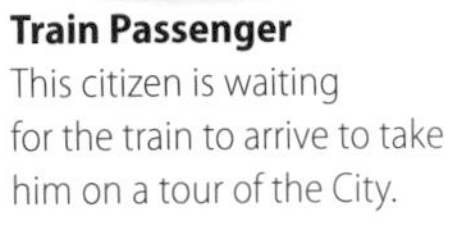

I'M KEEPING THIS BOOK SMOKE FREE!

Silver hard hat matches shades

Silver shades to protect eyes from the glare of fires

Radio to communicate with fellow workers

Fire department badge

Firefighter The brave LEGO City firefighters battle fires and rescue any people or animals that need their help.

Helmet with visor

Police badge

Policeman The citizens of LEGO City are safe thanks to the help of this Policeman.

Practical shirt

Delivery Man There are no new elements on this minifigure, although the combination of parts is new.

DID YOU KNOW?
Versions of the LEGO City policemen have been in production for many years, making that the highest volume minifigure to date.

LEGO
CITY
WARNING: CHOKING HAZARD. Small parts. Not for children under 3 years.
Ages/edades
5-12
7942
Off Road Fire Rescue
7942
131

Off-Road Fire Rescue (7942) One fire chief minifigure comes to the rescue in this set, which also includes a fire rescue truck and trailer, and firefighting equipment.

Gray beard
Anchor logo

Boat Captain This minifigure's torso is new, with an anchor logo on the pocket, and blue tie and pocket detail.

Sleeveless T-shirt to catch some rays

Life Guard This Life Guard is dressed for a day of sunbathing, and keeping the beach-goers safe, of course!

Essential tools for repair work
Cap keeps head warm

Harbor Worker This minifigure featured on day 10 of the City Advent Calendar.

Octan logo
OIL

Service Station Worker Wearing protective coveralls is a must when working at the Service Station.

Torso from Gravity Games theme first seen in 2004
Smiley face

Car Cleaner The LEGO City cars are squeaky clean thanks to this efficient worker and his scrubbing brush.

FLYING IS BETTER THAN GOING BY TRAIN!

Blue hat also comes in white
Airplane logo
Radio to communicate with colleagues

Airport Worker This happy Airport Worker makes sure all the passengers board their airplane on time.

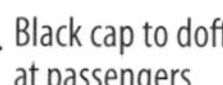
Black cap to doff at passengers

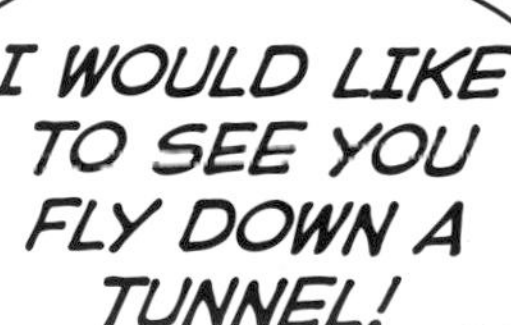
I WOULD LIKE TO SEE YOU FLY DOWN A TUNNEL!
Train logo

Train Worker This Train Worker features on Day 16 of the City Advent Calendar set (7907).

The LEGO briefcase first appeared in 1983.

Hard-wearing brush
Green pants

Sanitary Engineer The LEGO City streets are swept clean daily by this man and his brush.

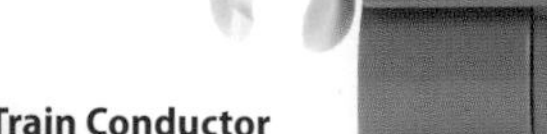
Bespectacled head
Notepad and pen

Train Conductor Calm, efficient, and friendly, this conductor is a firm favorite with the LEGO City citizens.

Briefcase full of important documents

City Worker This suited City Worker appears in only one set, Train Station (7997).

I'M WORKING ON A SPELL TO MAKE LEGO SETS BUILD THEMSELVES...
New hat with gold buckle and stars
Beard clips over a gray-and-white one printed on face
Potion, pouch, and amulet hang from belt charms

Good Wizard Four LEGO Castle minifigures and a Viking have previously used this head, with its stern but kind face.

2008

THIS YEAR WAS a memorable one in the history of LEGO® play. As well as being the 50th anniversary of the patent of the LEGO brick and the 30th anniversary of the LEGO minifigure, it brought fans an amazing array of new themes. LEGO® *Star Wars*® Clone Wars™ made its debut, along with the action-packed LEGO® *Indiana Jones*™. LEGO® Agents went on their first secret mission and the Vintage Minifigure Collection brought back favorites from the past. All in all, a year to remember!

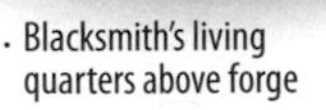
Blacksmith's living quarters above forge

Medieval Market Village (10193) Eight minifigures, a tavern, a forge, and a bustling market make up this set.

LEGO® CASTLE

The Crown Knights of LEGO Castle got a new enemy this year—the mighty Troll Warriors. Fortunately, they also acquired a new ally in the equally fierce Dwarf Miners. Six major LEGO Castle sets were released this year, plus three smaller sets. An exciting new Castle Advent Calendar also made its appearance as the holiday season approached.

New head with extra wide smile

Fantasy Era torso with crown buckle

Jester This all-new Jester lurks behind the day 24 window of the Castle Advent Calendar (7979). He is clearly having a happy holiday.

DWARVES

The brave dwarves appeared in four sets, including the impressive Dwarves' Mine (7036). The minifigures were armed with war hammers and battle axes—all elements from past Viking sets.

Broom popular with minifigure witches

Unlaced bodice—sweeping is energetic work!

Apron keeps dust off her skirt

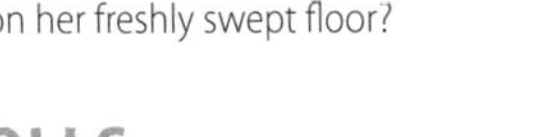

Maid The other face of this medieval minifigure Maid has a shocked look. Did someone get mud on her freshly swept floor?

Intricately braided beard

Dwarf Pawn In LEGO Castle Giant Chess (852293), Dwarf minifigures like this one serve as pawns.

Winged helmet exclusive to Dwarves

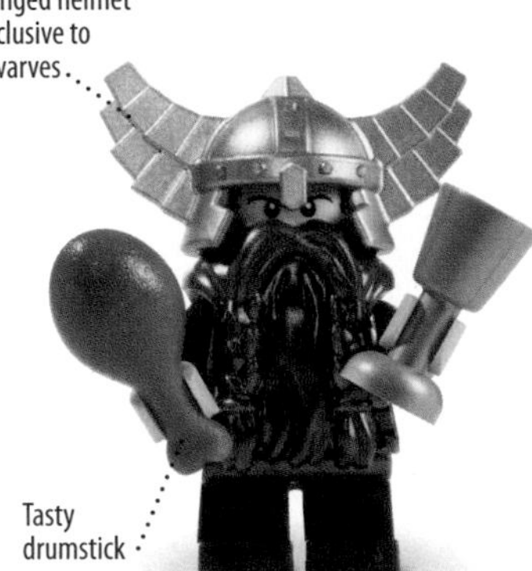
Tasty drumstick

Advent Calendar Dwarf This minifigure from the Advent Calendar is making the most of the festive fare.

TROLLS

Two kinds of Troll were made: regular minifigures and Giant Troll figures. Natural enemies of the Dwarves, Trolls battled the Crown Knights too, using siege engines and a warship.

Copper troll helmet with cheek guards

Belts, chains and buckles on chest

Copper Troll Pawn This Troll pawn is one of 33 minifigures in the LEGO Castle Giant Chess Set.

Silver-black variant of troll helmet
Troll symbol on buckle

Silver Troll Pawn Another Troll Pawn variant wears a breastplate with integral shoulder guards.

Evil Witch The potion bottles on this minifigure's belt may contain poison, or possibly her makeup!

Green eye shadow and black lipstick

Magic lightning bolt for zapping unsuspecting minifigures

Spider necklace

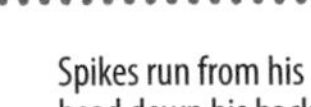
Spikes run from his head down his back

Hands attach via LEGO Technic pins

Giant Troll
At 3 inches (7.5 cm) tall, this musclebound, club-wielding Giant Troll is twice the size of a standard minifigure.

LEGO AGENTS

Agents replaced Alpha Team as the LEGO superspy theme, and leapt straight into action by sending secret operatives up against the evil Dr. Inferno. The eight sets were numbered ("Mission 1, Mission 2" and so on) and each included a comic strip on the package. Unlike Alpha Team, all of the henchmen minifigures in Agents had unique names and powers.

Agent Chase As team leader, Chase appears in six of this year's eight sets—more than any other Agents minifigure.

Reversible head

Reverse face has scared expression

Agent Trace Trace is the sole female Agent, and will remain so until next year.

Radio keeps him in touch with the team.

Powerful glasses for detailed work

Same head as standard Chase (this is the reverse face).

ID card attached to belt

Diver Chase Chase may be ready to go under, but he'll still come out on top in the Deep Sea Quest (8636).

Flat-top hair piece in reddish brown

Gun is hose nozzle piece

Agent Charge Unlike most Agents, Charge has only one face. No wonder he looks so angry about it!

Helmet with visor—he is an air, land, and sea pilot.

Agents logo on left of torso

Rocket Charge In Mission 2 (8632), Charge swaps his hair for a helmet to ride a hi-tech rocket cycle.

AGENTS

The Agent minifigures came equipped with jetpacks, speedboats, and an awesome Mobile Command Center (8635). They needed them all to fight not only Dr. Inferno and his minions but also a glow-in-the-dark octopus!

Agent Fuse This Agent minifigure gets his name because he is an expert in electronics, not because he has a short temper!

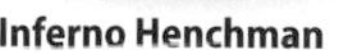

Robber's knit cap

Inferno Henchman There are no fancy robotic parts for this Henchman. He's just plain bad!

Gun made from camera and cones

Metal plate attaching arm to torso

Fire Arm The robotic arm of this minifigure is a huge double gun. He has a robotic eye, too.

Gold variant of hose nozzle gun

Eyepatch over damaged eye

Orange and black suit worn by male henchmen

Gold Tooth With gold teeth, hair, and gun, this must be one of the shiniest minifigure minions ever.

Four robotic eyes printed on face

Legs are robotic arm pieces

Spy Clops This multi-legged figure is a creation of Dr. Inferno. He is made up of 19 parts, including 6 helmet horns used as feet.

Unique face with thick monobrow

Break Jaw The helmet of this thuggish minifigure makes him look like he has a fierce underbite!

She gets her name from her claw hand

Same head as Evil Witch from LEGO Castle

Black is dominant color in outfit

Claw-Dette This wicked-looking minifigure is Dr. Inferno's right-hand woman. Or should that be his right-claw woman?

Mechanical arm and claw

THEY'RE JUST JEALOUS OF MY HAIR!

Unique hair piece is one of the most unusual ever

Badge design based on his own hairstyle

Dr. Inferno There are two variants of this minifigure, but only their claw color varies. This one has pearl light gray; the other has silver.

Clear, bubble style helmet

Slime drips printed on torso

Slime Face This henchman minifigure's head is colored trans-neon green to make it look like slimy green jelly.

Flat-top hair piece in black

Chainsaw piece in use since 1993

Saw Fist This cyborg henchman is aptly named! He is the only minifigure to use the LEGO chainsaw piece as a limb.

INFERNO AND CREW

The crazy, mixed-up doctor planned to conquer the world, aided by his team of minions with their futuristic weapons and gigantic laser cannon. They were a strange and scary lot, with names like Break Jaw, Slime Face, and Spy Clops. None of these minifigures would reappear after 2008.

2008

LEGO *INDIANA JONES*

The big name in LEGO adventure in 2008 was without a doubt Indiana Jones. Sets based on three of the hit movies arrived in stores this year (the fourth, *Indiana Jones and the Temple of Doom*, would be represented the following year). The play theme was an immediate hit, both with eager young builders just meeting the whip-cracking adventurer for the first time via *Indiana Jones and the Kingdom of the Crystal Skull*, and with their parents who remembered the original movies first released in the 1980s.

Brown fedora will become the Indy minifigure's signature hat
Tough leather jacket protects against the elements
Whip molded as coil but can be stretched out slightly.
Bag for stashing archaeological finds
Hair piece with side braids drawn back
Flower and bow detail on top
SNAKES, INDY! PLASTIC SNAKES!
Dark tan pith helmet
Gun not just used for self-defense
Dark tan clothes help him blend in with sand.
Hair piece used for most Harry Potter minifigures
Sweat caused by jungle heat (and nerves).
You won't forget his name—it's on his shirt!
JOCK
"Air Pilots" is printed on the back of the shirt.
Kepi keeps the sun out of his eyes.
Steel-rimmed specs—nothing escapes his eagle eye.
INDIANA? HIS NAME IS HENRY JONES JR.
Signature bow tie
Motorcycle helmet and goggles
Henry grasps treasure map
German soldier in hot pursuit
LEGO
INDIANA JONES
8-14
7623

Indiana Jones The same new Indy minifigure appeared across all three of 2008's Indiana Jones subthemes: Raiders of the Lost Ark, The Last Crusade, and the Kingdom of the Crystal Skull.

Marion Ravenwood Marion must escape the snakes because the reverse of her head is calm and smiling.

Satipo This untrustworthy jungle guide minifigure got just one chance to betray Indy: in Temple Escape (7623).

Jock The Temple Escape set also included this minifigure pilot with a distinctive torso, but a generic LEGO head.

Temple Escape (7623) Indy's minifigure faces all the traps from the opening of *Raiders of the Lost Ark*.

René Belloq Indy's rival shares his smirking face with another minifigure villain: Draco Malfoy from the LEGO® Harry Potter™ theme.

RAIDERS OF THE LOST ARK

Indy sought the Ark of the Covenant in this subtheme's five sets. Movie characters Indiana Jones, Marion, Satipo, and Belloq became minifigures. The only significant absence was Major Toht, who appeared in the LEGO Indiana Jones video games but never as a minifigure.

Kepi German Soldier This is one of five German Soldier variants in the theme. All have the same torsos and legs, but their heads and hats vary.

THE LAST CRUSADE

In the three sets of The Last Crusade, Indy and his father went on a quest for the Holy Grail and fans got their first Sean Connery minifigure (he played Indy's father, Henry James Senior, in the movie).

Motorcycle Chase (7618) In this set Indy and Henry Jones ride a motorcycle and sidecar that can divide into two parts.

Henry Jones Senior Judging by his natty suit and the diary in his pocket, Indiana's father values neatness and good record-keeping.

Motorcycle German Soldier This variant of the German Soldier minifigure appears only in the Motorcycle Chase set.

New head, old hair (that maybe needs combing)

Leather biker jacket for this motorcycle hero

Unique torso with name on jacket front

Mutt Williams Indy's long-lost son Mutt debuted in this subtheme. His minifigure was included in three sets: Jungle Duel (7624), Temple of the Crystal Skull (7627), and Peril in Peru (7628).

Dark blue pilot uniform

Pilot This Peruvian Pilot shares his head with both Satipo and the German soldier minifigure from the other two Indy subthemes.

THE KINGDOM OF THE CRYSTAL SKULL

An older, wiser Indy teamed up with a young man named Mutt on his strangest adventure yet—finding a mystical crystal skull. It was the largest subtheme, with seven sets, and featured new versions of Indy and Marion plus new minifigures Irina Spalko, Colonel Dovchenko, and more.

DID YOU KNOW?
Every set in the LEGO Indiana Jones theme features a minifigure of Indy himself.

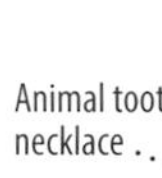

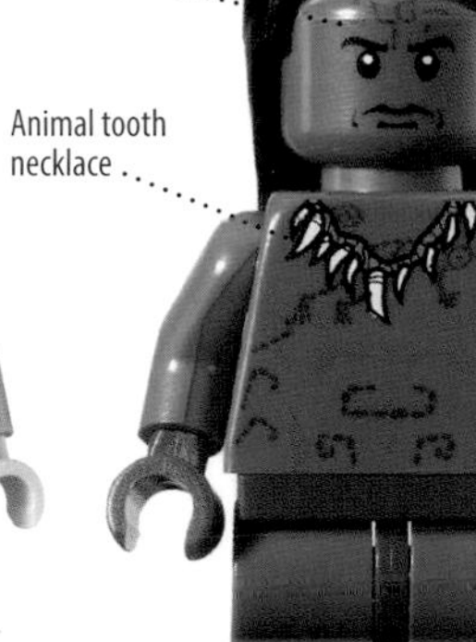

Green kepi-style hat

Soviet star symbol on buckle

Russian Guard The smirking minifigure head made yet another appearance on this sinister servant of the Soviet state.

Tattooed forehead

Animal tooth necklace

Ugha Warrior This Amazon tribesman minifigure came with and without hair. Either way, his appearance is pretty hair-raising!

Hat covers scars over right eyebrow

Automatic pistol

Colonel Dovchenko His face set in grim detemination, Dovchenko pursues his minifigure mission—to grab the crystal skull for Irina Spalko.

TELL ME ALL YOU KNOW ABOUT MINIFIGURES... NOW!

Ice-cold expression

No frills on this no-nonsense minifigure's shirt!

Irina Spalko On her relentless quest for power and knowledge, minifigure Irina maintains a cool (and new) head.

LEGO
INDIANA JONES
8-14
KINGDOM OF THE CRYSTAL SKULL

Temple of the Crystal Skull (7267) Ten minifigures and a temple full of booby traps are included in this set.

FIRST LEGO® LEAGUE

The 2008 *FIRST* LEGO League Challenge was Climate Connections, its theme being the effects of climate, and climate change on the Earth. Teams had to identify a climate problem in their area and use LEGO® MINDSTORMS® technology to design and build a working robot to solve it. Twelve accessory minifigures were included in the set.

Male Skier This minifigure's ski goggles have served as aviator, engineer, and miner's goggles in other themes.

Black crash helmet

Female Skier Four of the Climate Connections minifigures wear these clip-on skis. They are exclusive to the subtheme.

Skis clip onto standard feet

Gray hair shows he is middle aged.

Very bushy beard and mustache

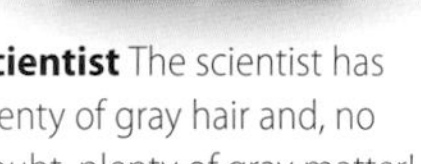

Scientist The scientist has plenty of gray hair and, no doubt, plenty of gray matter!

Yellow hands and face.

Female Scientist Like many scientists, this lab-based lady wears a white coat.

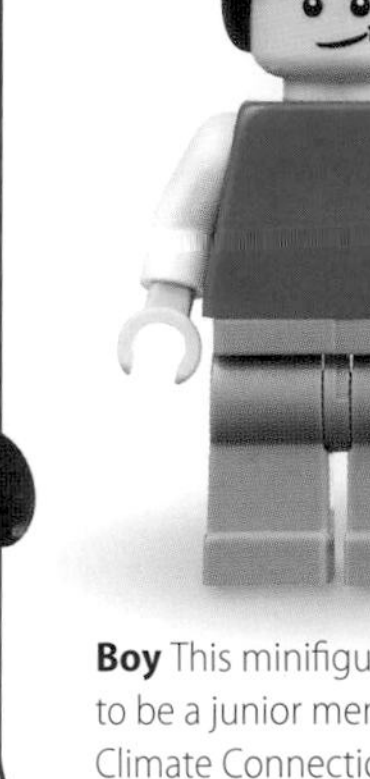

Simple clothes

Boy This minifigure is happy to be a junior member of the Climate Connections gang.

Same head as other female minifigures in the subtheme

Girl Only female head and hair distinguish this minifigure from the Climate Connections boy.

LEGO® RACERS

The LEGO Racers theme got a new licensed subtheme this year, based on the movie *Speed Racer*. All four of its sets focused on the heroic Speed Racer and his efforts to win the Casa Cristo 500 against the mysterious Racer X. More than a dozen new minifigures were introduced, including two versions of Speed Racer, his girlfriend Trixie, the villainous Cruncher Block, and Racer X.

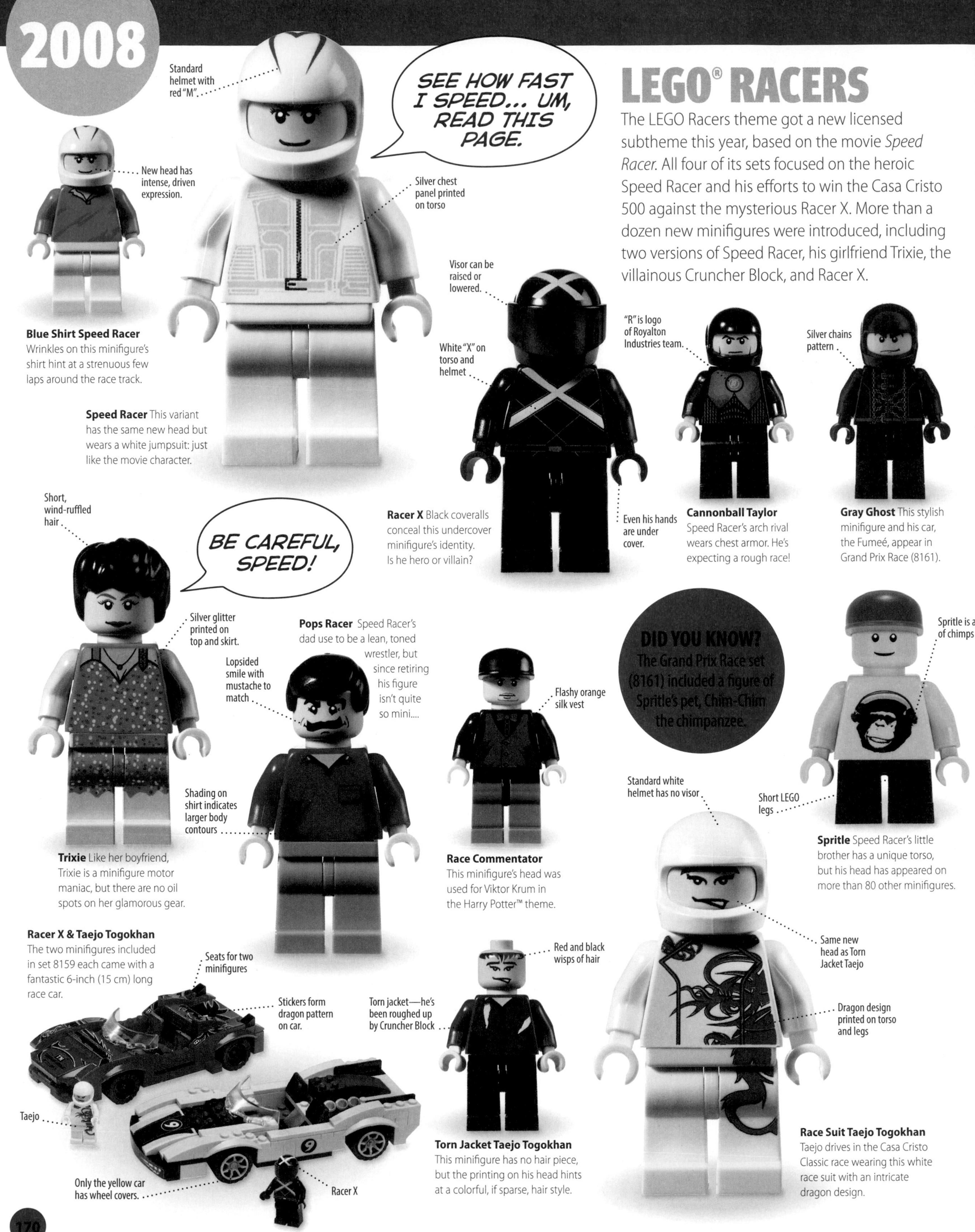
Standard helmet with red "M".
SEE HOW FAST I SPEED... UM, READ THIS PAGE.
New head has intense, driven expression.
Silver chest panel printed on torso
Visor can be raised or lowered.
White "X" on torso and helmet
"R" is logo of Royalton Industries team.
Silver chains pattern
Even his hands are under cover.
Short, wind-ruffled hair
BE CAREFUL, SPEED!
Silver glitter printed on top and skirt.
Lopsided smile with mustache to match
Shading on shirt indicates larger body contours
Flashy orange silk vest
Spritle is a fa
of chimps
Standard white helmet has no visor
Short LEGO legs
Same new head as Torn Jacket Taejo
Red and black wisps of hair
Dragon design printed on torso and legs
Seats for two minifigures
Stickers form dragon pattern on car.
Torn jacket—he's been roughed up by Cruncher Block
Taejo
Only the yellow car has wheel covers.
Racer X

Blue Shirt Speed Racer Wrinkles on this minifigure's shirt hint at a strenuous few laps around the race track.

Speed Racer This variant has the same new head but wears a white jumpsuit: just like the movie character.

Racer X Black coveralls conceal this undercover minifigure's identity. Is he hero or villain?

Cannonball Taylor Speed Racer's arch rival wears chest armor. He's expecting a rough race!

Gray Ghost This stylish minifigure and his car, the Fumeé, appear in Grand Prix Race (8161).

DID YOU KNOW? The Grand Prix Race set (8161) included a figure of Spritle's pet, Chim-Chim the chimpanzee.

Pops Racer Speed Racer's dad use to be a lean, toned wrestler, but since retiring his figure isn't quite so mini....

Trixie Like her boyfriend, Trixie is a minifigure motor maniac, but there are no oil spots on her glamorous gear.

Race Commentator This minifigure's head was used for Viktor Krum in the Harry Potter™ theme.

Spritle Speed Racer's little brother has a unique torso, but his head has appeared on more than 80 other minifigures.

Racer X & Taejo Togokhan The two minifigures included in set 8159 each came with a fantastic 6-inch (15 cm) long race car.

Torn Jacket Taejo Togokhan This minifigure has no hair piece, but the printing on his head hints at a colorful, if sparse, hair style.

Race Suit Taejo Togokhan Taejo drives in the Casa Cristo Classic race wearing this white race suit with an intricate dragon design.

KEEP READING... OR ELSE!

Threatening stare

Pinstriped vest and red silk tie

Dark blue pants match his shirt

Cruncher Block
This menacing minifigure works on the corrupt side of motor racing. He has a new, neat-looking torso and a new, rough-looking head.

New female head with steely gaze

Suit styled along masculine lines

Cruncher's Driver
Like many Speed Racer minifigures, Cruncher's car-driving henchmen has only printed hair.

Gold shades can't disguise his mean expression.

Belt buckle features two snakes design

Snake Oiler
Corrupt driver Snake Oiler is aptly named. His morals are lower than a snake's belly, and his torso features a snakeskin collar.

LEGO® FACTORY

The LEGO Factory theme started in 2005 and wrapped up this year with three sets, the only ones in the line to feature minifigures. Two were space themed and the third a Custom Car Garage (10200). Factory was tied to LEGO® Digital Designer, a software program that allowed for virtual LEGO building. Factory was replaced in 2009 by LEGO® DesignbyME.

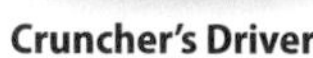

Semi-smiling expression

Coveralls printed on torso

Hot Rod Mechanic
This experienced Mechanic is quietly confident that he's done a good job.

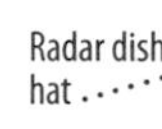

Silver star badge

Star Justice Astronaut
Two of these smiling minifigures are provided with Star Justice (10192).

Radar dish hat

Battle Droid arms from LEGO® *Star Wars*® theme

Star Justice Droid
This little helper robot and his variant buddy are made from small LEGO pieces, including tiles, dishes, plates, and levers.

Helmet with trident design from Aquazone theme

Plaid shirt often used in Town and City themes

Plaid Hot Rod Driver The three driver minifigures, including this plaid-shirted one, were made up of parts from a range of LEGO themes.

Orange torso with diagonal zipper detail

Orange Hot Rod Driver
The stubble-faced head of this minifigure has been in use since 2003.

Flat-top hairstyle

Naboo fighter pilot torso from LEGO *Star Wars* theme

Hot Rod Driver
A neat line in hair—goatee, sideburns, and a flat-top style—gives this minifigure his cool look.

Grinning skull face seen through transparent visor

Jacket is sticker on plain black torso.

Space Skull Commander
The nemesis of the Star Justice team is a gang of galactic looters called the Space Skulls. They are led by this malevolent minifigure.

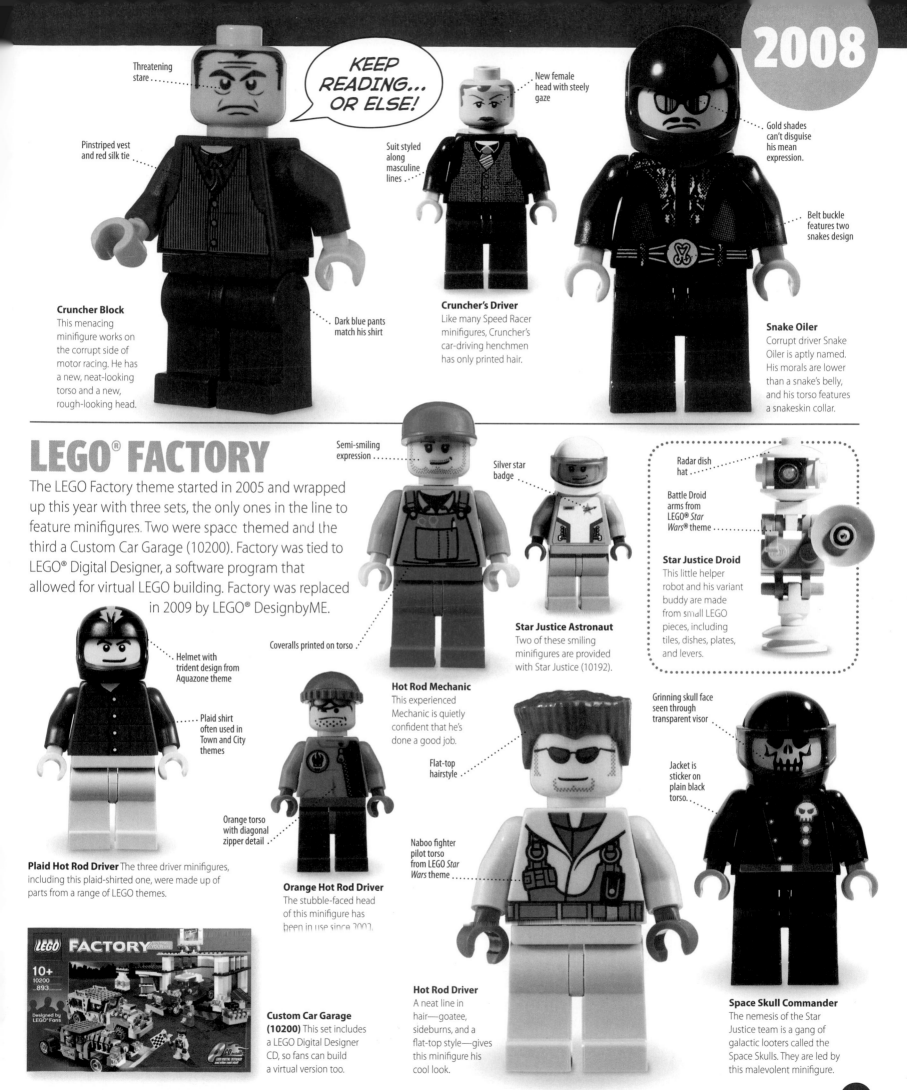

LEGO FACTORY
10+
10200
893
Designed by LEGO Fans

Custom Car Garage (10200) This set includes a LEGO Digital Designer CD, so fans can build a virtual version too.

2008

LEGO® *STAR WARS*®

LEGO *Star Wars* went from strength to strength in 2008. An exciting development was the launch of the first ever sets based on *The Clone Wars* TV series. Classic *Star Wars* was well represented too, with sets from Episode IV, Episode V, and the Expanded Universe. With so much to smile about, LEGO *Star Wars* fans may have found their only problem was keeping up with the new releases.

Rebel Trooper The first ever Rebel Trooper minifigure wears a new helmet exclusive to these troopers. Its clip-on visor, however, has been seen before.

Helmet chin strap printed on head

Short blaster gun is easy to handle when on the move

New torso with blue shirt and black vest

Crystals visible in lightsaber

Emperor Palpatine This Emperor Palpatine minifigure from the Death Star (10188) shows him in the black robes of a Sith Lord.

Like all Sith lightsabers, Palpatine's has a red blade

New bluish-gray head with heavily wrinkled face

Black gloves for handling dark deeds

Long black cloth cape

Head made in one-off black color.

Standard protocol droid design on torso

Imperial Protocol Droid Unlike most Protocol Droids, this minifigure has no name or model number. He will forever remain anonymous.

Other male minifigures have worn this female hair piece.

Belt holds blaster power cell reserves

Luke Skywalker Old parts are used for this minifigure, but in a new combination. Luke's 2007 head and hair top a standard stormtrooper torso and legs.

LEGO *STAR WARS* EPISODES IV, V, AND VI

The highlight of the year in classic LEGO *Star Wars* was the release of a fantastically detailed, multi-decked Death Star (10188). It came with 24 characters, six of which were exclusive to the set. These included Luke Skywalker and Han Solo in borrowed Stormtrooper armor, an Assassin Droid, and an Interrogation Droid.

New head and side part hair piece

WHEN DO I GET TO SING "SEND IN THE CLONES"?

Clone trooper-style armor

Obi-Wan Kenobi Like other Clone Wars minifigures, Obi-Wan has the big, cartoon-like eyes of his animated TV character.

Scared eyes—well, he has been kidnapped by Asajj Ventress!

Arms attach to bulbous body

Rotta the Huttlet This tiny baby Hutt figure can attach to other elements by a single stud.

Blue lightsaber shows he fights for the light side

A tense tussle has left his hair tousled

New torso with black tunic over brown shirt

Anakin Skywalker This heroic minifigure's new head is scarred and battle-worn. His hair and torso are new for 2008, too.

Green lightsaber used by Ahsoka in the Clone Wars

Detachable head piece has montrals (points)

Brown crop top matches belt and gloves

Ahsoka Tano A bright orange-colored torso and head mark out Anakin's Padawan as a minifigure member of the Togruta race.

Mask is not detachable as Plo Koon rarely removes it.

Head made from rubber rather than plastic

Undershirt seen at neck of Jedi robe

Plo Koon This minifigure Jedi Master has a unique head. He wears a special mask that protects him from breathing a harmful excess of oxygen.

THE CLONE WARS

LEGO *Star Wars* went storming into the Clone Wars era in 2008 with 10 new sets. New minifigure versions of Anakin Skywalker, Yoda, and Obi-Wan Kenobi were joined by a host of debuting characters, including Ahsoka Tano, Plo Koon, and General Grievous' MagnaGuards.

Red helmet markings are unique to this minifigure.
Kama fits over standard clone trooper legs.

Commander Fox This minifigure wears a new piece—the kama—which is a form of anti-blast leg armor.

Rangefinder fits onto any clone trooper helmet.

Plain helmet for low rank Clone Trooper

New clone trooper armor

Clone Trooper The 2008 standard Clone Trooper has a new head, torso, and helmet, and a new clip-on rangefinder.

LEGO
STAR WARS
9-14
7675

AT-TE Walker (7675) This set includes the iconic 6-legged Republic war vehicle, four minifigures, a Battle Droid, and Rotta the Huttlet.

Helmet has orange stripes and visor.

Pauldron protects upper body.

Commander Cody Like Captain Rex and Commander Fox, minifigure Cody wears a kama and carries two small blasters.

Five o'clock shadow—it's been a long mission
Small blaster pistol is a new piece for 2008.

Captain Rex All clone warrior minifigures have the same new head, except Rex. His has extra features—stubble and a scar on his chin.

DID YOU KNOW? All 2008 Clone Wars minifigures and figures are new and exclusive to the subtheme, except the Buzz droid.

Her twin lightsabers have unusual curved hilts.
Startling white face with blood red lips
First minifigure to wear the new cloth skirt

Asajj Ventress Making her minifigure debut in set 7676, this cold-eyed Sith assassin came with a killer variety of unusual new pieces.

Head and headwrap are one piece.
Electrostaff is unique to MagnaGuard minifigure
Photoreceptor attaches via tube in figure's torso

MagnaGuard Count Dooku's tall metal-bodied bodyguard cuts a menacing figure in his tattered cape.

Lever moves back and forth on base.

Radar dish piece

Spy Droid This assembly of brick, slope, dish, plate, and lever is in fact a highly dangerous spy droid.

Harley Quinn Harley had the Dark Knight's undivided attention in The Batcycle: Harley Quinn's Hammer Truck (7886). She and Batman were the only minifigures in the set.

New dual-colored jester cap
Domino mask
LEGO
Giant hammer for committing large-scale crimes
Diamond shapes printed on legs

LEGO® BATMAN™

The Caped Crusader was back this year for what were to be his last four sets until 2012. The big news was the release of an all-new minifigure. Harley Quinn—the Joker's sometime girlfriend and Poison Ivy's best buddy—arrived on the scene to give Batman some ha-ha-hard times.

Batman This updated Batman minifigure wears an outfit like that of the character in the newly released *The Dark Knight* movie.

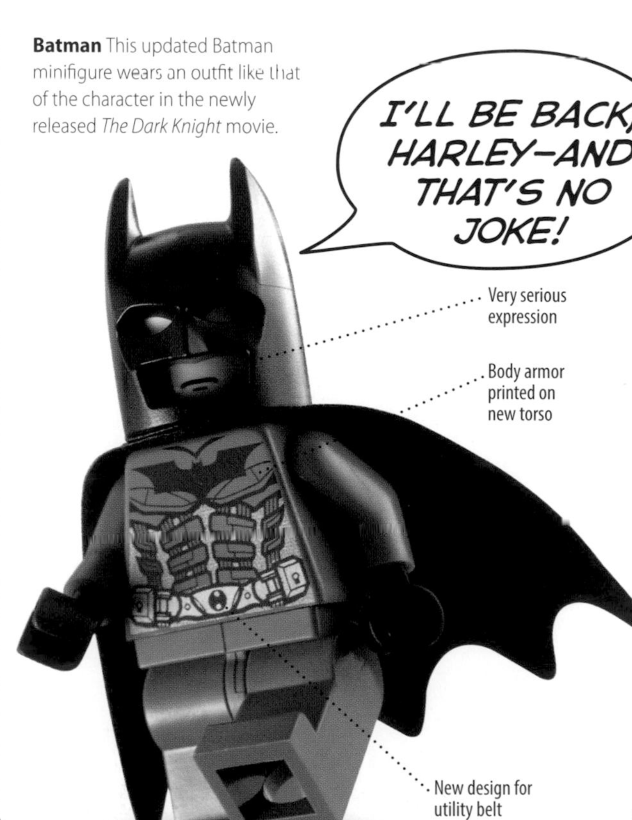
I'LL BE BACK, HARLEY—AND THAT'S NO JOKE!
Very serious expression
Body armor printed on new torso
New design for utility belt

Turning chopper blades

Tail rotor

Crash helmet often used for sporting minifigures

Coast Guard Platform (4210) Set 4210 includes three Coast Guard minifigures, their ocean base, a helicopter, and an oddly glum-looking rescuee.

THE OCEAN IS MY BEAT.

Floats enable plane to land on water

Life preserver is old piece in use since 1990

LEGO® CITY

LEGO City continued to be a busy place in 2008, and a safer one for its minifigure citizens, too. Not only was there a brand new Police Station in town, but the Coast Guard was back after many years away. The new Coast Guard minifigures kept watch on the shoreline of LEGO City, rescuing surfers and boaters from sharks, spills, and stormy weather.

Determined look—nobody gets lost at sea on his watch!

COAST GUARD

After a five year absence, Coast Guard returned under the LEGO City banner, with the minifigures sporting new blue and yellow uniforms. Eight sets included Coast Guard Platform (4210), Quad Bike (7736), Helicopter and Life Raft (7738), and Patrol Boat and Tower (7739).

Speedboat Pilot Under his life preserver, this minifigure wears the standard 2008 Coast Guard top with zippers, logo, and radio printed on it.

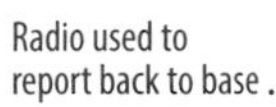

Diver mask flips down to cover eyes

Radio used to report back to base

Diver Minifigure overboard? No problem! This diver is fully equipped and ready to take the plunge.

Helicopter Pilot The pilot flies his chopper over treacherous seas to rescue minifigures from such hazards as snapping sharks!

Air hose attached to scuba tank on back

All coast guards have plain blue legs.

LEGO
CITY
5-12
7738
445

Helicopter and Life Raft (7738) Three Coast Guard minifigures and a stranded boater come with this set.

Shades guard against glare from sun on the water.

Kayaker The Coast Guard Kayak (5621) includes this paddling patroller, his kayak, an oar, and a buoy.

Alert, ever watchful expression

Fully waterproof jacket

Patroller This is one of two Patroller minifigures in the Coast Guard Patrol Boat & Tower (7739).

Cool orange sunglasses

Same helmet as Helicopter Pilot

Motorcyclist This minifigure was bagged with his bike and given away with a UK newspaper.

BREEZY TODAY, HUH?

"V" logo comes as a sticker to be applied to the torso.

Vestas Worker The worker minifigure drives the Vestas maintenance van.

WIND POWER

Sometimes, LEGO sets are made in conjunction with real companies. A limited edition set appeared in 2008 promoting Vestas, a Danish wind power company. Vestas Wind Turbine (4999) featured a maintenance van and a motorized wind turbine on a small house.

POST OFFICE

The Cargo subtheme entered its second year, with two of its four sets centered on delivering mail. Both the Postal Plane (7732) and Mail Van (7731) sets included a mailman minifigure.

Sunglasses popular with City minifigures since 2003

Both workers have this new torso, but old legs and heads.

Air Mail Worker The dedicated Air Mail Worker is very proud to be flying the flag (and the plane) for LEGO City Post Office.

Front of mail box opens

Glasses help him read badly-addressed mail.

Mail taken from mail box for delivery

New envelope logo for 2008 Post Office workers.

Mail Van Worker There's no chance of this Mail Van Worker deserting his post! He's never far from his trusty yellow van.

LEGO® VINTAGE MINIFIGURE COLLECTION

Old minifigures were suddenly new again with the launch of the LEGO Vintage Minifigure Collection. Each set in this series would feature five reissued minifigures, usually with little to no change from the original. The first set featured a Red Spaceman, Firefighter, Octan Driver, Mad Scientist, and a prisoner named Jailbreak Joe.

Astronaut wears the updated helmet, first seen in 1987

Classic planet logo on torso

Red Spaceman This minifigure from the classic Space theme was launched into the LEGO® Universe in 1978.

Mad Scientist Six years after his debut in the Studio theme, this minifigure shows no sign of regaining his sanity.

White lab coat and stethoscope

DID YOU KNOW? The original Jailbreak Joe minifigure was called Crazy Charlie in a 1993 TV commercial.

Octan Driver Fourteen sets (other than this one) have included this gas truck driver minifigure.

Octan
23768

Red cap with bill shades his eyes

Logo of Octan—the LEGO gasoline brand

Traditional striped convict shirt

Jailbreak Joe A veteran of five sets in the Police subtheme, Joe can rightly be called a serial offender.

Some earlier versions of Joe had white or black legs.

Fire helmet helps him keep a cool head at all times.

Five-button jacket

Firefighter This cheerful Firefighter got his foot on the first rung of the ladder in 1981's Town theme.

SPECIAL EVENTS

The big event for the LEGO Group this year was the 50th anniversary of the stud-and-tube brick, followed by the LEGOWorld 2008 celebration in the Netherlands. As ever, special events meant special minifigures that would become highly sought-after by fans.

Wispy red hair printed on head

White backpack

De Bouwsteen A Dutch group of Adult Fans of LEGO (AFOL) called De Bouwsteen gave out 750 of these minifigures to members at LEGOWorld 2008.

50
years

Anniversary Figure As befits a minifigure representing 50 years of the LEGO Group, this one bears the original and classic yellow head.

The "50" stands for fifty glorious years of LEGO bricks.

Classic head

Plain clothing—as a mascot, he represents all minifigures

Universe Promo As a promotion for 2008's LEGO Universe online game, the website mascot was finally made into a real minifigure.

LEGO® EXO-FORCE™

The anime-inspired EXO-FORCE theme came to an end in 2008, delivering seven sets that included a massive Hybrid Rescue Tank (8118). Minifigures making a final stand against their robotic foes included new versions of the EXO-FORCE battle machine pilots. Sensei Keiken also appeared for a second time.

Other side of head has angry expression.

Blue tubes run between the armor and belt.

Camo patterns feature on all 2008 pilot torsos

Ryo The 2008 version of repair expert Ryo is back in his orange suit, this time with a new, armored torso.

Reversible head with closed-mouth expression.

Ha-Ya-To The third and last Ha-Ya-To minifigure has the same head, hair, and legs as earlier versions, but his torso is new. He now wears body armor printed over a camouflage pattern suit.

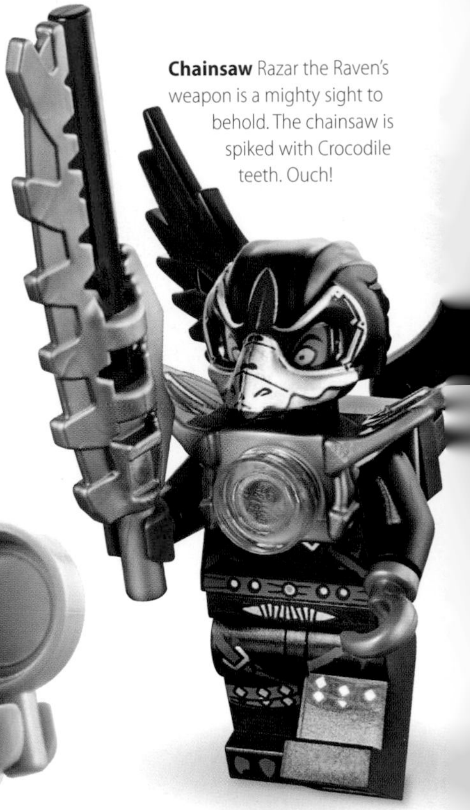

Chainsaw Razar the Raven's weapon is a mighty sight to behold. The chainsaw is spiked with Crocodile teeth. Ouch!

Seagull The Sea Captain's faithful friend perches on his hand when it wants a rest.

Frying pan Watch out! The Governor's Daughter is wielding a big silver frying pan and she looks pretty mad!

Maracas It's party time! Clip on the Maraca Man's colorful maracas and watch him shake them to the beat.

Backpack The brown pack loops around Sangye Dorje's neck, and has a handy pickax holder on the side. Snow shoes also help the Sherpa to cross the mountains.

Briefcase and ticket This Passenger minifigure looks business-like with his briefcase accessory. Clip his ticket to his hand and off he goes to board the train.

MINI GEAR

MINIFIGURES WERE given C-shaped hands so they could carry things—and boy, have they ever carried things! LEGO® minifigure gear can be practical, such as a sword for defending the king's treasure or a tool used on the job, or just fun, such as a piece of sports equipment or a magic wand. The kind of gear they carry helps to distinguish one minifigure from another and is great for role play. For example, the crook might have the stolen money in his hand but the police officer is ready for him with the handcuffs! Watch for new gear every year.

100

Money There's a sinister squid on the loose! The Squidman minifigure flees the scene of the crime, carrying his stolen loot in his hand.

Pom-poms The Cheerleader's hands fit securely inside her blue and white pom-poms.

Handcart The Railway Employee minifigure transports the passengers' luggage. He doesn't look very thrilled about it!

Parrot Pieces of eight! Every good pirate needs a parrot pal.

Sword LEGO Ninjago's Cole minifigure clutches tightly to the engraved hilt of his long katana sword.

Tarot cards The Fortune Teller is never seen without her trusty tarot cards. Printed on 1x2 tiles, one shows the sun and the other a tower.

Magic wand Abracadabra! Clip the Magician's wand into his hand and he's ready to conjure up a spell.

Tools The Harbor Worker is a busy man, but luckily tools like his handy wrench and mallet make life a little easier.

Trophy The Karate Master carries a golden miniature minifigure statuette. The perfect prize!

Paintbrush and palette The Artist's paint-splattered palette and brush accessories were brand new for 2011.

Steak and cleaver The Butcher's T-bone steak has a bone to make it easier to hold. The big cleaver and steak were brand-new accessories.

Pistols Frank Rock from LEGO Monster Fighters is a great shot with his twin silver pistols.

Police badge and handcuffs The Policeman's badge is printed on a 1x2 tile, like the Fortune Teller's tarot cards. His handcuffs have a cylinder-shaped piece for a firm grip.

HOW LONG DO I HAVE TO HOLD THIS? TAKE THE PICTURE ALREADY!

Pickax

Helmet with breathing gear and headlamps, first introduced in 1999 in the LEGO Rock Raiders theme.

Star logo

Doc The team's leader and also the medic, Doc has been on many adventures. His head is also double-sided—determined and grinning.

2009

IT WAS AN EVENTFUL year in the world of LEGO® minifigures. A new theme, LEGO® Power Miners, was launched, with the help of an animated mini-movie. LEGO® *Star Wars*® celebrated its 10th anniversary in Clone Wars style. Old favorites LEGO® Pirates were reintroduced after more than a decade's absence, and the LEGO® Space Police began patrolling the galaxy again. The microfigure also made its first appearance this year as LEGO® Games hit the shelves, giving board games an exciting LEGO makeover.

Duke
Rotating planetary drill
Doc
Energy Crystals

Thunder Driller (8960) With this powerful, double-geared drill, the Power Miners Doc and Duke can easily tunnel through solid rock.

LEGO POWER MINERS

Considered by many to be the follow-up to 1999 to 2000's LEGO® Rock Raiders, LEGO Power Miners would become one of the most popular LEGO play themes, until LEGO® Ninjago's arrival in 2011. It was the ninth play theme in which all the minifigure characters were given names.

Metal plate in forehead
Bomb logo

Rex This minifigure's job is to handle explosives, so he has a bomb logo on his uniform.

Safety goggles

Drill logo

Scar

Flashlight

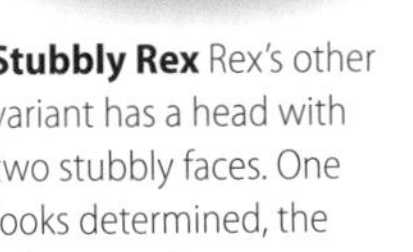

Stubbly Rex Rex's other variant has a head with two stubbly faces. One looks determined, the other scared.

Duke This veteran miner thinks he has seen it all—until he meets the Rock Monsters!

POWER MINERS

Doc, Rex, Duke, and Brains made up the team of minifigure miners in 2009. The brave Power Miners dug beneath the Earth, discovering amazing powerful crystals and fearsome Rock Monsters.

LEGO
POWER MINERS
8-14
8961

Crystal Sweeper (8961) The set features a working harvester wheel and four Power Miner minifigures.

Glasses with power lens
Boom! LEGO dynamite

Brains The Power Miners' scientist, Brains, can also be found in 2010's LEGO® Atlantis theme.

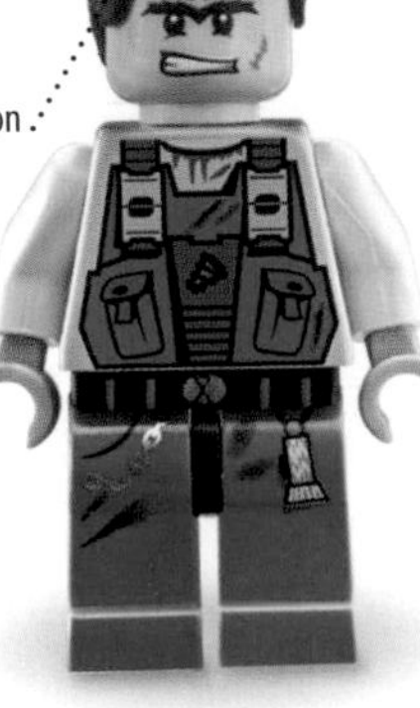

Hair piece seen on more than 80 minifigures

Variant with visor

Energy Crystal

Brains with Visor Another 2009 variant of Brains has a visor instead of safety goggles. Both variants have a test tube logo.

Duke with Hair This variant of Duke has no helmet, revealing a scarred, clean-shaven face.

Stored Energy Crystals
Articulated arms can launch rocks... or smaller rock monsters!
Crystalline teeth

Geolix Even when he's fighting, Geolix won't let his Energy Crystals go—he holds them on his back.

ROCK MONSTERS

The Rock Monster figures used all-new molds and came in five colors. Small versions were included with most sets, and two larger versions were included with the Fall 2009 releases.

Hinged mouth can open and close to gobble up crystals.

Glaciator Energy Crystals give this evil guy freezing ice powers. Brrrrrrrr!

Firox If this Rock Monster is allowed to eat an Energy Crystal it becomes super fast.

LEGO PIRATES

LEGO Pirates minifigures sailed the seas for the first time in 12 years. Eight new sets appeared in 2009, featuring Captain Brickbeard, along with a new female pirate, and new versions of the Imperial Guard. However, after the release of the exclusive Imperial Flagship (10210) in 2010, the line was discontinued.

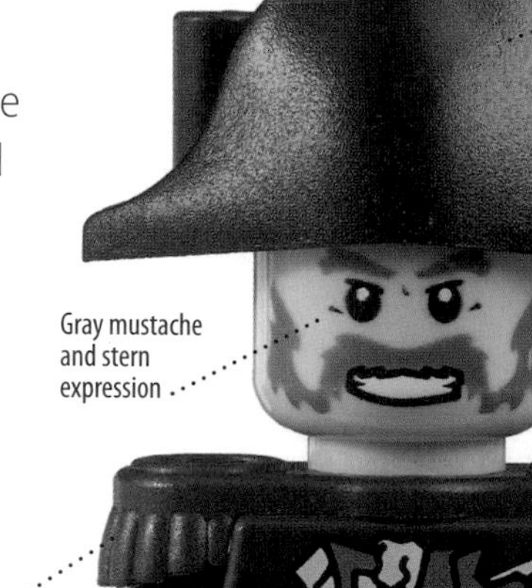
Bicorne hat
Gray mustache and stern expression
Red epaulets
Grand blue uniform

WE WILL HAVE TO SEARCH THE SEVEN SEAS FOR THOSE PIRATES!

PERHAPS TRY THE NEXT PAGE?

Governor This important minifigure is in charge of the Soldiers' Fort (6242). He resembles the Admiral, released in the same theme in 2010, but the naval leader has gold epaulets instead.

Red plume
This minifigure appeared in a battle pack and two games.

Plumed Hat Governor This variant of the Governor minifigure wears his hat the other way, and he has added a stylish red feather on top.

Tricorne hat

Nervous Officer This minifigure has good reason to worry—he's a lowly pawn in a LEGO Pirates chess set.

Impressive plume of red feathers
Blue epaulets
This soldier has a knapsack printed on his back.

Imperial Officer Attention! This soldier could win the prize for best turned out minifigure, thanks to his plumed hat and fine epaulets.

Goatee beard

Smiling Officer This soldier is also from LEGO Pirates Chess (852751). He is confident that the Imperial forces can win the game!

IMPERIAL GUARD

The new Imperial Guard had bearded faces and wore updated red jackets with blue epaulets. The Governor wore a blue jacket with red epaulets. In 2009, for the first time, the good guys sailed a bigger ship than the pirates.

Red plume and gold emblem
Flintlock musket

Imperial Guard This military minifigure wears an impressive plumed hat known as a shako.

DID YOU KNOW?
Four different versions of the Imperial Guard have appeared since 1989.

LEGO PIRATES CONTINUED

Brickbeard's Bounty (6243) Eight minifigures, including Captain Brickbeard and the Admiral's Daughter, feature in this set of the magnificent galleon.

Cutlass
Bicorne hat with skull and crossbones
Customary pirate's eyepatch
DON'T EVER CALL ME CAPTAIN REDBEARD!
Gold epaulets
Gold detail on outfit
Gold hook piece is new for 2009
Peg-leg

Captain Brickbeard The pirates' new leader replaces Captain Redbeard. This greedy pirate is only interested in one kind of treasure—gold.

Tricorne hat
Flintlock pistol

Tricorne Pirate This dastardly pirate wears a hat he "borrowed" from an Imperial Guard.

Green bandana worn at a jaunty angle
Matching green pants

Green Bandana Pirate This pirate doesn't see why he can't look good while being bad. His bandana and his pants match perfectly!

PIRATES

Captain Brickbeard led a crew of minifigure pirates in search of treasure. Most of the pirates had updated torsos and a variety of heads, hats, and leg colors. New elements included a gold hook on Brickbeard, a grizzled head with an eyepatch on another pirate officer, and a new castaway minifigure.

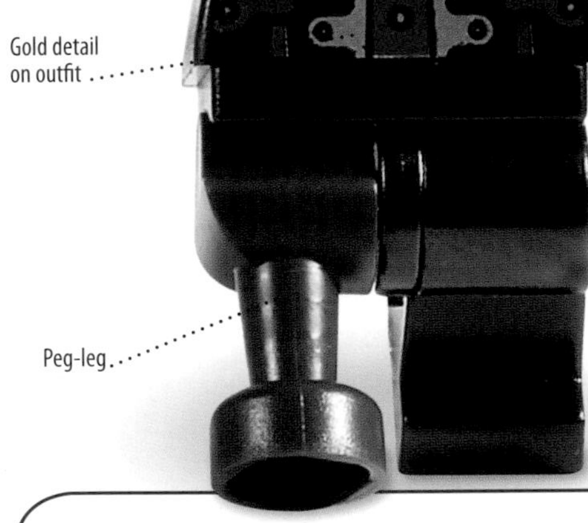

PIRATE VINTAGE COLLECTION

Two classic LEGO Pirate theme minifigures were reissued in 2009 as part of the Vintage Minifigure Collection.

The soldier was originally produced in 1989 and the pirate in 1996.

Vintage Soldier This minifigure retains all the original pieces of the 1989 minifigure.

The pirate's original vest was darker.

Vintage Pirate The LEGO designers kept all the details from the 1996 version, apart from the pirate's vest.

Long, brown hair
Eyepatch
Telescope
Treasure map

Female Pirate This treasure-hungry pirate debuts new head and torso pieces for this year. Her map tile has appeared in 15 sets since 2008.

Bodice
Dark green sloped piece

Female Pirate: Chess Piece This variant female pirate appears in the LEGO Pirate Chess Set. She has a sloped skirt piece instead of pants.

Loot Island (6241) The pirate's treasure map leads him to Loot Island. But first he must get past a crocodile and a catapult.

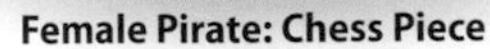

Castaway
Brick-flinging catapult
Treasure
Crocodile with moving jaw and tail

Tricorne hat
Striped tank top

Kraken Pirate This pirate must take his chances against the fearsome Kraken in set 6240.

Green bandana
Green and white striped tank top

Green Stripe Pirate This scurvy sea dog is exclusive to Cannon Battle (6239).

Blue bandana

Pirate Pawn He's smiling now but this pirate minifigure might soon be Imperial cannon fodder in the LEGO Pirates Chess Set.

Castaway In the 12 years since the last LEGO Pirates release, the castaway has had no hope of rescue. His pants have become ragged and his beard has grown shaggy.

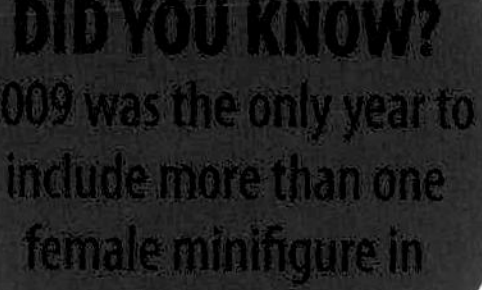

DID YOU KNOW?
2009 was the only year to include more than one female minifigure in the theme.

Fierce expression
Sharp knife is good for shaving pirate stubble

Red Bandana Pirate Most pirates have a very limited wardrobe—vest, or striped tank top, and bandana.

Anchor tattoo

Blue Bandana Pirate Popular pirate accessories include an anchor tattoo and some rope.

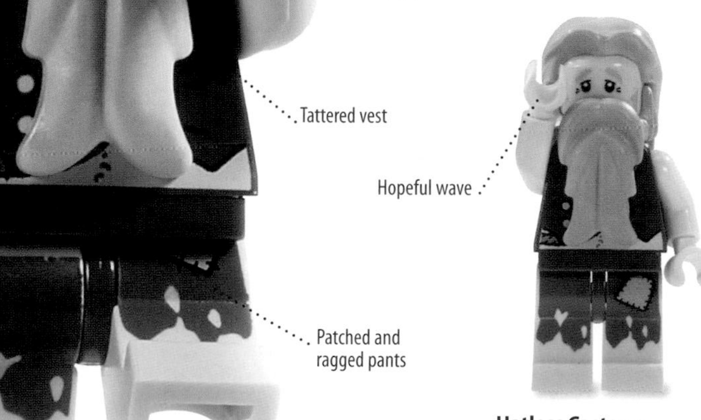
Blue bandana
Removable beard also seen on Professor Dumbledore from the LEGO® Harry Potter™ theme.
I CAN SEE MY SHACK FROM HERE!
Telescope—to search the horizon for ships.
Tattered vest
Patched and ragged pants
Hopeful wave

Hatless Castaway In this variant, the castaway's hat has been replaced by a hair piece.

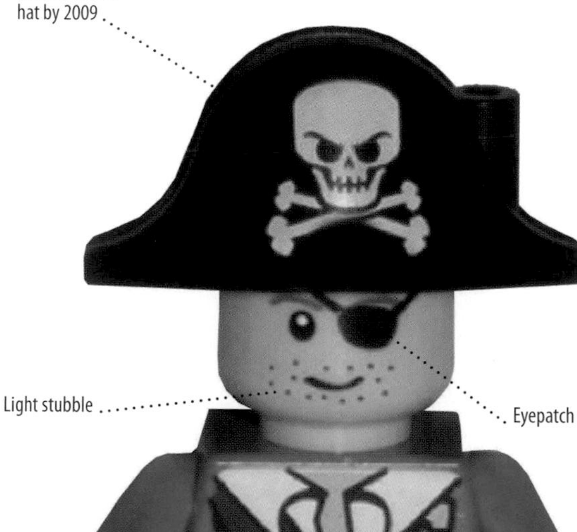
Brickbeard has also stolen this hat by 2009
ALL THIS TREASURE, YET WE CAN'T AFFORD A RAZOR.

EWW, CAN YOU SMELL FISH?

Light stubble
Eyepatch
Torso is unique to this minifigure
Black pants

Pirate Blue Jacket This young pirate has made a real effort with his look. Watch out Brickbeard—he could be after your job!

Tic Tac Toe Pirate Pirates like to play games—especially if they win! This minifigure is from a Tic Tac Toe (Noughts and Crosses) game.

MERMAIDS AND MORE

Two versions of the mermaid appeared in 2009—one as a ship's figurehead and one in the Pirates Advent Calendar. The Admiral's daughter was a new minifigure character this year.

Advent Calendar Mermaid This looks the same as the regular minifigure, except her tail is shorter.

Extra piece makes tail longer than on variant

Cutlass
Shell-design bikini top

Mermaid This fabled creature can be found on the prow of Brickbeard's Bounty (6243).

This hair piece can also be seen on Marion Ravenwood in the LEGO® *Indiana Jones*™ theme.
Old-fashioned white dress

Admiral's Daughter This damsel in distress can be found in the LEGO Pirates Chess Set and aboard Brickbeard's Bounty.

2009

HEY, DAD, WANT TO SEE THE MEDAL I GOT FOR DEFEATING YOU?

There have been two variants—the original had solid black pupils.

Celebration Luke Skywalker Available only as part of DK's LEGO *Star Wars Visual Dictionary*, this exclusive minifigure celebrates the rebels' victory over the Empire at the end of Episode IV *A New Hope*.

Exclusive torso with gold medal

Gun belt detail on brown pants

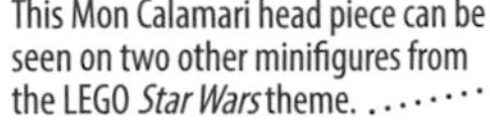

This Mon Calamari head piece can be seen on two other minifigures from the LEGO *Star Wars* theme.

Admiral Ackbar So far, the rebel leader has only appeared in three sets, so his minifigure is rare and very collectible.

Unique torso with Mon Calamari officer's uniform

LEGO *STAR WARS*

The tenth anniversary of LEGO *Star Wars* meant special minifigures. Among the treasures from this year were Luke Skywalker with a celebration medal, a chrome Darth Vader, a silver Stormtrooper magnet, the first minifigure appearance of Admiral Ackbar, and a new slave Leia magnet. Of these celebration minifigures, only Ackbar appeared in a standard LEGO set. The brave Ewoks also received a more realistic look.

The 2009 Wicket has detailed printing on his face.

Combined head-and-torso piece fits over standard torso.

Wicket W. Warrick Wicket was one of the first Ewoks to appear in minifigure form in 2002. This year, he's given a makeover—and is seen in his distinctive orange hood.

Underneath his helmet, the stormtrooper's head is blank.

This minifigure has the same helmet and torso pattern as a regular white stormtrooper.

Silver Trooper This shiny minifigure appears in a magnet set in 2009 and in an exclusive polybag for Toys 'R' Us in 2010.

KIDS, HUH? WHAT CAN YOU DO?

Underneath his shiny helmet lies Vader's scarred human face.

This version has a cape but no lightsaber.

Chrome Vader This 10th anniversary Darth Vader is shinier and more evil than ever, thanks to his chrome-black finish. Only 10,000 were produced.

The magnet variant is missing the slave neck chain.

The head, torso, and legs are identical to the 2006 minifigure.

Slave Leia This magnet variant is very similar to the minifigure released in the 2006 set Jabba's Sail Barge (6210).

CLASSIC SPACE

Four brave astronaut minifigures returned to outer space in 2009 as part of the Vintage Minifigure Collection. These minifigures were originally produced in the first five years of the Classic Space line. The reissued versions looked identical, apart from their helmets, which were given a more modern shape.

Black Spaceman This minifigure is on his first mission since 1984. Space hasn't changed a bit though!

New, sturdier helmet design

Blue Spaceman 1984 was the last time this astronaut blasted into space, so he can't wait to explore the stars.

White Spaceman This intergalactic explorer has been on ice since 1978. He can't wait to journey into the 21st century.

Classic Space insignia

Yellow Spaceman It's been 30 years since he last piloted a rocket, but it's a bit like riding a bike....

LEGO SPACE

Space adventures have been a part of LEGO fun for almost as long as there have been minifigures, with hundreds of Space sets produced since 1978. Whether it is peaceful exploration of Mars or battles against the forces of Blacktron, the stars have long beckoned to LEGO minifigures. In 2009, Space found some new frontiers, and some old friends.

Alien head piece also used on Rench in the Space Police III subtheme in 2010

A large skull is also printed on the back of Kranxx's vest.

Kranxx The leader of the Black Hole Gang, Kranxx is also a skilled pilot with a taste for high speeds.

Red light piece is used as a head

Mechanical claws

Police Droid
Not technically a minifigure, this Police Droid is made up of ten pieces, including two skeleton legs.

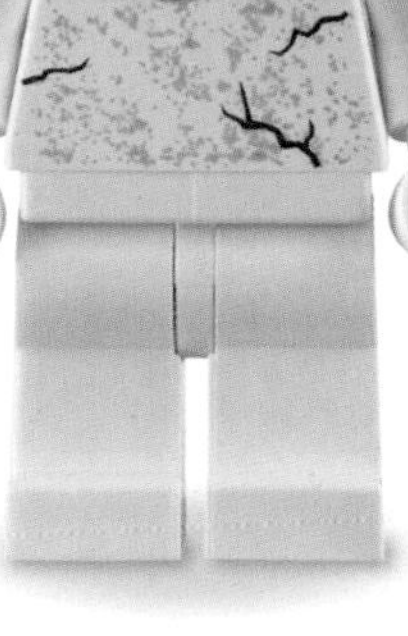

Unique torso with cracked marble details

Classic Space Statue
This statue of the first LEGO Space Astronaut features only in the Space Police III Galactic Enforcer set (5974). It's stolen by Kranxx and Slizer and the Space Police must get it back.

Spiked helmet on top of green alien head

Spiked armor printed on torso and legs

Slizer This spiky alien criminal is the chief mechanic of the Black Hole Gang.

Unique head piece

Red cape—to match his eyes

Scales and muscles printed on torso

Squidman This alien criminal is always thinking up schemes to make himself rich, but they usually fail.

Extra-large eyes

Torso extension piece

Extra arms

Frenzy This four-armed bad guy has a unique head piece featuring a huge, gaping mouth.

Visor can be used to hide his identity

Protective helmet

Symbol of the Black Hole Gang

Knee pads printed on legs

Snake This prolific criminal appears in five sets—more than any other alien villain in this theme.

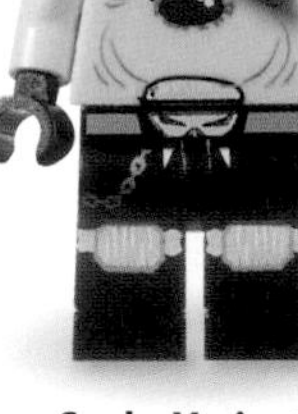

Eighth eye

Snake Variant
In Space Speeder (8400), slimy Snake appears without his visor.

Dual-sided head underneath the helmet. One side has two eyes, the other side has three.

Black uniform with "Octan" printed on it

Skull Twin Just one of these criminals would be bad, but unfortunately there are two evil Skull Twins. Double trouble!

LEGO
SPACE POLICE
7-14
5972

Space Truck Getaway (5972)
This Space Police van comes with two minifigures—one alien and one policeman.

FREEZE! KEEP YOUR TENTACLES WHERE I CAN SEE THEM!

Dual-sided head: smiling and scared

New silver armor for 2009

Communications Officer
Thanks to his headset, the Communications Officer can contact his Space Police colleagues wherever they are in the galaxy.

Black helmet with visor

Aggressive expression

Field Officer This officer is on a mission to track down the alien Frenzy. He should be worried!

Space Police badge

Rookie Officer This officer is on his first mission. He seems confident enough, but his alternative face looks scared.

Flick 'n fire missile launcher

Special Ops Officer
Orange glasses ensure that this minifigure looks good, even in space.

SPACE POLICE III

The intergalactic law enforcers were back after 11 years with a new play theme, chasing down the galaxy's worst thieves in 10 sets. Nicknamed Space Police III by fans, the theme featured numerous new alien heads, and every set included at least one alien minifigure.

Dual-sided female head: smiling and scared

Female Officer In 2009 the Space Police got their first female recruit. She wears the same unisex uniform as her male minifigure colleagues.

2009

LEGO® CASTLE

2009 was the last year of the fantasy-based LEGO Castle theme before LEGO Kingdoms took up the quest in 2010. In 2009, a mighty minifigure king and his knights battled the evil forces of the Troll King in three sets.

First hair piece to feature a hole for accessories
Medieval-style blue dress
Tattered cloak is new this year

Troll King This one-eyed minifigure is leader of the wicked Troll Warriors. He plans to capture the Crown King and imprison him in his Mountain Fortress.

Crown Queen The Queen has a dual-sided head: now she is happy and smiling, but she can easily turn to her annoyed expression if something makes her royally angry.

Golden sword

New plume of blue feathers

Detachable breastplate armor

Crown King The 2009 version of the King has new printing on his torso and legs, and a blue plume in his crown. However, unlike the 2007 version, this minifigure does not have a cape.

VINTAGE CASTLE

Three vintage minifigures were reissued this year: a Forestman and Knight from the classic Castle sets, and a ninja warrior from the Ninja sets.

Ninja head wrap later used in Ninjago play theme in 2011

Red Ninja The Red Ninja minifigure first adventured in 1999 in sets such as Ninja's Fire Fortress (3052).

Forestman This vintage Forestman was last seen in 1990 in the Crusader's Cart (1877) and Hay Cart with Smugglers (1680) sets.

Knight This noble minifigure debuted in 1978 as part of the Castle Mini Figures set (0016). He reappears, unchanged, as a vintage Knight for 2009.

Red feather
Simple hat
Classic Castle helmet
Armor and crest printed on torso

Red crown piece
Elusive diamond
Unique red outfit with gold details

Nightclub Willie Scott Ready for a performance at Club Obi Wan in Shanghai, singer Willie Scott wears a glamorous, Chinese-inspired outfit.

Black version of Indy's fedora hat

Grinning Gangster The two gangsters feature distinct but equally devious expressions. This one has a sneaky grin.

Slick, black suit with white tie

Revolver

Mustache Gangster This gangster sports a scowl and a long, thin mustache. He is determined to catch Indy, Willie, and Short Round.

Rock bin trap

Temple of Doom (7199) This set boasts many exciting features including a trap door, several booby traps, and glow-in-the-dark spikes.

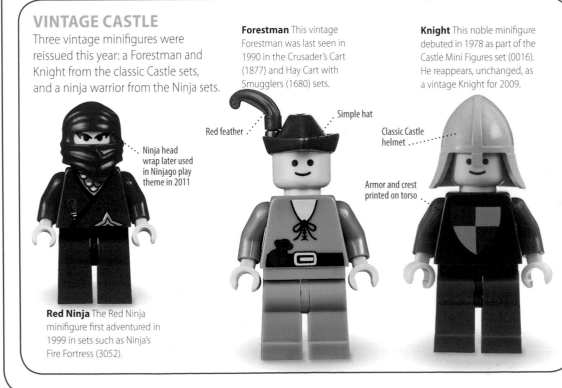

LEGO® *INDIANA JONES*™

The minifigure archaeologist with the famous hat was back in 2009 with two new sets based on *Indiana Jones and the Temple of Doom*—the only movie not featured in the theme's 2008 debut. The highlight of the 2009 theme was the Temple of Doom set (7199), featuring not only six new minifigures but also a thrilling temple/mine rollercoaster track build that was over three feet (nearly 1 meter) long.

The two versions of Willie have different blonde hair pieces
Dual-sided head—smiling and scared
Unique beading and fringing detail on torso and legs

Sacrificial Willie Scott
The Thuggee High Priest is planning to sacrifice this minifigure. Perhaps it's time for Willie to reveal the other side of her head piece—scared!

Indy is dressed up to visit Club Obi Wan in Shanghai.

Tuxedo Indiana Jones
The second version released in 2009 shows Indy dressed in a tuxedo, with his 2008 head piece.

Unique jacket and shirt design on torso

Short Round
Indy's *Temple of Doom* sidekick Wan Li or "Short Round" is only 11 years old so his minifigure has short LEGO legs. He appears in both 2009 sets.

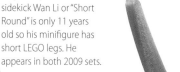

NEVER TRUST ANY PLACE THAT HAS "OF DOOM" IN ITS NAME.
New expression—sardonic grin
Sword
Indy's left arm has a shirtsleeve printed on it, but the right arm is bare.
Leather bag for the Sankara Stones
Gun holster printed on legs

Indiana Jones
The intrepid archaeologist minifigure keeps his trademark fedora, but he loses his leather jacket and even one of his shirtsleeves in 2009. He is searching for the powerful Sankara Stones.

DID YOU KNOW?
Short Round's LEGO legs can also be seen on Dobby in LEGO® Harry Potter™ (in tan), and the Ewoks in LEGO *Star Wars*.

THE HEROES

As with previous Indiana Jones releases, this theme featured two minifigure versions of Indy. He was joined by two versions of the nightclub singer Willie Scott and the diminutive minifigure of Short Round. This would be the final year of the Indiana Jones theme.

THE VILLAINS

The Temple of Doom set (7199) featured Mola Ram and two of his loyal Thuggee followers. The other set in this subtheme, Shanghai Chase (7682), included two gun-toting Shanghai gangster minifigures.

NOW THIS IS WHAT I CALL A HAT!

These detachable horns also appear on the Minotaur in LEGO Minifigures Series 6 from 2012.

Mola Ram The Thuggee High Priest has many unique details including his headdress (excluding the horns), his torso, and the red paint on his forehead.

LEGO INDIANA JONES 8-14 7199 TEMPLE OF DOOM

The Temple of Doom (7199) This set is based on the iconic scene from the film, and comes with six minifigures.

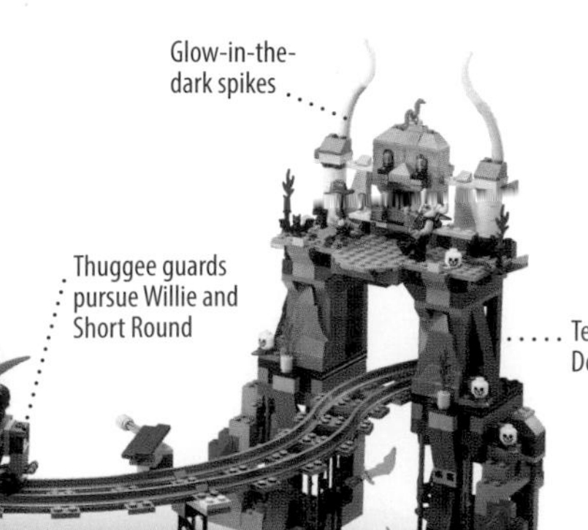

Glow-in-the-dark spikes
Thuggee guards pursue Willie and Short Round
Temple of Doom

Turban-style headdress
Large, curved sword
Unique head piece

Chief Thuggee Guard
The torso, with its bare chest, red sash, and ceremonial knife, is unique to this minifigure.

Rifle

Thuggee Guard
This guard's head piece and his torso are also unique.

Lava Dragon—Knight In this two to four-player game, the winner is the first knight to reach the top of a fiery mountain.

Minotaurus—Red Spartan Playing as red, blue, white, or yellow Spartans, the object is to travel to the center of a maze, avoiding the Minotaur.

Ramses Pyramid—Blue Explorer Blue, red, yellow, and orange explorers try to get to the top of Ramses Pyramid.

Ramses Pyramid—King Ramses The King, along with his eight mummies, tries to push the players back.

Lunar Command—Orange This two-player game was only released in the UK.

Lunar Command—Green Players must build space stations to launch a Lunar Rocket.

LEGO GAMES

Standing two bricks tall with a stud on the head, the microfigure burst onto the scene in 2009 in LEGO Games such as Lava Dragon, Minotaurus, Lunar Command, and the award-winning Ramses Pyramid.

Blue cap
He wears the same coveralls as the Farmer in the Farm set (7637).
GREAT CROP OF BRICKS THIS YEAR!

Farmer Blue Cap This farmer drives a red tractor in the Tractor set (7634) and carries his trusty shovel.

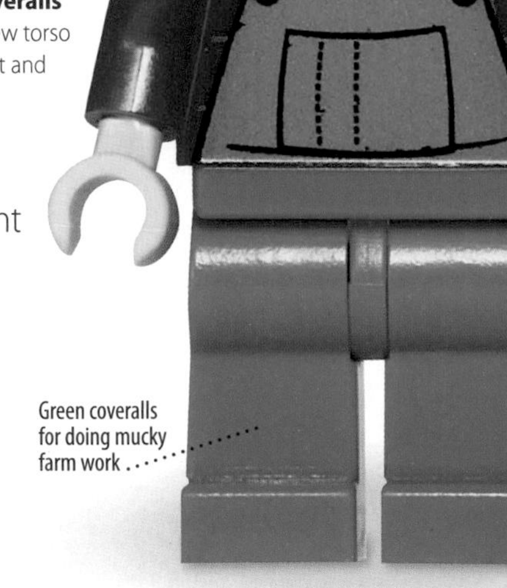
Tan sun hat
This head piece is popular in the LEGO City theme and is also used on several policemen and construction workers.
Printing continues on the back of the torso
Green coveralls for doing mucky farm work

Farmer Green Coveralls The Farmer has a new torso with a red plaid shirt and green coveralls.

LEGO® CITY

Farm made its first appearance in a LEGO System theme in 2009 as part of LEGO City. Five sets and eight new minifigures and various animals populated this line, which lasted for two years. Three of the minifigures were farmers, each with a different head and torso. Prior to this release, Farm was primarily a LEGO® DUPLO® theme for younger fans.

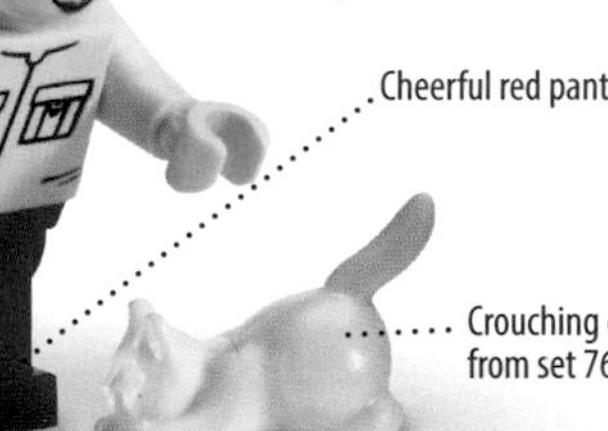
Cheerful red pants
Crouching cat from set 7637

Female Farm Hand The hardworking farm hand has some familiar parts: her shirt was worn by Cloud City Luke Skywalker in 2003.

Casual blue plaid shirt

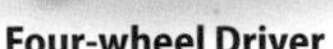

Four-wheel Driver This minifigure is taking his four-wheel drive with horse trailer for a spin in the country. He's no farmer!

Red cap
Coveralls keep clothes underneath clean

Male Farm Hand This farm hand wears blue coveralls that are also popular with LEGO janitors and mechanics.

Retro orange sunglasses

Camera

NEXT TIME, I'M GOING TO LEGOLAND!

New Hawaiian shirt is also seen on later City minifigures.

Lightweight tan pants

Tourist Scared Two other tourists appear in Robo Attack, as well as the evil Dr. Inferno.

THE TOURIST

Although essentially a City minifigure, this Tourist actually appeared in the LEGO® Agents set Robo Attack (8970). The unsuspecting out-of-towner finds himself in the path of a rampaging robot!

Happy, smiling face

Tourist Smiling The dual-sided head can be smiling or scared. It is unique to this minifigure.

Farm (7637) This set contains 609 pieces to make a grain silo, barn, cow pen, tractor, and mower, plus three minifigures.

Grain silo
Barn
Cow pen
Tractor

Farmer This happy farmer drives a mini tractor in the promotional set Mini Tractor (4899) released via newspapers and LEGO stores.

Tan fedora hat

Green coveralls with white shirt

This hat piece is more commonly seen as a construction helmet.

The horse cannot be disassembled.

Horseback Rider This well-dressed rider and her horse are found in 4WD with Horse Trailer (7635).

LEGO
CITY
5-12
7634

Tractor (7634) This red harvest tractor comes with one minifigure—the blue hat farmer.

DECK THE HALLS WITH LEGO BRICKS! TRA LA LA...

Pilot torso

Male Caroler The two carolers have a new head piece with an open, singing mouth, and rosy cheeks.

LEGO® SEASONAL

LEGO minifigures have always been a great holiday gift for LEGO fans. This group from the Winter Village Toy Shop and LEGO City Advent Calendar, featuring two exclusive caroler minifigures, were the first of many designed to double as holiday decorations. They did not appear in any other sets. One set in this festive line would come out each year from 2009 onward.

Unique caroler's head piece
Song book

Female Caroler The carol singer's double cloak should keep her warm during those chilly winter's nights.

Santa with Fireplace Perhaps not surprisingly, Santa can be found behind window 24 on the LEGO City Advent Calendar.

Sack for presents
Traditional Santa outfit and beard

Chimney
Stocking
Roaring fire

Red cap
Messenger pouch was first seen in various LEGO *Indiana Jones* sets from 2008.

Holiday Postman This minifigure appears behind the tenth window of the LEGO City Advent Calendar.

Hat piece often used for LEGO Police

Red jacket with horn logo printed on torso

Smart black pants

Postman This vintage minifigure hasn't delivered any LEGO mail since 1991, so he's probably got a sack full of letters waiting for him!

GOT MAIL!

This smiling post office worker was a reissue of a classic minifigure from 1982. He has appeared in six sets and was one of two post office minifigures released this year.

DID YOU KNOW?

The LEGO City Farm (7637) reappears later in a Space Police animation.

ULTIMATE FAN

This exclusive minifigure was a giveaway at the 2009 LEGO Fan Weekend in Skaerbaek, Denmark. Since then, it has become a very rare and much sought-after collectible!

LEGO
LEGO Fan Weekend
2009
LEGO logo and event details make this torso unique.

LEGO Fan Weekend 2009 The head, hair, and legs parts are common LEGO pieces, but the torso is unique with details of the 2009 event printed on it.

2010s

The 2010s launched with a bonanza for minifigure fans as the new collectible LEGO® Minifigures line added hundreds of colorful new characters, body components, and accessories to its ever-growing lineup. Minifigures burst onto the small screen as the martial-arts masters of LEGO® Ninjago and the battling beasts of LEGO® Legends of Chima™ had televised weekly adventures, while classic super heroes from comic books and movies ran, flew, and smashed their way into the spotlight. All that and alien invasions, dinosaurs, and monsters, too!

I LIKE LEGO CLUB. THWACK!
Underneath his removable hair and beard, the Caveman has a unibrow and a wide smile.
The spiked club is new for this minifigure.
Hairy chest and animal-hide clothes

Caveman This minifigure loves inventing things. If only he would invent a razor, then everyone could see his unique face!

2010

FROM THE SANDS of Persia to the depths of the ocean, LEGO® minifigures were everywhere in 2010. LEGO® *Star Wars*® celebrated the 30th anniversary of Episode V *The Empire Strikes Back*, while new licensed themes *Prince of Persia*™ and *Toy Story*™ combined Disney action and adventure with LEGO building know-how. Meanwhile, daredevil divers went in search of Atlantis, LEGO® Kingdoms brought the classic Castle theme back, and high-octane World Racers hit the track. And, not to be forgotten, the colorful, charming, and completely unique LEGO® Minifigures became the stars of their very own collectible theme.

LEGO MINIFIGURES

The collectible LEGO Minifigures theme was a major hit in 2010, with the first two series providing 32 exclusive minifigures to excited fans. Each character was packed individually in a series-colored polybag, so collectors wouldn't be able to tell which minifigure they were getting until they opened it.

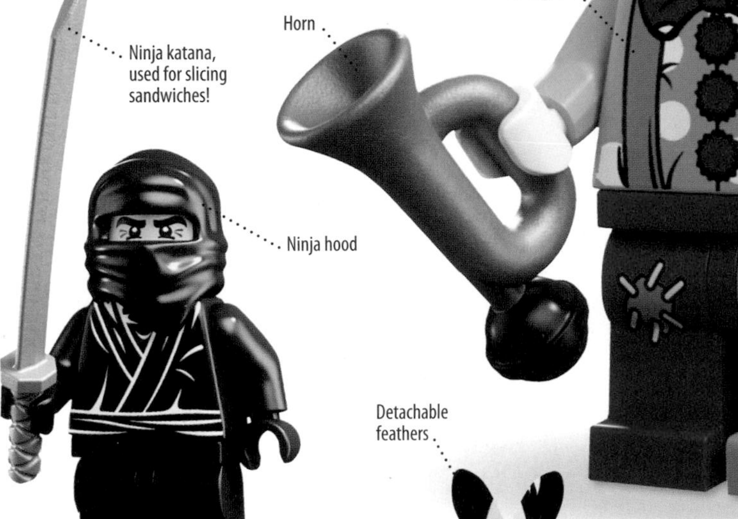

Clown face is unique to this minifigure
A black version of this hair piece can be seen on the Disco Dude in Series 2.
Torso and legs are also exclusive to this minifigure
Horn
Ninja katana, used for slicing sandwiches!
Ninja hood

Circus Clown This minifigure can't talk, but fortunately he can honk his horn.

Ninja He might look like a cool, scary Ninja but this minifigure is really a clumsy scaredy-cat.

Detachable feathers

Quiver of arrows attached to neck bracket

Bow was previously seen in the 1996 LEGO® Western theme

Tribal Hunter This minifigure specializes in finding things. Well, he'll never find a head, torso, and legs like his—they're unique.

Wrench

Head, torso, and legs are exclusive to this minifigure

PA7 70

License plate from a dismantled car

Demolition Dummy This unique minifigure has a one-track mind: he just wants to dismantle everything.

Skateboarder This minifigure likes to win, so it's a good thing that he was the clear favorite with kids in pre-launch consumer tests.

This dude can do some rad tricks!

SERIES 1

The Series 1 lineup featured nine new LEGO parts, but the smallest number of female minifigures of any LEGO minifigures release (three). Supply issues made this series of minifigures the rarest in the entire theme.

This hair piece is making its debut in blonde.
Hands fit inside pom-poms

Cheerleader "2, 4, 6, 8, who do we appreciate? LEGO!" The perky, pom-pom-shaking cheerleader is the first to feature rare side-printing on her legs.

Rare blue head piece with unique red mask printing
Cape has been seen on 17 other minifigures, including a 2002 Quidditch Harry Potter™

Super Wrestler Life's just one big wrestling match for this minifigure, and he's determined to win!

Spare bullets
This cowboy is toting two smoking pistols.
This is a light colored version of Indy's fedora from the LEGO® *Indiana Jones*™ theme.

Cowboy Don't be fooled by his unshaven, tough guy appearance; this minifigure is a darn-tootin' gentleman.

THE ONLY THINGS UP MY SLEEVES ARE MY WRISTS!

Mischievous expression
Wand with painted white ends

Magician That's not magic at the end of the Magician's wand, it's white paint—a rarity for a LEGO bar element.

DID YOU KNOW?

Some clever fans did know what they were getting—the bar codes on the 2010 polybags could be used to identify the minifigure inside.

Confused expression—this harmless Zombie isn't scary at all!
Turkey leg
Shovel

Zombie The LEGO Group's first-ever Zombie minifigure would be followed by four more in 2012's LEGO® Monster Fighters theme.

The Deep Sea Diver never takes his mask off, even on dry land.
Classic LEGO air tank is seen in orange for the first time
These flippers were first seen on the Coast Guard: Helicopter Rescue in the LEGO® City theme

Deep Sea Diver When he's not exploring the ocean, this minifigure makes do with splashing about in the bathtub!

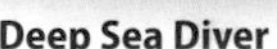
Syringe full of medicine
Unique torso printing with nurses' fob watch detail
Patient's chart

Nurse With her unique, caring face, the Nurse will make any minifigure feel better—whether they are sick or not!

Space helmet also seen in the LEGO® Space Police theme in 2010
Classic Space theme logo
Laser beam

Spaceman He's traveled far and wide, but the strangest place this Spaceman has ever been is LEGO Earth!

OH DEAR, I SNAGGED MY GREEN TIGHTS!

Red feather in hat
The Forestman has the same bow and arrows as the Tribal Hunter minifigure
Forest green outfit

Forestman Although many of his elements have been seen before, the Forestman's head and torso are new, and unique.

Metallic silver version of helmet used on Evil Robot in Series 8 in 2012
Unique torso with panel and gauge details
Claw piece instead of hand

Robot Underneath his rare metallic helmet, the Robot has a detailed face, with red photo-receptor eyes and a mouth-like speaker grille.

LEGO MINIFIGURES CONTINUED

SERIES 2

LEGO Minifigures Series 2 introduced more new minifigures and also redesigned some old ones, including the Vampire. The series included 13 new elements and innovations, such as giving the Mime three interchangeable heads. However, series 2 still had the identifying bar codes on the polybags.

Traditional beret, also seen on the Artist in Series 4.

Three alternate heads: smiling, sad, and very, very upset
The Mime is the only minifigure with three heads.

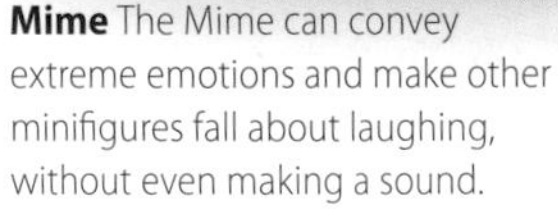

Mime The Mime can convey extreme emotions and make other minifigures fall about laughing, without even making a sound.

THIS ONE'S FOR ALL MY FANS OUT THERE!

New microphone piece

Exclusive pink outfit with silver details

Pop Star She might be one of the LEGO world's most popular singers, but the Pop Star is just a regular minifigure at heart.

New sombrero hat piece is unique to this minifigure

SHHH! THE FANS WANT TO HEAR MY MARACAS!

Unique poncho, made of two new patterned cape pieces

Maracas were specially created for this minifigure

Maraca Man When this colorful but mysterious character shakes his maracas, the other minifigures get into a party mood.

Unique lime green weightlifting suit
The weightlifting bar is made of three pieces.

Weightlifter
Dripping with sweat and his face straining with effort, the Weightlifter is determined to be the world's strongest minifigure.

DID YOU KNOW?
Series 2 is the only series to date not to include a minifigure with a sword.

Whip for taming lions

Hat also worn by the Magician in Series 1

Unique fancy red jacket and bow tie

Ringmaster It takes a certain type of minifigure to make sure that the lions are tamed, the clowns are funny, and the tightrope is tight. The circus Ringmaster is a busy man!

The first ever printed LEGO surfboard
Unique head with stubble and weatherbeaten wrinkle lines
The surfer's shorts and board have the same floral pattern.

Surfer His hair piece is a blond version of the Skater's in Series 1 and the Surfer is equally as focused on his board. He's also totally awesome, too!

Matching, warm blue hat
Racing vest with crossed skis logo
Both skis can be held in one hand
211
Ski poles can be clipped together

Skier The Skier might look good in his unique blue ski suit and cool, orange glasses, but he is actually a terrible skier.

GET UP AND GROOVE TO THE PLASTIC BEAT!
This head piece was also used on a rocker in a store-exclusive minifigure three-pack in 2012.
Retro record
Brick Fever
1970s outfit including medallion and white suit
Badge and walkie talkie printed on torso
Handcuffs are minifigure sized
Speeding ticket
Hair piece also used on the Vampire
Black belt
Trophy is the smallest scale model of a minifigure.
New, textured version of the witch/wizard's hat
Witch's broom
White pith helmet, also seen on Pippin Reed in the 1998 LEGO® Adventurers theme
LEGO field glasses
This shade of green is unique to the Witch's head.
New spear has a soft plastic tip
This hair piece was first seen on the Cheerleader in Series 1.
Magnifying glass actually works!
This is the first appearance of the sloped base in the Minifigures theme.
Rescue float can be gripped by two minifigures
Gold cobra-head staff, specially created for this minifigure
Stud so that decoration can be attached to the headdress
Helmet, head, torso, and legs are unique to this minifigure
Cape was later used in the LEGO Monster Fighters theme in 2012.
Shield has a handle on the back and a stud on the front
Unique fanged head, but this Vampire prefers smoothies to sucking blood!
Unique head, torso, and legs with Ancient Egyptian costume printing
Sandals printed on feet

Disco Dude
Remember when pop music was played on funky little vinyl things called records? No? The Disco Dude can!

Traffic Cop
Speeding minifigures, beware! This Traffic Cop is patrolling the LEGO highways ready to write you a ticket.

Karate Master
This martial artist minifigure can chop a LEGO brick in half with his bare hands. He's got a trophy to prove it!

Lifeguard All this minifigure thinks about is saving other minifigures. She doesn't even care how great she looks in her exclusive red swimsuit.

Explorer This eccentric globe-trotter has a unique head with monocle and bushy mustache. Despite his field glasses, he has a terrible sense of direction.

Witch This minifigure spells trouble. Watch out for her in 2012; she appears in a Halloween accessory set.

Pharaoh This minifigure was a king back in Ancient Egypt, but now he's all alone in the modern world, without a pyramid to call home. He wants his Mummy!

Vampire He's not the first LEGO vampire, but this Vampire is definitely the grooviest. He loves to throw parties—as long as they're at night, of course.

Spartan Warrior
He'd love to meet another Spartan minifigure to fight with, but the Spartan Warrior is just too unique.

2010

Dual-sided head: smiling and sad
1x1 round plates for juggling
WHY DID THE DRAGON CROSS THE ROAD?

LEGO® CASTLE

In 2010, the new LEGO Kingdoms series took over from the 2007-2009 LEGO Castle subtheme, focusing on a battle between the rival Lion and Dragon kingdoms. Eight new sets were released this year, featuring wizards, knights, fair damsels, and other new minifigures. A Kingdoms Advent Calendar was the jewel in the crown of this year's assortment.

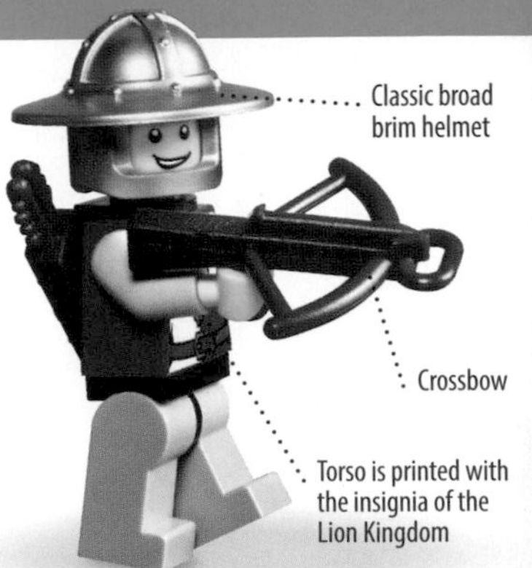

Classic broad brim helmet
Crossbow
Torso is printed with the insignia of the Lion Kingdom

Crossbow Knight This classic Knight minifigure has been updated with details of the Lion Kingdom.

If the Queen kisses him, this LEGO frog may turn into a prince!

Jester This medieval clown is only the second Jester minifigure ever created. The first wore a similar outfit in blue and red and was in the 2008 Fantasy Era sets.

LEGO
Kingdoms
5-12
7949

Prison Carriage Rescue (7949)
Three minifigures come with this set, which also includes a Dragon Knight warhorse, and prison carriage.

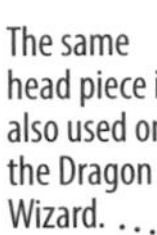

Red is the color of the Lion Kingdom.
The same head piece is also used on the Dragon Wizard.
Underneath the armor, the Knight's torso has a gold lion's head.

Lion Knight The armored Knight also features some exciting new elements, including his helmet, torso, legs, and light gray armor.

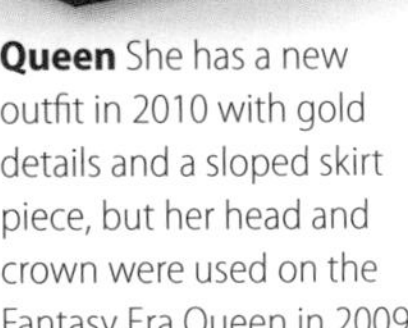

The Queen's dress has lace-up details printed on the back

Queen She has a new outfit in 2010 with gold details and a sloped skirt piece, but her head and crown were used on the Fantasy Era Queen in 2009.

Hair piece also seen on Hermione in the LEGO® Harry Potter™ theme

Lion Princess
The Princess' regal torso and matching sloped skirt piece are new for 2010.

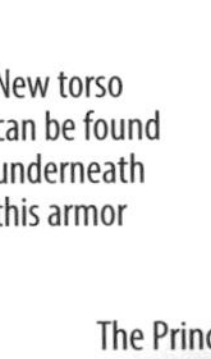

Gold crown with detachable plume of feathers
The same head piece can also be seen on the Blue Wizard.
Standard LEGO cape seen on more than 100 minifigures
New torso can be found underneath this armor
New printed legs with gold detail

Lion King As befits the noble leader of the Lion Kingdom, the King has many new elements, including a torso with Lion head medallion and fur trim pattern.

Head piece also seen on several City minifigures in 2011
Smiling head piece with chin dimple is new this year
The Prince wields a short sword.

Lion Prince The heir to the throne has the same torso and legs as the King, without the armor. The Prince only appears in the 2010 Kingdoms Advent Calendar.

LION KINGDOM

The heroic Knights of the Lion Kingdom featured a new helmet with a cross shape on the front and a new breastplate with a golden lion print. They were led by the Lion King, who had a new crowned head, a new torso, and new legs.

LEGO® PIRATES

The LEGO Group created this pirate exclusively for DK's *LEGO® Pirates Brickmaster*, a pirate-themed book with 140 pieces. An Imperial Soldier minifigure also came with the book.

Green bandana
Hairy chest
Peg-leg

Exclusive Pirate There's no doubt that this peg-legged pirate belongs on the sea. He has a new torso, which features an anchor tattoo and classic pirate vest.

Variant helmet with neck protector

Crossbow Knight Variant This Crossbow Knight has the same head piece and quiver of arrows as the other variant.

WHO ARE YOU CALLING A BLUE SANTA?

Head piece and beard also used on a 2011 Santa minifigure

Unique hat with star detail

Detachable hood

Blacksmith The Blacksmith's bearded head piece is new for 2010, but shared by other Kingdoms minifigures.

Chain Mail Knight This brave minifigure has chain mail armor. Ten other Knights in this theme have the same torso.

Broad brim helmet

Chain mail armor

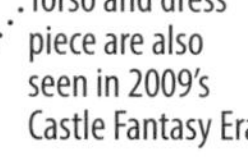

Torso and dress piece are also seen in 2009's Castle Fantasy Era.

Barmaid Only appearing in Day 16 of the Kingdoms Advent Calendar, the Barmaid's head piece is new this year.

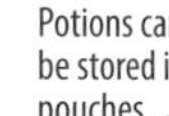

Potions can be stored in pouches.

Wizard Although he closely resembles Majisto from 1993 LEGO Castle, the 2010 Wizard has new legs and a stylish new hat.

VINTAGE CASTLE

This friendly Forestwoman minifigure originally came with the 1990 set Forestmen's Crossing (6071). It was reissued as part of the Vintage Minifigures series.

Forestwoman The 2010 Forestwoman is an exact replica of the 1990 version—all that's missing is her quiver of arrows.

Green corset detail on torso

DRAGON KINGDOM

The Dragon Kingdom had no king, so the Dragon Wizard minifigure usually acted as the leader. The Dragon Knights used the same helmet as the Lion Knights, but wore dark and pale green armor with a golden dragon on the breastplate.

Quiver of arrows

Broad brim helmet in shiny dark gray

Dragon Bowman He shares a head piece with his enemy, the Chain Mail Knight and also comes in the Green Dragon Knights Battle Pack (852922).

Flail weapon

I HOPE THIS THING DOESN'T HIT MY HEAD AGAIN!

This style of helmet is new this year.

Scale mail printed on torso

Flail Knight The detailed scale mail torso can be seen on six other Knights in this theme, but this Knight also wields a deadly flail.

Green is the color of the Dragon Kingdom.

Head shows teeth bared in fighting stance

Classic Dragon Knight This minifigure is ready for action! His sword is drawn and his Dragon shield is up.

Dragon shield

Dragon insignia

Dragon Knight One of five knights in the Green Dragon Knights Battle Pack (852922), the Dragon Knight features the new dragon torso printing.

The Dragon Knight wears a cape instead of armor.

Hat with dragon print is unique to this minifigure

This wizard is the only minifigure to have this beard piece in black.

Dragon Wizard This powerful minifigure would love to defeat the Lion Kingdom. He hates the Lion King and the Lion Wizard.

LEGO® ATLANTIS

Minifigure divers went in search of the mysterious city of Atlantis in this underwater play theme, but aquatic guardians were determined to stop them. Many exciting new elements and molds were introduced to create the amazing undersea creatures of LEGO Atlantis. The theme was a huge success, leading to more sets and minifigures in 2011. The new Atlantis elements also provided LEGO fans with colorful and unique pieces to use in their own creations.

Propeller blade attached to air tank
Eyepatch is unique to Ace minifigures
FIRST THING I DO IN ATLANTIS? VISIT THE SWIMMING POOL!
Standard issue green diving flippers

Ace Speedman The leader of the Salvage Crew, Ace Speedman pilots the Neptune Carrier. He wears a distinctive eyepatch—his eye is fine, he just thinks an eyepatch looks cool!

Dual-sided head piece: serious and scared

Dr. Jeff Fisher This marine biologist minifigure is hoping to discover new creatures in Atlantis. He has a unique head piece with glasses and a mustache.

ATLANTIS DEEP SEA SALVAGE CREW

The lime-green and silver Atlantis minifigures featured a new breathing apparatus mold, new torsos (printed front and back), and new heads. All but two of the Atlantis sets came with specially molded portal keys, which were the object of the divers' quest in the 2010 storyline.

Dual-sided head: smiling and annoyed
Sam is the only female diver
Harpoon gun

Professor Samantha Rhodes Although not technically a member of the Salvage Crew, scientist Sam Rhodes tags along because she is determined to prove that Atlantis exists.

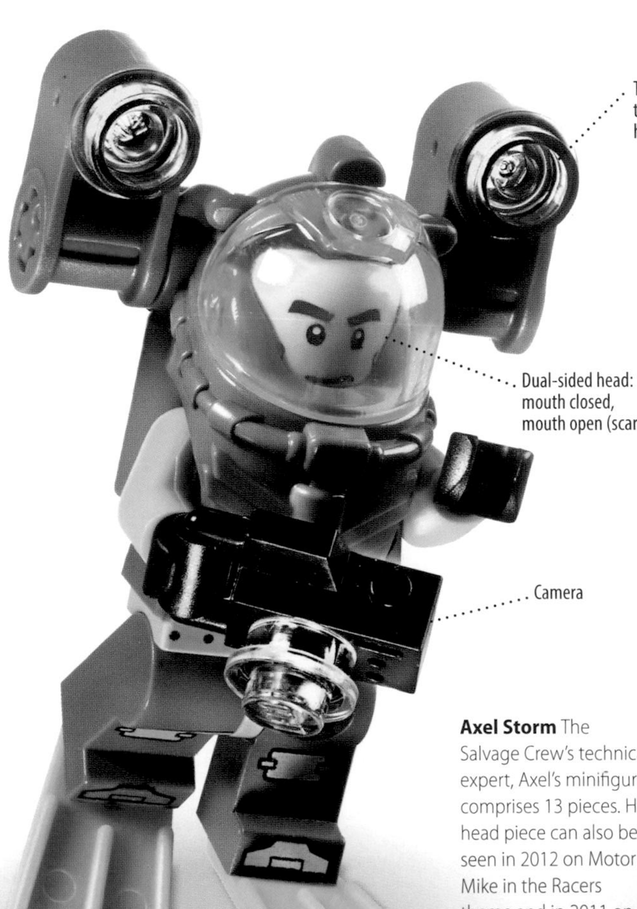
Two vertical lamps attached to air tank—a variant Axel has horizontal lamps
Dual-sided head: mouth closed, mouth open (scared)
Camera

Axel Storm The Salvage Crew's technical expert, Axel's minifigure comprises 13 pieces. His head piece can also be seen in 2012 on Motor Mike in the Racers theme and in 2011 on the Lion Knight in the Castle theme.

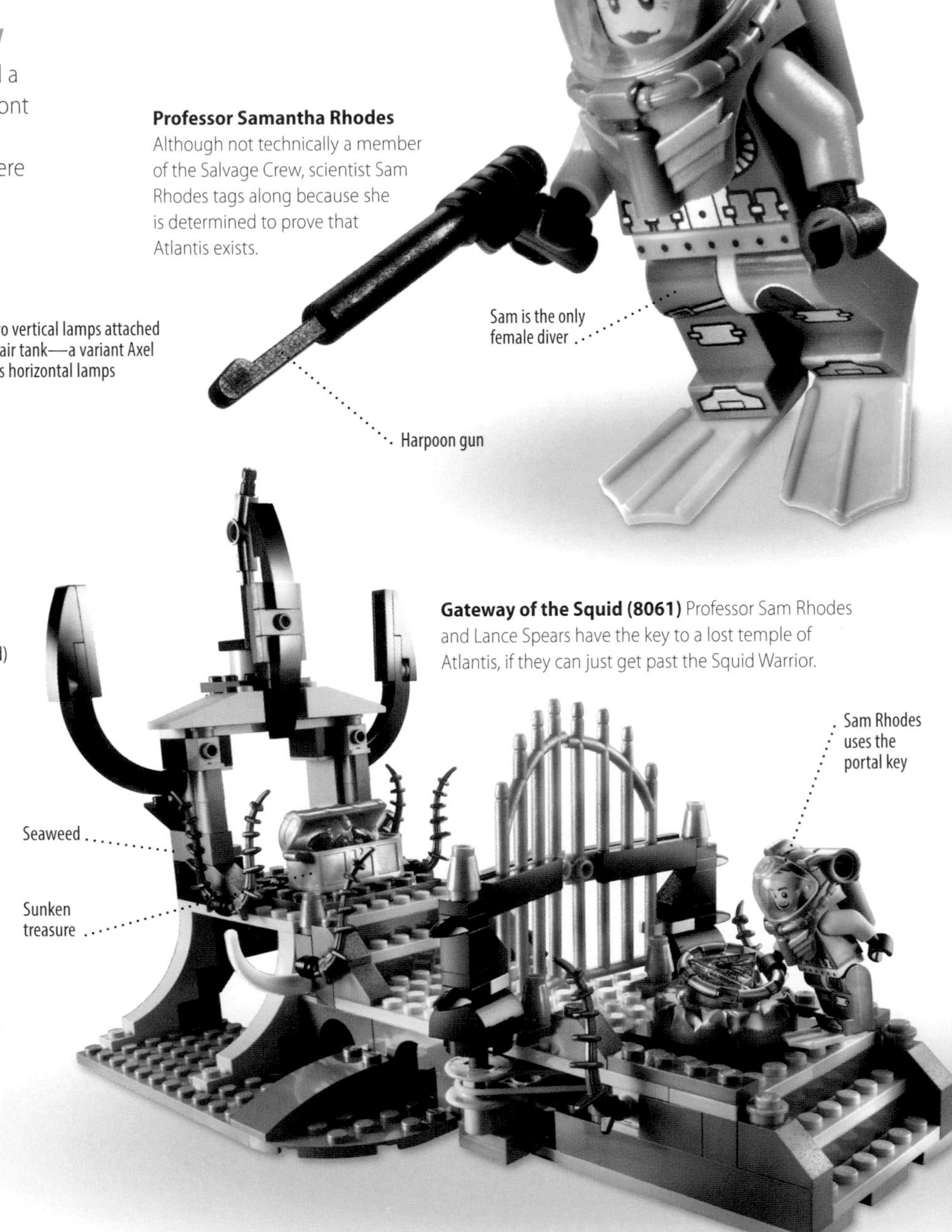
Seaweed
Sunken treasure
Sam Rhodes uses the portal key

Gateway of the Squid (8061) Professor Sam Rhodes and Lance Spears have the key to a lost temple of Atlantis, if they can just get past the Squid Warrior.

NOBODY WARNED ME ABOUT THE BAD JOKES WHEN I SIGNED UP
Standard issue air tank and helmet
All the divers wear gray diving suits with green arms
Dual-sided head: smiling and nauseous
There is no standard minifigure head underneath, unlike Viktor Krum's 2005 LEGO Harry Potter minifigure.
Gold and black speckled helmet
Trident
Gold and black speckled breastplate
Portal key
LEGO ATLANTIS
8-14
8078
Like the other underwater warriors, the Squid Warrior wields a gold trident—new for 2010.
Headgear reflects the shape of a manta ray fish
Detachable headgear
Unique torso
Detachable headgear
New tentacle piece, instead of regular legs
Portal key

Bobby Buoy This rookie is on his first mission. His torso and legs are standard issue for the Salvage Crew and his dual-sided head is either smiling or surprised.

Lance Spears The First Mate of the Salvage Crew is famous for his bad jokes. He appears in four sets, more than any other crew member.

DID YOU KNOW?
Atlantis was the first LEGO play theme to feature 3D content on its website.

Shark Warrior
Comprising three unique pieces, the Shark Warrior has the head of a shark but the torso and legs of a human.

Portal of Atlantis (8078) The team can get to Atlantis, if they can beat the Squid and Shark Warriors, and the Portal Emperor. The set features seven minifigures.

UNDERSEA GUARDIANS

Atlantis featured some of the most innovative minifigure designs to date, particularly its fierce underwater warriors. The Portal Emperor included a new helmet with a never-before-seen gold and black speckled paint pattern.

Portal Emperor
This minifigure is made of five parts, four of which are unique. Only his breastplate appears on another minifigure—the Atlantis Temple Statue in 2011.

Manta Warrior
Featuring unique head, headgear, and torso pieces, this Manta Warrior is a fearsome foe for the Salvage Crew. His trident can fire blasts of electricity!

Squid Warrior Instead of legs, the Squid Warrior has a new tentacle piece. The piece was also used on the 2011 Alien Commander in the LEGO® Alien Conquest theme.

LEGO® HARRY POTTER™

LEGO Harry Potter reappeared after a two year absence in 2010 with six sets. Rebranded for the new movie *Harry Potter and the Half-Blood Prince*™, most of the minifigures had been released before. One set, The Burrow (4840), was brand new and taken from that film.

Hair piece is a dark brown version of the ones used on Draco Malfoy
Unique torso and head

Fenrir Greyback™ This snarling werewolf has bared teeth for biting other minifigures, even if there isn't a full moon.

Unique head
White wand piece
Unique torso

Voldemort™ Look out, Harry Potter! He Who Must Not Be Named looks more evil than ever in 2010. He can be found in Hogwarts Castle (4842).

This version has raised eyebrows and deeper lines on his cheeks.
Elegant suit and cravat are unique

Lucius Malfoy™ As with the 2005 version, the Malfoy minifigure head piece has a Death Eater mask on the other side. However, both sides have been updated for 2010.

Dementors have a skeleton body underneath their tattered robes.

Dementor The gray and green 2004 Dementor figures were scary enough, but the spooky 2010 ones are terrifying. Their gaping mouths look ready to suck out a minifigure's soul.

Long, curly hair piece is unique
Torso and skirt piece are decorated with silver and blue details

Bellatrix Lestrange™ The evil personality and unique style of one of Voldemort's most loyal supporters is brought to life as a minifigure for the first time in 2010.

DARK LORD AND FOLLOWERS

The vicious (and redesigned) Lord Voldemort had new minifigure allies this year. Joining his wicked crew were witch Bellatrix Lestrange and vicious fiend Fenrir Greyback, plus a reimagined Lucius Malfoy.

Harry Potter The microfigure has Harry's distinctive scar and glasses, and Gryffindor uniform.

Hermione Granger The young witch wears a slight variation of the uniform seen on Harry.

Albus Dumbledore The Hogwart's Headmaster is still an imposing figure, even at micro size.

Slytherin House Player This generic microfigure wears the green uniform of Slytherin.

LEGO® GAMES HARRY POTTER™

Harry Potter Hogwarts was a new board game released in the summer of 2010. Nine characters debuted as microfigures, including four generic students from each house.

QUIDDITCH™

Game on! 2010 saw new minifigures of Harry Potter and Draco Malfoy in redesigned Quidditch robes, and a new character, Marcus Flint.

2010 Quidditch minifigures have a helmet that can be placed on the head when the hair piece is removed.

Marcus Flint The Slytherin captain wants to win the Quidditch Cup. His unique head piece shows his gap-toothed determination.

Tan hair piece is unique to both 2010 versions of Draco
Gloved hands
Green is the color of Slytherin house.

Draco Malfoy For 2010, Malfoy's Quidditch minifigure has a new dark green uniform and white pants. His dual-sided head can look worried or smug.

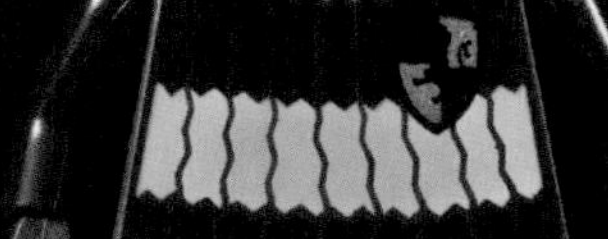
Lion badge denotes Gryffindor house
Only four other minifigures wear the same colored robe.
Gloved hands

Harry Potter Unique to Quidditch Match (4737), this version of Gryffindor's scarlet Quidditch uniform appears twice—on Harry and on Captain Oliver Wood, also released in 2010.

Head piece is updated but the beard piece is unchanged.

Dumbledore™ In 2010, Dumbledore's purple robes are replaced in light blue, with silver and purple details.

The professor is depicted frowning.

Professor Snape™ This version of the Potions professor wears an all-black outfit and no longer glows in the dark.

First appearance of a dark green witch's hat

Professor McGonagall™ Harry's Transfiguration teacher has a new dark green outfit and robe in 2010.

Dual-sided head has goggles on other side

Madam Hooch™ The flying instructor hasn't been seen since 2002, but she is back with an updated minifigure.

This is Flitwick's only appearance.

Professor Flitwick™ The Charms professor's tiny stature is reflected in his short LEGO legs.

TEACHERS AND OTHERS

Four new minifigures joined the supporting cast this year: Professor Flitwick, Argus Filch, and Ron's parents Arthur and Molly Weasley. The Molly minifigure went through numerous prototypes before the final look was achieved.

Hair piece also seen on Dumbledore
Crumpled outfit is unique to this minifigure

Argus Filch™ Making his first appearance in 2010, the Hogwarts caretaker has a hefty collection of keys hanging from his belt.

Unique head and torso

Arthur Weasley It was easy for the LEGO designers to make Mr. Weasley look like his sons—they just used the same red hair piece as Fred and George's minifigures.

Hair piece also used on Mary Jane Watson in the 2004 LEGO® Spider-Man™ theme

Molly Weasley Ron Weasley's caring and hard-working mother is portrayed in a unique minifigure with a lined face and homely apron.

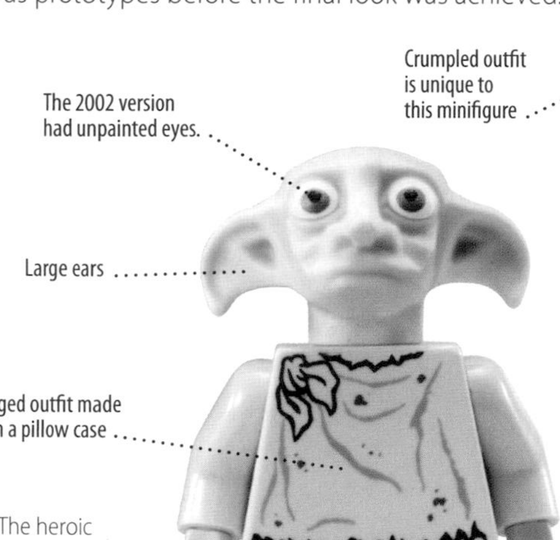
The 2002 version had unpainted eyes.
Large ears
Ragged outfit made from a pillow case

Dobby™ The heroic house-elf's minifigure had an impressive makeover in 2010. His unique head mold and authentic outfit bring his character to life.

Movable hands

Hagrid™ A head taller than most other minifigures, this version of Hagrid the Hogwarts gamekeeper appears in one set in 2010 and two more in 2011.

Hogwarts Castle (4842) The fourth LEGO version of the famous wizarding school was released in 2010.

Plain head piece underneath helmet

Gryffindor Knight Statue This statue of a Knight appears in the Gryffindor common room in Hogwarts Castle (4842).

STUDENTS

All of Harry's friends got minifigure redesigns this year. The only new minifigure was Luna Lovegood, complete with reversible head with Spectrespecs on one side and a smile on the other.

This variant has black pants and the Gryffindor house crest

Hermione Granger™ This minifigure is a variant of the Triwizard version released in 2005.

Wavy hair piece

Ron Weasley™ Harry's best friend has a new haircut in 2010, and a dual-sided face featuring a terrified expression.

Spectrespecs
Exclusive pink jacket
Unique skirt over pants design

Luna Lovegood™ She's a unique character in many ways, and Luna Lovegood is also the only Ravenclaw student to appear as a minifigure.

Same torso and legs as Hermione, Ron, and Ginny

Harry Potter™ In set 4842, this version of Harry Potter comes with his Invisibility Cloak.

Dual-sided head: frowning and smiling

Ginny Weasley™ Ron's sister's minifigure looks much more grown up than its 2002 version.

2010

LEGO® WORLD RACERS

World Racers was a new theme in 2010, the first racing-related theme since *Speed Racer* to have minifigures and a story behind it! World Racers pitted two teams—the Backyard Blasters and the Xtreme Daredevils—in a bruising series of races all over the globe.

Another variant has the same helmet but with a red visor.

Torso exclusive to Bart Blaster variants

Racing Helmet Bart Blaster There are four variants of this minifigure released in 2010, each with different helmets.

Detachable goggles

Unique torso with Backyard Blasters logo

Aviator Helmet Bubba Blaster This monobrowed minifigure has three variants.

All the Backyard Blasters have the same legs.

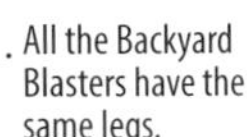

Helicopter is in the Backyard Blasters' team colors

Blizzard's Peak Helicopter This helicopter features in Blizzard's Peak (8863). The Backyard Blasters sneakily use it to try to win a race.

Aviator-style helmet

Aviator Helmet Bart Blaster This determined driver has a dual-sided head—scowling and half covered by a balaclava.

Dual-sided head: determined and scared

Spiked Helmet Bubba Blaster This variant wears the same helmet worn by Slizer in 2009's Space Police theme.

BACKYARD BLASTERS

The Backyard Blasters were the "bad guys" of this theme. Bart, Billy Bob, and Bubba would try anything to beat their opponents. The team drove large, chunky vehicles with an array of explosive and destructive weapons, such as giant cannons and saws.

Spiked Helmet Billy Bob Blaster This minifigure is the team's mechanic. He has three variants.

Spike helmet also worn by Bubba variant

Tools printed on torso

Helmet with red visor

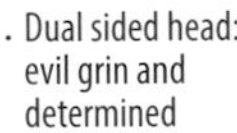

Dual sided head: evil grin and determined

Torso is unique to all variants of this minifigure

Red Visor Billy Bob Blaster Underneath his helmet, Billy Bob has red eyes and an unusual glasses pattern.

CREW AND OFFICIALS

Other minifigures came along for the World Racers ride—three Team X-Treme crew members and three race officials. The latter minifigures had little to do, since no one was paying attention to the rules anyway....

Orange legs also used on rebel pilot Luke Skywalker from the LEGO *Star Wars* theme in 1999.

Race Official The three versions of the race officials had the same torso but different heads and head gear.

Each crew member variant has the same torso.

Crew Member Three crew members were released with different heads.

LEGO
World Racers
8-14
8863
5

Blizzard's Peak (8863) This is the only set to include all three minifigures from the Backyard Blasters team.

Team logo on helmet
I FEEL THE NEED... THE NEED FOR SPEED
Removable goggles
Leg pattern features on all X-Treme team members

Dirtbike Helmet REX-treme
Rex has four variants. Three are distinguished by their helmet, but the fourth, from a promotional set, has plain white legs.

Lime green helmet is exclusive to variants of Dex and Max
Radar detail

Green Helmet DEX-treme
The three Dex variants all feature the same torso with radar detail on the front and belt detail on the back.

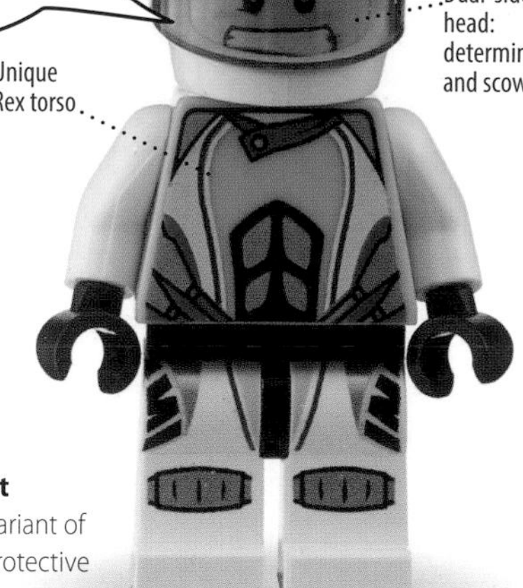
ME TOO. NOW WHERE DID I PUT MY KEYS?
Dual-sided head: determined and scowling
Unique Rex torso

DID YOU KNOW?
The World Racers theme was replaced by Racers—Air Stompers in 2011.

Standard Helmet REX-treme This variant of REX-treme has a protective visor on his helmet.

Sports helmet also seen on skateboarder minifigures

Sports Helmet REX-treme World Racers is a tough theme, and Rex's face has the scars to prove it!

TEAM X-TREME DAREDEVILS

MAX-treme, DEX-treme, and REX-treme made up the heroes of World Racers, driving sleek vehicles armed with an array of missiles. All three featured new, dual-sided heads and torsos printed front and back.

Visor can be worn up or down
Black gloves to protect hands

Standard Helmet MAX-treme
The two sides of his head are grinning and determined, but thanks to his shades it can be hard to tell what Max is really thinking.

Max wears goggles and sunglasses!
A red bandana completes Max's cool look

Dirtbike Helmet MAX-treme
If there is one thing Max is sure of, it's that sunglasses always look cool. That's why he wears them whatever the weather, on each of his three variants.

LEGO® SEASONAL

The holidays meant more fun minifigures this year. The unusually undressed Santa minifigure is from the LEGO City Advent Calendar. He's fresh from the bathtub! The two female minifigures are variants from the holiday-themed Winter Village Bakery (10216).

Full red lips and black eyebrows

Winter Village Female
This minifigure wears a popular red sweater—13 other minifigures also have it.

Santa keeps his hat on, even in the bath!
Nude yellow torso and legs

Bathtub Santa
He makes an unusual appearance on day 18 of the 2010 LEGO City Advent Calendar, but by day 24 Santa is dressed again.

Brown eyebrows and thinner, smiling mouth

Cake box

Winter Village Female Variant Only eagle-eyed fans would spot the difference between this minifigure and the one above—her face.

2010

Head piece is the same as rebel pilot, Zev Senesca

Torso seen on two more Clone pilot minifigures in 2010

Captain Jag
Brave Captain Jag is one of three similar Clone pilot minifigures released in 2010. Only his helmet is unique.

Unique torso and head

Exclusive Twi'lek head tails

Aayla Secura Twi'lek Jedi Knight Aayla Secura makes her only minifigure appearance in 2010 in the Clone Wars set Clone Turbo Tank (8098).

Head piece is the same as the 2008 Clone Trooper, although Senate Commandos are not clones

Exclusive white markings denote rank of captain.

Senate Commando Captain
Tasked with guarding Chancellor Palpatine and the Senate, this minifigure's elite status is reflected in his unique helmet and torso.

Lightsaber

Printing also continues on the back of the torso

Luke Skywalker The fifth variant of Luke as an X-wing pilot features more details on his g-suit and helmet. The g-suit is also worn by fellow rebel Zev Senesca, also released this year.

LEGO *STAR WARS*

2010 proved to be a great year for LEGO *Star Wars* collectors, as new characters and new versions of fan-favorites entered a galaxy not-so-far-away. Ruthless bounty hunter Boba Fett was back with a more movie-accurate look, and Aayla Secura, Cad Bane, and Bossk showed up as minifigures for the first time.

Bossk The Trandoshan bounty hunter's reptilian head piece and flight suit torso were specially created for this minifigure. Bossk is exclusive to two sets.

Unique sand-green head

Flight suit has breathing apparatus printed on the back

Blaster rifle

Detachable range finder

Battle damaged helmet with new, battle-scarred head underneath

Blaster with technic piece on barrel

YOU'RE WORTH A LOT OF CREDITS TO ME.

Removable jetpack on back

Boba Fett This new variant of the famous bounty hunter is only available in *Slave I* (8097). The minifigure has a new torso and cape.

Underneath his helmet, Boba Fett has a plain black head piece.

Printing represents an early stage production minifigure

Limited Edition Boba Fett
Designed to represent a LEGO prototype of Boba Fett, this promotional minifigure was given away as part of the 30th Anniversary of *Star Wars: The Empire Strikes Back*.

Trademark wide-brimmed hat

Detachable breathing apparatus

Cad Bane All the elements of the ruthless Duros bounty hunter, apart from his legs, are new for 2010 and exclusive to this minifigure.

LEGO
STAR WARS
7-12
8128
Cad Bane's Speeder
NEW

Cad Bane's Speeder (8128) This set contains a speeder for Cad Bane with two flick-fire missiles.

LEGO CITY

LEGO City Traffic was a new subtheme of LEGO City focusing on the day-to-day life of a real city. This casually dressed minifigure came from Public Transport (8404), which was released as a LEGO fan choice.

City Traveler This minifigure's torso and tousled center part hair piece are new in 2010, but his head has been seen on more than 60 other minifigures.

White hoodie with blue pockets

Hair piece also seen on Dastan in the LEGO *Prince of Persia* theme

Set 8404 contains a bike, a tram, a bus, a street sweeper, and a sports car

LEGO ADVANCED MODELS

Since 2000, LEGO builders wanting a bigger challenge had looked to the Advanced Models theme. These LEGO sets were larger in size and piece count, and generally used more advanced building techniques. Popular Advanced Model subthemes in 2010 included Modular Building and Space.

SPACE

The Space Shuttle Adventure (10213) was the second ever LEGO Space Shuttle set. It featured a male and a female astronaut and one ground crew member. This set was updated in 2011 as Shuttle Expedition (10231).

These torso and legs are also used on many airport workers

Shuttle Crew Member
The Astronauts are assisted in both versions of the Space Shuttle set by this minifigure.

Female has red lips

Female Astronaut
The only difference between the male and female minifigures is the head piece.

AEJ-S81

Detachable gold visor

Male Astronaut
This torso is exclusive to the Male and Female astronauts in set 10213. Both heads are dual-sided.

Blank face with features on back

Wedding dress used again on a Town bride minifigure in 2011

Mannequin Bride
The Bride's torso and skirt piece were first seen on the Admiral's Daughter in the Pirates theme in 2009.

Standard black suit, also seen on a Town chauffeur in 2013

Mannequin Groom
Although he is shown with a blank face, the Mannequin has features printed on the rear of his head.

MODULAR BUILDINGS

The huge clothing store known as the Grand Emporium (10211) was the fifth Modular Building to be released. It featured the wedding mannequins, a cashier, a window cleaner, a child, and two shopper minifigures.

LEGO SPECIAL EDITIONS

Standard sets are not the only place minifigures can be found. Minifigures have been used as promotional items, pack-ins with books and video games, and even appeared in LEGO® Education sets. Unique minifigures such as the LEGO® Club Max are rare and highly collectible. Nothing says LEGO building like a minifigure, and fans around the world know it!

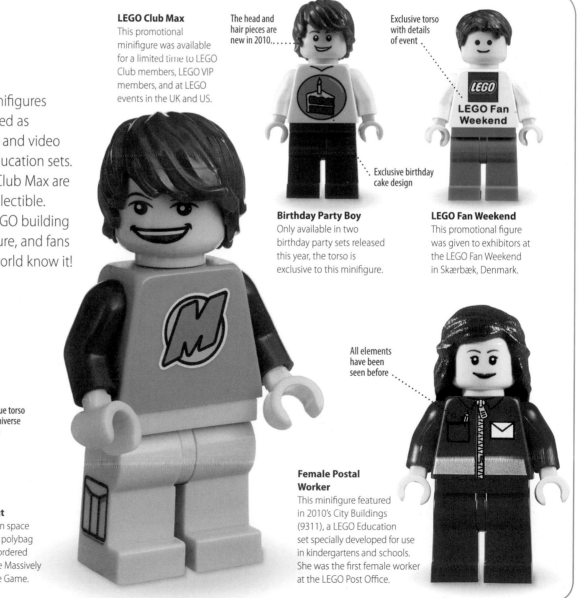

LEGO Club Max
This promotional minifigure was available for a limited time to LEGO Club members, LEGO VIP members, and at LEGO events in the UK and US.

The head and hair pieces are new in 2010.

Exclusive birthday cake design

Birthday Party Boy
Only available in two birthday party sets released this year, the torso is exclusive to this minifigure.

LEGO
LEGO Fan Weekend

Exclusive torso with details of event

LEGO Fan Weekend
This promotional figure was given to exhibitors at the LEGO Fan Weekend in Skærbæk, Denmark.

New and unique torso with LEGO® Universe Nexus insignia

Nexus Astronaut
This limited edition space traveler came in a polybag for fans who pre-ordered the LEGO Universe Massively Multiplayer Online Game.

All elements have been seen before

Female Postal Worker
This minifigure featured in 2010's City Buildings (9311), a LEGO Education set specially developed for use in kindergartens and schools. She was the first female worker at the LEGO Post Office.

RARE MINIFIGURES

SOME MINIFIGURES are harder to find than others. But just what makes them so rare? There can be a few reasons why a minifigure might be scarce. Some are produced in very limited numbers only, as part of a competition. Others are available for a limited time promotion, or with the purchase of a certain item. Finally, there are some that may appear many times in sets, but only once with a certain look or accessory. The minifigures here are just a small sample of the rarest ones that only the most dedicated, or fortunate, collectors possess.

Captain America Toy Fair This promotional comic book variation was given away at the New York Toy Fair in 2012 to promote the new LEGO® Marvel Super Heroes theme.

Iron Man Toy Fair Only 125 exclusive copies of the red hero were given away at the 2012 Toy Fair in New York.

Mr. Gold A mere 5,000 copies of this dashing golden-colored Minifigure were released in 2013, making him even more desirable!

De Bouwsteen Just 750 of these red-haired guys were given out by De Bouwsteen, a Dutch AFOL (Adult Fan of LEGO) group, to members at LEGOWorld 2008. The minifigure came with a certificate and was produced with special permission from the LEGO Group.

LEGO Universe Nexus Astronaut This exclusive spaceman was given to lucky fans who pre-ordered the LEGO Universe game in 2010.

RED SOX

Red Sox Baseball Player The smallest addition to the team, this little minifigure was made exclusively available at the Boston Red Sox's Fenway Stadium in 1999.

LEGO
LEGO Fan Weekend
2009

LEGO Fan Weekend 2009 This smiley fellow was given away in small numbers at a Fan Weekend in Denmark. The minifigure is actually made from easy to find parts, but it's the unique printed torso that makes it a real collectible catch!

Gold C-3PO Looking sophisticated in all his 14 carat glory, just two gold versions of C-3PO were produced for the 30th anniversary of *Star Wars*® in 2007. Sterling silver and bronze versions were also created.

Boba Fett This extremely rare and highly sought after minifigure was only released in one exclusive set, Cloud City (10123) in 2003. The rare printing on his arms and legs makes him even more special.

DON'T TELL ANYONE, BUT SPINJITZU MAKES ME DIZZY!
Detachable beard covers goatee printed on head
Traditional Japanese hat
Spinner
First release minifigure wears black obi sash

Sensei Wu Ninja practice the art of Spinjitzu—spinning at high speed—to fire up their energy. The Sensei Wu minifigure comes with a spinner, as do those of his student Ninja.

LEGO
NINJAGO
Masters of Spinjitzu
8-14
2507

Fire Temple (2507) As well as a temple and dragon, the Fire Temple set supplies seven minifigures: Kai DX, Lord Garmadon, Sensei Wu, Zane, Nya, Samukai, and Kruncha.

Bushy eyebrows
Earth symbol held in place by cords

Cole As the Ninja of Earth, the Cole minifigure wears black to represent the soil that makes up his element.

2011

THIS WAS A BIG YEAR for the LEGO Group. LEGO® Ninjago, its most successful play theme ever, was introduced; aliens invaded Earth in the new Alien Conquest line; LEGO® City launched a successful space program; bold adventurers went on a Pharaoh's Quest; and LEGO® Master Builder Academy taught fans new and better ways to build. And with new sets appearing in the LEGO® Atlantis, LEGO® SpongeBob Squarepants™ and LEGO® *Stars Wars®* themes, action continued from the depths of the ocean to the furthest reaches of outer space, and everywhere in between!

LEGO NINJAGO

LEGO Ninjago was one of the most ambitious play themes ever launched, and its success proved to be beyond anyone's expectations. Combining colorful and exciting Ninja sets with a social game (Ninjago Spinners), it spawned a successful TV series and a best-selling graphic novel line. Originally planned to be a three year line, Ninjago's popularity later led to it being extended to a fourth year.

Scarred eyebrow
Lightning symbol

Jay Although only their eyes are seen, the Ninja minifigures all have distinctive features. Jay, the Ninja of Lighting, has a scarred eyebrow.

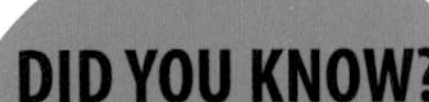

DID YOU KNOW?
Although the Kai minifigure has scars around his left eye, these marks were not present in the TV series.

Red robes indicate that Kai is the Ninja of Fire.
Dragon breathing fire design
Tail of dragon printed on legs

Kai DX This later version of the Kai minifigure bears a golden dragon design. It shows that he has tamed a dragon and attained Dragon Extreme (DX) status.

NINJA

The four Ninja minifigures each wear different colored robes tied to their element: red for Fire, blue for Lightning, white for Ice, and black for Earth. The colored robes were featured in play theme sets and spinner packs.

Ice symbol on robe
Gray sash keeps robes in place

Zane The Ninja of Ice, Zane, wears all white robes. He is the fourth of the four original Ninja minifigures in the LEGO Ninjago theme.

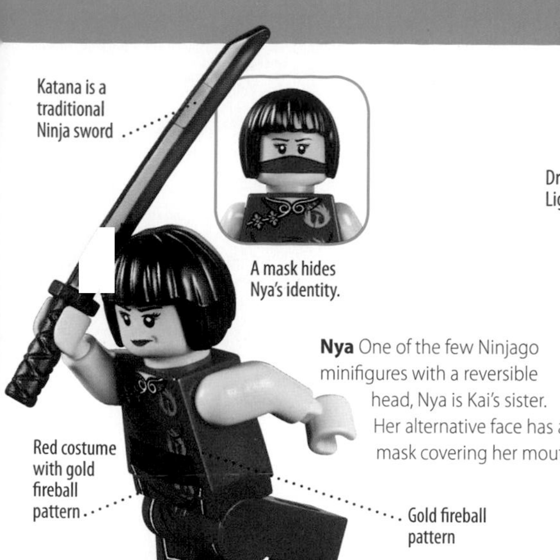
Katana is a traditional Ninja sword
A mask hides Nya's identity.
Red costume with gold fireball pattern
Gold fireball pattern

Nya One of the few Ninjago minifigures with a reversible head, Nya is Kai's sister. Her alternative face has a mask covering her mouth.

Blue head wrap unique to Jay minifigures
Dragon spits Lightning bolt

Jay DX Like the other DX minifigures, DX Jay has his name and symbol printed on the back of his torso and new legs with the sash tied on his right.

DID YOU KNOW?

DX (Dragon Extreme) versions of Cole and Zane were released in spinner battle packs.

Jay Microfigure The game pieces are ¾ inch (19mm) tall—about half a minifigure's height.

Skeleton General A vivid purple color marks out the single Skeleton General.

Skeleton Guard Skeleton Guards block the path of the Ninja around the board.

Cole Microfigure Like all microfigures, Cole loses his limbs but not his facial features.

LEGO® GAMES NINJAGO

Ninjago joined the LEGO Games lineup in 2011, with a board game featuring 10 microfigures. The object of the game is for the Ninja to recapture their temple from the Skeleton Army.

SKELETONS

Soldiers of Lord Garmadon, skeleton figures each have a unique weapon. They appear in both play theme sets and in spinner packs. Despite their fearsome look, they play a comic role in the story.

Removable armor
Metal plate replaces lost eye
New boots leg piece

Kruncha The General Kruncha figure wears a military cap that cannot be removed.

Frakjaw This Frakjaw figure hides his metal-plated head firmly under his hat.

Nuckal The skeleton figures have vertical grip arms—their hands are rotated 90 degrees to their arms.

Ubiquitous bamboo hat
Protective chestplate of a skeleton general

Wyplash His torso may be standard skeleton issue, but the General Wyplash figure's worm-eaten head and bone armor are all his own.

Dual-colored jester hat
Cracks and holes in head

Bonezai Like the Ninja, each skeleton has his own theme. Bonezai is the Skeleton of Ice.

Krazi Skeleton Krazi's hat was last seen on a jolly court jester in 2009's LEGO® Castle theme.

Chopov The first Chopov figures were hatless, but he later gained this simple black helmet.

Turbo Shredder (2263)
The 10-inch (25.5 cm) long Turbo Shredder dwarfs its Frakjaw skeleton driver. It comes with a pursuing Jay and Cole.

Jaws open and close as tracks turn
Exhaust flames
Bone decoration

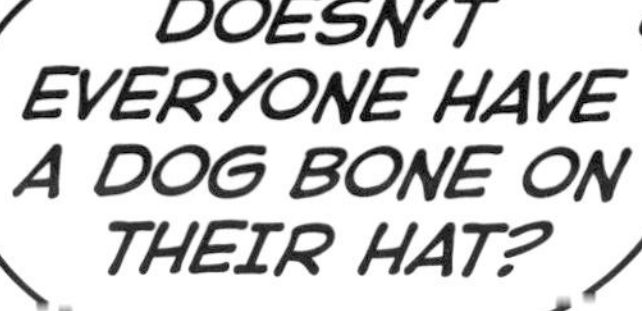
DOESN'T EVERYONE HAVE A DOG BONE ON THEIR HAT?

Removable bone trophy
Gnashing teeth
Silver Samurai helmet

Lord Garmadon Nemesis of the Ninja, Garmadon cuts a suitably sinister minifigure in black. The bone on his helmet marks him out as the commander of the Skeleton Army.

VILLAINS

Lord Garmadon's plot to escape the underworld would lead to a conflict that spans all Ninjago. Aided by General Samukai and the Skeleton Army, Garmadon quests for the Four Golden Weapons of Spinjitzu.

2011

LEGO® PHARAOH'S QUEST

A brave team of minifigure adventurers battled an ancient Egyptian Pharaoh in this play theme that lasted for one year. Pharaoh's Quest featured six sets and 12 new minifigures. The sets also included six mystical treasures, such as swords and scarabs, all but one of which were colored gold.

Pistol—mainly for self-defense
Cross-body bag to store finds

Helena Tova Skvalling Two versions of Helena's minifigure exist—one with yellow hands and one wearing brown gloves.

Earnest expession
Map
Unwieldy pickax

Professor Archibald Hale The pith helmet may be old hat, but the bespectacled head is brand new for the Professor Hale minifigure.

Extravagant sideburns
MUMMIES. WHY DID IT HAVE TO BE MUMMIES?

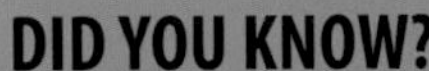

Mac McCloud Mechanic Mac isn't afraid of a bit of dirt, as his oil-stained minifigure shows.

Rifle

Jake Raines With a wry grin, bold stare, and facial scar, this dashing minifigure conveys Jake Raines' fearless nature.

READY FOR ADVENTURE

Professor Hale is aided by a team of brave minifigure heroes. Their names all refer to types of weather—a homage to the names of the original LEGO® Adventurers, including Johnny Thunder and Charles Lightning.

DID YOU KNOW? The LEGO rifle has appeared in more than 70 sets since it was introduced in 1996.

Battle spear
Mummy wrappings
Wings attach to minifigure's neck

Flying Mummy The falcon headdress of this minifigure represents the god Horus.

LEGO® MASTER BUILDER ACADEMY

This special program is designed to teach young builders the techniques used by the real LEGO Master Builders and the model designers who create official LEGO sets. It is broken into separate levels, each of which addresses particular skills. Every level comes with an exclusive minifigure whose color matches that of its level.

LEGO MBA Level 1 logo on shirt
Aviator's cap and goggles

Level 1 Minifigure A minifigure in lime green presents Skill Level 1—the easiest.

LEGO MBA Level 2

Level 2 Minifigure This minifigure's helmet is part of his gear from the Level 2 Auto Designer kit.

PHARAOH FOE

The heroes' enemy is evil pharaoh Amset-Ra. His forces include jackal-headed Anubis Guards, Flying Mummies with beak-shaped headdresses, and dim but dedicated Mummy Warriors.

Striped headdress worn by pharaohs

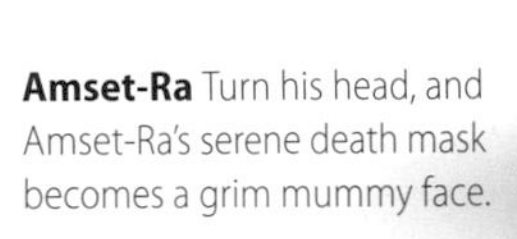

Amset-Ra Turn his head, and Amset-Ra's serene death mask becomes a grim mummy face.

Bluish-gray mummy skin

Symbol of power to control snakes

Mummy Snake Charmer This variant of the Mummy Warrior minifigure wears snake-themed headgear.

Jackal-head mask

Sword with scyth-like blade

Scarab-shaped shield

Anubis Guard No standard minifigure heads lurk under the jackal masks of the Anubis Guard.

Scorpion Pyramid (7327) This features seven minifigures, including three explorers on the hunt for treasure.

LEGO
PHARAOH'S QUEST
8-14
7327
Scorpion Pyramid
792 pcs/pzs

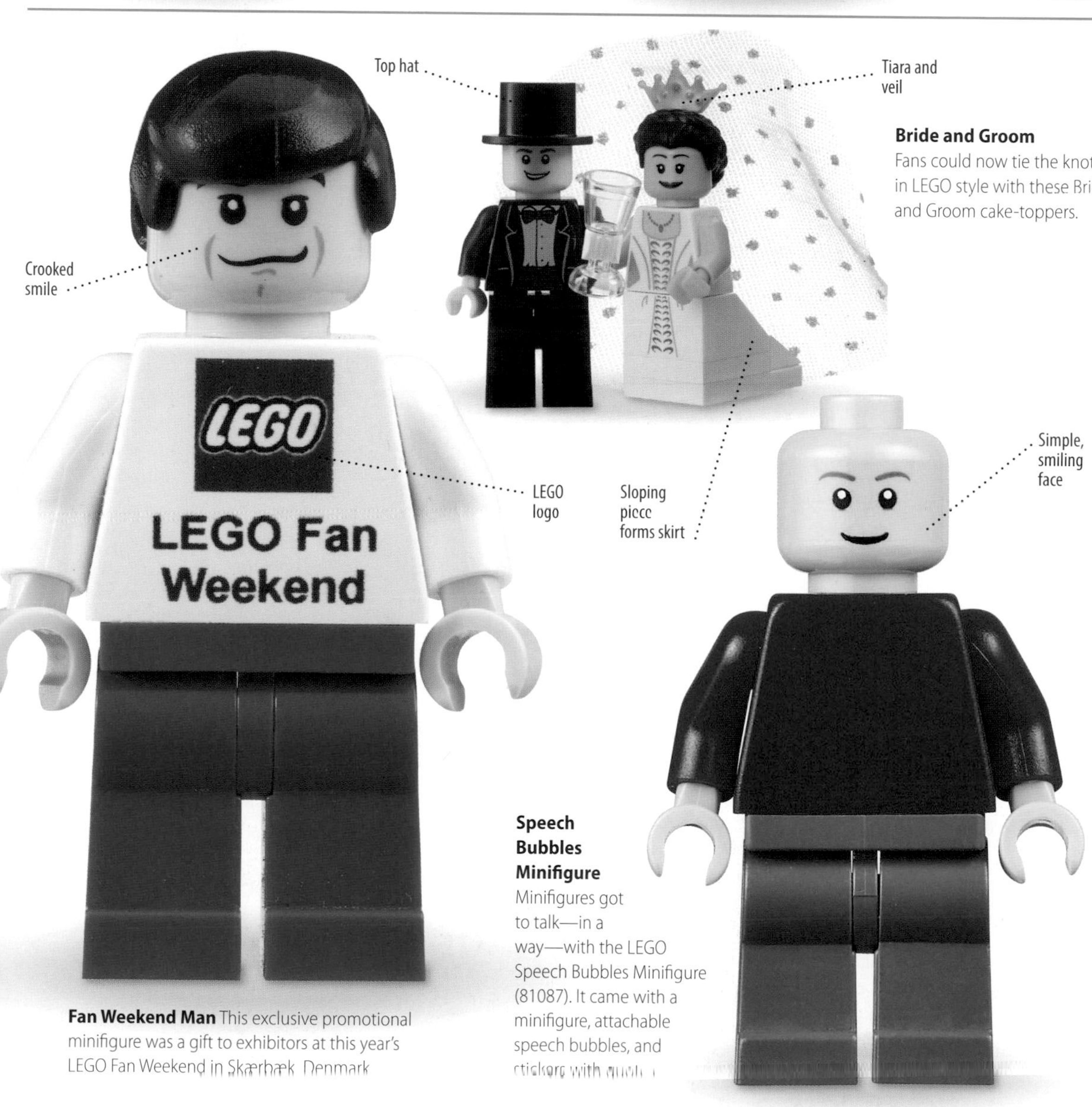
Top hat
Tiara and veil
Crooked smile
LEGO
LEGO Fan Weekend
LEGO logo
Sloping piece forms skirt
Simple, smiling face

Bride and Groom Fans could now tie the knot in LEGO style with these Bride and Groom cake-toppers.

Fan Weekend Man This exclusive promotional minifigure was a gift to exhibitors at this year's LEGO Fan Weekend in Skærbæk, Denmark.

Speech Bubbles Minifigure Minifigures got to talk—in a way—with the LEGO Speech Bubbles Minifigure (81087). It came with a minifigure, attachable speech bubbles, and stickers with

Shaggy bangs
Missing eye

Werewolf Some microfigures recur in several games, but the Werewolf appears only in Waldurk Forest.

Dark Druid Druids may be either Heroes or Monsters. The Dark Druid is among the Monsters.

Goblin General Goblins are Monsters easily identified by their green faces and red eyes.

Ranger The Ranger is a bow-wielding Hero who can defeat a Monster up to five spaces away.

LEGO® GAMES HEROICA™

LEGO Games plunged into the fantasy world of HEROICA™ in 2011, with microfigures of heroes and monsters scattered across a total of five games. The HEROICA™ line would last until 2012.

MINIFIGURE MANIA

Some LEGO minifigures do not fit into a theme, but they are no less popular. They have played a part in all sorts of celebrations, from topping cakes at weddings to being a giveaway at LEGO Fan Weekends in Denmark. The fellow in the red and blue even came with his own speech bubbles—he always had something to say.

2011

Mature features

ADU issue azure blue suit

Helmet protects his powerful brain

ADU logo

Detachable jet pack

ADU Sergeant Gray facial hair and wrinkles mark this minifigure out as the senior ADU member.

Computer Specialist Orange glasses protect this geeky minifigure tech-expert's eyes from screen glare.

ADU Rookie The slightly over-confident Rookie isn't laughing on the other side of his face!

ALIEN DEFENSE UNIT

The brave minifigures of the ADU have new torsos, printed legs, a belt pattern on the hips, and reversible heads. The team includes a prominent female minifigure who appears only in Earth Defense HQ (7066).

THOSE ALIENS HAVE MADE THEIR LAST CROP CIRCLE!

Smudgeproof makeup

Breathing apparatus

Double-barrelled blaster gun

High-grip gloves

Female ADU Soldier This glamorous minifigure is the only female in the ADU.

Helmet with clear visor

Protective vest

ADU Pilot All ADU team minifigures, including this pilot, have belts printed on their hips rather than their torso.

LEGO® SPACE

Aliens invaded Earth for the first time in a LEGO line in this one-year Alien Conquest theme. The strange aliens and their UFOs were opposed by the Alien Defense Unit, who drove the invaders off Earth at the end of 2011. The Alien Conquest story crossed over into numerous other play themes, including LEGO City Space.

CIVILIANS

The Aliens need brainpower to make their ships go, and they have realized that Earth people are a good supply. These civilian minifigures all have reversible heads so they can look scared when the Aliens appear.

Specs for spotting toxic spills

Radio to transmit warnings

Scientist Cleaning up alien toxin is this green-spattered Scientist's job.

LEGO
ALIEN CONQUEST
8-14
7066
Earth Defense HQ
879 pcs/pzs

Earth Defense HQ (7066) With 855 parts, the Earth Defense set is the largest in the LEGO® Alien Conquest subtheme.

Shocked expression

Clipboard

Briefcase

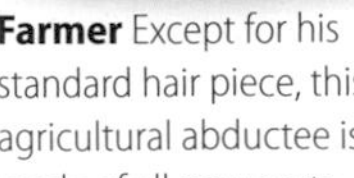

Sharp, sleek hairdo

Microphone

Farmer Except for his standard hair piece, this agricultural abductee is made of all new parts.

Businessman This city slicker's other face shows him *after* he's seen the aliens....

Lotta Brix A new head and torso grace this pushy news reporter minifigure who is about to get the full scary story!

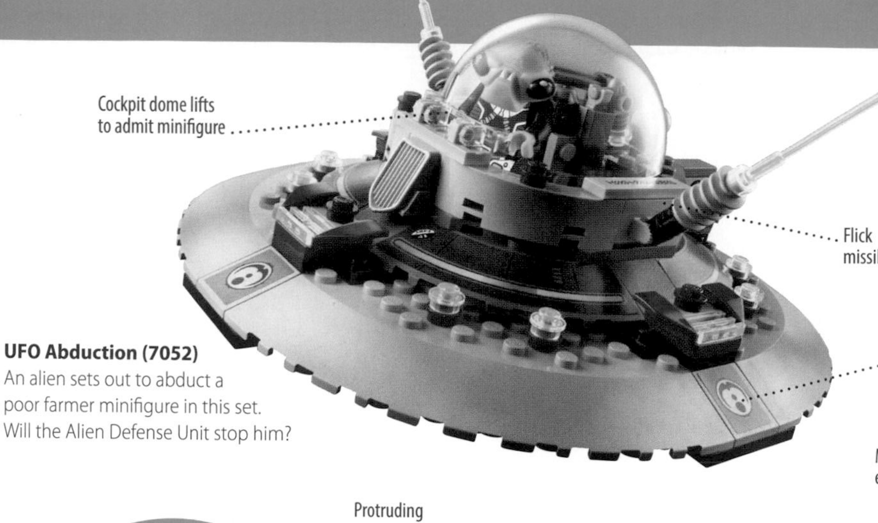
Cockpit dome lifts to admit minifigure
Flick missile
Alien symbol

UFO Abduction (7052) An alien sets out to abduct a poor farmer minifigure in this set. Will the Alien Defense Unit stop him?

Semi-transparent brain

Mechanical eye

Mechanical arm with barb

Metal peg-leg

Alien Android The easily-fazed android sports the standard Alien Conquest Alien colors—black, magenta, silver, and lime green.

DID YOU KNOW?
LEGO designers try to use traditional minifigure parts for new characters, but sometimes they make brand-new parts, such as these alien heads.

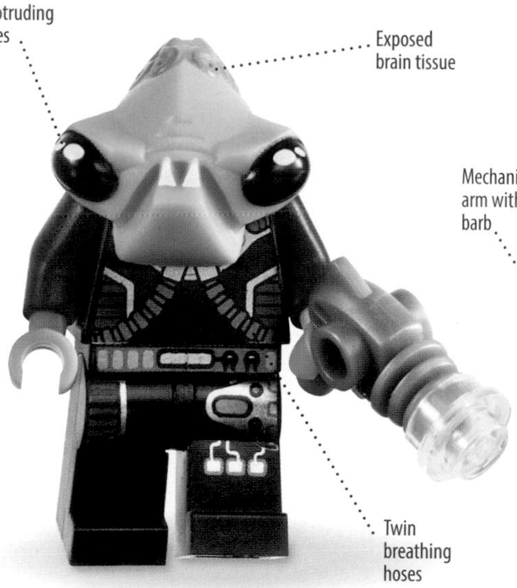
Protruding eyes
Exposed brain tissue
Twin breathing hoses

Alien Pilot A hover-bike, a jet-copter, and a UFO have all been flown by the Alien Pilot.

ALIENS

Four new Alien minifigures were introduced in this line, with new head pieces and new torsos. Their ray guns had previously only appeared in the collectible Minifigures theme. The Alien Commander has tentacles instead of standard LEGO legs.

Alien Commander Separate brain and face elements make up the head of the self-styled "Supreme Overlord" alien.

I RULE AN EMPIRE, BUT I CAN'T FIND PANTS THAT FIT!

Gold epaulets show rank

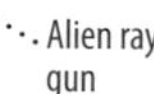

Alien ray gun

Six tentacles swirl around him

Alien Clinger The Alien Clinger can fit onto any civilian minifigure's head. Once in place, it sucks out their brainpower to fuel the Alien ships.

Very small brain
Pronounced underbite
GOOD GRIEF, COMMANDER, SHOW SOME DIGNITY!

Alien Trooper This ferocious minifigure is the land soldier of the alien invaders.

YOU KNOW, I AM A SERIOUS ACTOR...I JUST LIKE MONKEYING AROUND.

LEGO® MINIFIGURES

The second year of the collectible LEGO Minifigures series featured three assortments, totalling 48 new minifigures. The bar code—which in the past allowed some people to guess which minifigure was in a package—was removed, so the selection was truly random. Forty-eight new parts featured this year.

It's *very* warm inside the gorilla suit!

Standard minifigure head visible through mask

Giant banana

Gorilla Suit Guy This minifigure is not a real gorilla—just a guy dressed up in a suit!

Pointy elfin ears

Longbow and arrow

Scale mail armor

Stag head emblem on shield

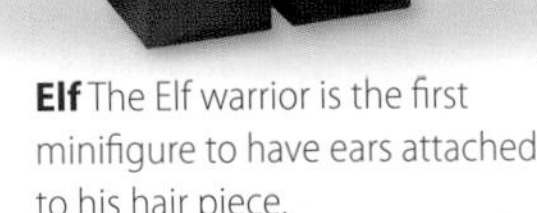

Elf The Elf warrior is the first minifigure to have ears attached to his hair piece.

Green flesh exposed

Loose bandages

Venomous scorpion

Mummy The scorpion held by the Mummy minifigure has appeared in 50 sets since its 1998 debut.

Visor hides mechanical right eye

Ray gun acts as holder for light beam.

Lethal red light beam weapon

Mechanical claw hand

Peg-leg

Space Villain Sinister black, silver, and red elements make up this spacefaring cyborg-gone-bad.

DID YOU KNOW?

Series 3 featured the first ever appearance of a LEGO elf minifigure.

Tennis racket

Tennis outfit printed on torso and legs

Tennis Player This new female minifigure wears traditional tennis whites.

Line and reel attach to rod

Prize catch

Waterproof coveralls

Fisherman The Fisherman is the first minifigure to wear this new white beard.

SERIES 3

Series 3 featured nine new parts. The most popular minifigures are the Elf and the Fisherman. The Fisherman is believed to be rare in the assortment. Each minifigure came with a display plate.

Katana has octagonal design on hilt.

Helmet first used in 1998 Ninja line

Extended shoulder guards

Samurai armor skirt

Samurai Underneath this minifigure's removable armor is a flower-patterned Samurai robe.

Chief's feathered headdress

Beaded cloth printed on legs

Tribal Chief It looks like the Tribal Chief had a happy day's hunting with his giant spear.

Upturned alien eyes

Breathing tubes

Space Alien Lime green is the LEGO Group's go-to color for aliens. This one has a contrasting red tongue.

Minifigure head logo

Dollar sign medallion

Shiny, gold-topped microphone

Boom box

Rapper An eighteen-carat smile and slotted shades give the Rapper minifigure his cool, urban style.

Adhesive bandages on head

Monster Unusually, the Frankenstein Monster has a detachable head top.

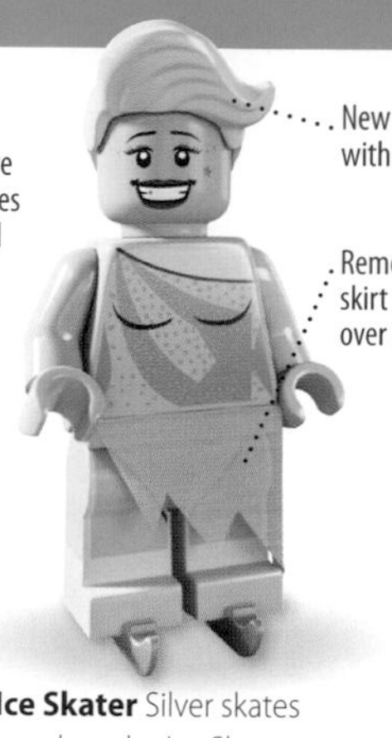
New hair piece with forelock
Removable skirt fits over legs

Ice Skater Silver skates attach to the Ice Skater minifigure's feet.

Sailor hat unique to this minifigure
Telescope for spotting land

Sailor This skilled seafarer is the first—and currently, only—collectible minifigure to have a winking facial expression.

Glowing eyes
Torn shirt reveals hairy body

Werewolf This minifigure's bone will later adorn the hair of a Cave Woman in Series 5.

Plumed hat with turned-up brim
Rapier with cup-shaped hilt

Musketeer The fleur-de-lis on the Musketeer's torso is a classic symbol of French royalty.

SERIES 4

Nineteen new parts made their debut in Series 4. New accessories included the electric guitar, Artist's palette, and Kimono Girl's fan. The Crazy Scientist would prove to be the rarest figure in this series.

I CAN'T GET THROUGH DOORS WITH THIS HAT ON!
Helmet has detachable horns
Heavy ax
Round shield with knot pattern

Viking More than 30 minifigures have worn a version of this Viking's helmet since its introduction in 2005.

Artist's floppy beret
Paint splashes on legs

Artist The painter's raised eyebrow suggests he is gazing critically at his work.

Green pointy hat
Rod for fishing in the garden pond
Short, LEGO legs

Lawn Gnome The beard of the Lawn Gnome minifigure also appears on the face of another Fisherman in Series 3.

DID YOU KNOW?
Series 4 Minifigures featured more back printing and decorated accessories than any previous series.

Bright orange hazard suit and helmet
Radioactivity warning symbol

Hazmat Guy Judging by his terrified expression, the Hazmat Guy minifigure is in the wrong job.

Tousled, post-game hair
Minifigure-shaped trophy
Octan
Lion crest of Brick Kickers team

Soccer Player The soccer player minifigure's jersey bears the logo of his team's sponsor—the LEGO gas station brand, Octan.

Traditional Japanese makeup
Folding fan

Kimono Girl
A delicate floral pattern adorns the kimono of this graceful minifigure.

Protective goggles
Vial of chemicals
White coat with chemical spill

Crazy Scientist He has a new torso, head, and hair, but this Scientist's legs have been in production since 1978.

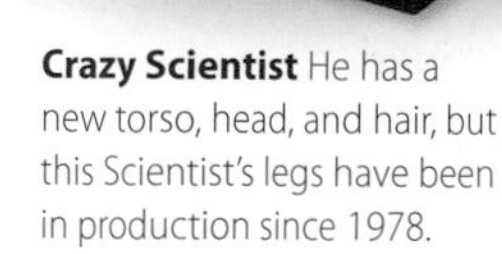

Team logo
Hockey puck

Hockey Player
This minifigure's huge visor does little to conceal his aggressive expression.

2011

LEGO MINIFIGURES CONTINUED

Gladius based on real gladitorial sword

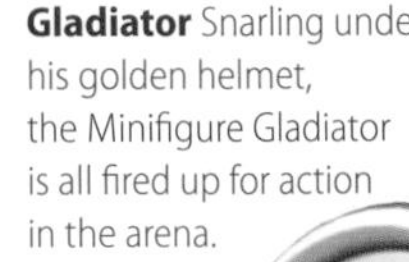

Gladiator Snarling under his golden helmet, the Minifigure Gladiator is all fired up for action in the arena.

Classic round Roman shield

Eyes peer out of lizard mouth
Yellow scales on torso
Spiky back and tail piece attaches to neck

Lizard Man This LEGO lizard sheds his skin. His hood can be removed to reveal a smiling Minifigure face.

Freshly honed ax
Banana to pacify unruly apes
Chimpanzee

Zookeeper The zoo workers' chimp friend will reappear with 2012's Jungle Boy Minifigure.

Lumberjack This breezy Minifigure has his plaid shirt printed on both sides of his torso and his arms.

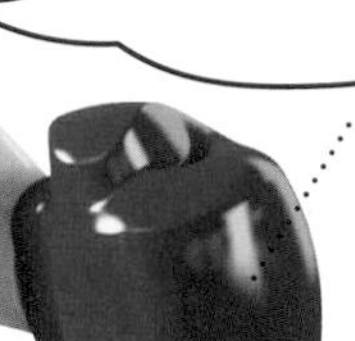

THIS SERIES IS A KNOCKOUT!

Minifigure hands replaced with a new glove element

Boxer The Boxer packs a real punch in his flashy all-red gear. Instead of regular minifigure hands, he has two boxing gloves.

SERIES 5

The Series 5 Minifigures featured 20 new parts and had an international flavor, including a British Detective and Royal Guard, an Egyptian Queen, and a Roman Gladiator.

Fish caught through hole in ice

Ice Fisherman A fur design is printed on the Ice Fisherman's legs and torso, and molded on his hood.

PARDON? I CAN'T HEAR ANYTHING WITH THIS HAT ON!

Tall bearskin-style hat

Deerstalker hat
Tweed coat

Detective When this Minifigure sleuth is on the case, no brick is left unturned.

Royal Guard Nothing catches this fine, upstanding Minifigure off guard. No one knows what he keeps under his hat though...

Venomous green snake
Winged scarab printed on hair

Egyptian Queen The ancient Queen's snake has appeared in 65 other sets and in five colors.

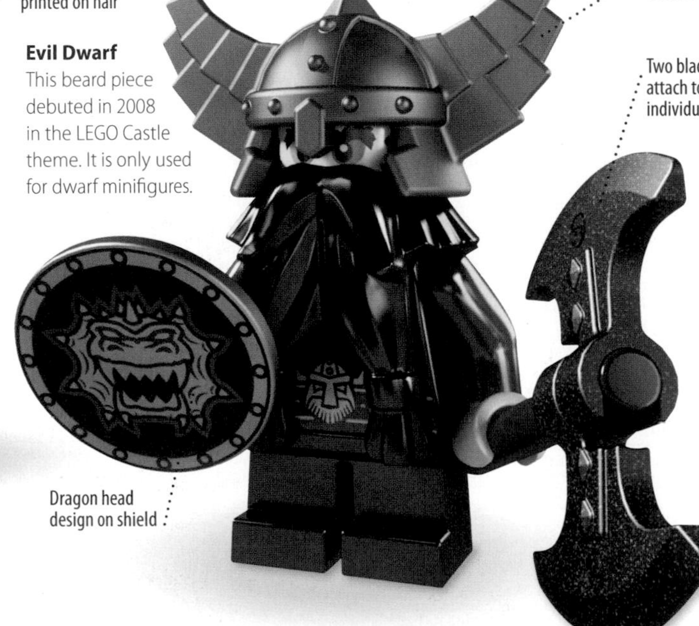

Winged metal helmet
Two blades attach to ax individually
Dragon head design on shield

Evil Dwarf This beard piece debuted in 2008 in the LEGO Castle theme. It is only used for dwarf minifigures.

Rock club

Cave Woman One of the locks on the Cave Woman's hair piece acts as a clip to attach her bone ornament.

Flower printed on bowler hat
Custard pie for throwing

Small Clown Short of leg but not of arm, the Small Clown Minifigure pitches a mean custard pie.

LEGO® HARRY POTTER™

The LEGO Harry Potter theme featured two sets related to *Harry Potter and the Deathly Hallows*™ in 2011, as well as the largest LEGO Harry Potter set to date, Diagon Alley (10217). This year saw the release of 28 minifigures, with some, including Narcissa Malfoy, Mr. Ollivander, and the Weasley twins appearing in minifigure form for the first time.

Ron Weasley™ The 11th Ron minifigure has had his old bowl haircut restyled into a shaggy side-part.

Reds and browns color scheme

Two-colored hair piece

Narcissa Malfoy™ Narcissa's sleek minifigure has fancy blue-gray embroidery on both sides of her torso.

Dress print emphasizes small waist

Witch's hat with buckle

Professor Sprout A sprig of leaves adorns the torso of Hogwarts' Herbology teacher.

LEGO
Harry Potter
Ages/edades
7-14
4867
Hogwarts™
466 pcs/pzs
WARNING: CHOKING HAZARD.

Hogwarts (4867) The Hogwarts set contains seven minifigures, including a new one—Professor Sprout.

Lightning bolt scar

Familiar Harry Potter hairstyle

White bow tie and dress shirt

Yule Ball Harry Potter DK's book *LEGO® Harry Potter™ Building the Magical World* comes with this minifigure, looking suave in his Yule Ball dress robes.

Conductor's cap is a purple version of a police hat

Hollow, lined cheeks

Stan Shunpike This Knight Bus conductor minifigure has a shaven head, unlike his 2004 predecessor.

Magic wand

Teeth gritted in concentration

Knitted sweater with hood

Neville Longbottom™ Unlike the 2004 version, Neville's new minifigure has a reversible head.

Side braids drawn back

Zippered sweater

Casual pants

Hermione Granger The new 2011 Hermione minifigure has swapped her school uniform for casual clothes.

DID YOU KNOW?
The strip of paint on some minifigures' torso pegs (underneath the head piece) helps the printing machine recognize which side of the torso is the front and back.

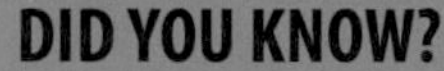

KNIGHT BUS
KB

Triple-decker

Style based on that of 1950s London bus

Shrunken head

Open door with footplate

The Knight Bus (4866) The Knight Bus is an update of an earlier 2004 set (4755). It includes minifigures of Harry, Stan, and driver Ernie Prang.

LEGO® DC UNIVERSE™ SUPER HEROES

Super Hero excitement started to build in July with the announcement at San Diego Comic-Con that the DC Universe would be coming to LEGO sets in 2012. Batman and Green Lantern minifigures were given away at that show as a free promotion, with a Superman minifigure offered at New York Comic-Con that fall.

Green Lantern logo

Green Lantern On one side of the Green Lantern minifigure's head is this fierce snarl; on the other is a confident smirk.

Sideswept hair with front curl
Famous "S" symbol
Muscles printed on torso
Red cape
WHAT AM I? I'M... PLASTIC.
Bat cowl
Grimly set mouth
Bat logo
Highly detailed utility belt
Five-pointed cape

Superman The promotional Superman minifigure would later reappear in 2012's Superman vs. Power Armor Lex (6862).

Batman Another Comic-Con exclusive, this Batman minifigure bears the logo from the recent movies instead of the classic black and yellow one.

DID YOU KNOW?
So far, the Green Lantern minifigure has never appeared in a LEGO set.

LEGO ATLANTIS

The adventure beneath the sea continued in 2011, as the minifigure heroes of LEGO Atlantis found the lost city itself, complete with a Poseidon statue that turned out to be its Golden King. The King would be the only Atlantis minifigure to appear as a microfigure in the LEGO® Game Atlantis Treasure. Ten minifigures and five sets rose from the depths this year.

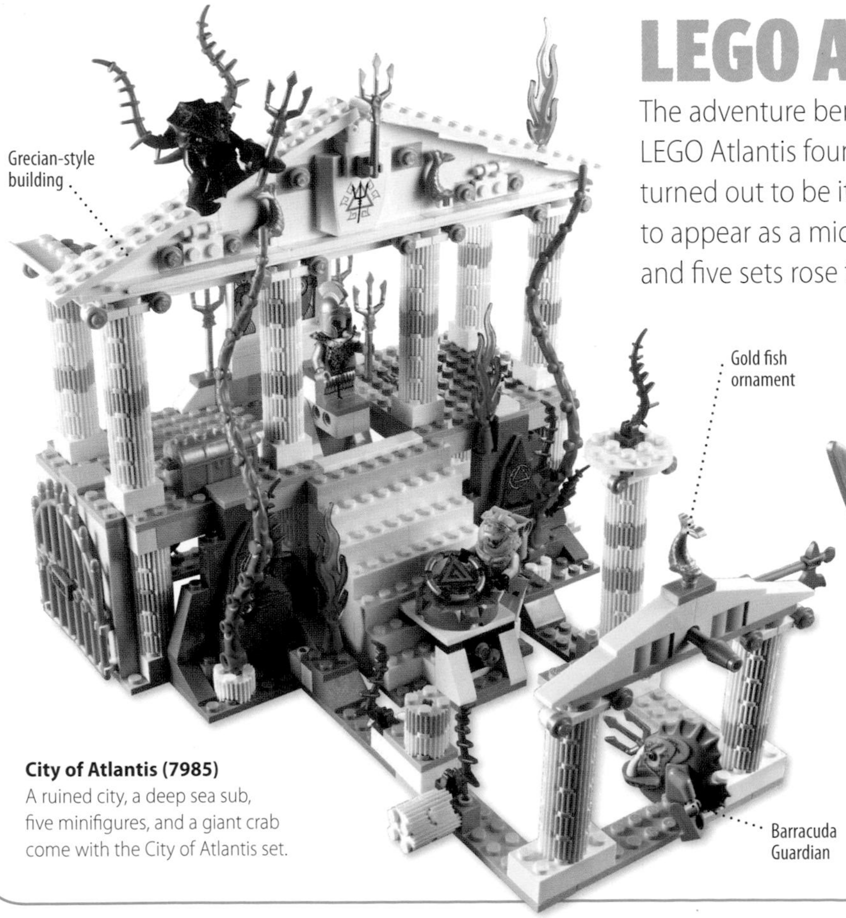

Grecian-style building

Gold fish ornament

Barracuda Guardian

City of Atlantis (7985)
A ruined city, a deep sea sub, five minifigures, and a giant crab come with the City of Atlantis set.

Spartan warrior's helmet

Poseidon Statue A yellow, human face on the reverse of its head is this minifigure's only non-gold part.

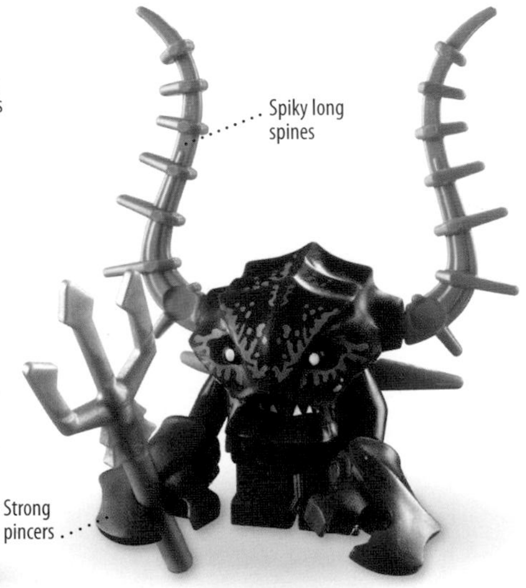

Spiky long spines

Strong pincers

Lobster Guardian This fierce fellow guards the temple with a golden trident gripped in one of its big claws.

LEGO® CASTLE

LEGO® Kingdoms was a subtheme of the LEGO Castle line, and featured the Lion Kingdom battling the evil Dragon Kingdom. Five sets were introduced in 2011, with a dozen minifigures, many of whom appeared in more than one set. The Lion King, Milkmaid, Stableboy, and Farmer's Wife were all exclusive to their sets.

Defending the realm is easy with a big, shiny sword.
Red-and-white jester hat
I THINK I'M IN THE WRONG CENTURY.
Fur-trimmed torso with royal chains
Dark red cloth cape

Female Jester For the first time a female minifigure gets to play the fool!

Lion King This royal minifigure shares his crown with many other monarchs, including King Mathias from LEGO® Knights' Kingdom in 2004.

Mill Village Raid (7189) In this set, three minifigure peasants defend their mill, barn, and livestock from a trio of Dragon Knights.

LEGO
Kingdoms
Ages/edades
7-14
7189
Mill Village Raid
663 pcs/pzs
WARNING:

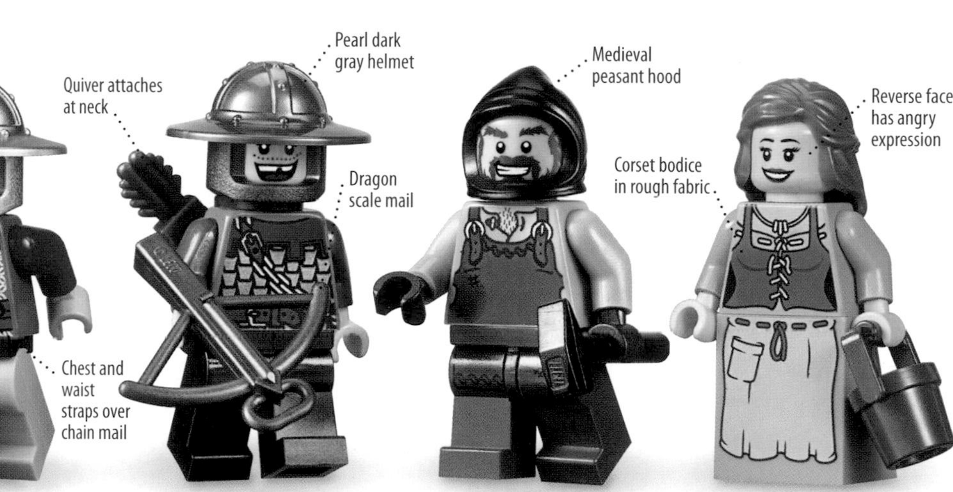
Quiver attaches at neck
Pearl dark gray helmet
Dragon scale mail
Medieval peasant hood
Corset bodice in rough fabric
Reverse face has angry expression
Chest and waist straps over chain mail

Lion Knight This minifigure wears a brimmed helmet like the Dragon Knight, but in shiny silver.

Dragon Knight Of the six Dragon Knight variants released this year, only this one is missing a tooth.

Blacksmith That hammer could easily be used as a defensive weapon by the Blacksmith minifigure.

Milkmaid The last thing this minifigure maid wants is an arrow hole in her milk bucket accessory!

LEGO® BRAND STORE

2011 saw the tradition of exclusive LEGO sets offered at LEGO Brand Store openings continue. These sets featured one or more minifigures, some specially made for the sets, others reissues of classic minifigures. Several new stores opened this year in North America, Canada, Denmark, and the UK.

DID YOU KNOW?
Exclusive store minifigures often feature back printing with the year and the name of the store.

Hard hat protects against falling bricks
Construction vest with pockets
Helmet with nose guard
I'M ON A KNIGHT SHIFT.
Lion head emblem
Chain mail pattern
Long side bangs
Pretty yellow flowers

Misson Viejo Worker Unusually for a Brand Store minifigure, this construction worker from Mission Viejo, California, has a new head.

Sunrise Lion Knight The Sunrise, Florida, Knight has a new torso, but his other parts are all reused.

San Diego Lady This minifigure from San Diego, California, wears a tank top worn by four other Brand Store minifigures so far.

Curved top to helmet
Breathing apparatus
Lightweight armor
Black gloves

Shadow ARF Trooper A new, black Advanced Recon Force Trooper came free with some online purchases as part of a *Star Wars* Day promotion.

I USED TO STYLE WOOKIEE HAIR IN MY OLD JOB.

T-shaped visor
Twin blaster guns

Mandalorian A detailed new head, with glaring blue eyes, is concealed by the minifigure soldier's helmet.

Unique ponytail plugs into stud on head

Orange jumpsuit

Aurra Sing Aurra's torso and legs are printed with an ammo vest and holsters.

8-horned head top piece

Savage Opress A yellow pattern on Opress' head represents clan tattoos.

Bowcaster

Embo The printed radar dish helmet is unique to the Embo minifigure.

Head piece and hair piece have both been seen before

Padmé Naberrie This is the first update of the Padmé minifigure since the *Star Wars* theme's debut in 1999.

Rare double-ended lightsaber
Yellow eyes of dark side devotee
New torso details for fourth Darth Maul minifigure

Darth Maul There are red tattoos on Maul's head piece, otherwise it is the same as Opress's, Maul's minifigure brother.

LEGO *STAR WARS*

The LEGO *Star Wars* theme went from strength to strength this year, with both fan-requested minifigures and minifigures based upon The Clone Wars appearing. Some characters, such as the crimson R-3PO, had never before been seen in LEGO form. Others became exclusive minifigures unlikely to reappear in future sets. All of this helped make 2011 a great year for LEGO *Star Wars* collectors.

DID YOU KNOW?
The R-3PO minifigure uses the same mold and printing as C-3PO. Only its color is different.

Sniper rifle

Removable head bandage

Patched-together armor

Dengar Bounty-hunting has left its mark on Dengar's battle-scarred minifigure.

Photoreceptor eyes
Pattern also on back of torso

R-3PO This protocol droid minifigure is only available with the Hoth Echo Base set (7879).

New, tousled hair piece
Breathing mask on reverse face joins air tube

Bacta Tank Luke The latest Luke Skywalker minifigure shows the hero ready for immersion in a healing bacta tank.

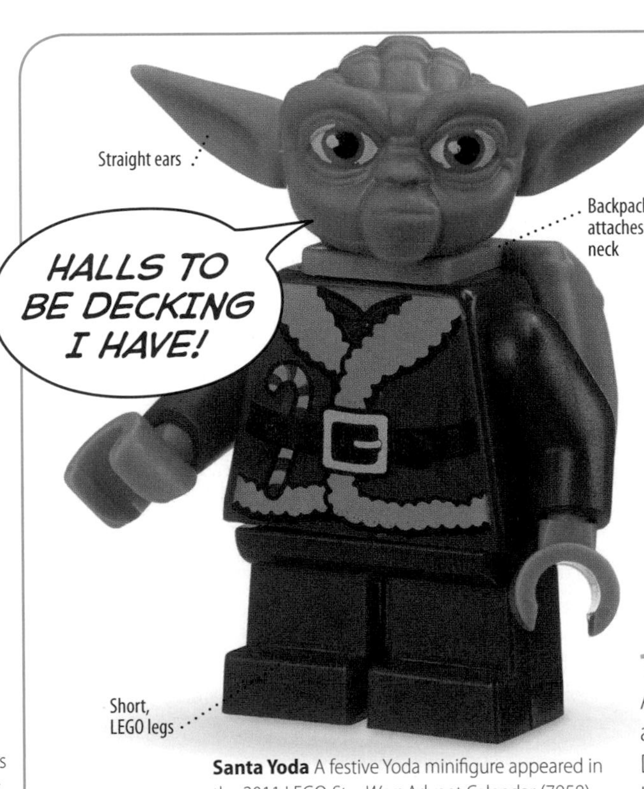
Straight ears
HALLS TO BE DECKING I HAVE!
Backpack attaches at neck
Short, LEGO legs

Santa Yoda A festive Yoda minifigure appeared in the 2011 LEGO *Star Wars* Advent Calendar (7958).

Hair parts on different side from adult Han
Medal given to Han in Star Wars: A New Hope movie
Short LEGO legs

Young Han Solo This Han minifigure came only with the *Star Wars*®: *The Padawan Menace* Blu-Ray DVD.

Han Solo with Medal Another exclusive Han minifigure came with DK's *LEGO® Star Wars® Character Encyclopedia.*

THREE OF A KIND!
All three of these were limited-edition exclusives, appearing as promotional minifigures with LEGO *Star Wars* books and DVDs, or as part of the 2011 LEGO *Star Wars* Advent Calendar. Hard to find they are!

LEGO® TRAIN

The Mærsk Container Train (10219) left the station in 2011, with a diesel engine and two container cars. It came with three train worker minifigures, all with the same body but with different heads. This was a follow-up to the re-release of the Mærsk Container Ship (10155), which also came out this year.

High-visibility vest

Mærsk Train Workman This gray-bearded minifigure wears a Mærsk-blue construction helmet, first seen in 1980.

Bright blonde hair
Fur-lined hood
Same head as Lion King from Kingdoms subtheme in 2010
Long winter skirt
Snow pants

Customer The seven minifigures in the Winter Village Post Office set include this late-running customer.

Snow Shoveler This minifigure keeps warm in a new fur-trimmed hood.

Santa Holiday Set 3300002 came with this bushy-browed Santa.

LEGO® SEASONAL

This year's addition to the Winter Village line was the Post Office (10222)—minifigures finally had somewhere to go to buy holiday cards! Meanwhile, Santa Claus was a giveaway with purchase at the LEGO Shop online.

Reversible head with smile or frown
White envelope logo worn by PO staff

Post Office Worker The Winter Village Post Office set featured a female PO worker—the second ever to appear in a LEGO set.

EXCLUSIVE MINIFIGURE

A LEGO activity book linked to the LEGO City Harbor subtheme contained stories, puzzles, and this happy Diver minifigure.

Lime green flippers

Diver This minifgure's happy-looking head has so far appeared on six other minifigures since 2010.

LEGO® ADVANCED MODELS

The Pet Shop (10218) was the first Modular Building set to include two structures—a three-story pet shop and a townhouse. This was the sixth set released for this line. LEGO fans blasted off into outer space again with Shuttle Expedition (10231), which was a slightly revised version of the Space Shuttle Adventure set (10213) from 2010.

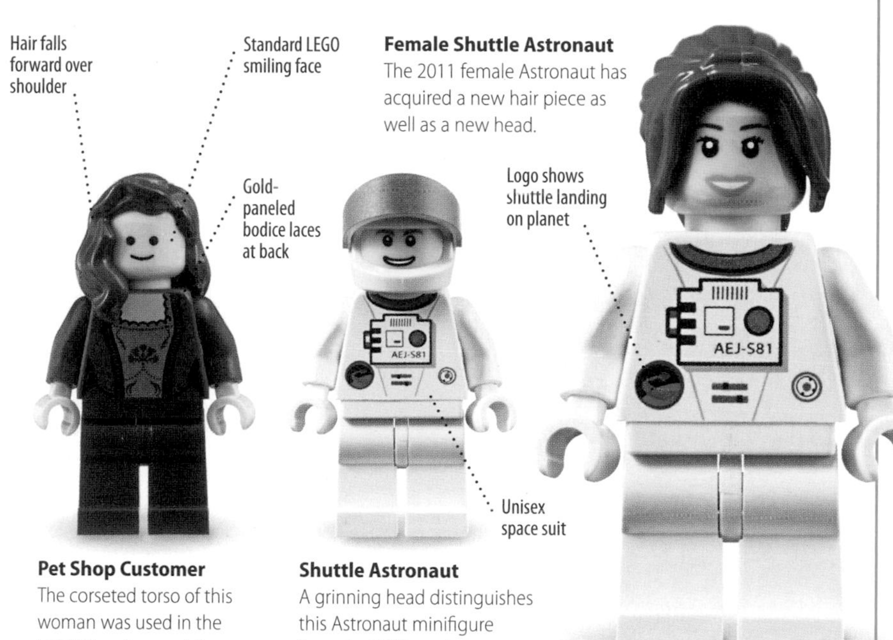
Hair falls forward over shoulder
Standard LEGO smiling face
Gold-paneled bodice laces at back
Logo shows shuttle landing on planet
Unisex space suit
AEJ-S81

Female Shuttle Astronaut The 2011 female Astronaut has acquired a new hair piece as well as a new head.

Pet Shop Customer The corseted torso of this woman was used in the LEGO Kingdoms subtheme.

Shuttle Astronaut A grinning head distinguishes this Astronaut minifigure from the 2010 version.

Pet Shop (10218) There are four minifigures in the Pet Shop set—a shop owner, a woman, a little girl, and a painter with coveralls and paint roller.

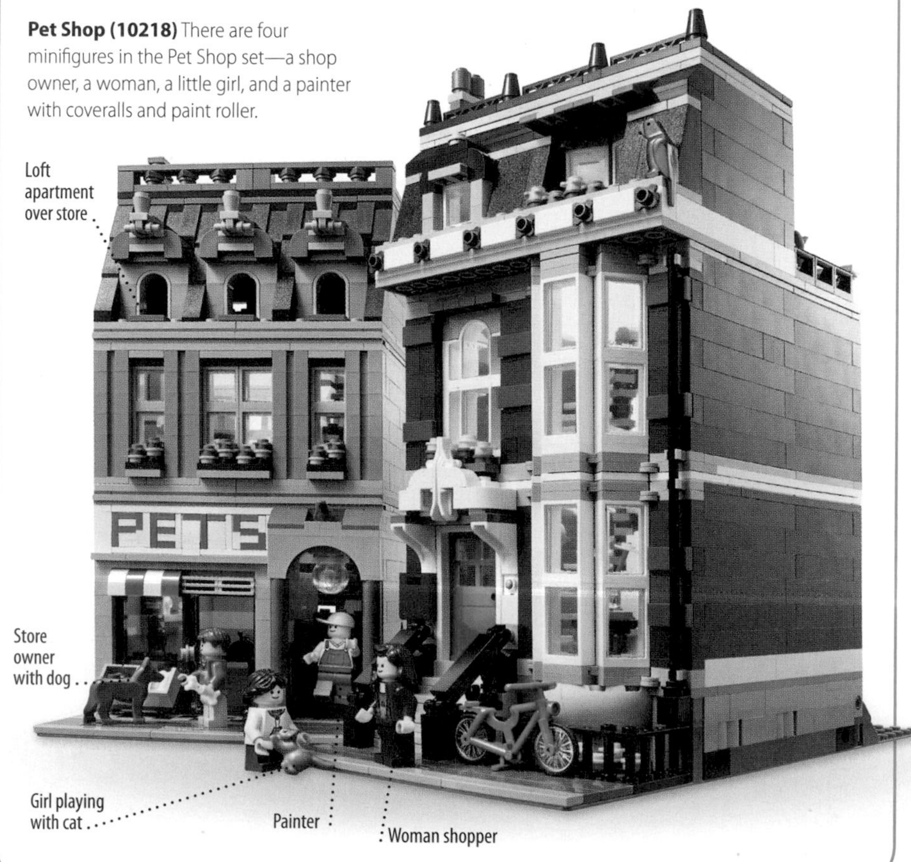
Loft apartment over store
PETS
Store owner with dog
Girl playing with cat
Painter
Woman shopper

BEYOND THE MINIFIGURE

ALONG WITH THE RED 2x4 brick, the minifigure is the most iconic symbol of LEGO® building. So it's no surprise that it has shown up in many places besides LEGO sets. Minifigures have been banks, magnets, keychains, and clocks, and oversized minifigure heads have been used as storage for LEGO bricks! Minifigures have appeared in much bigger scale as blow-molded figures or as sculptures made from LEGO pieces. You can even find them in your kitchen, as ice cube and popsicle trays. Yes, minifigures are everywhere!

Minifigure lantern.

LEGO City minifigures coat rack.

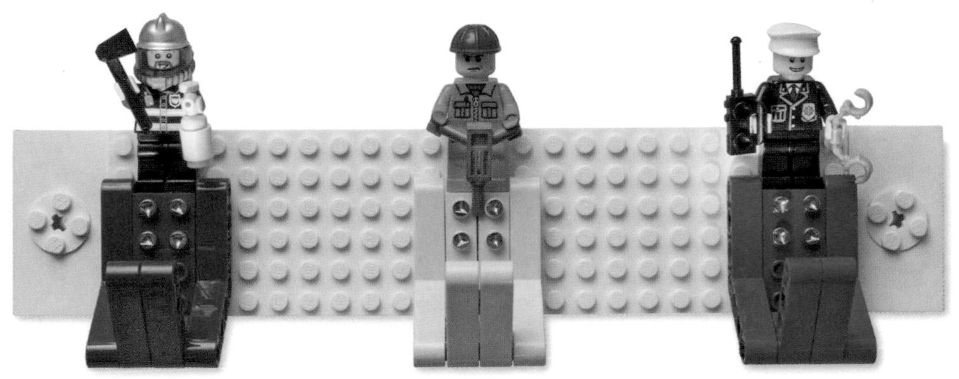

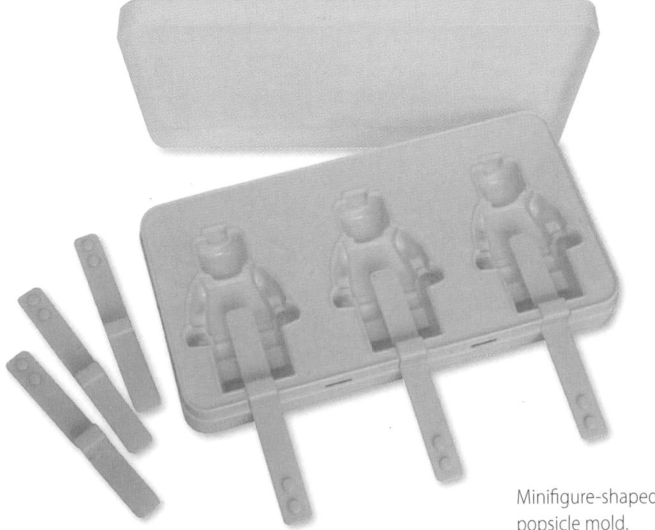

Minifigure-shaped popsicle mold.

Minifigure head salt and pepper shakers.

PM 12:38
7:30
LEGO

Giant brick-built astronaut based on a LEGO Mars Mission minifigure.

LEGO Monster Fighters Lord Vampyre minifigure digital clock.

LEGO Legends of Chima keychain.

Minifigure head storage box.

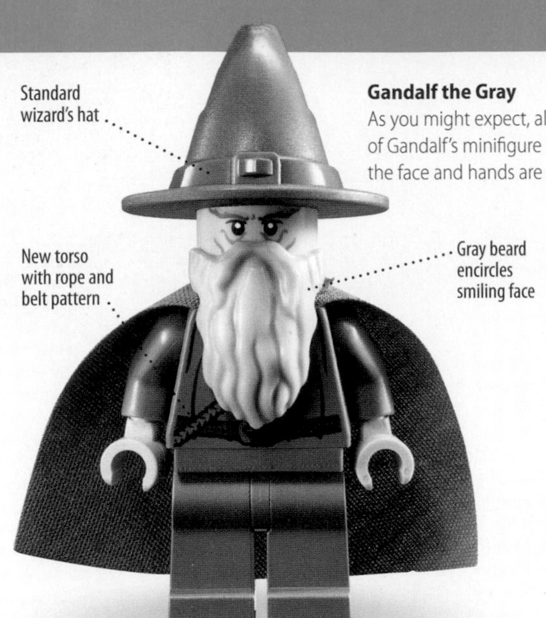

Standard wizard's hat

New torso with rope and belt pattern

Gray beard encircles smiling face

Gandalf the Gray As you might expect, all parts of Gandalf's minifigure but the face and hands are gray.

Dark brown hobbit hair

Gray cloak

Frodo's other face has an expression of pop-eyed terror!

Short sword is a new weapon for 2012

The One Ring fits over the minifigure's hand.

Frodo Baggins Frodo is the main character in the theme, and his minifigure appears in four of the seven sets.

Tousled reddish brown hair

Carelessly tied scarf

Pippin Hobbit minifigures, like this mischievous Pippin, all have the same new hair piece but in different colors.

Reverse of head has shouting mouth

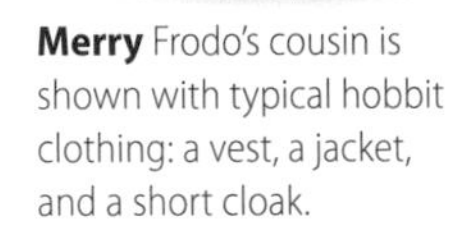

Merry Frodo's cousin is shown with typical hobbit clothing: a vest, a jacket, and a short cloak.

Reversible head with hobbit hair piece

Samwise Gamgee Careful hobbit Sam wears both a belt and suspenders!

2012

EXCITEMENT PEAKED in 2012, with adventure stepping up to the next level. New licensed themes LEGO® *The Lord of the Rings*™, LEGO® DC Universe™ Super Heroes, and LEGO® Marvel Super Heroes spawned some of the most sought-after building sets yet. Brand new play themes such as Monster Fighters delighted fans, while continuing favorites LEGO® Ninjago, LEGO® Minifigures, LEGO® *Star Wars*®, and LEGO® City found new ways to spark their imaginations. Of the huge number of new and refreshed minifigures released this year, many represented some of the greatest characters in fiction. Little surprise, then, that 2012 became a banner year for collectors of every age.

LEGO *THE LORD OF THE RINGS*

It was one of the most hotly anticipated LEGO play themes launched in 2012, with seven sets based on the three hit *The Lord of the Rings* movies. All the major characters appeared as minifigures, with new heads, torsos, and printed legs. The many new elements included swords, shields, and helmets, and an entirely new element was created to represent the One Ring.

DID YOU KNOW?
Three variations of the Frodo minifigure appeared in the 2012 sets.

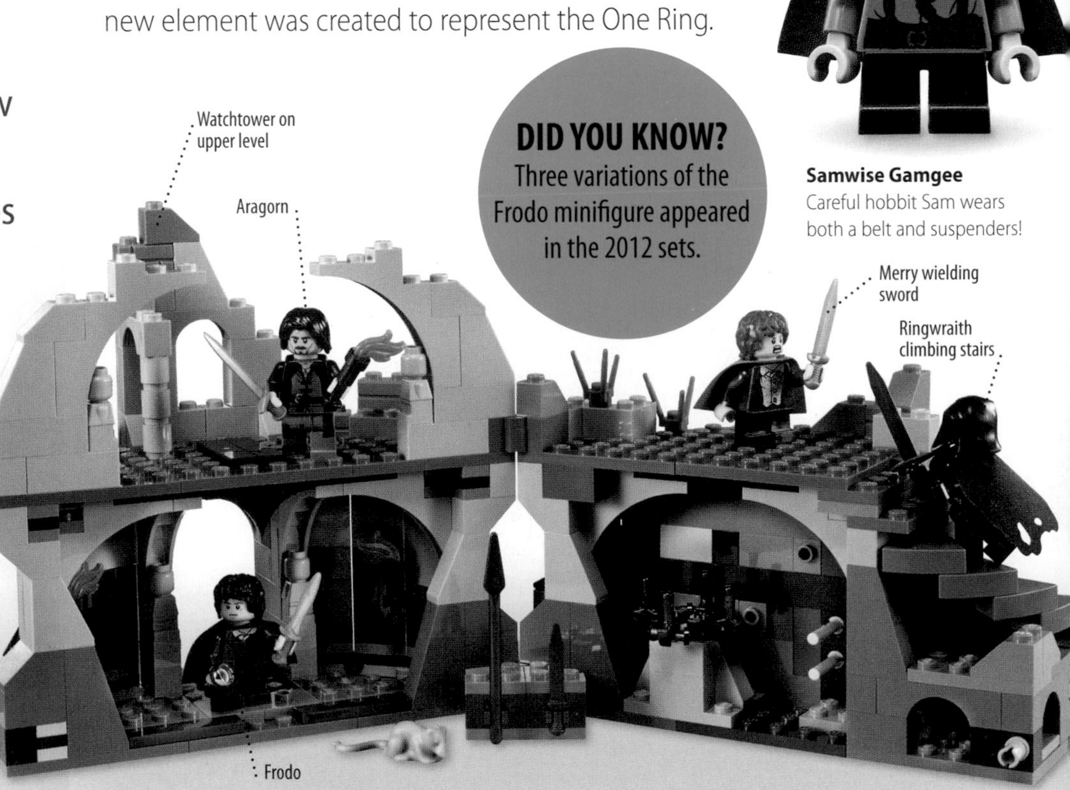

Watchtower on upper level

Aragorn

Merry wielding sword

Ringwraith climbing stairs

Frodo

Attack on Weathertop (9472) In this set, heroic Frodo, Aragorn, and Merry minifigures are menaced by two sinister Ringwraiths.

GOLLUM

This small LEGO figure requires a minimum 2x2 brick to stand on because of his hunched shape. He appears in two variants and in two sets, one from 2013's *The Hobbit* theme and one from *The Lord of the Rings*.

Arms must be attached
Head and body are one piece

Gollum The other (equally precious) variant of Gollum has sinister narrowed eyes.

Pointed greatsword
Evenstar pendant printed on torso
Flame and telescope form torch
Shirt tails on torso extend to legs

Aragorn Brave Aragorn has a new torso, legs, and reversible head, but his hair piece has been worn by at least 18 other minifigures since 2010.

Full length cloak
Ornate helmet with cheek protectors
Braided dwarfish beard
Breastplate covers entire torso
Gold crest on helmet
Scale mail pattern on legs

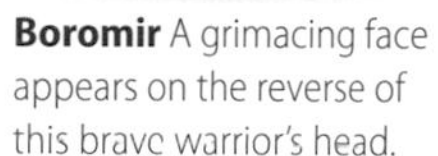

Boromir A grimacing face appears on the reverse of this brave warrior's head.

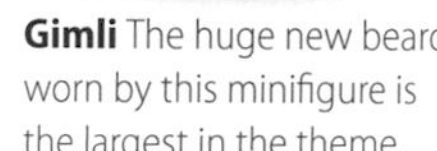

Gimli The huge new beard worn by this minifigure is the largest in the theme.

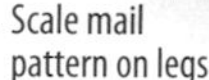

King Théoden The heroic Rohan king minifigure has new ornate legs, helmet, torso, and breastplate.

EXCLUSIVE ELF

This exclusive version of Second Age Elrond was available only with pre-orders of LEGO® *The Lord of the Rings™: The Video Game.*

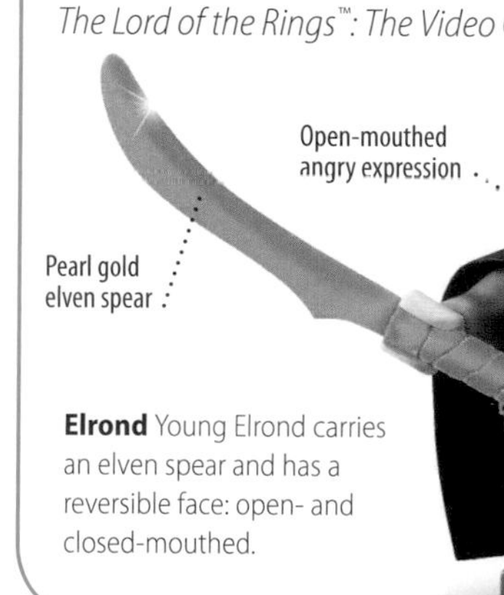

Same hair piece as fellow elves Legolas, Haldir, and Tauriel, but in brown
Open-mouthed angry expression
Pearl gold elven spear

Elrond Young Elrond carries an elven spear and has a reversible face: open- and closed-mouthed.

Legolas This minifigure's new hair piece is worn by all 2012 elves in this theme and for *The Hobbit* in 2013.

Elvish ears attached to hair piece
Standard bow and arrow
Elven tailcoat
Gold icons on helmet

Éomer The new Rohan helmet reappears for the Éomer minifigure, this time in pearl light gray.

Ornate armor detailing printed on legs and torso
Dressed for battle

Haldir Haldir has similar elvish features to Legolas, but wears armor instead of a tailcoat.

White hand of Saruman

In set 9476, the Uruk-hai can be found with a handprint on his helmet.

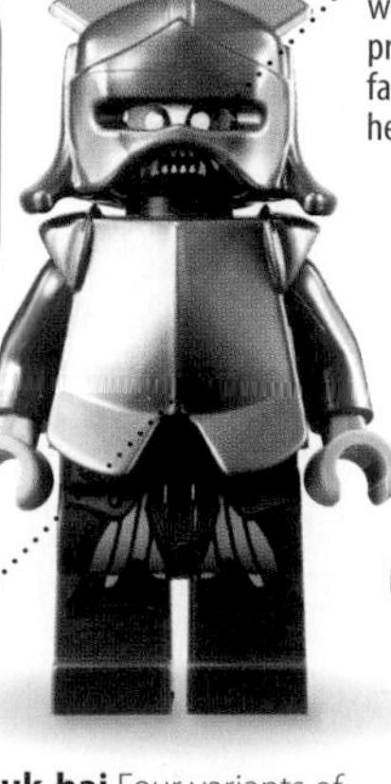

Terrifying war paint printed on face beneath helmet
Standard gray breastplate piece

Uruk-hai Four variants of these fierce warrior creatures have been released, with and without helmets and armor.

All-black outfit includes tattered cloak and hood

Ringwraith The shadowy Ringwraiths, also known as Nazgûl, have only appeared in one set to date (9472).

2012

Unique head has sad expression on other side.
One-off torso
Purple cape
Tiara is part of hair piece
Halter top with gold trim
Star spangled shorts
Angry expression
Stylish black suit
Cowl piece in use since 2006
Headband visible through cowl eyeholes
Utility belt is larger than on other Batman minifigures
I TAKE CRIME APART, BRICK BY BRICK.
Five-pointed cloth cape
Electro pattern on cowl
Bat logo in blue
Electrical wires and plates printed on legs and torso
Lined cheeks give serious expression
Expensive gray business suit
WHICH ROBIN AM I? I GET CONFUSED.
Cord printed on torso represents cape attachment.
Lightning bolt symbol
Reverse of head has expression of open-mouthed alarm.
"R" logo appears on all Robin minifigures.
Black cape is the same as Batman's.
Bat wing tail fins
Batman in cockpit
Black on yellow bat logo
Hubcaps same color as bat logo

Bizarro This rare minifigure of Superman's troubled clone was a prize in a raffle at the 2012 San Diego Comic-Con.

Wonder Woman The minifigure Amazon warrior comes complete with a golden lasso accessory.

Lex Luthor Lex is one of three minifigures in the Superman vs. Power Armor Lex (6862).

SUPERMAN

The giveaway Man of Steel from 2011's San Diego Comic-Con made a welcome return in 2012. This time he was packaged with Wonder Woman and Lex Luthor who, unlike Superman, were new and exclusive to the set.

LEGO® DC UNIVERSE™ SUPER HEROES

After releasing a few exclusive minifigures at Comic-Cons in 2011, the DC Universe burst into life with an explosion of LEGO minifigures in 2012. It was the first year that non-Batman DC sets joined the assortment, a trend that would continue in 2013. New characters, including Wonder Woman and Lex Luthor, made their debuts and old favorites got an exciting new look.

Electrosuit Batman This minifigure is exclusive to *LEGO® Batman™ The Visual Dictionary* published by DK.

Batman Two variants of this minifigure exist: this one and another with a new-style cowl.

DID YOU KNOW?

In post-July issues of set 6864, the Batman minifigure wore a new style of cowl.

BATMAN II

The Dark Knight returned in five sets this year, with a new minifigure head and torso. Many other minifigures were similarly refreshed for 2012, including Poison Ivy, The Joker, The Riddler, Two-Face, and Catwoman.

Bruce Wayne Batman's alter ego shares his new head with a less heroic minifigure from the LEGO Marvel Super Heroes theme: Loki.

Robin The first new Boy Wonder minifigure since 2008 wears all red instead of the classic red and green.

Shazam Another San Diego Comic-Con raffle prize, this is the only Shazam minifigure ever made.

Batmobile and the Two-Face Chase (6864) This set comes with two vehicles, five minifigures, and a bank with a safe.

Joker's henchman pilots the helicopter
"J" for Joker
Joker face emblem
Laughing gas bomb
Whip to whisk stolen goods into her grasp
Zippered catsuit printed on torso
Classic jester hat
Parti-colored legs
Wrestler mask printed on head
Old hair piece appears in green for first time
NEW HEAD, NEW TORSO... SAME SENSE OF HUMOR! HA HA HA!
Face painted with sinister clown makeup
Skin bleached white by accident with chemicals.
Torso printed with lime vest, bow tie, and squirty flower.
White hands match face
Clothes in 2012 Joker colors
DC Universe
LEGO
SUPER HEROES
7-14
6860
The Batcave
COMIC BOOK INCLUDED
New head has a pupil missing on the scarred side.
Same hair piece as 2006 Two-Face
Bowler hat in light gray
Riddler's question mark motif
Leaves printed on hair piece
Leaves emit potent pheromones
Knit cap loved by many thugs
Jacket in Two-Face colors
Crease details on suit
Crowbar resembles a question mark
Split colors continue on back of legs and torso

Batwing Battle Over Gotham City (6863) This Joker helicopter, a Batwing with flick missiles, and three minifigures are included in this set.

Catwoman The feline minifigure has a new torso, mask, and head complete with purple lipstick.

Harley Quinn Aside from her classic hat, the Joker's mischievous minifigure sidekick has all new parts.

Bane Tubes that carry a strength drug to Bane's brain are printed on the back of his torso and head.

The Joker It's smiles all around for the Joker. His new head has a different kind of grin on the reverse.

The Batcave (6860) The Batcave set includes both Batman and Bruce Wayne minifigures, along with Robin, Poison Ivy, and Bane.

The Joker's Henchman This minifigure shows his loyalties by wearing Joker colors—purple and lime.

The Riddler Three question marks on this minifigure's new torso and hat leave no doubt as to this trickster's identity!

Two-Face Bold new colors give this updated good guy/bad guy minifigure an eye-catching look.

Poison Ivy A printed vine trails its leaves all over this minifigure's torso and legs.

Two-Face's Henchman Two-Face now has two goons—this one and a cool character in shades.

DID YOU KNOW?
The Riddler's hat is a gray version of the one debuted by the 2011 collectible LEGO Minifigures Small Clown.

2012

LEGO MARVEL SUPER HEROES

Spider-Man had first spun his webs in a LEGO set in 2002. Ten years later he was back—this time as Ultimate Spider-Man—along with a whole wave of Marvel characters making their minifigure debut. They included the X-Men, the Avengers, and some of their most formidable foes!

Flaming red hair
Symbol of phoenix rising from flames

Phoenix This minifigure shows fiery X-Men telepath Jean Grey in her classic costume as Super Hero Phoenix. Her reversible head has two faces; one friendly and one fierce.

Scabbard on back holds two katanas
Muscled torso
Extra utility belt on leg

Deadpool A black and red mask is printed directly onto the minifigure mercenary's head.

Sideburns printed on head.

Claws attach to minifigure hands

Wolverine The X-Men's wild mutant minifigure has a hair piece previously seen only on vampires.

Gray eyebrows show his age.
First minifigure to wear cape in medium lilac color
Gray platform

Magneto The platform supplied with this X-Men foe minifigure represents the metal disk on which he flies.

X-MEN

Wolverine was the first X-Men mutant to achieve minifigure status, in Wolverine's Chopper Showdown (6866). Phoenix would show up next, as a promotional giveaway at San Diego Comic-Con in July of this year.

LEGO
MARVEL
SUPER HEROES
6-12
6866
COMIC ADVENTURE INCLUDED
MARVEL
X-MEN

Wolverine's Chopper Showdown (6866) In set 6866, Wolverine needs his chopper motorbike to escape the Magneto and Deadpool minifigures in their helicopter.

HEY DOC OCK, CAN YOU SCRATCH MY BACK?

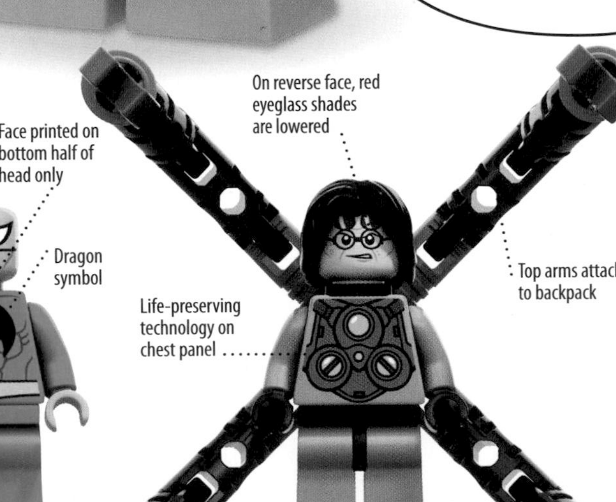

Face printed on bottom half of head only
Dragon symbol
On reverse face, red eyeglass shades are lowered
Top arms attach to backpack
Life-preserving technology on chest panel

Iron Fist The symbol on this minifigure's torso shows that he fought the magic dragon Shao Lao.

Doc Ock The Doc Ock minifigure has four arms that are all detachable and posable.

Small spider logo

Mask has rounded eye shapes and black webs

The usual red Spidey gloves

Spider-Man The new Spidey minifigure is modeled on the cartoon version from *The Ultimate Spider-Man* animated TV series.

Large white eyes
Black suit is really a living alien being!

Black Suit Spider-Man Raffle winners at the 2012 San Diego Comic-Con got this special minifigure as a prize.

SPIDER-MAN

Spidey and martial arts master Iron Fist teamed up to take on Dr. Octopus in Spider-Man's Doc Ock Ambush (6873). It was one of three sets to include minifigures based on characters from the Ultimate Spider-Man TV series.

DID YOU KNOW?
The 2012 Doc Ock minifigure is made up of an amazing 26 parts.

AVENGERS

The Avengers smash hit movie became an exciting LEGO play theme in 2012, with four action-packed sets. Black Widow, who appeared only in Quinjet Aerial Battle (6869), was the most sought after minifigure.

Only Thor has this hair piece in light yellow.
Unique torso with circular armor plates
Tail fins
SHIELD jet flown by Hawkeye
SHIELD
Flick missiles
Mask printed on head
Round repulsor beam on chest
No metal plates on knees
Gold mask fits over helmet
Repulsor beam
Unique horned helmet
Armor based on *The Avengers* movie costume
Strap for archer's quiver
Gloved hand for holding bow
Black, tousled hair
Well-muscled torso
HULK SMASH BIGGER HULK!
Printed mask has white eye covers
Curved red-and-white panel
Eyebrows and lipstick colors match hair
Chitauri alien mask
Weapon holsters strapped to both legs
Head, torso, and legs are one piece
Detachable hands turn at wrist
"A" for America (but it could also be for Avengers)
Massive arms must be attached
Pants molded on figure as well as printed
Striped panel is straighter than on Toy Fair variant

Thor The Norse god minifigure wears a snarl of rage on the other side of his head.

Toy Fair Iron Man Just 125 minifigures like this one were given away at the International Toy Fair in New York.

Hulk's Helicarrier Breakout (6868) This set includes Thor, Hawkeye, and Loki minifigures, a Hulk figure, part of the helicarrier, and a SHIELD jet.

Iron Man Transparent bricks attach to Iron Man's hands to represent repulsor beams.

Loki The god of mischief is the only Marvel minifigure to have an unprinted back.

Hawkeye A black archer's bow is this sharp-shooting minifigure's accessory.

Toy Fair Cap A special promotional Captain America minifigure came packaged as a set with Iron Man at the International Toy Fair in New York.

Black Widow Unlike the movie character, this sleek minifigure wears one belt diagonally.

Alien General The Chitauri alien minifigure's armor plating also extends to the back of his torso.

Incredible Hulk This Hulk minifigure was an exclusive gift-with-purchase at LEGO Stores and the online LEGO Shop.

Captain America This figure has blue pants and blue arms.

Large Hulk Huge, specially molded hands enable the large Hulk to grip standard minifigures by their legs.

HULK GROW!

The Hulk figure in Hulk's Helicarrier Breakout (6868) is far from mini. He's been scaled up to match Hulk's relative size in the movie. Call him a minifigure and he'll get angry, and you wouldn't like him when he's angry....

Spacious cockpit
Claw marks on tiger pattern
Tow chain with hook
Jaws can fit minifigure inside
Harness
T-Rex

T-Rex Hunter (5886) The T-Rex Hunter set comes with two minifigures, a helicopter, a scout vehicle, and a T-Rex with posable arms, legs, head, and tail. Both the 16-inch-long (40.65 cm) helicopter and the 11-inch long (28 cm) T-Rex dwarf the two minifigures.

Bandolier holds vials of dino tranquilizer
Utility vest holds screwdriver and radio

Dino Truck Driver This battle-scarred but cheerful driver appears in four 2012 LEGO Dino sets.

"Tracer" Tops A chin dimple and cool shades give Triceratops-hunter Tracer his rugged look.

LEGO® DINO

Deep in the jungle, LEGO adventurers discovered dinosaurs that had somehow survived into the modern era. Armed with tranquilizer guns, the minifigure heroes tried to capture the dinos alive in the seven-set theme. Each set came with a dinosaur, at least one hero minifigure, and a vehicle.

Aviator cap and goggles
Beads of sweat
Dino logo on undershirt
Chuck's long-range camera
Nervous expression
Tousled hair
Field glasses for spying dinosaurs
GPS device to help locate T-Rex
Belt holds pocket for pen and paper

Dino Pilot The disheveled but determined pilot has flown a variety of LEGO Dino helicopters and planes.

Chuck "Stego" Jenkins A new head is introduced for this wildlife photographer. He clearly has bigger things to worry about than shaving.

ID tag necklace
Loosely tied scarf
Belt pocket

Josh Thunder This minifigure hero is a descendant of Johnny Thunder from the LEGO® Adventurers theme.

Sue Montana Ponytailed Sue is ready to face the action dressed in hardy safari gear.

Tranquilizer gun
Jacket with harness

Ocean Interceptor Hero This sandy-haired minifigure from the Ocean Interceptor set shares a head with three of the firefighters in 2012's LEGO City theme.

Fedora shields eyes from sun
T-REX... MMMM, TASTES LIKE CHICKEN!
Vest laced up with string
Wild and bushy red mustache
Belt holds gun and compass

Rex Tyrone If you want a rampant Raptor roped, Rex is your man. His fedora hat—in a variety of colors—has also been worn by bandits, gangsters, cowboys, and, of course, Indiana Jones.

LEGO® HARRY POTTER™

The LEGO Harry Potter theme had run for 11 magical years, but in 2012 it finally came to an end. No sets were released, but Harry himself popped up to take his final bow in the form of an exclusive minifigure appearing in DK's *LEGO® Harry Potter™: Characters of the Magical World*.

Matching shirt and tie

Harry Potter™ Harry's minifigure looks all grown up in his new dress robes from the Slug Club Christmas party.

Pearl gold shoulder armor
Gold details on black robes
Silver emblem on head wrap denotes ZX status
Shoulder armor piece can hold two katanas
Diamond pattern on robes
LEGO
NINJAGO
8-14
9450
915
INCLUDED
Samurai helmet with spiked crest
Ice Energy design
Ice pattern
Protective mask
Extended shoulder pads
Brown leather leg armor

Exclusive Lloyd ZX DK's bestselling *LEGO® Ninjago Character Encyclopedia* came with an exclusive cover gift—this minifigure of Lloyd with ZX status, wearing elemental robes.

Lloyd ZX One of just two Ninjago minifigures to have a reversible head is the heroic Green Ninja—a.k.a. Lloyd Garmadon.

Epic Dragon Battle (9450) Lloyd ZX is one of seven minifigures in the Epic Dragon Battle set.

NRG Zane Zane's NRG-level minifigure wears a new ice-blue robe.

Samurai X This mystery minifigure has mostly new elements, but under that visor is a familiar face. It's Nya!

DID YOU KNOW?

All Serpentine tribes carry small, hand-held vipers that they use as toxic weapons.

Cobra-type hood

Scale pattern

Long, trailing tail

Skales A hypnotic pattern adorns General Skales, leader of the Serpentine Hypnobrai tribe. Like other Serpentine general minifigures, Skales has a tail rather than legs.

LEGO NINJAGO

Now in its second year, Ninjago upped the action as the Ninja challenged the tribes of the Serpentine. The snakes featured new modified serpent heads, new scaly torsos, and new printed legs. Kai's sister, Nya, returned this year clad in samurai gear in Samurai Mech (9448).

I WONDER IF THE DINO FOLKS ARE HIRING?
Boa crest on hood
Gray scale markings
Ready to grip Constrictai Fang Blade

Snike Short, unposable legs set the tunneling Constrictai apart from the other Serpentine tribes.

Scale pattern

Extra large fangs

WHAT DO YOU MEAN, "CHEER UP?" I'M ALREADY SMILING!

Necklace made of fangs

Fang-Suei This minifigure's head is made from the same mold as that of his Fangpyre comrade, Chokun.

Head spikes

Battle scars on torso

Lizaru Venomari tribe members, such as Lizaru, have prominent venom-filled fangs.

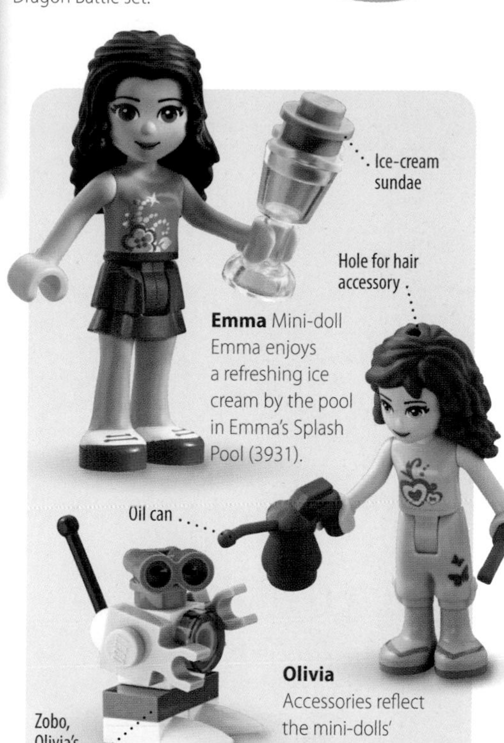
Ice-cream sundae
Hole for hair accessory
Oil can
Zobo, Olivia's robot

Emma Mini-doll Emma enjoys a refreshing ice cream by the pool in Emma's Splash Pool (3931).

Olivia Accessories reflect the mini-dolls' hobbies—in Olivia's case, science.

LEGO® FRIENDS

The new LEGO line for girls, LEGO Friends, proved to be an incredible success. Larger than standard minifigures and more stylized, the characters in these sets are known as mini-dolls.

Shirt and tie suggest older age group

Andrea A top with a musical note design is a perfect fit for songbird Andrea.

Peter In the theme's launch year, its only male mini-doll was Peter, Olivia's father.

Stephanie The mini-dolls come with a range of cute animal friends, including Daisy, Stephanie's pet rabbit.

2012

LEGO MINIFIGURES

The LEGO collectible Minifigures line returned for its third year in 2012, with 48 new minifigures spread over three series. As in previous years, many new elements were featured in each of the series.

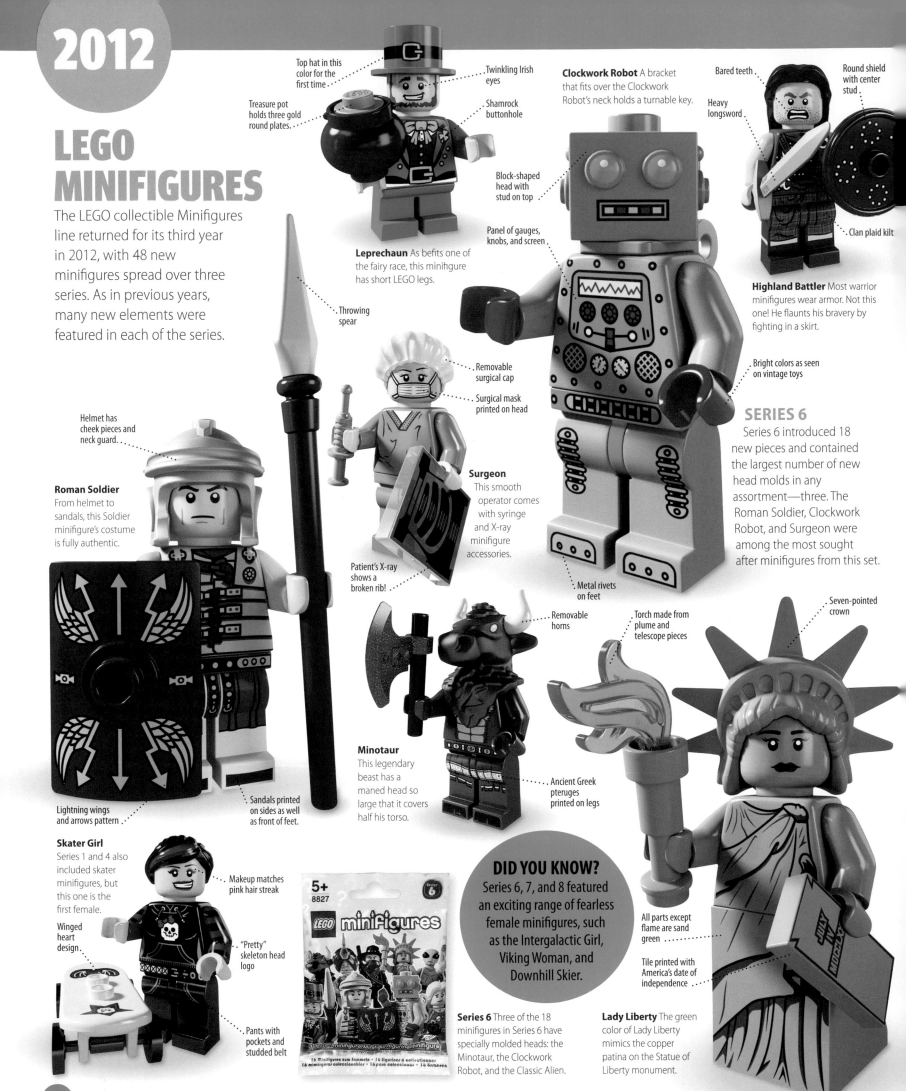

Top hat in this color for the first time

Twinkling Irish eyes

Treasure pot holds three gold round plates.

Shamrock buttonhole

Leprechaun As befits one of the fairy race, this minifigure has short LEGO legs.

Bared teeth

Heavy longsword

Round shield with center stud

Clan plaid kilt

Highland Battler Most warrior minifigures wear armor. Not this one! He flaunts his bravery by fighting in a skirt.

Clockwork Robot A bracket that fits over the Clockwork Robot's neck holds a turnable key.

Block-shaped head with stud on top

Panel of gauges, knobs, and screen

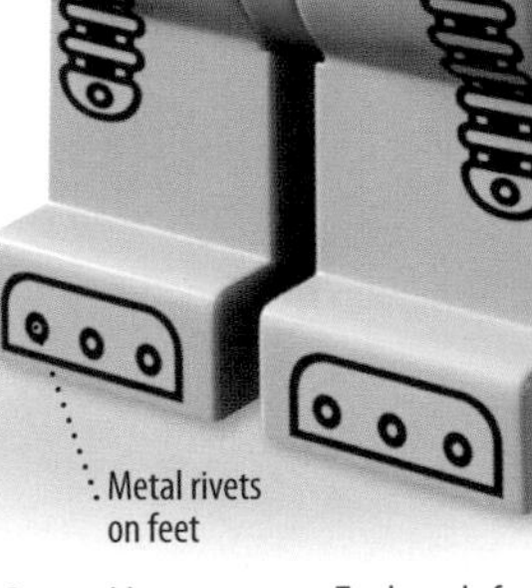

Bright colors as seen on vintage toys

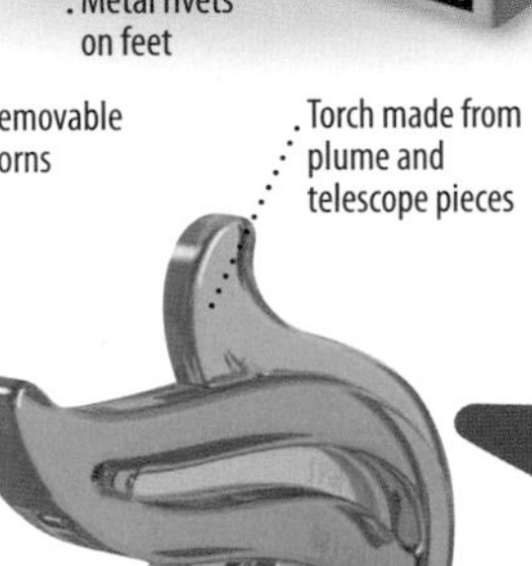

Metal rivets on feet

SERIES 6

Series 6 introduced 18 new pieces and contained the largest number of new head molds in any assortment—three. The Roman Soldier, Clockwork Robot, and Surgeon were among the most sought after minifigures from this set.

Throwing spear

Removable surgical cap

Surgical mask printed on head

Surgeon This smooth operator comes with syringe and X-ray minifigure accessories.

Patient's X-ray shows a broken rib!

Helmet has cheek pieces and neck guard.

Roman Soldier From helmet to sandals, this Soldier minifigure's costume is fully authentic.

Lightning wings and arrows pattern

Sandals printed on sides as well as front of feet.

Removable horns

Ancient Greek pteruges printed on legs

Minotaur This legendary beast has a maned head so large that it covers half his torso.

Torch made from plume and telescope pieces

Seven-pointed crown

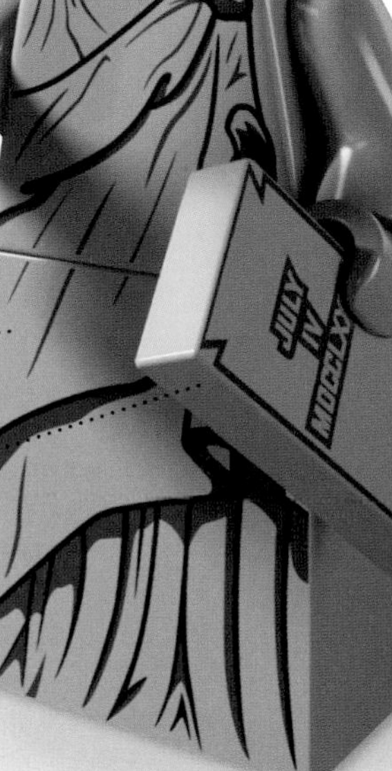

All parts except flame are sand green

Tile printed with America's date of independence

Lady Liberty The green color of Lady Liberty mimics the copper patina on the Statue of Liberty monument.

Skater Girl Series 1 and 4 also included skater minifigures, but this one is the first female.

Makeup matches pink hair streak

Winged heart design

"Pretty" skeleton head logo

Pants with pockets and studded belt

5+
8827
Series 6
LEGO minifigures

Series 6 Three of the 18 minifigures in Series 6 have specially molded heads: the Minotaur, the Clockwork Robot, and the Classic Alien.

DID YOU KNOW?

Series 6, 7, and 8 featured an exciting range of fearless female minifigures, such as the Intergalactic Girl, Viking Woman, and Downhill Skier.

HUD (Head Up Display)
Open helmet; visor details are printed on face
Double-barreled blaster gun
Gold shell crown
Fish tail with silver scales
So far only this little minifigure has worn this hood in red.
Rubbery basket used in LEGO Friends theme.
Head piece has rabbit ears
Giant carrot accessory
Green warpaint
Gold spear
Eagle feathers design
Swim cap so tight it has wrinkles
Winner's medal
Blue mouth guard protects smile
Boxing gloves are not removable
Helmet and hair molded as one piece
Team GB sash
New Santa hat
Short, detachable beard
Glaring red eyes
Sack bulging with gifts
Helmet has antennas
RESISTANCE IS... JUST GOING TO BE FRUSTRATING FOR YOU.
Standard Skull
Ruff is separate
Claw arm
Laser weapon made from ray gun and red bar
Magenta ski coordinates with jacket.
Goggles shield eyes from glare
Ski pole
Detachable plume
Helmet is also metallic gold

Galaxy Patrol This heroic minifigure patrols deepest space wearing a suit of deepest blue.

Ocean King The stormy sea king's gold trident is right out of the LEGO® Atlantis theme.

Grandma Visitor This is the first female in the LEGO Minifigures theme to have short legs.

Bunny Suit Guy A veggie diet has put a spring (or a hop) in this minifigure's step.

Aztec Warrior This Aztec knight wears a gold Eagle helmet and feathered breastplate.

Swimming Champion The swimmer's medal would resurface in the Team GB subtheme.

SERIES 7

When Series 7 hit the stores, it brought 16 new parts and more printing than any LEGO Minifigures collection to date. Its rarest minifigures were the Aztec Warrior, Bunny Suit Guy, and Ocean King.

Brawny Boxer Team GB's lion head logo appears on the Brawny Boxer's headguard.

Horseback Rider The Rider's helmet will later be worn by two minifigures in the LEGO Friends theme.

TEAM GB

Nine minifigure athletes were produced to commemorate the 2012 London Olympic Games. Each came with a white stand and gold medal. All of these minifigures were available only in the United Kingdom and Ireland.

Santa Santa's sack accessory can be gripped by minifigure hands or attached to a brick.

Actor Alas, poor Actor! He wears a hair piece usually reserved for female minifigures.

Evil Robot Robot armor covers this minifigure's torso and legs. Under his helmet, his face is silver metal with rivets.

Conquistador This seeker of gold wears a metallic gold breastplate over his dark red torso.

Downhill Skier Colors taken from the LEGO Friends theme adorn this minifigure's gear.

SERIES 8

Series 8 had a more even distribution of minifigures than past releases, making it easier for fans to collect a complete set. The Alien Villainess and Downhill Skier are perhaps slightly more difficult to find.

LEGO CITY

LEGO City left town for a while in 2012, with the introduction of the City Forest Police subtheme. New Forest Police minifigures and their adversaries appeared in seven sets, including a new Forest Police Station (4440). Forest firefighters also got four sets. Ranger, pilot, and crook minifigures featured new heads and torsos, and firefighter minifigures had new torsos.

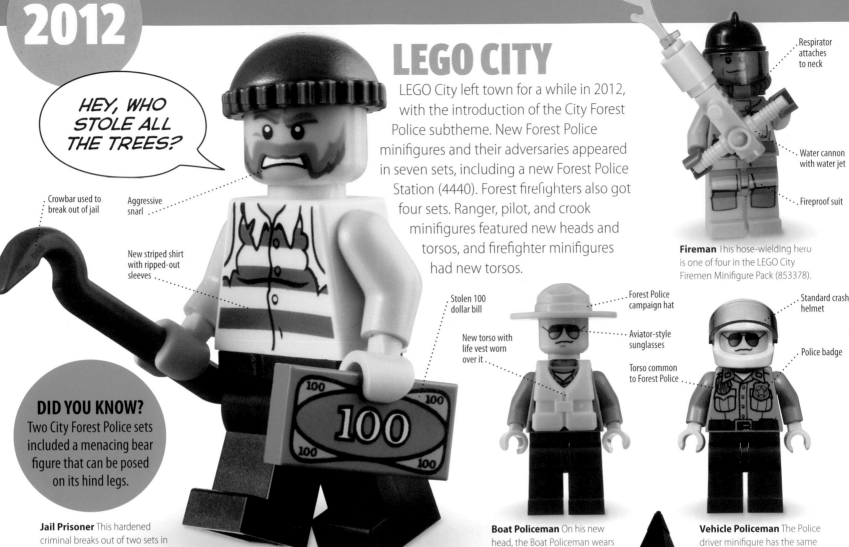

HEY, WHO STOLE ALL THE TREES?

Crowbar used to break out of jail

Aggressive snarl

New striped shirt with ripped-out sleeves

Stolen 100 dollar bill

Jail Prisoner This hardened criminal breaks out of two sets in the City Forest Police subtheme.

DID YOU KNOW?
Two City Forest Police sets included a menacing bear figure that can be posed on its hind legs.

Respirator attaches to neck

Water cannon with water jet

Fireproof suit

Fireman This hose-wielding hero is one of four in the LEGO City Firemen Minifigure Pack (853378).

Forest Police campaign hat

Aviator-style sunglasses

New torso with life vest worn over it

Boat Policeman On his new head, the Boat Policeman wears a new hat made just for 2012's Forest Police.

Standard crash helmet
Police badge
Torso common to Forest Police

Vehicle Policeman The Police driver minifigure has the same new head. He only appears in Police Pursuit (4437).

LEGO® ADVANCED MODELS

LEGO Advanced Models are highly complex models, mainly vehicles or buildings, that take a lot of skill to put together. The LEGO Town Hall was one of 2012's three Advanced Models. In it, the Mayor minifigure performed a wedding for a happy Bride and Groom who appear in this set only.

Gray hair suggests mature character
Pinstripe jacket
Plain blue pants

Mayor This pinstripe jacket has been worn by three other businessmen minifigures so far.

Traditional top hat
Blue tie and pocket linings

Groom The Groom, like all Town Hall minifigures, has the standard smiley LEGO face.

Hair piece has long French braid at back.
Long sleeves
Plain white slope for skirt

Bride The Bride has opted for a timeless white gown for her big day.

Janitor minifigure sweeping roof
Mayor makes announcements from the balcony
1891
Shield flanked by croissant-shaped decorations

Town Hall (10224) This set includes Mayor, Bride, Groom, Secretary, Janitor, News Woman, and two child minifigures.

Double-ended saberstaff
Zabrak tattoos on face
Pattern on both sides of torso
Yellow eyes on chrome silver head
Exposed wires on torso

Darth Maul This shirtless Darth Maul minifigure was a free-with-purchase give-away.

TC-14 The only existing female protocol droid minifigure was the second promotional giveaway.

"REVENGE OF THE FIFTH"

The unofficial *Star Wars* Day on May Fourth was followed by a cleverly-titled "Revenge of the Fifth" day. To celebrate, the LEGO Group offered two exclusive minifigures free with online and instore purchases.

New hair piece with integral gold headdress
Gold patterns on royal robe
IF YOU ONLY KNEW HOW LONG IT TAKES TO PUT ON THIS GET-UP....
Unique new piece for skirt

Queen Amidala This is the first Padmé minifigure to show her dressed as the Queen of Naboo.

LEGO *STAR WARS*

The big news for LEGO *Star Wars* in 2012 was the arrival of Queen Amidala. Padmé Amidala (or Padmé Naberrie) minifigures had been around since 1999, but this was her first appearance as queen. It featured in only one set, Gungan Sub (9499). Other highlights of the year were a more detailed Gamorrean Guard and the debut of bounty hunter Boushh.

Leia unmasked
Helmet with breathing mask and vision enhancer
Thermal detonator
Bar and telescope combine to form Force pike

Boushh Removing this minifigure's helmet reveals its true identity. It isn't Boushh the bounty hunter at all—it's actually Princess Leia in disguise!

Helmet dented by past battles

Gun is pistol set in a lightsaber hilt

Boba Fett A new Boba minifigure has orange kneepads and silver boots

Short blaster gun

Dotted mouth

Armor printed on new torso

Stormtrooper The 2012 Stormtrooper has a new head with a black balaclava hidden under his old standard helmet.

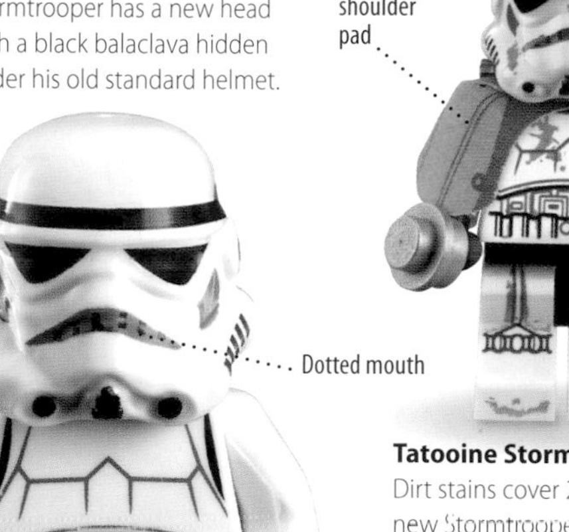
Spatters on classic helmet
Orange pauldron shoulder pad

Tatooine Stormtrooper Dirt stains cover 2012's second new Stormtrooper.

DID YOU KNOW?
Padmé has appeared in five minifigure versions, two of them under her family name of Naberrie.

LEGO
STAR WARS
9-14

Jabba's Palace (9516) The nine characters in Jabba's Palace include a spider-like B'omarr monk.

Ax head clips to bar to form vibro-ax.
Armor one piece with head

Gamorrean Guard This minifigure is a redesign of a much less detailed one from 2003.

JABBA THE HUTT

This second version of Jabba is more detailed than the one that appeared in 2003, and features a head that can swivel 360 degrees. His hands are capable of holding minifigure accessories.

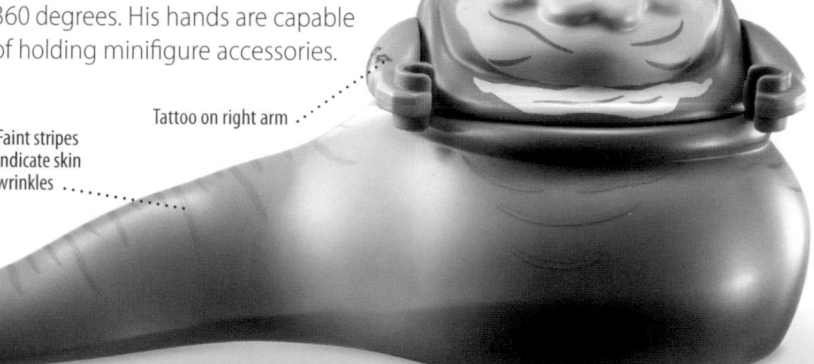
Tattoo on right arm
Faint stripes indicate skin wrinkles

Jabba the Hutt The head and torso of this Hutt figure are made as one piece.

LEGO® BRAND STORE

The tradition of producing special minifigures for LEGO Brand Store openings continued in 2012. The three minifigures shown here formed an exclusive pack at the grand opening of the Oakridge Centre store in Vancouver, BC, Canada. They are now very hard to find.

White ascot scarf

Captain Brickbeard The popular pirate pops up again at the Vancouver store opening.

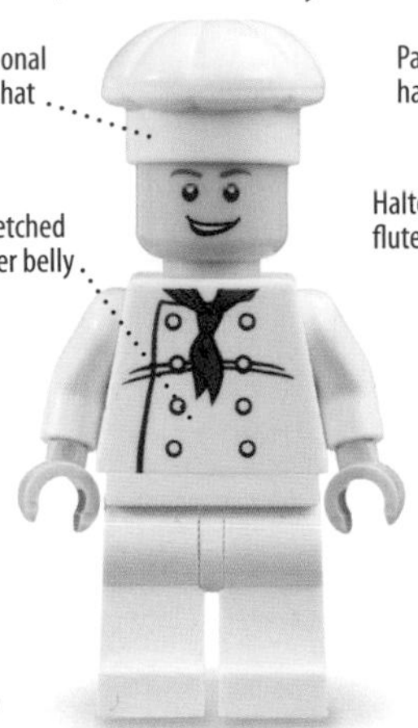
Traditional chef's hat
Jacket stretched tightly over belly

Chef Also in the mix is this Chef minifigure, who seems to enjoy his own cooking.

Part-braided hair piece
Halter top with fluted hem

Orange Woman A bright orange outfit matches this minifigure's bright smile.

LEGO® MASTER BUILDER ACADEMY

Level 3 of LEGO Master Builder Academy launched this year, introducing a new orange-clad minifigure. There were three sets: The Lost Village (20206), The Forbidden Bridge (20207), and The Dark Lair (20208). Fans were encouraged to build sets from their own stories and learned how to create details such as stairways and arches.

Level 3 MBA Minifigure Orange is the color for this year's Level 3 minifigure.

LEGO® MONSTER FIGHTERS

The LEGO Monster Fighters theme focused on Lord Vampyre's evil plan to use the powerful Moonstones to help monsters to rule the world. Only the valiant Monster Fighters could stop him! Heroes and Monsters clashed in nine sets in this one-year line. Although some of the Monsters had appeared in previous LEGO sets, they all got new heads and torsos for this play theme.

Blunt-ended foil keeps vampires at bay
I KNOW THE MONSTERS ARE OVER THERE... THAT'S WHY I'M OVER HERE!
New color for bowler hat this year
Unique steam-powered artificial leg
Harpoon clips to topknot
Crossbow
Garlic and stakes attached to belt

Dr. Rodney Rathbone The dapper minifigure team leader appears in three Monster Fighters sets.

Ann Lee Ann's two faces—one smirking and one scowling—both bear a scar left by a witch's nail.

Hammer held by steam-powered artificial arm
Bushy beard and eyebrows
Pink moonstone coveted by zombies
Slicked-back hair
Twin pistols

Jack McHammer Jack's hammer was first wielded this year by the Thor minifigure in the LEGO Marvel Super Heroes theme.

Frank Rock Biker Frank rarely takes his shades off, but his alternative face shows him with uncovered eyes.

Blunderbuss weapon topped by pearl gold cone

Telescopic eye

Silver bullets to take down werewolves

Major Quinton Steele This old-school minifigure hunter has werewolf teeth as a trophy on his printed belt.

FIGHTERS

All five Monster Fighter minifigures in the theme feature new heads, new torsos, and new printed legs, and all appear in at least two sets.

Unique head with bared teeth

Glow-in-the-dark claws attach to minifigure hands

Werewolf Both the torso and legs of the minifigure Werewolf are printed with ripped clothing.

DID YOU KNOW?
360 million minifigures were manufactured in Billund, Denmark in 2012.

Detachable head cover with fins

Seaweed and scales pattern on legs

Swamp Creature Big, froglike eyes peer through eyeholes in this minifigure's head cover.

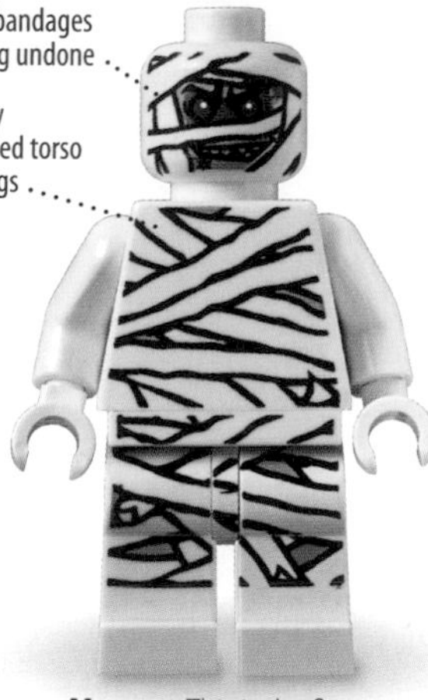

Head bandages coming undone

Tightly wrapped torso and legs

Mummy This is the first Mummy minifigure with glow-in-the-dark details.

Lord Vampyre's Bride The bloodthirsty Bride featured in two sets, including the huge Haunted House (10228).

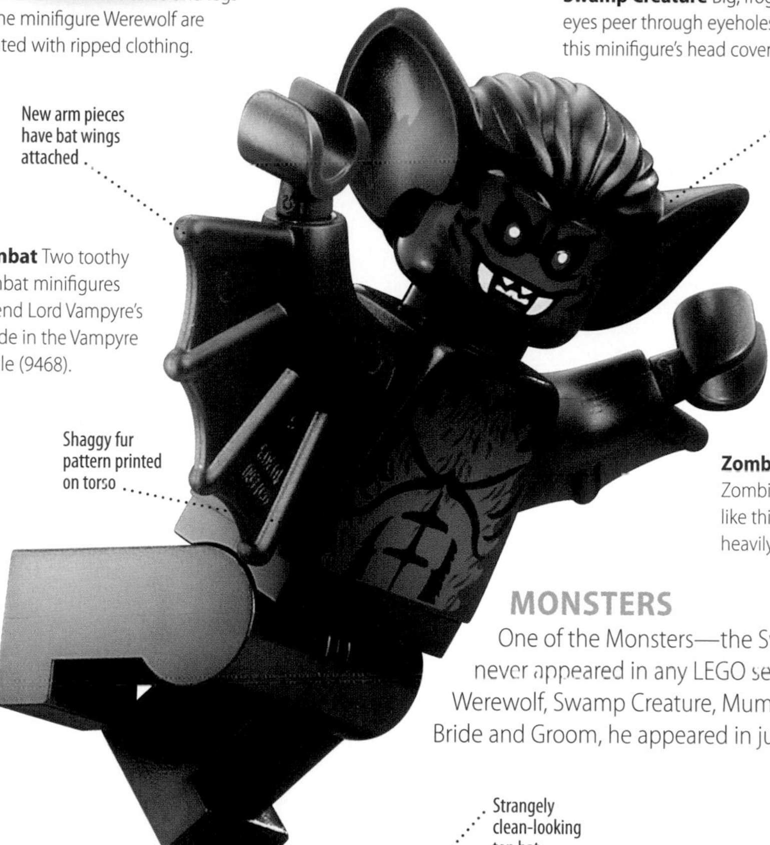

Blood red sloped skirt piece

New arm pieces have bat wings attached

Hair piece has huge bat ears attached

Shaggy fur pattern printed on torso

Manbat Two toothy Manbat minifigures defend Lord Vampyre's abode in the Vampyre Castle (9468).

Dead, white eyes

Tattered driver's livery

Zombie Driver Zombie minifigures, like this one, feature heavily in the theme.

LEGO
Monster Fighters
8-14
9467

The Ghost Train (9467) This set includes two monster fighter minifigures plus three spooky glow-in-the-dark ghosts.

MONSTERS

One of the Monsters—the Swamp Creature—had never appeared in any LEGO set prior to this. Like the Werewolf, Swamp Creature, Mummy, and the Zombie Bride and Groom, he appeared in just one set in the theme.

Dull, lifeless hair

New torso with torn dress

Sloped piece for wedding gown skirt

Zombie Bride This minifigure Bride is definitely not the life and soul of the wedding party.

Strangely clean-looking top hat

Mismatched arms

Zombie Groom The badly-groomed Groom has a torso that looks old, but is in fact brand new.

Special bat moonstone accessory

Hair piece has widow's peak

Cloth cape with huge, pointed collar

Lord Vampyre A red moonstone gives Lord Vampyre power over all other Monster minifigures.

LEGO® CUUSOO

LEGO CUUSOO is a special program that allows fans to design sets and submit them online to the LEGO Group. The best designs may be made into real LEGO sets. The Hayabusa Unmanned Asteroid Explorer (21101) was the second CUUSOO set produced, and the first available worldwide. It featured this minifigure of a Hayabusa project manager.

Jacket worn by Mayor in Advanced Model Town Hall set this year.

Junichiro Kawaguchi The only minifigure in the Hayabusa set (21101) is the space project's manager.

COMPUTER-ANIMATED MINIFIGURES

IN 1997, THE LEGO GROUP INTRODUCED the world to pizza delivery boy Pepper Roni in the first LEGO® PC game (*LEGO Island*)—and animated versions of LEGO minifigures have been cropping up in their own video games and television shows ever since. The process begins with a detailed sketch of the minifigure, which is then transformed into a computer-generated image (CGI). Recent hits include the LEGO® *Legends of Chima*™ and LEGO® *Ninjago* TV series and LEGO® *Star Wars*® *The Yoda Chronicles* mini-series, all of which feature minifigures who can use facial expressions and movement to express themselves in new and exciting ways.

LEGO® *Indiana Jones*™: *Raiders of the Lost Brick* (2008) This mini-series contained details from all four Indiana Jones films alongside in-jokes and LEGO humor.

***The Adventures of Clutch Powers* (2010)** Starring heroic minifigure Clutch Powers, a character created for the film, this was the first full-length movie to feature minifigures.

LEGO® *Star Wars*®: *The Padawan Menace* (2011) Created in close collaboration with Lucasfilm, this 22-minute feature included a cameo by George Lucas.

LEGO *Ninjago* (2011–2012) A two-episode mini-series was followed by two seasons of episodes in 2012, centering on a team of trainee Ninja.

LEGO *Legends of Chima* (2013) Unleash the power! This TV series is based on the mythical animal tribes' continuing fight over the mystical CHI.

LEGO® *Star Wars*®: *The Yoda Chronicles* (2013) This three-part mini-series focuses on the adventures of Yoda, his fledgling Padawans, and other favorite *Star Wars* characters.

PC CD-ROM
LEGO
ISLAND

LEGO® *Island* (1997) Players had an island full of missions and new minifigures to meet in the LEGO Group's first video game.

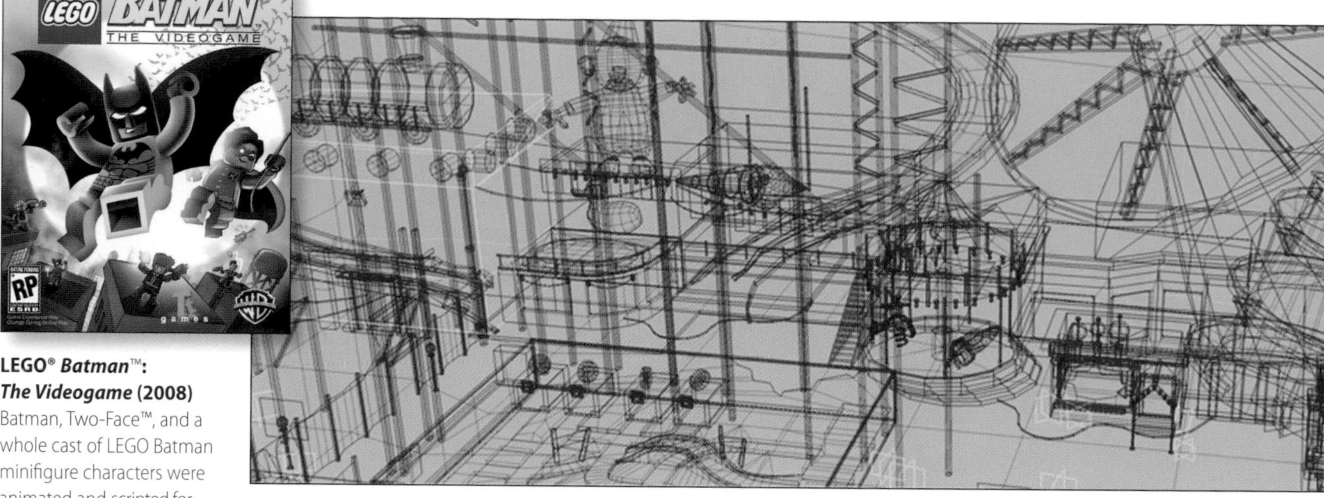

LEGO® *Batman*™: *The Videogame* (2008) Batman, Two-Face™, and a whole cast of LEGO Batman minifigure characters were animated and scripted for the video game.

Setting the scene When designing a video game, a 3-D wire-frame is produced of the game environment.

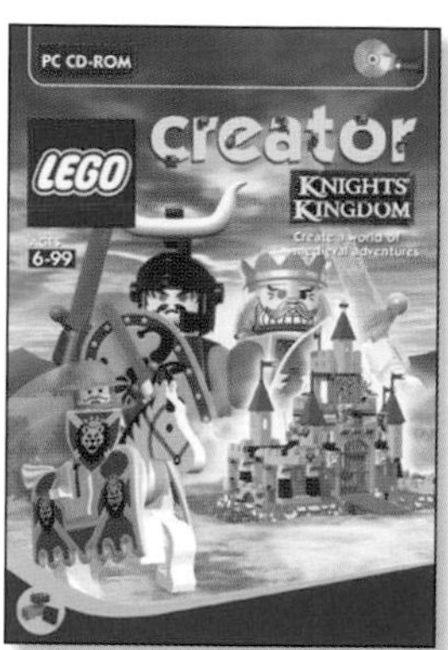
PC CD-ROM
LEGO
creator
KNIGHTS' KINGDOM

LEGO® *Creator: Knights' Kingdom* (2000) Players can use virtual bricks to build a medieval kingdom.

The final details The 3-D wire-frame design is filled in and shaded before light, color, and textures are added.

XBOX 360
LIVE
LEGO
INDIANA JONES 2
LUCASARTS

LEGO® *Indiana Jones*™ 2: *The Adventure Continues* (2009) Gamers could build their own levels in this game based on the adventures of all four movies.

Rough wire-frame rendering of Two-Face.

Pixelated minifigures Following initial concept sketches and paintings, every element of the game is created on a computer. The designers use a digital library of every LEGO piece ever created.

Wii
LEGO
STAR WARS III

LEGO® *Star Wars*® III: *The Clone Wars*™ (2011) This game combines the epic stories and characters of *The Clone Wars* TV series with exciting gameplay.

LET ME AT THOSE CROCS!
This pearl gold CHI harness gives Longtooth awesome power.
The battle scar on his unique head mask makes him look especially tough!

Longtooth This older foot soldier has spent many years on the Lion Tribe's front line, where all the "action" is—and his minifigure has the battle scars to prove it!

LEGO LEGENDS OF CHIMA

Tribes of intelligent animals clash over a mysterious source of power called CHI in this exciting new theme. Its story centers on the battle for control of CHI between the powerful Lion and Crocodile Tribes, which then draws other tribes of Chima into battle. In 2013, LEGO Legends of Chima featured more than 30 new minifigures, all with completely new designs and accessories.

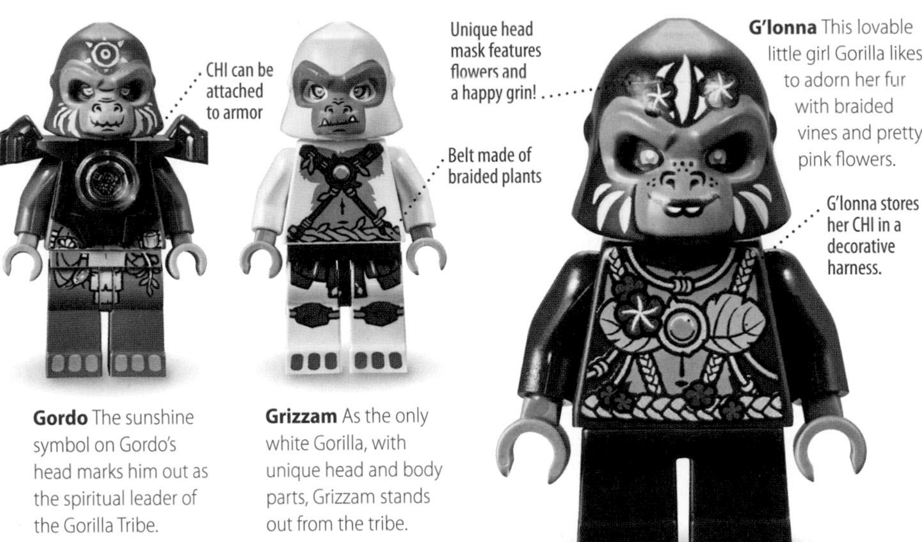
CHI can be attached to armor
Unique head mask features flowers and a happy grin!
Belt made of braided plants
G'lonna stores her CHI in a decorative harness.

Gordo The sunshine symbol on Gordo's head marks him out as the spiritual leader of the Gorilla Tribe.

Grizzam As the only white Gorilla, with unique head and body parts, Grizzam stands out from the tribe.

G'lonna This lovable little girl Gorilla likes to adorn her fur with braided vines and pretty pink flowers.

2013

LEGO® FANS WERE INTRODUCED

to a whole new world of play in 2013 with the launch of LEGO® Legends of Chima™, a fantasy theme set on a world where animals rule and the power of CHI is the key to peace… or empire. But there were plenty of other high-stakes conflicts going on this year, as the Ninja of Ninjago battled a Stone Army, LEGO® Galaxy Squad fought off a bug invasion, and two new licensed themes—LEGO® Teenage Mutant Ninja Turtles™ and LEGO® *The Lone Ranger*™—took the battle between good and evil to new heights.

HEROIC TRIBES

The brave Lions, quirky Eagles, and laidback Gorillas are allied in an effort to preserve peace and harmony in Chima. They want to ensure fair distribution of CHI for all tribes—even their hostile enemies!

Only Laval is important enough to wear this unique head mask!
Powerful CHI staff is a symbol of his high status in the tribe.
CHI-orb-encrusted crown
Only Lagravis wears this elaborate CHI armor in pearl gold
Royal armor features Lion Tribe symbols

Lagravis Laval's father commands great respect as king of the Lion Tribe. The aging leader is the only Lion minifigure with gray hair.

Laval Dressed in a gleaming gold crown, a regal cape, and dark-blue battle armor, Laval looks the part of royal prince of the Lion Tribe!

Pointed gold leader crown

Ewald As leader of the Eagles' Ruling Council, Ewald is the brains rather than the brawn in battle, so he wears a stately robe instead of battle armor.

Jagged scales poke through his gold head mask

King Crominus The gruff, tough king of the Croc Tribe has gold teeth to match his royal head mask.

I'M THE KING—DO WHAT I SAY AND MAKE IT SNAPPY!

Eagles have the same wings as the Ravens, in white

Lower body is a sloped piece instead of legs.

Legs feature feathers, talons, and Eagle Tribe armor

Eris The gleaming gold tiara on Eris' head shows that she is the daughter of one of the Eagle Tribe's Ruling Council Members.

Only Croc royalty wear capes

Vine necklace has a place for storing CHI

TIME TO CHI UP!

Sharp claws

Crawley This formidable foot soldier's tough scales provide natural body armor, so all he wears in battle is a red bandana and a loin cloth.

Red robe features animal bones—which Chima creature could they be from?

CHI-firing blaster

Battle scar from fighting on the Croc Tribe's front line.

Crug stores his CHI on his belt

Crug Take cover! This is one of the Croc Tribe's biggest, strongest, and most dangerous minifigures—especially with his powerful CHI blaster in hand!

VILLAIN TRIBES

Motivated by greed, the Crocodiles want to seize control of all the CHI in Chima. They persuade the ferocious Wolves and sharp-tongued Ravens to side with them and do battle against the Lions and their allied tribes for power.

Unique head mask features flashy gold decoration and red feathers

Rawzom The Raven Tribe doesn't have many rules, but it does have a ruler. This minifigure's gold-plated head markings distinguish him as the "boss."

Rawzom has the same legs as Razcal, with Raven-symbol knee pads and sharp talons.

Head mask with beak and feather texture fits over a regular minifigure head piece

Battle scars over both eyes from numerous dogfights

Wakz Bushy eyebrows and white whiskers mark this minifigure out as the oldest warrior of the Wolf Tribe.

Worriz is the first minifigure to wear this jagged cape.

Rizzo might have lost his eye in battle—or maybe he sold it for something more profitable!

Double-sided face shows eyes wide with CHI power.

The LEGO® DC Universe™ Super Heroes Riddler has the same purple hands in 2012.

Peg-leg is also worn by an Alien Android in 2011 in the LEGO® Alien Conquest theme

Worriz His minifigure's gray cape shows that Worriz is the lead negotiator of the Wolf Tribe, but that doesn't mean he is the boss—all members of the pack are equal.

Wakz wears scary-looking fangs on his leg straps.

Razcal This minifigure is in charge of valuing the Ravens' stolen treasures. The gold markings on his head mask suggest that he keeps some for himself!

Rizzo This ragtag Raven has a silver peg-leg and eye patch made from scavenged metal.

LEGO® MINIFIGURES

The LEGO Minifigures collectible series continued into 2013 with the release of series 9, 10, and 11 (the Series 11 Minifigures were still top secret at the time of writing this book). Series 10 was the first of the popular assortment of characters to include a limited-edition minifigure that fans would have to search for, adding a new level of fun to the collecting!

Hard helmet protects equally hard head
Armor found on battlefields

Alien Avenger Underneath this trooper's armor is the text "SHAMI," the nickname of LEGO designer Fédéric Andre.

New worker's cap

Plumber The Plumber's brand-new plunger accessory has a hard handle and rubber cup that can actually suction onto things.

Award for her role in "The 7-Stud Brick"

I'D LIKE TO THANK MY DESIGNER.

Diamond pendant

Hollywood Starlet This icon of the plastic screen wears a stylish dress with precisely 372 stars printed on it.

Gray version of Caveman's club from LEGO Minifigures Series 1

Watchful eye

New hair piece features painted coins and scarf

Fancy dress details

Fortune Teller The Fortune Teller's tarot cards represent triumph (the Sun) and a change of structure (the Tower).

Armored girdle with a cyclopean skull

Cyclops Beneath his green head piece, Cyclops has a two-sided head—the other side has a squinting eye.

DID YOU KNOW?

The Chicken Suit Guy's mask and wings were hand-sculpted by members of the LEGO Minifigures team.

SERIES 9

The first series to be released in 2013 combined historical figures and those of myth in a new 16-character collection. Both the Cyclops and the Heroic Knight were among the easier ones to find, while the Hollywood Starlet and Fortune Teller proved more elusive. Other minifigures in this series included a Roman Emperor and a Waiter.

Wings instead of arms
Claws for pretending to scratch the soil

WHY DID I CROSS THE ROAD?

Chicken Suit Guy Excluding classic LEGO skeletons, this is the first minifigure to have a torso-and-arms that is the same from the front and back.

New sword piece with detailed hilt

New print detail on shield

Heroic Knight This Knight's silver visor is a classic element from the LEGO® Castle theme.

Traditional British court dress
Brand new gavel

Judge The ceremonial wig worn by this formidable character is new this year.

Hair is braided with bark
Symbol shows affinity with the woods

Forest Maiden The new hair piece created for this tree-loving minifigure is made from soft plastic.

Mermaid As with all LEGO merpeople, this Mermaid sports a tail piece that is unique to her. It appears in pale blue for the first time.

I FEEL LIKE A FISH OUT OF WATER HERE...

Unique blonde hairpiece also seen in other colors on Elizabeth Swann and the mermaid Syrena in the LEGO® *Pirates of the Caribbean*™ theme

New tail piece design also worn by the Ocean King in LEGO Minifigures Series 7

Grippable starfish makes its first ever appearance in dark orange

Battle Mech Beneath his helmet, this futuristic fighter's face bears a visor and out-of-this-world orange and gray markings.

New armor piece has jetpack connections on the back

Policeman Criminals beware! The Policeman is ready to enforce the law, alongside the Traffic Cop from LEGO Minifigures Series 2.

Policeman's badge bearing his ID number—2101

Soft plastic handcuffs

Roman Emperor This royal minifigure bears a golden crown never worn by anyone else. A good thing too, as he has no desire to share his Empire!

Scroll tile complete with Latin writing

Sandals for walking in hot, dusty climes

Tattered top hat

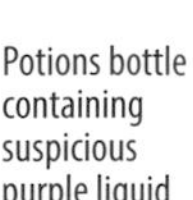

Potions bottle containing suspicious purple liquid

Mr. Good and Evil This character has a split personality after an experiment went wrong. Even his clothes and face are divided—one side torn and messy, the other side neat and tidy.

Helmet with unique star printing

Roller Derby Girl Don't try to stop this roller skater—her super fast wheels mean she's not going to slow down for anything!

New roller skate design can attach to LEGO studs

WHAT A GRAPE JOB I HAVE!

Wine bottle

White gloved hands can grasp serving tray

Waiter This is not the first waiter minifigure to be produced by the LEGO Group, but with his formal jacket and mustache, he is certainly the most suave.

2013

LEGO MINIFIGURES CONTINUED

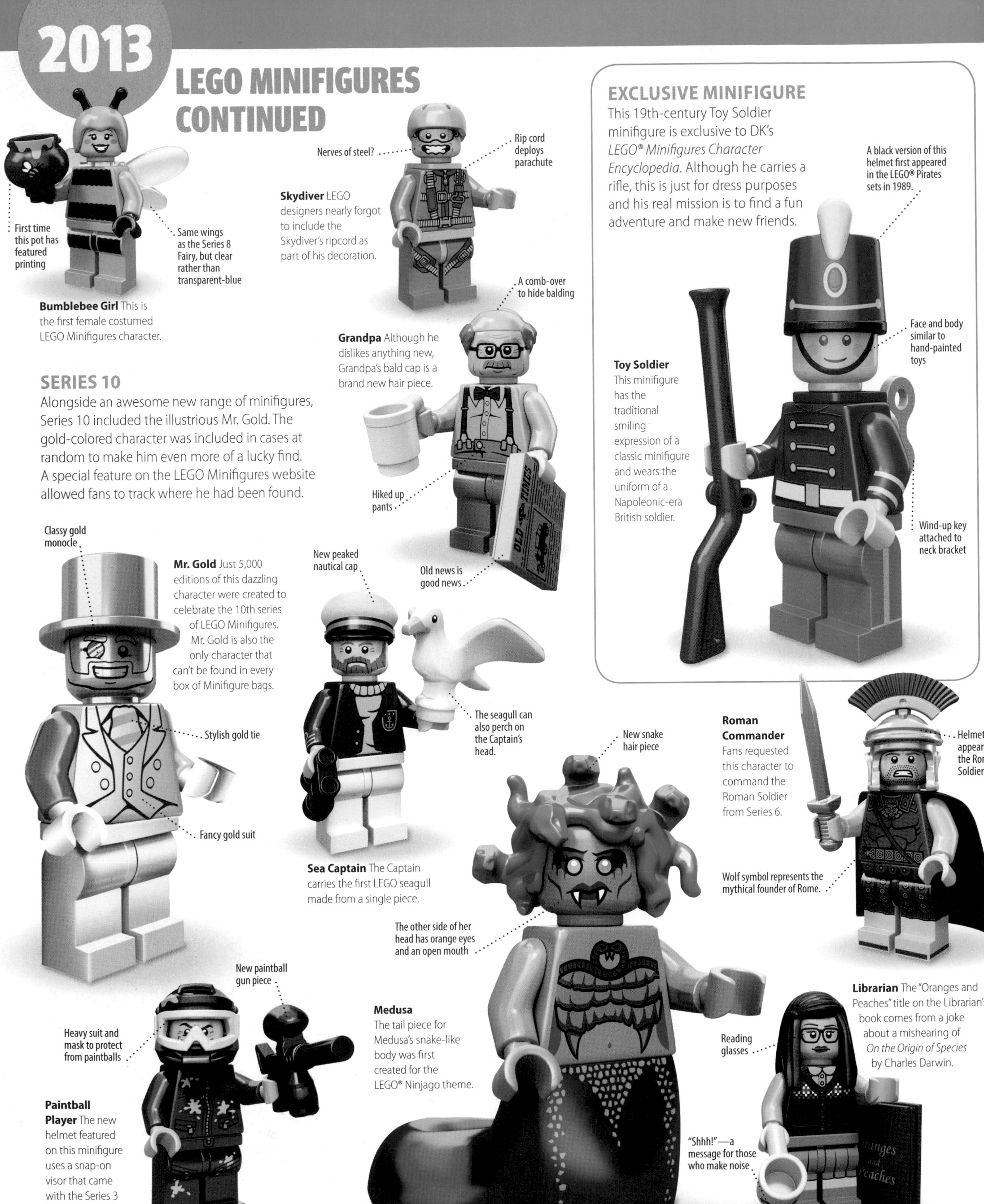

First time this pot has featured printing
Same wings as the Series 8 Fairy, but clear rather than transparent-blue
Nerves of steel?
Rip cord deploys parachute
A comb-over to hide balding
Hiked up pants
Old news is good news
Classy gold monocle
New peaked nautical cap
Stylish gold tie
Fancy gold suit
The seagull can also perch on the Captain's head.
New snake hair piece
The other side of her head has orange eyes and an open mouth
New paintball gun piece
Heavy suit and mask to protect from paintballs
Reading glasses
"Shhh!"—a message for those who make noise
Wolf symbol represents the mythical founder of Rome.
A black version of this helmet first appeared in the LEGO® Pirates sets in 1989.
Face and body similar to hand-painted toys
Wind-up key attached to neck bracket

Bumblebee Girl This is the first female costumed LEGO Minifigures character.

Skydiver LEGO designers nearly forgot to include the Skydiver's ripcord as part of his decoration.

Grandpa Although he dislikes anything new, Grandpa's bald cap is a brand new hair piece.

SERIES 10

Alongside an awesome new range of minifigures, Series 10 included the illustrious Mr. Gold. The gold-colored character was included in cases at random to make him even more of a lucky find. A special feature on the LEGO Minifigures website allowed fans to track where he had been found.

Mr. Gold Just 5,000 editions of this dazzling character were created to celebrate the 10th series of LEGO Minifigures. Mr. Gold is also the only character that can't be found in every box of Minifigure bags.

Sea Captain The Captain carries the first LEGO seagull made from a single piece.

Medusa The tail piece for Medusa's snake-like body was first created for the LEGO® Ninjago theme.

Paintball Player The new helmet featured on this minifigure uses a snap-on visor that came with the Series 3 Snowboarder.

Roman Commander Fans requested this character to command the Roman Soldier from Series 6.

Helmet fi[rst] appeared [in] the Roma[n] Soldier

Librarian The "Oranges and Peaches" title on the Librarian's book comes from a joke about a mishearing of *On the Origin of Species* by Charles Darwin.

EXCLUSIVE MINIFIGURE

This 19th-century Toy Soldier minifigure is exclusive to DK's *LEGO® Minifigures Character Encyclopedia*. Although he carries a rifle, this is just for dress purposes and his real mission is to find a fun adventure and make new friends.

Toy Soldier This minifigure has the traditional smiling expression of a classic minifigure and wears the uniform of a Napoleonic-era British soldier.

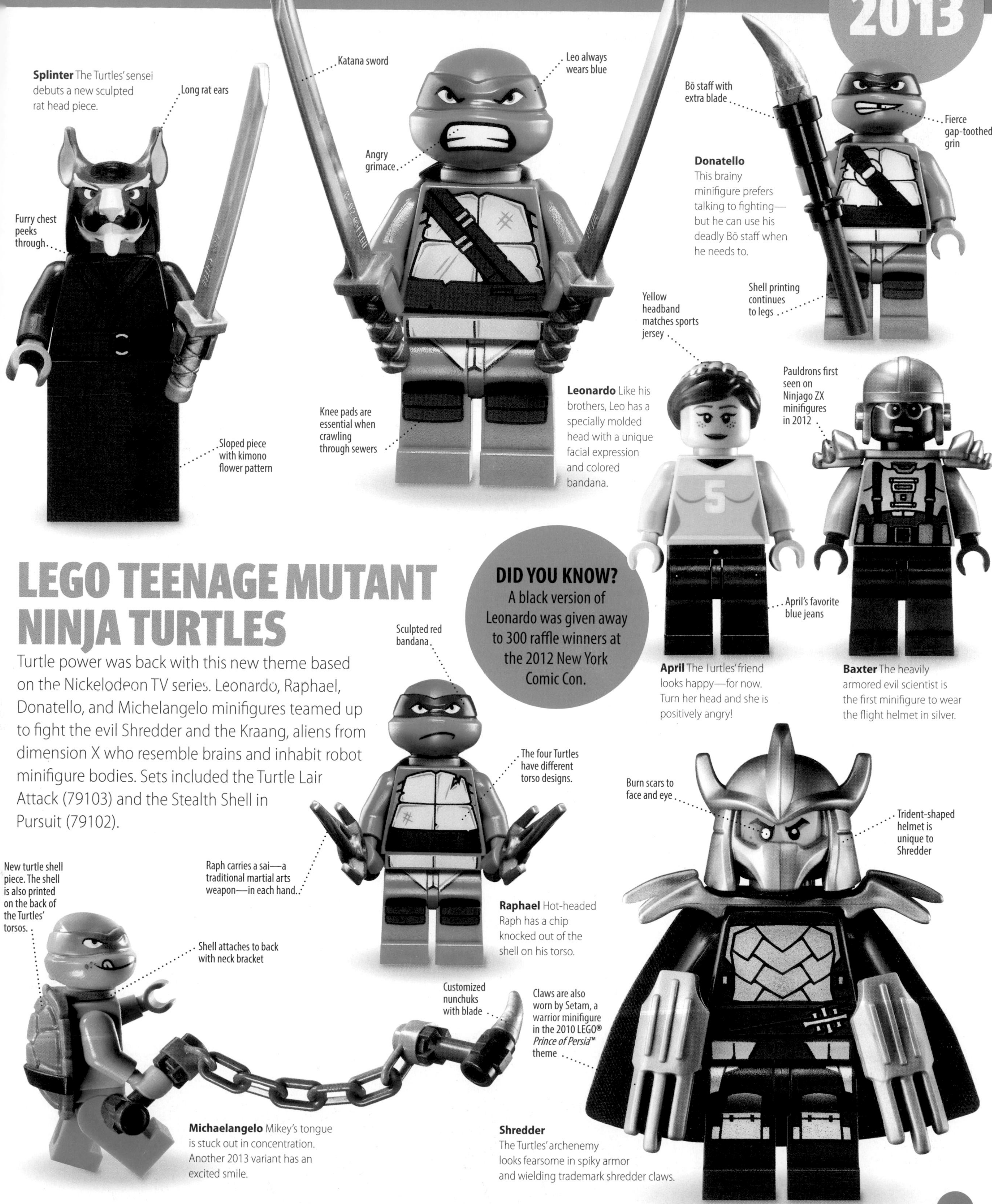
Long rat ears
Furry chest peeks through
Sloped piece with kimono flower pattern
Katana sword
Leo always wears blue
Angry grimace
Knee pads are essential when crawling through sewers
Bō staff with extra blade
Fierce gap-toothed grin
Shell printing continues to legs
Yellow headband matches sports jersey
Pauldrons first seen on Ninjago ZX minifigures in 2012
April's favorite blue jeans
Sculpted red bandana
The four Turtles have different torso designs.
Raph carries a sai—a traditional martial arts weapon—in each hand.
Burn scars to face and eye
Trident-shaped helmet is unique to Shredder
New turtle shell piece. The shell is also printed on the back of the Turtles' torsos.
Shell attaches to back with neck bracket
Customized nunchuks with blade
Claws are also worn by Setam, a warrior minifigure in the 2010 LEGO® *Prince of Persia*™ theme

Splinter The Turtles' sensei debuts a new sculpted rat head piece.

Leonardo Like his brothers, Leo has a specially molded head with a unique facial expression and colored bandana.

Donatello This brainy minifigure prefers talking to fighting—but he can use his deadly Bō staff when he needs to.

LEGO TEENAGE MUTANT NINJA TURTLES

Turtle power was back with this new theme based on the Nickelodeon TV series. Leonardo, Raphael, Donatello, and Michelangelo minifigures teamed up to fight the evil Shredder and the Kraang, aliens from dimension X who resemble brains and inhabit robot minifigure bodies. Sets included the Turtle Lair Attack (79103) and the Stealth Shell in Pursuit (79102).

DID YOU KNOW?
A black version of Leonardo was given away to 300 raffle winners at the 2012 New York Comic Con.

April The Turtles' friend looks happy—for now. Turn her head and she is positively angry!

Baxter The heavily armored evil scientist is the first minifigure to wear the flight helmet in silver.

Raphael Hot-headed Raph has a chip knocked out of the shell on his torso.

Michaelangelo Mikey's tongue is stuck out in concentration. Another 2013 variant has an excited smile.

Shredder
The Turtles' archenemy looks fearsome in spiky armor and wielding trademark shredder claws.

2013

Elvish ears attached to hair piece

Unique orange elf hair piece

Armed with two daggers

Camouflaged warrior clothing printed on torso and legs

Tauriel The Elven Guard of Mirkwood is the only female minifigure to be released in the LEGO *The Hobbit* theme to date.

Same hair piece as 2012 Legolas, with braid running down back

Legolas Greenleaf This version of the elf appears in just one set, dressed in forest attire for Escape from Mirkwood Spiders (79001).

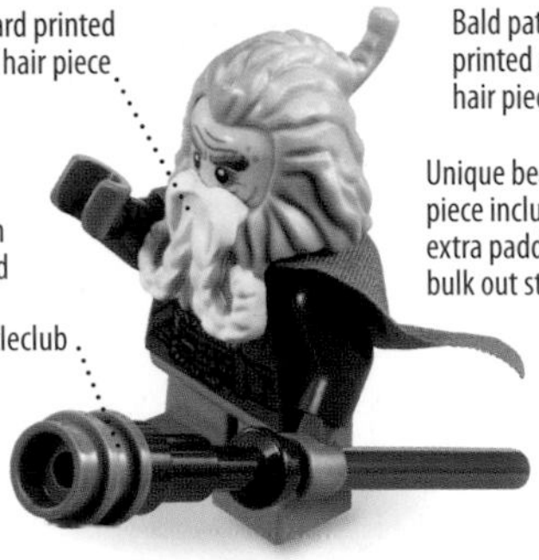

Golden chain mail

Mean orange eyes

Spiked bone collar

Hi-rise pants printed on torso and legs

Yazneg Scars and wrinkles mark the torso and bare head of the Orc commander minifigure.

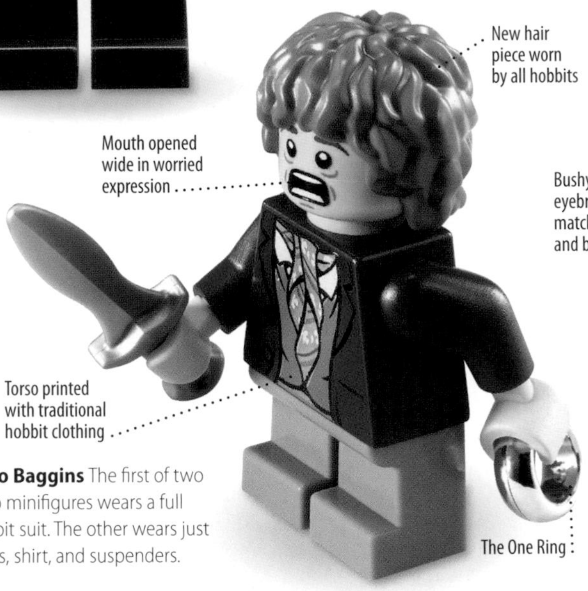

White beard printed onto gray hair piece

Arms uniquely printed in pearl gold

Battleclub

Oin The many dwarves in the LEGO *The Hobbit* theme all have beard and hair pieces unique to each individual figure.

Bald patch printed on hair piece

Tasty sausage

Unique beard piece includes extra padding to bulk out stomach

Bombur This dwarf minifigure is accompanied by accessories displaying his first love: food.

New hair piece worn by all hobbits

Mouth opened wide in worried expression

Torso printed with traditional hobbit clothing

The One Ring

Bilbo Baggins The first of two Bilbo minifigures wears a full hobbit suit. The other wears just pants, shirt, and suspenders.

Hair piece includes ponytail on the reverse

Bushy orange eyebrows match hair and beard

Nori Instantly recognizable by his unique star-shaped hair and beard piece, Nori joins his dwarf friends for The Goblin King Battle (79010).

LEGO® FRIENDS

Following on from its massive success in 2012, the LEGO Friends returned in 2013. Twenty-three new sets continued to expand the world of Heartlake City and the adventures of the original five girls.

Glasses printed on unique face

Legs also seen on Stephanie's soccer outfit

Andrew Sea-loving Andrew wears an all-blue outfit complete with a boat motif.

Wears the same skirt as Anna's mini-doll, but in white

Ms. Stevens The teacher at Heartlake High is one of several brand-new mini-dolls for 2013.

Surfer hair piece is the same as Andrew's, but black rather than blond

Legs also used on Peter's mini-doll figure in 2012

Matthew The third male mini-doll to feature in the theme, artistic Matthew attends Heartlake High.

Chain mail seen through shirt opening

Thorin Oakenshield Dwarf leader Thorin shares his new hair piece mold with minifigures Kili and Fili, also from *The Hobbit* theme.

LEGO® THE HOBBIT™

Based on the prequel films to *The Lord of the Rings* trilogy, the first launch of LEGO *The Hobbit: An Unexpected Journey* featured eight sets depicting movie scenes. All of the major characters were represented, with Gandalf, Gollum, and Legolas also appearing in *The Lord of the Rings* sets. It was a fantastic year for hobbits and dwarves, who also turned up as microfigures in a new LEGO game.

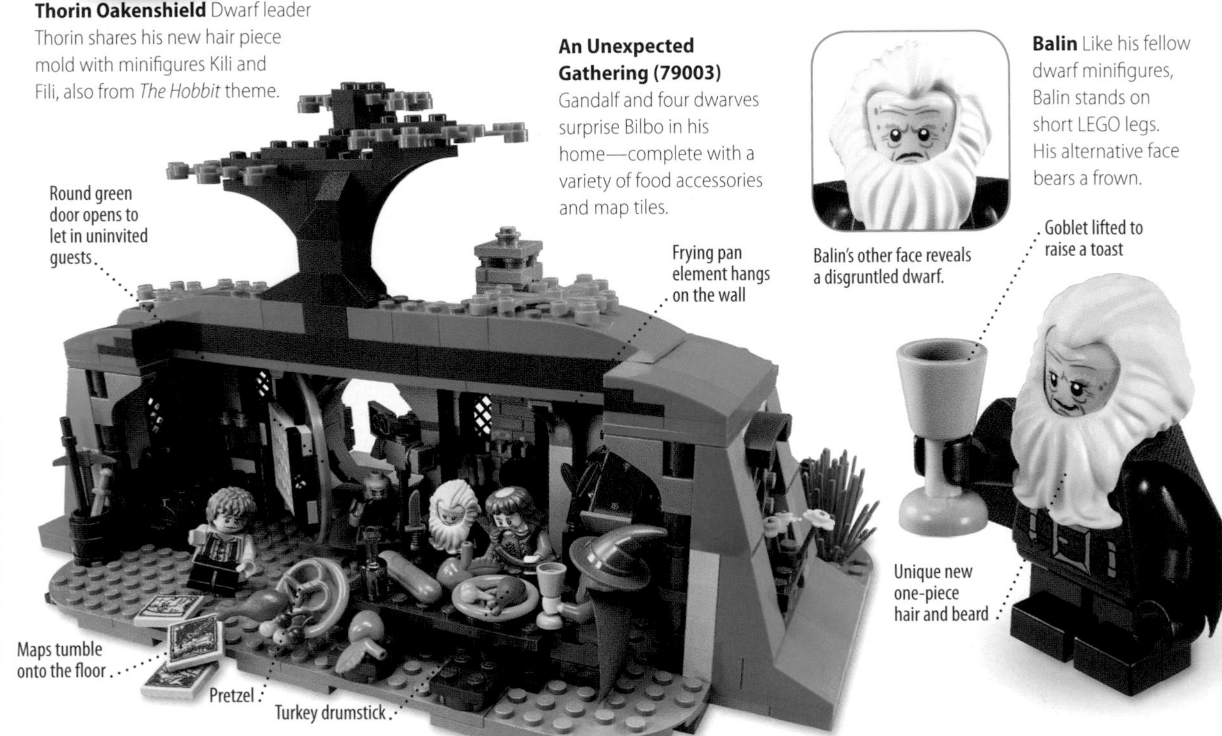

Round green door opens to let in uninvited guests
Frying pan element hangs on the wall
Maps tumble onto the floor
Pretzel
Turkey drumstick
Goblet lifted to raise a toast
Unique new one-piece hair and beard

An Unexpected Gathering (79003) Gandalf and four dwarves surprise Bilbo in his home—complete with a variety of food accessories and map tiles.

Balin's other face reveals a disgruntled dwarf.

Balin Like his fellow dwarf minifigures, Balin stands on short LEGO legs. His alternative face bears a frown.

Worried expression

Brown jacket, with red vest, as in 2012

Frodo Baggins The adventuring hobbit comes with a new, double-sided face in 2013, and no longer wears a cape.

Frodo's other face displays an angry scowl.

LEGO
THE LORD OF THE RINGS
9-14
79007
656 pcs/pzs

The Battle of Black Gate (79007) Gandalf the White and Aragorn minifigures must face the Mouth of Sauron and a duo of menacing Orcs.

New hair piece similar to Elrond's, but without the braided detailing

Double-sided face can be either smiling or frowning

Elven dress printed on torso and sloped piece

Arwen This elf became the first female minifigure of the theme, appearing alongside her father Elrond in set 79006.

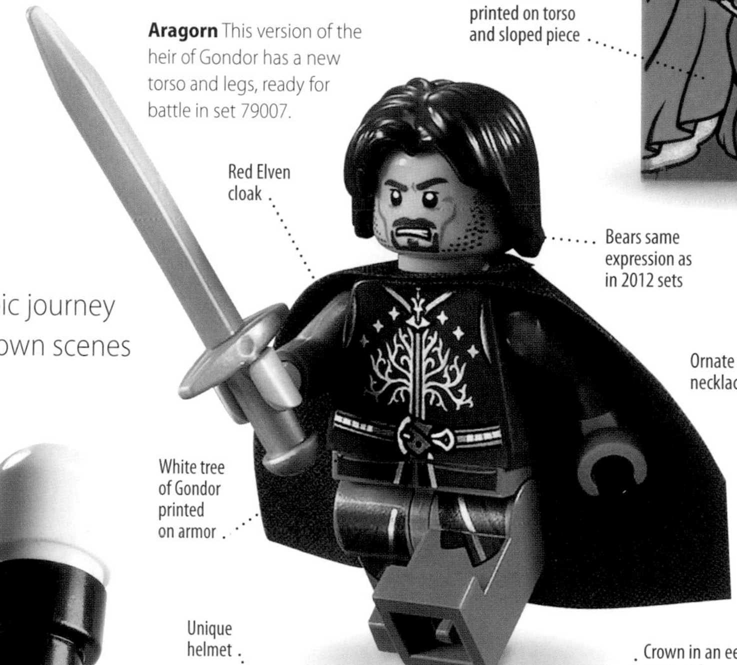

LEGO® THE LORD OF THE RINGS™

The most famous fantasy series of all continued its epic journey in 2013. Five more sets depicted some of the best-known scenes from all three movies. New versions of minifigures were revealed, and even more joined the action, with many featuring new headgear and hair pieces. The adventure was set to continue with new releases later in the year.

Aragorn This version of the heir of Gondor has a new torso and legs, ready for battle in set 79007.

Red Elven cloak

Bears same expression as in 2012 sets

White tree of Gondor printed on armor

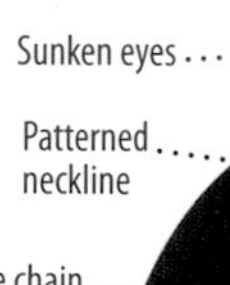

Sunken eyes

Patterned neckline

Ornate chain necklace

Gríma Wormtongue
The evil adviser to King Théoden looks sinister in his dark, subdued robes.

Wrinkled face partly concealed by bushy beard

Black and white wizard's staff

Saruman
Saruman the White battles Gandalf the Gray in The Wizard Battle (79005).

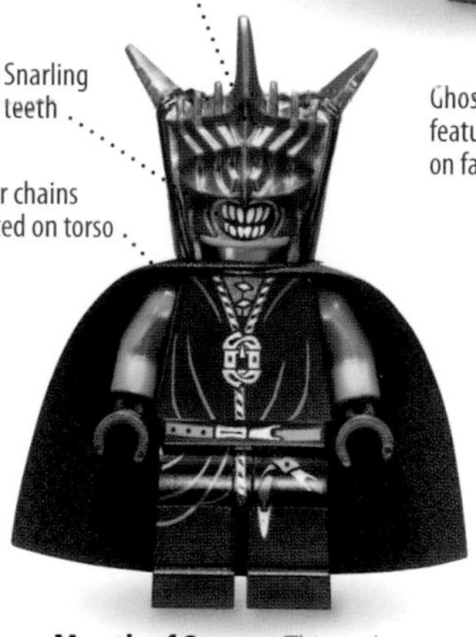

Standard cloth cape, in white

Unique helmet

Snarling teeth

Silver chains printed on torso

Mouth of Sauron This evil messenger makes one exclusive appearance. The face beneath his helmet has a mouth but no eyes.

Crown in an eerie green color

Ghostly skeleton features printed on face and torso

King of the Dead The leader of the Soldiers of the Dead marshals his minifigure troops to battle in Pirate Ship Ambush (79008).

Braided hair with silver detailing

Orange fabric cloak

Long red coat continues on to legs

Elrond The Third Age version of Elrond shows him to be older, with silver lining his hair, and dressed for life in Rivendell rather than battle.

Helmet also worn by 2012 Uruk-hai minifigures

Evil orange eyes

Mordor Orc This 2013 variant of the Orc wears his usual scowl but no hair piece so that he can don a helmet for fighting in set 79007.

Gandalf the White His cloak and clothes might be all-new, but Gandalf's distinctive bushy eyebrows and kindly eyes are clearly visible beneath his new white hair and beard piece.

White wizard's staff

Simple belt detailing on torso

LEGO® DC UNIVERSE™ SUPER HEROES

Batman returned to the world of LEGO building this year, accompanied by Superman. The Caped Crusader battled his foes in a new version of Arkham Asylum (10937) and teamed up with Aquaman against Mr. Freeze. Superman was kept busy challenging General Zod in sets based on the *Man of Steel* movie.

Aquaman
Usually seen wielding his powerful trident, Aquaman wears a belt with the symbol of Atlantis on it.

Muscular torso with scales

Arctic Batman
Wearing an Arctic camouflage Batsuit in preparation for taking on Mr. Freeze, this variant is exclusive to Arctic Batman vs. Mr. Freeze: Aquaman on Ice (76000).

Dual-sided head: frowning or determined

White headband worn underneath cowl

Movie Batman Exclusive to set The Bat vs. Bane: Tumbler Chase (76001), this minifigure features a copper belt and black Batman logo.

Cape is shorter than previous variants

Staff

Robin The addition of a hood rather than a hair piece makes this variant of Robin look unusually scary!

New suit with silver and gold detail

Superman Something has made Superman angry—one side of his dual-sided head features red eyes.

Hair piece is the same as the Black Widow from the LEGO® Marvel Super Heroes theme, seen in 2012

Lois Lane Making her debut in minifigure form this year, Lois appears in Superman: Black Zero Escape (76009).

Gray buttoned vest and shirt

TIME FOR ANOTHER "FOWL" CRIME!

DID YOU KNOW?

This is the first minifigure appearance of Dr. Harleen Quinzel, although she was seen as Harley Quinn in 2012.

Freeze gun

Eye can now be seen through monocle

Silver fish accessory

The Penguin Back to rain on Batman's parade, this version of the Penguin features a new torso, legs, and head piece.

2013 head piece features more wrinkles than the 2006 variant

Mr. Freeze
Minus his trademark goggles, Mr. Freeze's icy blue eyes are revealed. His helmet was first seen in 2011 in the Atlantis theme.

2006 variant is wearing a black wizard hat

Sunken red eyes

Scarecrow
The nightmarish Scarecrow has a new, more detailed head, and a dark brown wizard hat.

Harley Quinn costume poking through

ID badge

Head piece first seen in 2012

Inmate jacket

Dr. Harleen Quinzel
The obsessed psychiatrist looks happy to be next to her "Puddin," The Joker. Her hair piece can be interchanged with a red and black jester's hat.

The Joker Even though the Joker is locked up in Arkham Asylum, he just can't stop smiling. The back of his torso reads "inmate 109370."

The other side of head features red eyes
General Zod's emblem: a sideways omega symbol

General Zod There are two variants of General Zod: in the other, he is wearing his combat armor.

Radio to call for backup

Colonel Hardy All decked out in his military armor, the Colonel minifigure is featured in Superman: Battle of Smallville (76003).

Torso features silver "F" insignia

Faora General Zod's right hand woman is seen here without her battle armor—but she still looks scary!

Head piece also seen on Lex Luthor
Muscular torso

Tor-An It's clear to see whose army Tor-An belongs to—his torso is similar to General Zod's, but with a silver "T" insignia.

DID YOU KNOW?
Pepper Potts wears the Iron Man Mark 42 armor in Malibu Mansion Attack (76007).

LEGO® MARVEL SUPER HEROES

The armored Avenger flew into battle in sets based on the movie *Iron Man 3*. From his Malibu mansion to a high-speed chase over water, Tony Stark challenged the forces of the Mandarin with the help of War Machine. Other minifigures this year included Dr. Doom, Nova, Venom, and Ultimate Spider-Man.

Iron Man
This minifigure has an updated torso, with arc reactor and gold Heartbreaker armor.

Arc reactor

Transparent blue jets

Shoulder gun
Dual sided head: neutral and angry
WHEN DO I GET A MOVIE?
"Danger" printed on torso

A variant is capeless, and has a different torso, legs, and arms

Beard also seen on Professor Dumbledore (in gray) from the LEGO® Harry Potter™ theme

The Ten Rings insignia is printed on torso

The Mandarin Iron Man's archenemy is ready for a showdown in Iron Man vs. The Mandarin: Ultimate Showdown (76008).

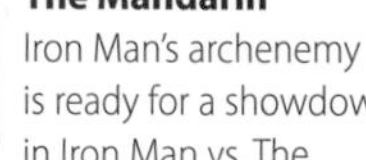

War Machine Wearing the same helmet as Iron Man, but in gray, this minifigure comes with a shoulder gun and transparent red repulsor and jets.

Freckled face

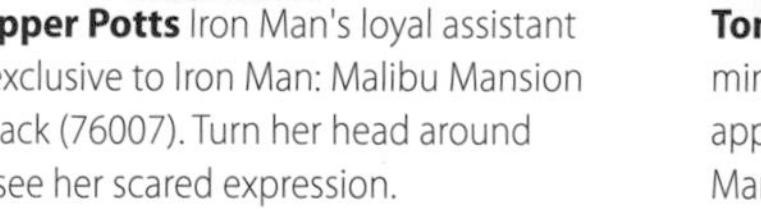

Pepper Potts Iron Man's loyal assistant is exclusive to Iron Man: Malibu Mansion Attack (76007). Turn her head around to see her scared expression.

Dual sided head: confident and scared

Tony Stark The first ever minifigure of Tony Stark appears in Iron Man: Malibu Mansion Attack (76007).

2013

LEGO® *STAR WARS*®

The biggest news from the LEGO *Star Wars* universe this year was the release of *The Yoda Chronicles*, an animated mini-series created by the LEGO Group, featuring the wise green Jedi Master and other favorite characters. Adding to the excitement were debuts of a host of new characters in minifigure form and new versions of familiar minifigures, including Yoda and Darth Maul.

Beard-like tendrils
Trans-clear wings
Gold armor printing
Pistol accessory
Prominent head crest
Same hair piece as Draco Malfoy from the Harry Potter™ theme, but in white.
Life-support system for changing altitudes
Eye markings not seen on 2010 variant
The Gran species has three eyes
Same head piece as Professor Snape from the Harry Potter™ theme
Two-sided face has a snarling expression on the other side.
Bulbous eyes
Long droopy ears of the Ortolan species
Technic pin piece placed over barrel
Wrench for fixing starfighter equipment
Alternate face shows the pilot looking nervous
Other side of face shows visor removed
Rebel insignia
Loose white straps
Life-support chest pack printing is more detailed than Luke's 2010 flight suit
Printed braid is longer than 2002 variant
New hair piece exclusive to Padmé
Two-sided head piece also shows Padmé with a smirk
Printed eyes seen on Classic Yoda for the first time
Small curved ears
Pockets and straps printed on legs

Poggle the Lesser With his specially sculpted head, the Archduke of Geonosis makes his debut in Duel on Geonosis (75017).

Jango Fett The redesigned variant of the renowned bounty hunter features silver armor and knee pad printing on the legs.

Coleman Trebor Making his minifigure debut in AT-TE (75019), the Vurk Jedi Master's gray head piece is specially molded.

General Rieekan This brave rebel general appears for the first time in 2013, sporting a new thermal jacket to keep him warm on icy Hoth.

Count Dooku With distinctive eyebrows and slicked-back hair, the third incarnation of Dooku bears a close resemblance to actor Christopher Lee, who played him in the movies.

TIE Bomber Pilot The elite Imperial Pilot features new more-detailed printing on his helmet and torso.

Ree-Yees With a three-eyed head created just for him, this lawless creature works on Jabba's Sail Barge (75020).

CLASSIC *STAR WARS*

Among the many sets released this year were the all-new Rancor Pit (75005), and a new version of Jabba's Sail Barge (75020). The Rancor Pit set was designed as an add-on to Jabba's Palace (9516) released in 2012.

A-Wing Rebel Pilot This redesigned pilot, who first appeared in 2000, has a completely new helmet and a new dark-green flight suit.

Snowspeeder Luke Wearing a pressurized g-suit, Luke is ready for action against the Imperial forces in the Battle of Hoth (75014).

Max Rebo Jabba the Hutt's musician is entirely blue, although his specially molded head is a lighter blue than the rest of his body.

Clone Trooper Captain Wielding a heavy rifle, the Clone Trooper Captain features red printing, denoting his rank.

Classic Yoda It's all about Yoda in 2013! He has a new molded head piece, featuring a focused expression.

Episode II Anakin Skywalker This variant of Anakin features him wearing Hawkeye's hair piece from the LEGO Marvel Super Heroes theme.

Padmé Amidala Padmé may look happy, but her back features scratch marks made by the Nexu beast in the Geonosian Arena.

THE CLONE WARS

The Clone Wars raged throughout LEGO *Star Wars* in 2013 with new sets including Z-95 Headhunter (75004) and the Mandalorian Speeder (75022), which featured a new Darth Maul minifigure.

Huge bounty hunter blaster rifle

Rako's trademark facial tattoo

Rako Hardeen Obi-Wan's minifigure has been transformed to look like Rako, the bounty hunter out to get him.

Togruta have striped head-tails

HEADS OR TAILS... OR BOTH?

Turn Ahsoka's face and her expression changes to a huge grin.

Ahsoka wields two lightsabers to defeat the Umbarans.

Ahsoka Tano The 2013 minifigure features the same hair piece as her younger 2010 self, but she has a more grown-up look with new head, torso, and leg printing.

LEGO
STAR WARS
8-14
75024
362 pcs/pzs

HH-87 Starhopper (75024) This long-ranged starfighter set features three new minifigures, including Rako Hardeen and Cad Bane.

Special Forces Commander An exclusive elite minifigure came with *The Yoda Chronicles* book, published by DK.

Helmet similar to those worn by Stormtrooper minifigures.

Protective armor continues to legs

THE YODA CHRONICLES

In 2013 the LEGO Group released Jek-14's Stealth Starfighter (75018), which was based on the three-part animated mini-series. It featured the first character to be created by The LEGO Group—in conjunction with Lucasfilm—the mighty Jek-14.

Double-sided head shows eyes crackling with power.

Jek-14 The Force-enhanced clone is the first minifigure to have a transparent arm.

Arm projects Force shields and lightning

Unique white lightsaber hilt

Modified clone trooper helmet

Different head mold than Classic Yoda in a brighter green, with longer ears and cartoon-like eyes.

White tufts of hair can be seen on the back of his head

Clone Wars Yoda This variant of Yoda features new torso printing with a hood on the reverse.

Two-sided head piece also shows Obi-Wan with a stern expression

Jedi robes extend to legs

Obi-Wan Kenobi This calm Jedi minifigure prefers to use his lightsaber to defend, rather than to attack.

Four arms means Krell can wield two double-bladed lightsabers at the same time

Pong Krell A custom-made head piece was designed to show this all-new minifigure's distinctive jowled features.

Krell has an extended torso with an additional pair of arms

Deadly darksaber

Cyborg Darth Maul Darth Maul now walks on powerful cybernetic legs. Nothing can stop this fierce Sith warrior!

New shirtless torso for 2013

Claw-like robotic legs

LEGO® BRAND STORES

These three minifigures were offered to 300 lucky customers in a promotion at the grand opening of the LEGO Store in Watford, United Kingdom. Packaging for the range featured Watford Junction railway station.

Signalling paddle

LEGO Friends Mia also rode this skateboard in 2012

Passenger Dressed warmly for a long wait, the Passenger looks happy that his train isn't delayed.

Station Master This busy worker lets the train driver minifigures know when the train is ready to depart.

Skateboarder The Skateboarder isn't allowed to ride his board at the station.

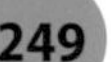

2013
Each of the Ninja received a new elemental sword this year
Silver, three-point crown shows he has reached ZX status
WOW, WHO'S YOUR TAILOR, KOZU?
THIS GUY IN THE UNDERWORLD.
Blue-and-silver color scheme for the Ninja of Lightning
Kozu is armed with two scimitar swords
He wears a red version of his boss's horned samurai helmet
Elaborate red-and-white armor covers his torso extension piece.
Armor down to his knees
Lower body is a standard minifigure torso
This jagged sword element is only carried by the Ninjago warriors.
Unique gold head
Protective shoulder pauldrons
Sword hilt is a telescope piece

Jay Kimono This new variant of Ninja Jay wields a powerful new Lightning blade!

General Kozu Look out, Ninja! Lord Garmadon's scariest soldier is twice the size of a regular minifigure thanks to his unique torso extension piece.

Garmatron (70504) Packed with Dark Matter missiles and with General Kozu at the helm, this battle machine is ready to fire at the ninja and Ninjago City!

LEGO NINJAGO

Entering its third year, Ninjago ramped up the action as the Ninja faced off against Lord Garmadon and an army of ancient stone warriors. The Ninja minifigures now wore elemental robes and carried powerful new weapons, but it would take the appearance of a gold Ninja and an awesome new Dragon to finally end the latest threat to the world of Ninjago.

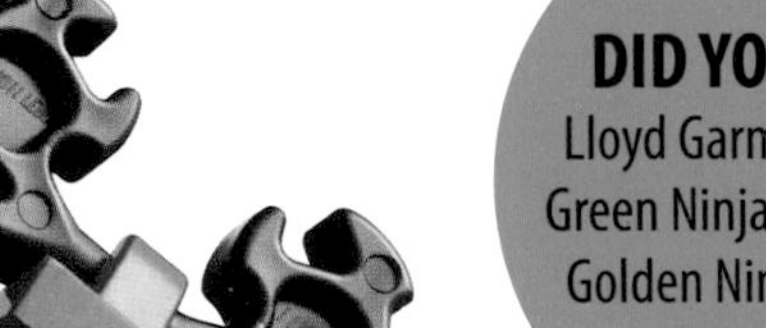

Green and gold elemental robes

Lloyd Golden Ninja When Lloyd Garmadon turns into the Ultimate Spinjitzu Master, he becomes gold from minifigure head to foot!

DID YOU KNOW?
Lloyd Garmadon was the Green Ninja, becoming the Golden Ninja for the first time in 2013.

New helmet with crest and mask
Horned staff matches his intimidating helmet
Evil-looking red eyes
This torso extender piece was first introduced on his 2012 variant
Purple belt extends from lower torso to leg piece

Lord Garmadon The evil, four-armed brother of Sensei Wu has a special torso extender piece to accommodate his extra limbs!

Ice-white Ninja head wrap

Zane Kimono Ninja of Ice Zane wears a black, white, and gold kimono for the first time in Garmatron (70504).

Arms are in Kai's elemental color.
Gold warrior symbol

Kai Kimono Kai and his fellow Ninja minifigures wear their elemental robes when they battle Lord Garmadon and his Stone Army.

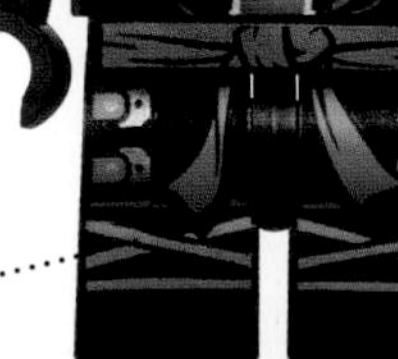

Ninja leg wraps

Cole Kimono This variant of Cole has ZX (Zen Extreme) Ninja status, but he wears a formal kimono instead of his regular ZX robes.

LEGO® SPACE

Got a flyswatter handy? 2013 saw the launch of a new Space subtheme: LEGO Galaxy Squad. Summoned to Earth by Lord Vampyre from the LEGO Monster Fighters theme, the alien bugs swarm through space—and only Galaxy Squad can stop them! The subtheme features Red, Blue, Green, and Orange teams versus a powerful (if not too smart!) menace.

Dual-sided head features breathing equipment when turned.

Ray-gun, cocked and ready for bug-shooting

Solomon Blaze The leader of the Blue Squadron wears a scope over his right eye to help him spot enemy bugs.

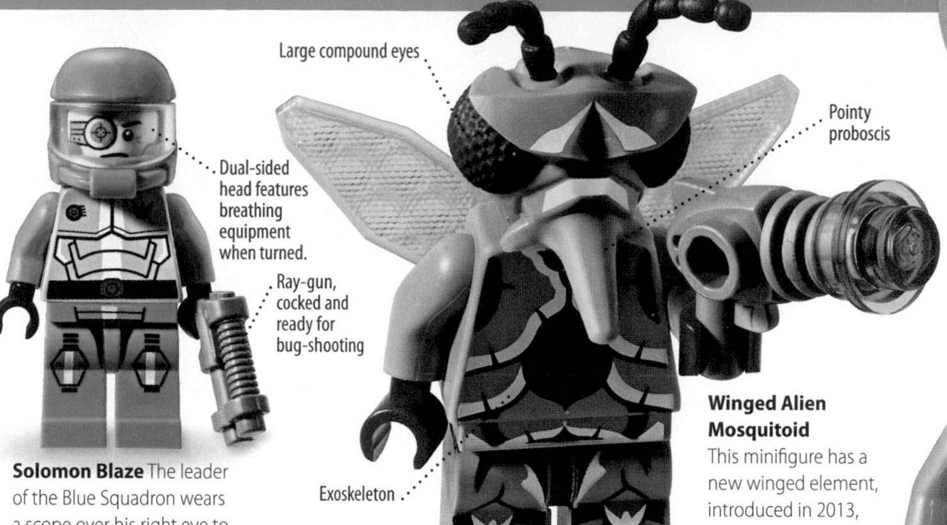

Large compound eyes

Pointy proboscis

Exoskeleton

Winged Alien Mosquitoid
This minifigure has a new winged element, introduced in 2013, which attaches with a neck bracket.

Exclusive head features thick eyelashes and blue lips

Squad armor extends down to legs

Ashlee Starstrider
This Orange Squadron team member wears the latest fashion in space—blue lipstick!

Billy Starbeam
As leader of the Red Squadron, Billy tells his team what to do—which is always to get the bugs. Zap!

Only Billy wears this helmet in red.

Chuck was first to wear this helmet in bright green.

Minifigures wear flight suits in the color of their squadron.

Chuck Stonebreaker
This minifigure is angry. Very angry. He hates the color green.

Helmet design first seen in 2010 sets

Scope

Armored knee pads

Max Solarflare This minifigure sometimes wishes he belonged to the Orange squadron—at least his uniform would match his beard.

Wide, translucent visor for clear visibility

Galaxy Squad symbol

Jack Fireblade
The most fun Jack had this year was obliterating bugs in the Bug Obliterator (70705).

Four eyes on head piece

Alien Buggoid
This Alien minifigure is small, but he has a big secret weapon—his Star Slicer vehicle (70703).

Sonic gun

Alien Mantizoid If his face isn't enough to scare the Galaxy Squad, then this Alien's two sharp blade weapons certainly will!

Sharp fangs

Armor

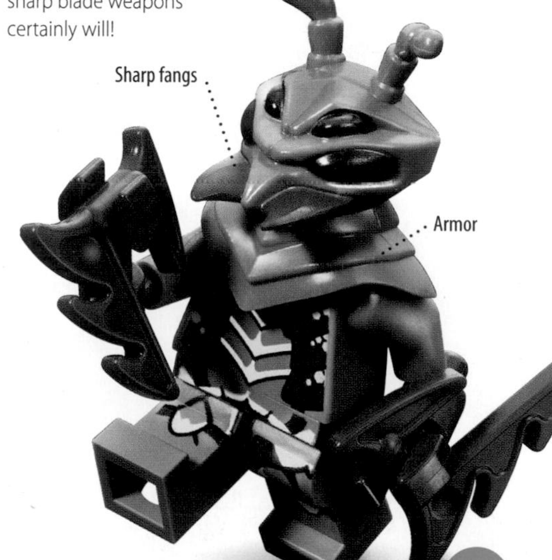

LEGO® CITY

Police and Fire took center stage this year, with a new Elite Police Force providing a lot of the action. Chase McCain and the Elite Police team tackle the toughest crimes and criminals, both in LEGO City sets and in a 2013 video game. Meanwhile, the Fire team got a new Fire Station (60004).

This fireproof helmet has been worn by minifigures since 1978.

New torso features a utility belt and air pressure gauge for breathing equipment

Reflective stripe

Firefighter This minifigure is wearing the regulation LEGO City firefighter uniform from 2013.

Conspicuous red crowbar

City Burglar
Could you pick this minifigure out in a police lineup? His unique head with stubble and a scowl might help!

New striped torso features a rope for scaling buildings

NO CRIMES HAPPEN WHILE I'M ABOUT...

Bulletproof police vest offers protection from gun-toting criminals

Police radio

Chase McCain
This Chase first appeared in 2013, but an exclusive variant was also given away with pre-orders of the LEGO *City Undercover* video game in 2012.

The 2012 variant wore black pants

Index

OIL

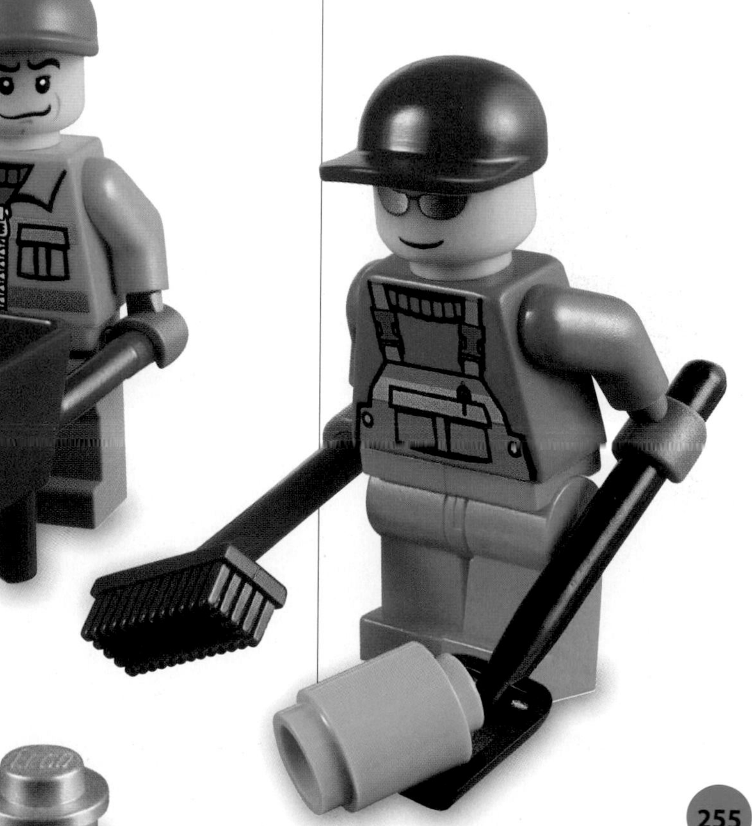

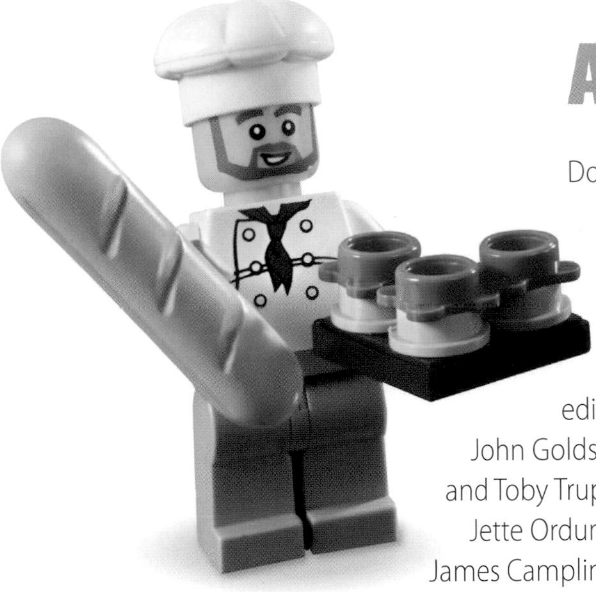

Dorling Kindersley would like to thank the following people for their help in producing this book:

Hannah Dolan, Gaurav Joshi, Rahul Ganguly, Emma Grange, Zoe Hedges, Lauren Nesworthy, Rosie Peet, Garima Sharma, Claire Sipi, and Lisa Stock for editorial assistance; Liam Drane, Ian Ebstein, Anna Formanek, John Goldsmid, Jon Hall, Mary Lytle, Lisa Robb, Clive Savage, Rhys Thomas, and Toby Truphet for design assistance; Edel Schwarz Andersen, Kristian Reimer Hauge, Jette Orduna, Elsebeth Søgaard, Randi Sørensen, and Tara Wike at the LEGO Group; James Camplin and Lucy Boughton for additional consultancy help; Joseph Pellegrino for additional photography on p221; Huw Millington and the brickset.com community; and, lastly, all the wonderful LEGO fans and collectors from across the world who lent us their minifigures to be photographed: Ann and Andy at minifigforlife.com, Jeremy Allen, Suzanne Allen, Carl Olof Andersson, Bozó Balázs, Daniel Cooley, Prentice Donnelly, Helen Floodgate, Lluís Gibert, Tim Goddard, Doug Harefeld, Ben Johnson, Wesley Keen, Giles Kemp, David Kirkham at minifigsandbricks.co.uk, Simon La Thangue, Richard Lawson, Mark Lee, Brandon Liu, Stefano Maini, David McClatchey, Neal McClatchey, Huw Millington, Jon Roke, Caroline Savage, Harry Sinclair, Joseph Venutolo, Sophie Walker, Adam White, and Mark Willis.